THE DZOGCHEN PATH

DZOGCHEN PEMA KALSANG RINPOCHE

TRANSLATED BY CHRISTIAN A STEWART

MAHASANDHI PUBLISHING

Mahasandhi Publishing
5 Corinthian Court
West Hill Road
Cowes
Isle of Wight
U.K.

www.dzogchen-monastery.org

© 2018 Mahasandhi Publishing

Cover calligraphy 'Guard Your Mind' by Dzogchen Pema Kalsang Rinpoche
Design and typeset by Mahasandhi Publishing

All rights reserved. No portion of this book may be reproduced by any means without prior permission from the publisher.

THE DZOGCHEN PATH
By Dzogchen Pema Kalsang Rinpoche
Translated by Christian A Stewart

First edition

ISBN: 978-0-9568596-2-4

CONTENTS

Translator's Foreword 1
Brief Introduction to Dzogchen Pema Kalsang Rinpoche 3

   The Expression of Worship and the Request to Listen 11
Teaching Day One 15
   Goodness of the Beginning – the Introduction 27
      Explanation of the Title of the Root Text 27
      The Four Dharmas of Necessity and so forth 30
   Homage and the Pledge of Composition 32
   Goodness of the Middle – the Meaning of the Text 37
      Unification of the Four Times 37
   Part One, the Prayer to Invoke the Lama 43
      Invoking the Outer Lama 43
      Invoking the Inner Lama 45
The Common Outer Preliminaries 49
   1) Difficulties of Finding the Freedoms and Endowments 53
      The Nature of Freedom 53
      The Endowments of Dharma 55
Teaching Day Two 69
   Difficulties of Finding a Precious Human Rebirth 74
   Eight Unfree Incidental Circumstances 74
   Eight Unfree States that Cut the Mind Off from Dharma 80
   2) Impermanence of Life 85
      General Impermanence 85
      Impermanence according to the Root Text 88
   3) Karmic Cause and Effect 103
      Negative Actions to be Abandoned 103
      Positive Actions to be Adopted and their Results 108

- Teaching Day Three 119
  - 4) Defects of Samsara 131
    - The Suffering of Samsara 131
    - Individual Sufferings of the Beings of the Six Realms 133
- Teaching Day Four 159
  - 5) Benefits of Liberation 167
  - 6) How to Follow a Spiritual Teacher 171
    - Examining the Lama 171
    - Following the Lama 178
    - Emulating the Lama's Realisation and Conduct 182
    - How to Abandon Negatives from the Student's Perspective 183
- Teaching Day Five 197
- The Unique Inner Preliminaries 205
  - Part Two, Taking Refuge 205
    - Classifications of Taking Refuge 207
    - The Three Jewels 208
    - How to Take Refuge 219
    - Taking Refuge according to the Root Text 223
    - How to Visualise the Field of Merit 233
- Teaching Day Six 239
  - Part Three, Arousing Bodhicitta 245
    - The Lineage of Bodhicitta 250
    - The Benefits of Arousing Bodhicitta 251
    - The Meaning of Arousing Bodhicitta 253
    - The Definition of 'Bodhisattva' 254
    - Classifications of Bodhicitta 254
    - Taking the Bodhisattva Precepts 255
    - The Main Practice of Arousing Bodhicitta 257
    - The Bodhisattva Precepts 258
    - The Precepts of Refraining, Gathering, and Benefitting 259
    - The Precepts of Aspiring Bodhicitta 266

The Precepts of Engaging Bodhicitta	273
Teaching Day Seven	275
Part Four, Meditation and Recitation of Vajrasattva	283
The Four Powers	283
Vajrasattva Purification according to the Root Text	285
Part Five, The Mandala Offering	301
How and Why to Offer the Mandala	301
The Trikaya Mandala	304
Part Six, Gathering the Accumulation of the Kusali	311
The Significance of Chod	311
Chod Accumulation according to the Root Text	311
Teaching Day Eight	319
Part Seven, Guru Yoga	329
Visualising the Accumulation Field	329
Invoking Enlightened Mind by means of the Seven Vajra Lines	337
Offering the Seven Branches	340
Accomplishing the Nature of the Four Vajras	346
Part Eight, Prayers to the Lamas of the Lineage	353
Supplementary Prayers of Aspiration	356
Part Nine, Taking the Four Empowerments	365
How to Bring the Practice Session to a Close	367
The Goodness of the End – the Conclusion	371
Part Ten, Prayers of Dedication	371
Part Eleven, Special Prayers of Aspiration	372
Concluding Words	373
The Root Text, the Sublime Path to Omniscience by Jigme Lingpa	385

Translator's Foreword

This teaching on the Longchen Nyingtik *Sublime Path to Omniscience* by Jigme Lingpa was given by Dzogchen Pema Kalsang Rinpoche in the Lotus Ground Retreat Centre, Dzogchen Monastery, Tibet, in the summer of 2009. The Tibetan transcript was prepared by Khenpo Shesha Kunzig, and republished in 2018 as volume thirteen of the *Collected Works of Dzogchen Pema Kalsang Rinpoche*, under the title *ngag 'don rnam mkhyen lam bzang gi ljags khrid chos rje pad mi zhal lung* by Gansu Nationalities Publishing House.

This English translation was prepared based on both Lama Rinpoche's oral teaching and the transcribed text. My numerous questions were patiently answered by Lama Rinpoche personally, his nephew and director of the Lotus Ground Retreat Centre, Mura Rinpoche, and Khenpo Ngedon Dorje. Many thanks go to Renaud Samyn, whose generosity enabled this translation to come about, and to my editor and mother of this life, Anna Sherwell. Royalties from the sale of this book go directly to Dzogchen Monastery and its numerous beneficial projects. May this virtue enlighten all beings!

Christian A Stewart
August 2018

Lotus Ground Retreat Centre
Dzogchen Monastery, Tibet
www.dzogchen-monastery.org

Brief Introduction to Dzogchen Pema Kalsang Rinpoche

Having received an intense and enlightening education with some of the most eminent masters of the 20th century, while still a teenager, Dzogchen Pema Kalsang Rinpoche became twelfth throne holder of Dzogchen Monastery. Throughout the bleak period of the 1960s and '70s, he managed to maintain and practise the Dharma in secret, and as soon as circumstances permitted, he completely rebuilt Dzogchen Monastery, Shirasing Buddhist College, and established the Lotus Ground Great Perfection Retreat Centre. He now devotes his time to teaching Dzogpa Chenpo to tens of thousands of students from all over the world, and to date, thirty-two volumes of his teachings have been published in Tibetan.

Pema Kalsang Rinpoche was born in the summer of 1943 in Dzachuka, Eastern Tibet, the homeland of many exceptional masters, including the great bodhisattva Patrul Rinpoche and the incomparable scholar Mipham Rinpoche. Lama Rinpoche's mother was the sister of the accomplished Dzogchen master Adro Socho, and she bore many signs of a dakini. Rinpoche's maternal uncle, the fourth Mura Rinpoche Pema Norbu, named the child Pema Kalsang.

When Pema Kalsang reached the age of five, Dzogchen Kontul Rinpoche, who had been very close to the second Pema Banza, travelled to Dzachuka and arrived at the family camp. As soon as the young Pema Kalsang saw the master, he went to him very joyfully, as if he was a good friend. He also recognised the knife strapped to Kontul Rinpoche's belt, saying 'That's mine!' The knife had belonged to the second Pema Banza. The names of Rinpoche's parents, his place of birth, and other details were found to correspond with the prophesies of Jamyang Khyentse Choki Lodro, the sixth Dzogchen Rinpoche, and other genuine masters, and Pema Kalsang was recognised as the third incarnation of Great Khenpo Pema Banza.

The first Dzogchen Pema Banza, also known as Padma Vajra or Pema Dorje, was considered the most learned master of his time. He presided as Head Khenpo in Shirasing Buddhist College for many years, and in the latter part of his life, lived and taught in the Dzogchen Lotus Ground. He was amazingly realised, and in particular, in visions of the wisdom body of All-knowing Jigme Lingpa, attained indications of realising the ultimate lineage, thereby receiving direct transmission of the Heart

Essence teachings. Great Khenpo Pema Banza had many eminent students, including Mipham Rinpoche, Jamyang Khyentse Wangpo, the fourth Shechen Gyaltsab, Do Khyentse, the third Dodrupchen, Adzom Drukpa, the fifth Shechen Rabjam, and the treasure revealer Lerab Lingpa.

Pema Banza is in turn considered to be the emanation of Zurchen Choying Rangdrol, who was the Tantra master, root guru, and Dzogchen master to none other than the Great Fifth Dalai Lama. He is a very important and influential figure in Tibetan Buddhism, numbering many eminent masters of the seventeenth century among his students.

While Pema Kalsang Rinpoche was growing up, he lived and studied with his root guru Khenpo Yonten Gonpo, and the sixth Dzogchen Rinpoche, in the Lama Palace of Dzogchen Monastery. Together they also travelled to the monastery of Dzongsar Khyentse Jamyang Choki Lodru to receive empowerments of the old and new traditions, Sutras, Tantras, and treasure texts. In 1955, Lama Rinpoche, together with Khenpo Yonten Gonpo and the sixth Dzogchen Rinpoche, travelled to Central Tibet and Tsang on extensive pilgrimage and met many great lamas, including a young 14th Dalai Lama. Following their return, from the age of fourteen to sixteen, Lama Rinpoche lived in the Long Life Retreat Centre above the Dzogchen valley with great Khenpo Pema Tsewang, who taught him personally. This was to be the last opportunity Lama Rinpoche had to study with his masters.

In the autumn of 1958, when Lama Rinpoche was seventeen, Dzogchen Rinpoche took him to Gyalgi Drakkar, the retreat centre of Great Khenpo Tupten Nyendrak. With tears in his eyes, Dzogchen Rinpoche requested the khenpo to give Lama Rinpoche seventeen long life empowerments, corresponding in number to the years of his age. Dzogchen Rinpoche said to the khenpo, 'Very soon the Buddhist tradition will face great obstacles, and destruction. At that time don't worry about me, focus your attention on this young one', and he pointed to Lama Rinpoche. It was only a few days later the political situation deteriorated into violence.

During the winter of the following year, Lama Rinpoche, Dzogchen Rinpoche, and Khenpo Gonre were imprisoned in Dege for political re-education. At one stage, because he was still only a boy, Lama Rinpoche was allowed to return to Dzogchen. This was the last time he saw either Dzogchen Rinpoche or Khenpo Gonre. Lama Rinpoche himself recalls a brief exchange he had with Dzogchen Rinpoche several years earlier:

> One day, as we were sitting together, Dzogchen Rinpoche turned and said to me quite emphatically, 'I have no other heir but you. Do you

understand?' I didn't know it at the time, but later I realised what Rinpoche said to me that day was prophetic.

The next twenty years brought terrible suffering, even before the turmoil of the Cultural Revolution. Dzogchen Monastery and Shirasing Buddhist College were completely razed to the ground and Lama Rinpoche was sent to live in Dzogchen village. From 1959 to the late 1970s, under extreme duress and with no personal freedom, Lama Rinpoche was allotted the heaviest manual labour, forced to move earth and stones, make roads, and build houses for the Chinese. During the worst years, not only was he allocated heavy work during the day, but the evenings were filled with terrible political education sessions. Every so often, Lama Rinpoche was arrested and threatened with imprisonment, or even death, if he did not conform. He was often singled out as an object of intimidation, repression, and struggle. During the years of the Cultural Revolution, Lama Rinpoche was accused of various anti-revolutionary crimes, and forced to live in conditions worse than anyone else. It was only many years later that he was given the less demanding work of tailoring. In the words of Lama Rinpoche himself:

> More devastating than all of this was the complete waste of the crucial time when my youthful mental faculties were at their sharpest. My progress in studying general areas of knowledge and science, and in particular the traditions of Tibetan Buddhism, came to an abrupt end under the Cultural Revolution. The little knowledge I have of Dharma does not extend beyond that which I had when I was sixteen years old. If I had completed my education, I believe I would certainly have been able to write a few more Dharma-related books and leave a positive legacy which would benefit many future generations. However, the lives of my parents and family were taken when I was young, and my holy tutors, spiritual companions, and master khenpos were separated from me by force, leaving me alive but orphaned from their wisdom and love.

During this time, Lama Pema Kalsang Rinpoche prayed day and night for the revival of the precious Buddhist teachings. He risked everything to store secretly even the smallest piece of scripture or representation of the Buddha which came into his possession. He did not waste any time resting from the exhausting daily labour, but tirelessly practised the approach and accomplishment of the yidam, and the practices of generation, perfection, and Great Perfection. In this way he embraced the bad conditions into the path of Dharma to enhance his realisation.

In Rinpoche's own words:

Despite all the physical and mental hardship and suffering that I endured, I also realised many beneficial aspects of these experiences, true teachers which cannot be found in the words of books. These included true renunciation of samsara, realisation of the impermanence and unreliability of worldly pursuits, the way to find inner happiness from undefiled samadhi, and non-separation from the lama who resides in the centre of the heart.

During the years 1978 and 1979, limited freedom to travel was allowed, and Lama Rinpoche took the opportunity to make pilgrimage to almost all the important holy sites of the Central and Tsang regions of Tibet. Travelling widely on foot, he managed to recover many important texts and statues which had escaped destruction. These he saved, and often carrying them on his back, brought them back to Dzogchen. In this way, he managed to preserve many sacred items which otherwise would have been lost or stolen.

Returning to Dzogchen, Lama Rinpoche gathered resources to build a small mantra wheel house on the site of the ruined Dzogchen Monastery, where only a few collapsed walls remained. This was barely permissible at the time, but he managed to complete its construction. Eventually, Lama Rinpoche was able to move back to the monastery grounds where he lived in a tent. Small pujas began to be held in makeshift buildings, and finally monks were permitted to wear robes once again.

In 1981, Lama Rinpoche began reconstruction of the ground floor of the Dzogchen Lama Palace. He based the design on the original building and began construction on the original site, finishing it the same year. This was the crucial first step in the revival of Dzogchen Monastery.

In the same year, Lama Pema Kalsang Rinpoche and Zankar Rinpoche, managed to get permission to establish the first Tibetan language college of Sichuan Province, on the original site of Shirasing Buddhist College. Lama Rinpoche went to great lengths to invite senior non-sectarian masters, the remaining holders of the Dzogchen teaching lineage, to give instruction on Tibetan language and other key subjects. Because Dzogchen is historically such an important seat, these eminent lamas and khenpos were willing to act as school teachers in the new Tibetan Language School.

At first the school was merely a few tents pitched on the site of the original college. Only later was it possible for basic classrooms and accommodation to be built. The school served as a lone outpost of learning and culture to educate a generation of Tibetans who otherwise would have had no opportunity to receive an education, or even study their own language. At that time, becoming a monk or nun was prohibited, so the school also served as a refuge for young men and women, where they were able to dedicate themselves to concentrated study. Later, the Tibetan Language School was moved to Dartsedo in Kham (Chn. Kanding), where it continues to provide comprehensive learning opportunities for young Tibetans; opportunities which are still very difficult to find elsewhere in the region.

In 1982, at the age of thirty-nine, Lama Rinpoche set out to travel on pilgrimage to India, but on the way was involved in a terrible car accident. He was seriously injured and almost died. In Lama Rinpoche's own words:

> I had managed to survive all the obstacles that threatened my life. I was the only one left of all the lamas and monks who had lived in the Lama Palace of Dzogchen. That I was able to continue to work for the Dharma at a time of extreme decline was certainly due to the power of Dzogchen Rinpoche's prayers, and the blessings of Khenpo Tupten Nyendrak's seventeen long life empowerments.

Lama Rinpoche was forced to spend a year in hospital where he underwent multiple operations to pin together broken bones, some of which had to be repositioned over and over again. Not disheartened, Lama Rinpoche recovered his strength, and relying on two walking sticks, travelled to India and Nepal, working for the teachings and making pilgrimage to all the major holy sites. During this time he was also reunited with His Holiness the 14th Dalai Lama. From India he visited Europe and the United States, where he gave teachings to many fortunate Westerners.

Having returned to Dzogchen, Lama Rinpoche took responsibility for the completion of the upper floors of the Lama Palace, as well as the reconstruction of the Grand Temple of Dzogchen Monastery. Despite the physical hardships, he once again joined in the manual labour on the construction site. Lama Rinpoche was also able to build a golden reliquary stupa to enshrine the relics of the sixth Dzogchen Rinpoche, which he had risked his life keeping hidden for twenty-five years. The stupa is now enshrined in the newly rebuilt Dzogchen Lama Palace.

From a prophecy of the Great Treasure Revealer Pema Namdrol Lingpa:

> On the supreme fearless lion throne
> Of Shri Singha Dharma Centre,
> Padma's mind emanation, named Pema,
> Will illuminate like the sun
> The excellent and enlightened qualities
> Of all the Buddha's teachings,

And the thousand-petal lotuses
Of many young Pemas will bloom.

This prophecy was fulfilled when reconstruction of the great Buddhist College of Shirasing began in the fortunate dragon year of 1988. Lama Rinpoche used the small amount of money he received in compensation from his road accident to start the building work. In the past, the college was a highly specialised establishment accommodating only fifty or so of the most exceptional and promising tulkus and monks, together with the most eminent khenpos and lamas. Lama Rinpoche saw the opportunity for expansion, and constructed buildings to accommodate five hundred monks, and a large temple which could hold a thousand people. Again, Lama Rinpoche laboured personally on the construction to the extent that the soles of his feet cracked open.

When the building was complete, he invited many of the surviving senior and most learned masters from all schools of Tibetan Buddhism to revive the teaching lineages, and so Shirasing Buddhist College attracted students from all traditions. This was a very fragile time for the Dharma in Tibet, but Lama Rinpoche managed to bring up a new generation of monks, tulkus, and khenpos in the true Dharma, educating them to the highest possible standard. He spent the next ten years living in the college, focused on educating the younger generation, so there would be qualified teachers to spread the Dharma in the future.

Lama Rinpoche also revived the tradition of ordination in Tibet, and was the first master to give the vows of ordination in Samye Monastery after the Cultural Revolution, in the same temple where the first ever Tibetans became monks. Travelling extensively, he was invited to give teachings and empowerments in the great monastic seats of Dorje Drak, Mindroling, Palri, Jigme Lingpa's seat at Tsering Jong, Samye, and Drigang, as well as over a hundred of Dzogchen's branch monasteries. Lama Rinpoche also established extensive community aid and education programmes through his charitable organisation, the Kalsang Foundation.

In 2003, Lama Rinpoche completed the Lotus Ground Great Perfection Retreat Centre in Dzogchen Pema Tung, the site of his previous incarnation Pema Banza's retreat centre. It is from here that he now shares the blessings of one of the closest and most pure Longchen Nyingthig lineages in the world. Only five lineage holders connect All-knowing Jigme Lingpa with Lama Rinpoche, all of whom were truly eminent masters.

Despite being still very active in teaching, writing, and travelling, Lama Rinpoche now spends most of his time in silent retreat, rising early every day to engage in sessions of prostration, writing, and meditation.

Working with all the tremendous hardships and challenges he has faced throughout his life, Lama Rinpoche fully embodies the activities of Buddha body, speech, and mind. With his body he rebuilt Dzogchen Monastery from the foundations up, with his speech he teaches the enlightened view of the Great Perfection, and with his mind he never ceases to benefit all sentient beings by transmitting realisation of Dzogchen Great Perfection.

The Expression of Worship and the Request to Listen

Nature of all the buddhas of the three times, Lord of the families and oceanic mandalas, supreme protector holy lama whose kindness has no equal, I bow down utterly, touching my head to the immaculate dust below your feet. With tremendous devotion of my three doors I pay homage and take refuge. I pray, bless the mindstream of myself and all other sentient beings.

> Never growing tired of gazing upon the blossoming lustrous smile of your sublime countenance,
> The vivid anthers of the radiant marks and characteristics becomes nectar to the eyes of all beings.
> The corolla of your compassion completely embraces the vast sphere of the three realms.
> White Lotus Lord Buddha, reside in and nurture the ocean of my mind today.
>
> In Sukhavati is Amitabha, in Potala is Avalokiteshvara,
> In the world is the Lotus King. To beings they appear separate, but
> The activities of the three kayas are combined in one nature –
> Glorious Buddha Lotus Born,
> Especially loving to beings of the Land of Snows with your rays of affection, to you I pay homage.
>
> Endowed with the combined might of the adornments of the world, the Six Ornaments and Two Supreme Ones,
> Compassion, learning, and realisation;
> Through hidden yogic discipline in holy forests,
> Yogi of the great expanse who realised samsara and nirvana as the dharmakaya,
> I pray at the feet of Drimey Ozer.
>
> Knowing all there is to know, treasure of compassion towards beings,
> Emanation of Drimey Ozer, depository of mind treasures,
> Sky-yogi of the luminous great expanse,
> I pray at the feet of Jigme Lingpa.

The Dzogchen Path

Empowered master and teacher of the profound treasures of
Padmasambhava all-knowing in the three times,
Emanation of Sangye Lingpa held in a secret manner,
I pray at the feet of Kunsang Shenpen.

Manifestation of the compassion of Arya Lokeshvara,
Supreme guide of beings travelling to the land of liberation,
Meaningful to all who have a connection, yogi of the great expanse,
I pray to Jigme Gyalwe Nyugu.

Single unified emanation of the inseparable compassion
Of Padmasambhava, embodiment of the victorious ones of the
   three times,
And Vimalamitra who attained the vajrakaya rainbow body,
I pray to Migyur Namkhai Dorje.

Upholder of the victory banner of theory and practice
Of the tradition of the Great Vidyadhara Orgyen,
Dharma Lord possessing a treasury of precious enlightened
   qualities,
I pray at the feet of glorious lama (Orgyen Tenzin Norbu).

Exalted manifestation of the inseparable compassion
Of Dawa Drakpa, mighty scholar of the exalted land, and
All-knowing Lord, actual Manjushri of the Land of Snows,
I pray to spiritual master Shenpen Choki Nangwa.

You received blessings of the three lineages, perfected the great
   power of enlightened intent,
Mastered the four visions, and attained the kingdom of the
   dharmakaya.
Primordial protector in the guise of a man,
I pray to Jigme Yonten Gonpo.
Bless me with transference of realisation of enlightened mind.

SHI! From the unexcelled palace of dharmadhatu,
The very essence of all buddhas of the three times,
I pray to the supreme root lama,
Who showed my mind to be the actual dharmakaya.
Turn my mind and others' to the Dharma.

Whoever lives on Mt. Meru – nature of supreme gold – Mandara:
   gods together with harm-bringers,

Expression of Worship and the Request to Listen

And whoever of the nagas living underground illuminating the darkness with the light of their serpent's hood jewels,
Whichever supremely joyful vidyadharas, who live gloriously among snow mountains,
In order to listen to teachings that enable entrance to the holy door of liberation, all of these, come here!

Whoever has become a student of the One Gone to Bliss,
Wherever in the ten directions of the thousand-fold universe,
Come here at this time,
All who wish to listen to a rain of holy Dharma!

In all worlds in the extent of space,
Gods, nagas, harm-bringers, gandharvas, demi-gods,
Kumbhandas, kinnaras, reptiles and so on,
All those with miraculous minds, come here!

Delightful to listen to for a thousand aeons,
Bringing eternal bliss to whoever hears it,
The harmonious speech of the One Gone to Bliss, the sound of nectar-like Dharma,
I am imparting this, so listen with faith and respect!

Eternal supreme refuge of whomsoever,
The enlightened qualities of the Three Jewels are inconceivable;
Knowing these, the full maturation is likewise inconceivable.
Even for the count of millions of billions of kalpas,
It is difficult to find mere mention of the name of the Precious Jewels.
So, for complete liberation of myriad preciousness,
Listen with respect to this profound teaching of the Victorious One!

The language of the gods, nagas, harm bringers,
The kimbhandas, and all human languages,
The languages of all wandering beings, however many,
May this teaching translate into all these languages!

Teaching Day One

Having finished last year's Dharma teaching session, after a period of one year, through the compassion of the buddhas and lamas, we have once again gathered together here, in the Lotus Ground of Dzogchen Monastery. Although the human body, and life in general, are neither permanent nor stable, I trust everyone here continues to remain in good health. Particularly in the degenerate age, at this final time of the decline in lifespan, we live as if in a buffeting gale of harmful, undesirable negative conditions, so there are many people who were with us last year who are not here today, extinguished like oil lamps in the wind. Therefore, if we measure the extent of the impermanence and unreliability of our situation, it is such good fortune that we are able to be here today to enjoy the holy Dharma. This is due to previously accumulated merit remaining undiminished, and the kind compassion of the essence of refuge, the Three Jewels.

Now, if we are happy, it is due to the compassion of the Precious Jewels. If we are miserable, it is the karmic result of a previous life. This is the thinking of a faithful Buddhist who has convinced faith in cause and effect. In addition, it is the unmistaken mode of thinking of someone dedicated to following the Mahayana path of Dharma. In the course of one person's life, the times we think 'I'm happy' are when coarse feelings of suffering are few. The occasions when we think 'I'm miserable', strong feelings of suffering have descended upon us. In this way, the two: happiness and misery, are connected together like the two sides of a saddlebag. They are like the turbulent white clouds of the season between autumn and winter, in as much as, hidden behind all happiness is misery; on the far side of every lofty mountain there is a downward slope. This is the general nature of worldly activities.

No one here today is exempt from this mixture of happiness and misery. We pass our lives among steep mountain passes and treacherous defiles, and what is more, our life is continually being exhausted by time. What is known as 'time' is a vast enemy who gobbles up the three realms and their contents. Having been consumed by time, there is not one composite thing that is not totally eradicated. If we divide time into past, present, and future, as the past falls behind us, all activities pass and are abandoned on the path we left behind. As activities of yesterday and the days previously become nothing but the subject of today's memories, so these accounts of the past, the refuse and rubbish of old things, get put out with the garbage. Many years from now, most past activities will have left no trace.

In respect of future plans, we imagine what will happen: 'After this, let's do that...' 'tomorrow and next year...' 'in the future I want this kind of...' The wheel of time turns moment by moment, a brief moment is a click of the fingers, a longer interval is the length of a human life, but ultimately, from the perspective of when both come to end, in the moment they cease, they are the same. What we call 'this moment now' is our perception of the present between the past and the future, but in fact there is not one moment that is not included in one of the two: past or future.

If we do experience delusory dream-like perceptions once momentarily, then, as we just mentioned, having been consumed by this great fearsome enemy 'time' that devours everything, there is nothing in the universe of the three realms – three states of existence, either the outer container or the inner contents – that is not swallowed whole. Whether ourselves or others, whether of high, low, or middling status, from the gods Brahma, Indra, or Vishnu, down to the short-lived insect that came into existence last night, we are all prey to the fangs of the demon of impermanence. We do not know when those jaws will gobble us up, and we will disappear into the demon's belly.

While we are alive and death is not imminent, look at ourselves – first at the time we were children, then while we were young, and finally when youth has passed. If we compare photos from the beginning, middle, and end of a person's life, we can clearly understand the stark changes human beings undergo.

I once wrote a poem on the back of one of my own pictures:

> First a child with a top-knot of black hair,
> Later a young man with beautiful conch-white teeth,
> Finally the body of an old monk with a shaven head.
> Who can trust this transitory, illusory show?

I also wrote:

> At the very end, when I become
> A collection of bones and skin, and a few specks of dust,
> The one to experience the results of my good and bad karma
> Will again be something else; this delusory phenomena is
>   perplexing!

In this way, life is a phenomenon of change. Under the influence of time, changing from moment to moment, the wheel of suffering of old age, sickness, and death turns. To recount the changes in the life of someone is a sad story. If we talk about anyone's life, of course it is full of pain and despair: 'He didn't fulfil his ambition, she failed to accomplish anything. If they hadn't done that, this would never have happened...' In the beginning people died, in the end a fortune was lost. Aside from all that, there are tales of beatings, killings, cold, hunger, and misfortune; things we wanted but did not achieve; sickness, pain, aging, and so on. In short, if we recall our past, all we can say of our entire history, the story of former human generations, seems to be comprised of only suffering.

If we think about the present time, almost everything we do also sows the seed for us to experience future suffering. Of course it does! All we ever do and have in mind are bad intentions: hatred, ways to deceive, methods to cause harm, ways for ourselves to win and our opponents to lose. It is rare for both thoughts and actions to be positive without the admixture of any faults. This being the case, for us samsaric beings, we live within the truth of suffering which harms us directly, and the truth of the all-pervasive origin of suffering, which harms us indirectly.

How is that so? If we are currently experiencing the result of previous all-pervasive karma and afflictive emotions, the cause for suffering to come in the future is that we are currently under these negative influences, so we continue to sow the seeds for future suffering. If we take an honest look at ourselves, this is something we can recognise.

Regarding this, Shantideva said:

> We desire joy, but ignorance
> Destroys our joy like an enemy.

If at this time we consider our situation, it is as if we have been carried off by a vast river and thrown out onto a stony ridge. Understanding how to evaluate the past and consider the future, in addition to making the most of this opportunity we have gained to make positive change, this is also a chance to consider our happiness and misery, both current and into the future. We have met with the opportunity of a great method of gaining a jewel, the value of which we cannot begin to estimate, so do not feel hopeless, thinking 'I'm a householder, and not only that but I've got a female body...' Whether male or female, we can all attain liberation. Male or female, our human body has the six elements. In addition, if the eighteen or thirty-four freedoms and endowments are complete, then this is something even the baby boys and girls of the heavenly realms cannot achieve. This is called attaining a 'particular physical basis better than the gods'. As it is said:

> A modest female rebirth, but high realisation.

On the basis of a female physical body, it is possible to develop the realisation of the Buddha. And, if you are a man, do not feel hopeless thinking 'I'm just some guy...' You have the six chakras, right? The object of our aspiration prayers is to attain a human body. It is the basis from which the thousand buddhas of this fortunate aeon are born and attain enlightenment. Also, some may be thinking 'I used to be a monk, I've appropriated monastic offerings. By not protecting my vows, I've fallen to the ranks of a lowly householder. Whatever I've done, nothing has been achieved. There is no one worse than me here.' But do not lose hope! You believe in cause and effect, without developing any wrong views. You have not disparaged the Dharma or lamas. If you have not transgressed, impaired, violated, broken, or lost the Secret Mantra vows, then you have not done inexpiable deeds.

The Buddha taught:

> The flowers of campaka may become old, but
> One hundred ordinary flowers are no rival.
> However lowly my followers may become,
> One hundred ordinary people are no rival.

Of the four defeats, one of them may have occurred, however if you have not let all of them be lost, benefit and merit have still been gained. You may wear layperson's clothes, but by not becoming contaminated by killing, stealing, and so forth, you can maintain the vows of a lay person purely. However you say it, there is a difference between someone who has engaged with the Dharma and someone who has not, just as in the above quotation. What need is there to mention a monk practitioner who, having donned the victory banner of saffron robes and taken the vows of a novice and fully ordained monk, maintains them appropriately?

As it is said:

> The Lord of the three states of existence has taken rebirth a hundred times,
> But only held the victory banner of saffron robes this once.

That goes without saying. In particular, a group of four or more fully ordained monks represents the Sangha of the Precious Jewels. They are the object of veneration, the field of offering. There is no teaching of Sutra or Tantra not included within the three trainings, and there is no other path of practice.

In this case, everyone here without exception possesses positive karma and good fortune, having previously accumulated merit – we have established this by way of both scripture and reasoning, so that now, with happiness and joy, everyone here can enjoy the nectar of holy Dharma. This enjoyment of the supreme medicine to clear away the disease of afflictive emotions is a shared positive karma we have accumulated together, by the strength of which we are brought together by one teaching, gathered together in one Dharma hall.

If we illustrate our individual previous karmic propensities, based solely on positive and negative, then, when Dzogpa Chenpo is taught, there is reference to two aptitudes: sharp and dull. This refers to those whose mind state is either of objective appearances or of self-manifest rigpa. Because of differences in understanding of those with sharp or dull faculties, then the result of practice differs from person to person, but this mainly depends on the amount of effort they put into devotion and pure vision. This being the case, in short, this sun of the holy Dharma, like the celestial sun that orbits the four continents, shines upon everyone with no distinction of status or class, so whoever basks under the sun is able to do so. There is no prejudice or partiality involved, however a north-facing cave does not receive any sunlight, because it does not have the correct outlook to receive it.

The Buddha taught numerous Dharma teachings, for example the teachings given by means of the spoken word. There are also teachings given in the language of non-humans – gods, nagas, harm-bringers, gandharvas, rakshasas, and so forth. But if our mindstream is corrupted with wrong views, even if the Buddha himself were to appear, there would be nothing he could do, as is told in the stories of Devadatta and Sunaksatra. Additionally, the Buddha taught the inexpressible ultimate truth free of all description, the suchness of Dharma, through unspoken means. If you know how to receive it, it is possible to receive this inexpressible ultimate Dharma taught throughout the continuous wheel of eternity. In addition, he also taught instructions based upon symbols and miracles. If you know how to realise these, the symbols and signs of the phenomenal world arise as Dharma. This also is a secret, profound, unceasing miracle of the Victorious One.

In terms of the teacher who teaches Dharma with this kind of miraculous speech, some beings to be tamed are taught by a dharmakaya teacher, some are taught by a sambhogakaya teacher, and some by a nirmanakaya teacher – particularly beings of the degenerate age like us. In this regard 'we' all cannot be subsumed in one encompassing category. How can an ordinary person measure the capacity of another? For the sake of a sentient being like me, the Buddha appears in the form of a spiritual teacher, taming like by like. They have the same face, hands, and actions as us. They are like a person. The way they eat, the way they dress, and so on – it is all the same, even down to their way of speaking, which conveys their message. This is so that we may think, 'If I practise, I will surely achieve something like this.' Therefore, the Buddha appears in the form of a lama and teaches the Dharma.

In that way, as the lama is the representative of Buddha speech, he also must be the representative of Buddha body. In this way, if we can meditate that our lama's mind is inseparable from Buddha mind, which does not waver from the ultimate sphere, then we can draw forth blessings. Not only that, when our lama is teaching Dharma, if we can make offerings with faith and devotion, the merit is particularly great.

What is the reason it is so great? The blessings of the Buddha at that time reside in the lama, so we need to be able to draw forth those blessings with our faith and devotion, and also by gathering the accumulations, and purifying obscurations. Moreover, if we have faith, we can actually see the Buddha's enlightened form. For example, Magadha Sangmo said:

> Protector of all sentient beings without exception,
> And subjugating deity of a host of terrible maras,
> Knowing all realities as they are, without exception,
> Bhagavan with your retinue, come here I pray!

By reciting these four lines, it is as if we can invite the Buddha with his retinue, instantly from a far off place. In actual fact the Buddha does not leave, or stay, or pass away. Forever looking to benefit sentient beings, in his omniscient nature, there is nothing that the Buddha does not see, including each individual sentient being's past, present, and future karma and habituated obscurations, even the very slightest. Therefore, if invited, he will come to anyone, and he can be seen.

Guru Rinpoche taught:

> For everyone with faith, there is a Padmasambhava.

And also:

> For those with faith, Padmasambhava rests at their door.

We have been born in a land that has the Dharma, met with a time when the Dharma is widespread, and we have the freedom of opportunity to hear and practise the Dharma. These circumstances are found only very rarely and are very meaningful. Not only that, but since the Dharma began to spread again in this region, here in Dzogchen Lotus Ground we have received very many empowerments, transmissions, and teachings. Thinking 'What tremendous fortune!' this is an appropriate time to repeatedly arouse thoughts of happiness and joy.

If just the water from the vase used when receiving empowerments was saved up, there would be a copious amount. This forms our karmic connection together. However, it is difficult and rare to practise all the teachings we have received. When that is not possible, that which we have received is not really very useful. If that is the case, first, from this day forward we need to know how to begin to practise. There is no way not to understand this. What is it we must understand? We need deep understanding of the benefit given by these teachings that we have received. To give an example, in our daily lives we need to eat food and wear clothes. In the same way, we also need to practise the Dharma. If we ask, 'What is the benefit of eating food?' it is in order to fill our stomachs, so we are relieved of the suffering of hunger, and nourish our bodies. Similarly, we wear clothes to keep our bodies warm and avoid the suffering of cold, protecting our physical health, and so on. Likewise, we wear attractive ornaments in order to look smart and appear beautiful.

Practising the Dharma is also the same, but of much more importance. Crucially, it benefits our mind and brings us happiness inside. Because this mind of ours is the driver on the journey through both samsara and nirvana, if we can learn to control it and establish ourselves on the virtuous path of the three doors, we can attain lasting happiness, now and in the future, for ourselves and others. We do it in order to be able to cut back the root of suffering: non-virtuous thoughts and actions. This enables us to abandon harming others, together with its basis, and also to become able to accomplish benefit for others, together with its basis.

To do this we do not need to look far into the future, to the very end of a long period of many lifetimes. By relying on the swift path of the extraordinary Dharma, in this lifetime we can accomplish benefit for ourselves and others. If we do not know how to practise this, it is as if we do not know what we should be eating, and so we end up consuming something inedible, just like the person from some small nomadic valley who is said to have eaten a wax candle thinking it was pork fat! Still, eating a candle may not be that harmful and while we probably would not die, if medicine and poison do become confused, and we were to consume something poisonous, then that would be a grave mistake. Similarly, if we do not know how to practise the Dharma, then in addition to not bringing any benefit, it may become the basis for harm.

Therefore, for whatever action or activity we undertake, we need to attain the beneficial result, and to attain this, we need to understand correctly the manner of accomplishment, without any error. Therefore, the perfect path that is unmistaken, and the method to travel this path of happiness for ourselves and everyone, is called 'receiving and practising the Dharma'.

So now, as we teach and listen to this Dharma, it is taught in the *Sutra Requested by Devaputra Holder of Jewels*:

> All of the Dharma, Buddha's words and the treatises,
> His good teachings and their commentaries –
> By the power of these, this teaching of the Buddha,
> Will remain in this world for a long time.

This holy Dharma of the victorious perfect Buddha which benefits beings, has two aspects: teachings that the blessed Buddha actually gave in person, and commentaries by his followers on their intended meaning. If the eighty-four thousand divisions of the Dharma are grouped together, they are included within the twelve aspects of excellent speech. If these are again grouped together, they are included within the three collections of scriptures: Sutra, Vinaya, and Abhidharma. Based on teaching, hearing, and contemplating these, by means of the three trainings: discipline, samadhi, and wisdom, the doctrine of teaching and realisation is maintained by practice. Thus the root of happiness and comfort for all beings, the teaching of the Buddha, 'will remain in this world for a long time'.

What does this teaching imply? If there was no basis of the practice of discipline, there would be no foundation whatsoever to speak upon. Beyond that, if hearing, contemplating, and teaching the Dharma and its commentaries had not spread, it is said, 'Where the holy Dharma has not spread, from there it will be eclipsed'.

The teachings of the Victorious One and their commentaries, the representations of the Precious Jewels in scripture form, previously only belonged to wealthy households. But if the five volumes of teachings or our thirteen major philosophical texts are not studied or practised, they are of no use – just a mess of pages. If they are left piled up their whole life, never opened, then although it could be said the Dharma is present in that place, actually this represents nothing more than a mere symbol of the doctrine. For example, when the sun has passed behind the westerly mountains, as it finally sets, a red glowing light is left on the mountain top. This is known as the 'dying sun'. Just like this, except for saying the teachings exist, without studying them, there is no further benefit.

Anything dying does not have the complete qualities of something alive, however there is also another reason to use the term 'dying sun'. In the period of the intermediate bardo state of becoming, having cast aside the coarse physical body, based on the aggregates of the four names, when we roam yearning for the mere smell of sustenance, there is no sun or moonlight, just total blackness, insipid grey, and dull reddishness. This example resembles these visions which arise from the three poisons.

What is the reason for discussing this? The point is, it is very important to listen, contemplate, teach, and hear the authentic Dharma. The holy Dharma is generally summarised to consist of the Buddha's teachings and the commentaries on his intent. In particular there is the Sutrayana and the Vajrayana. In the Sutra tradition there is the Foundational Vehicle and the Great Vehicle, and the Vajrayana consists of the outer and inner tantra traditions. This teaching that we are listening to is Vajrayana. In Vajrayana there are three outer tantra sections, called Kriya or Action Tantra, Upa or Conduct Tantra, and Yoga Tantra. In inner tantra there are also three sections, called Mahayoga, Anuyoga, and Atiyoga, of which we are studying supreme Atiyoga.

Also, if we classify the three great views into ground, path, and result, then the ground view is Mahamadhyamaka, the path view is Mahamudra, and the resultant view is Dzogpa Chenpo. Therefore, all of the three great views are included within the resultant teaching of Dzogpa Chenpo. What is more, this place is Dzogchen, and this teaching is Dzogchen. As the name of the teaching has been adopted by the people, and the name for the people has been applied to the place. In the place where the three Dzogchens are gathered, we are discussing the practice of Dzogchen.

This teaching of Dzogchen is the pinnacle of the nine vehicles, the subject of our teaching. If we discuss it in terms of the expressions of the tantras of words, there are six million, four hundred thousand tantras of Dzogpa Chenpo, and so on, a very large number. The quintessence of these tantras, the Buddha's final testament, the testaments of vidyadharas, and the hidden secrets, are ultimately combined together into Vimalamitra's *Secret Heart Essence*, and Padmasambhava's *Heart Essence of the Dakini*. These earlier Heart Essences form the basis of the *Four Volumes of the Heart Essence*, together with the *Ultimate Essence of the Lama*, which is also included with them. In three visions of the wisdom magical form of All-knowing Victorious Longchenpa, elucidation of the intent of the innermost quintessence of these was transmitted to one person, as enlightened blessings of the mind transmission. Thereby, sounds and visions arose of symbols and scriptures, and the three transmissions became complete in him.

Who was this person? He was the latter All-knowing One, Rigzin Jigme Lingpa. His mind treasure, from the sky treasury set of teachings, is the later Heart Essence known as the *Heart Essence of the Great Expanse*, which in modern times is widespread throughout the four continents pervaded by sun and moonlight. So it is a section of this Dharma that we are studying today.

These teachings of Dzogpa Chenpo exist as individual lineages of empowerment, guidance, and direct instructions, and our current section of liberating guidance consists of both the stages of preliminaries and main practice. According to the tradition of guidance, regarding the preliminaries, there are texts like the *Introduction to the Preliminaries – Words of my Perfect Teacher*. In terms of the tradition of recitation, there are texts like the *Sublime Path to Omniscience*, which we are discussing now. What is more, according to the earlier tradition in Dzogchen Monastery, based on practise of the *Dzogchen Heart Essence of the Dakini*, thirteen practitioners attained the rainbow body, the sign of ultimate accomplishment. This happened right here, in this very monastery.

An example of the guidance text for the *Heart Essence of the Dakini* is the comprehensive *Pure Path of Liberation*, and the recitation for this is also called the *Pure Path of Liberation*, which starts 'OM, myself and the sentient beings of the three realms...' When I was a child of five or six, this is what my writing tutor got me to practise writing out, and it was also the recital that was done without fail as village rites. In the past, in the monastery there was what was known as 'making the winter vow' when, apart from one or two of the important groups of lamas, it was forbidden to let smoke rise into the sky during practice sessions. Also, our way of life in the monastery was governed by the eighteen sacred precepts. Practising the *Heart Essence of the Dakini*, there was the established discipline of engaging in one hundred day retreats. Later, the story of how this became just a nominal representation of what it used to be is known by the old folks here.

The primary guidance text on the main practice of the *Heart Essence of the Great Expanse* is the *Khridyig Yeshe Lama*, with the supporting teachings of the real reference points of the innermost enlightened intent, which are the *Four Heart Essences* together with the auxiliary teachings, plus the seventeen Dzogpa Chenpo tantras, and so on. What we are teaching and listening to at this time is the recital text of the *Dzogchen Heart Essence of the Great Expanse Preliminaries*. The real root of this preliminaries recital text is the unique inner preliminaries of taking refuge and arousing bodhicitta onwards, which are the mind treasure of All-knowing Jigme Lingpa. The text preceding that, the recitals of the six common outer preliminaries, was added by Dodrupchen Jigme Trinle Oser, who was one of the Four Jigmes from Kham, the chief heart disciples of All-knowing Jigme Lingpa.

The lineage I hold is transmitted down from Jigme Trinle Oser himself, and chiefly from Jigme Gyalwe Nyugu. Jigme Gyalwe Nyugu's testament fell to Migyur Namkhai Dorje, who passed it to Orgyen Tenzin Norbu, who passed it to Choje Shenpen Nangba, who passed it to Jigme

Dadrin Yonten Gonpo. The lineage that I have been given was transmitted like this.

The lineage of the Four Jigmes is widely transmitted, but all four of them are included among the lamas of Drupwang Dzogchen Monastery. These days, the lineage of the Heart Essence is found everywhere, however it has always propagated from this key monastic seat alone. Some are students of a lama, and some are students of students. Like the difference between a tree trunk and its branches, in short they can all be represented by 'the tree'.

If the preliminaries are not completed first, then the purpose of the main practice will not be fulfilled. These days there are many, here and abroad, Easterners and Westerners, who all say they are practising the main practice of Dzogpa Chenpo. There may be many, but if they have reached the key point of true practice, it is an essence of emptiness and compassion. Therefore, be certain that there is no way the fire of emptiness can be present without the smoke of compassion. To say this is actually present, with regard to either ourselves or others, is a rare thing.

Why is this rare? It is due to lack of a good firm foundation in the preliminaries. When the accumulations are not gathered and the obscurations are not purified, it is difficult for special qualities to grow without cause. How can a result that is causeless ripen? It is like a picture hung without a wall, or trying to install a roof without walls or pillars.

If, having accumulated and purified through the preliminaries, and if based upon the key points, maturation of one's mindstream is good, then by relying on guru yoga in connection with this, by the strength of devotion, the blessings of the lineage are received. With this, based on the crucial practice points of the main practice, culmination can occur. Not only that but, the root of blessings is the lama, therefore blessings of the three roots, along with accomplishments and enlightened activity, come to be attained together.

GOODNESS OF THE BEGINNING – THE INTRODUCTION

EXPLANATION OF THE TITLE OF THE ROOT TEXT

We are studying the preliminaries recital text in the manner of practical guidance, which has three parts:

1. The goodness of the beginning, the introduction.
2. The goodness of the middle, the meaning of the text.
3. The goodness of the end, the conclusion.

Of the goodness of the beginning, the introduction, it is the time to explain the subsidiary topics of exposition. These are:

a) Stating the title.
b) Expressing homage.
c) The pledge of composition.

In connection with stating the title, the meaning of the title needs to be explained, so the title is:

The Sublime Path to Omniscience, Recital for the Preliminaries of Dzogpa Chenpo Heart Essence of the Great Expanse, Arranged in Proper Order.

What is the meaning of the 'dzog' in 'Dzogpa Chenpo'? When we have finished reading sutras and commentaries, at the end are often the words 'dzog so'. In that way, the words 'dzog so' taken literally means 'the end', but that is not the actual meaning. Although it may be the end of one read-through, if we were to say 'that's the end' it would be inauspicious, and the interdependent connection of words would not be positive, therefore in its place the meaning of 'fully complete' is added in one word which means 'perfect'. Alternatively, 'finished for the moment' is written, so 'for the moment' is added to limit the negative connotation. In short, 'dzog' has the meaning of 'complete' or 'inclusive'.

At this stage, when saying 'Dzogpa Chenpo', what is complete? What is thoroughly perfect? All phenomena subsumed in the appearances and possibilities of samsara and nirvana comprise vast rigpa wisdom – great luminosity-bliss, a nature of unseparated appearance-emptiness, the foundational continuum of the essence of enlightenment, the state in which there is nothing which is not subsumed, and which is fully complete, or entirely perfect. Therefore the word 'dzog' is used.

How are both samsara and nirvana complete? From the state of unwavering dharmadhatu, the expression of delusory samsara's myriad joys and miseries arises, like clouds appearing in the sky. So, in this way, samsara is complete within the state of rigpa. This samsaric perception is one manifestation of it.

How is nirvana complete? As delusion dissolves into the ground, it is the state of the undeluded original way of abiding. For example, in the sky, originally without transition or change, it is as if a transient gathering of clouds of delusion has dissolved into the expanse of the sky. Enlightenment is the actualisation of having the two purities, which is also complete within rigpa. Therefore it is taught nirvana is complete within rigpa. In this way is it 'dzogpa' or 'perfect'.

In addition, the reason for saying 'chenpo' or 'great' is as follows: All enlightened qualities and activities of the Buddha bodies and wisdom are intrinsic, in the manner of the sun and sunlight. This kind of great perfection has the nature of wisdom that completely pervades samsara and nirvana – vajra of the sky pervading space in its entirety, unchanging. Therefore it is called 'great' or 'chenpo'. So that is Dzogpa Chenpo.

This kind of subject, the actual Dzogpa Chenpo of the three: ground, path, and result, and the three: view, meditation, and conduct, and so on, is codified by the words of expression of Dzogchen, from the limitless numbers of which, this is a time to teach the *Heart Essence of the Great Expanse*.

What is the meaning of 'great expanse'? Generally, 'great expanse' is taught to be large and extensive, like a vast sky. Here this is taught to be connected with the name of the All-knowing Victorious Longchen Rabjam. 'Longchen' or 'great expanse' has the meaning of profound emptiness, and 'rabjam' or 'immensity' indicates the vastness of apparent phenomena. Therefore, the first indicates Dzogchen trekcho, and the second, spontaneously accomplished togal. In summary, all the tantras, scriptures, and direct instructions of Dzogpa Chenpo are included in the secret treasury of Victorious Longchenpa's enlightened mind, in the same way as all of the world's rivers flow into the ocean.

As All-knowing Victorious Longchenpa accepted Jigme Lingpa with his wisdom form, blessings of realisation of the mind transmission were transmitted into Jigme Lingpa's mind. Thereby Longchenpa's secret mind treasury became widespread, and in reliance on these transmissions of the Dzogpa Chenpo teachings, the later All-knowing One, Rinzin Jigme Lingpa, founded the tradition. As a source of water is traced to the glacier, so the Dharma fortune of the later Heart Essence is called the *Heart Essence of the Great Expanse*.

Dividing the Heart Essences between earlier and later does not signify a higher or lesser spiritual approach, nor more or less the importance of their key points. It is merely divided between earlier and later times. Between the preliminaries and main practice of the *Dzogpa Chenpo Heart Essence of the Great Expanse*, we are studying the preliminaries. Between the guidance on the preliminaries, and the recital text arranged for convenience to be practised regularly, this is the recital text.

The title mentions it is 'arranged in proper order.' Generally, there are three types of transmission:

1) Mind transmission of the victorious ones.
2) Rigpa transmission of the vidyadharas.
3) Aural transmission of mundane individuals.

In addition to these, three transmissions of the early translation school's important treasure category are added:

1) Transmission of prophetic authorisation.
2) Transmission of empowered aspiration.
3) Transmission of the dakini's entrustment.

By opening each section of the teaching that comes from the category of treasures and possesses the six transmissions, the seal of indestructibility is placed upon them. Until these are placed into the hands of a karmically destined doctrine master, they remain held under a seal of secrecy. When the time has come to benefit beings, for the karmically destined person who has accomplished the power of prayers and aspirations, the power of their previous karmic propensity is awakened. Receiving the extraordinary blessings of the great master Padmasambhava and others, they reveal the treasure.

Not only that, the treasure revealer also reveals the concealed general sequence of the tantra, transmission, or direct instruction for each individual characteristic Dharma treasure. Straightening out any kinks, they rearrange any mistakes in the sequence to put it in the correct order, and fill in any parts that are not complete, so as to make it suitable for recitation and practice. This is called 'compile into good order', so this kind of correct compilation of a treasure text is said to be 'arranged in proper order'.

The above narrative background of the source of this teaching indicates the necessity of having a general outline of the title. Following this, to focus on specifics, like a handle, the real name to hold onto is *Sublime Path to Omniscience*.

What is the meaning of 'omniscience'? All phenomena that exist, as they are, without exception, are known instantly in direct perception. This is the characteristic of omniscience. Therefore, the truth of profound emptiness, how things exist, and the totality of limitless knowable phenomena, is all known. Who possesses such omniscient wisdom? It is the perfect Buddha, Transcendent Perfect Conqueror, who has cast far away the stains of things to be abandoned in their totality, and actualised all enlightened qualities of things to be realised without exception. It is he who has put an end to all faults, and possesses all good qualities.

If we similarly wish to actualise the true level of manifest enlightenment that does not dwell in the extremes of samsara or nirvana whatsoever, then we will not be able to accomplish or actualise it without depending on this kind of excellent path. Therefore, in order to lead sentient beings to be tamed onto the holy path of liberation, the Victorious One taught eighty-four thousand gates of the Dharma, to accord with the individual mental capacities of sentient beings. To say this again in summary: the three turnings of the wheel of Dharma are for the three types of beings to be tamed. The ultimate goal of all those paths is the same – the accomplishment of perfect enlightenment. However they differ in the speed of the path, the level of hardship, and the number of methods.

Our path belongs to the Mahayana in general, and specifically to the Vajrayana. In addition, it is the extremely swift path of luminosity Dzogpa Chenpo. By following it, those with diligence can actually attain buddhahood in one lifetime, so it truly is a sublime path. Therefore, this text is called the *Sublime Path to Omniscience*.

THE FOUR DHARMAS OF NECESSITY AND SO FORTH

Additionally, what are the four Dharmas, the ancillaries of necessity, and so on? They are:

1) The expressed.
2) The necessity.
3) The connection.
4) The ultimate necessity.

With regard to what is to be expressed, the first of our topics of discussion is the six aspects of guidance of the common outer preliminaries. These are the common spiritual approach mind trainings, which consist of:

- The four mind changers.

Together with:

- The benefits of liberation from samsara.
- How to rely on the expert guide to the path, the spiritual teacher who teaches the path to liberation.

Subsequently, we will address the unique inner preliminaries, which are not common to the Foundational Vehicle. These are:

- The entrance to the path, taking refuge.
- The actual entrance to the path, arousing bodhicitta.

Following that, we will learn the practices which are not common to the lower Vajrayana yogas:

- The method to purify obscurations of the path, meditation and recital of Vajrasattva.
- Gathering the accumulations, the mandalas of the three kayas.
- The auxiliary mandala, the kusali's accumulation of merit by giving the body as an offering.

Then lastly, we will study:

- The method to strongly arouse the wisdom of realisation in the mindstream, the profound path of guru yoga.

These constitute the common and unique preliminaries. In short, by accumulation and purification the mind is made workable. Consequently, through devotion, blessings are drawn forth into the mind with the special means of direct instructions, which are arranged to be easy to engage with. Of the four Dharmas of necessity, this is the expressed.

What is the necessity? Having entered the path of Secret Mantra Dzogchen, those Dzogchen practitioners with sharp faculties actualise liberation and holy enlightenment. They do so by having first completed this practice of the preliminaries, then by progressing with the main practice. Also, those with extremely sharp faculties can attain liberation by means of just this path of the preliminaries, so actualisation of non-abiding wisdom is the necessity.

As for the ultimate necessity, it is the need of the necessity, which is for all mother-like sentient beings, infinite as the sky, by travelling this path, to be established in enlightenment.

Also, the words of this teaching are connected to the meaning, so by practising the meaning of the expressed subject, the truth of the goal can be accomplished. This is the connection, thus completing the four Dharmas of necessity.

The above concludes the first section: stating the title, together with the ancillaries, as part of the discussion of the goodness of the beginning, the introduction.

HOMAGE AND THE PLEDGE OF COMPOSITION

Second is the expression of homage. The start of the root recital text reads:

> **Although primordially enlightened, your unceasing forms tame beings in any way necessary.**
> **You display various miracles, yet are free from aggregates, elements, sense-fields, and dualistic grasped-grasping.**
> **Although appearing in human form, you are actually a buddha, blazing with a thousand light rays of wisdom and compassion.**
> **Not just in this life, you are my refuge forever; I rely on you [Khyentse Ozer], bless me!**

The first line reads:

> Although primordially enlightened...

Primordially, or originally, there were not even the words 'samsara' or 'nirvana', 'liberation' or 'delusion', in the unchanging ground expanse, the pure realm of inseparable samsara-nirvana. From this, the single sphere of rigpa emptiness, realisation-free wisdom that knows its own nature, was purified of the ground of non-rigpa delusion and became enlightened with the six special qualities. Thus this indicates the dharmakaya.

> Your unceasing forms tame beings in any way necessary.

Both naturally abiding, primordially pure expanse of emptiness, and natural luminosity, spontaneously accomplished rigpa, manifest possessing the two purities, inseparably. From this pure realm of inseparable appearance-emptiness and the unity of bliss-emptiness, manifestations endowed with the five certainties – the form of the sambhogakaya and its pure realm, retinue, and activities – are displayed unceasingly. Of the two forms of the rupakaya, this indicates the single sambhogakaya.

> You display various miracles, but are free from aggregates,
> elements, sense-fields, and dualistic grasped-grasping.

In accordance with the dispositions, capacity, and intent of individual beings to be tamed in any way necessary, you display various miracles, in the manner of a reflection of the moon in water. These manifest in the form of spiritual teachers, or alternatively houses and towns, medicine and sustenance, birds and animals, food to nourish the hungry, nectar to quench the thirst of the parched, a place to sleep for visitors, an escort to protect from danger, and so on. In short, to benefit sentient beings, when buddhas and bodhisattvas act for their sake, they manifest various miracles according to the inclination of the minds of beings. However, they are free from the five aggregates, twelve sense-fields, eighteen elements, and so on, of delusional dualistic grasped-grasping. This 'display of various miracles' is taught to be the nirmanakaya.

> Although appearing in human form, you are actually a buddha,
> blazing with a thousand light rays of wisdom and compassion.

What does this third line imply? Expanse and wisdom, non-dual object and perceiver, inseparable primordial purity and spontaneous accomplishment – this is the enlightened mind of the Buddha. This vast pure expanse is the ultimate subject of the three collections of scripture and the four classes of Tantra – the holy Dharma. The vast pure expanse of inseparable expanse and rigpa is both the Buddha and the Dharma. Those who realise the enlightened intent of these are the Arya Sangha, therefore:

> Because the Buddha embodies the Dharma,
> He is also the ultimate Sangha.

The one who possesses the combined intent of the Three Jewels and the three kayas is the lama. Therefore, for this reason it says:

> Although appearing in human form, you are actually a buddha.

This kind of lama is the essence of all refuges combined, manifesting in order to benefit beings to be tamed in the degenerate age. The Buddha himself said:

> Do not grieve Ananda, do not lament!
> In future times I will manifest in the form of spiritual teachers
> To bring benefit to yourself and others.

That kind of appearance in the form of a human being is, in general, a manifestation appearing in the form of a spiritual teacher, and specifically, in the case of the master who supplemented this recital text, Dodrupchen Jigme Trinle Ozer, his lama is:

> Actually a buddha, blazing with a thousand light rays of wisdom and compassion.

In Tibetan, rays of wisdom and compassion are 'khyentse ozer', which is the name of All-knowing Jigme Lingpa. What is the meaning connected with this name 'khyentse'? Having perfected the expressivity of the realisation of wisdom knowing reality just as it is, realised in the profound way things exist just as they are, with the wisdom of knowing all things in their entirety, to know the essential point of all knowable phenomena without confusion, is wisdom or 'kyhen'. In unseparated unity from this is compassionate love or 'tse', in the form of light rays or 'ozer'. In the degenerate age, for the teachings of the Secret Mantra, he came like the Second Buddha, lord of the family himself. To explain this in terms of Vajrayana, the embodiment of the five buddha families combined is the Sixth Victorious One, the actual Vajradhara.

> Not just in this life, you are my refuge forever; I rely on you
> [Khyentse Ozer], bless me!

This vow is pledged, not just for this single life or rebirth, but for the entire chain of future lives – until the bodhisattvas have emptied samsara or the sky has collapsed – to abandon selfish intent in order to work for the benefit of sentient beings. Emulating the conduct of Samantabhadra and the activities of Manjushri, which was without any limit, this is just as the aspiration Bodhisattva Manibhadra made:

> Let my pure conduct have no limit!
> Let my enlightened qualities also be measureless!
> By maintaining immeasurable conduct,
> May I accomplish all of these miracles!
> However far space extends,
> Sentient beings are equally limitless;
> The extent of their karma and afflictive emotions
> Is the extent of my prayers of aspiration!

Goodness of the Beginning – The Introduction

The meaning of the expression of homage is: 'In my successive lifetimes you are my refuge forever. Embodiment of all victorious ones combined, I rely on you, holy lama. Bless your faithful and devoted student with transmission of the trifold secret of your body, speech, and mind, and especially realisation of the enlightened intent of your wisdom mind, so I may be inseparable from you!'

With this opening stanza, the *Recital for the Preliminaries of Dzogpa Chenpo Heart Essence of the Great Expanse* expresses the meaning of both the pledge of composition and the connection that engages with the main meaning of the text.

This concludes the goodness of the beginning, the introduction.

Goodness of the Middle – The Meaning of the Text

Unification of the Four Times

Now, for the goodness of the middle, the meaning of the text, the *Recital for the Preliminaries* is taught generally in seven parts. But, before we talk about the main meaning of the text, because this time we are discussing things in the manner of practical guidance, when we practise we need to do so in four daily sessions. This is the instruction on the unification of the four times:

1) Sealing the appearances of the day.
2) Gathering the key points of the senses at dusk.
3) Placing what is knowable into the vase at midnight.
4) Making wisdom luminosity at dawn.

Sealing the Appearances of the Day

The first method is to seal the appearances of the daytime. During the day, whatever forms, sounds, and so on – the apparent objects of the six senses – appear or arise, do not let them come under the distracted, delusional influence of habitual grasping or attachment: afflictive emotions, negative karma, or indifference. Except for merely thinking 'this is...' do not let your three doors come under the influence of distracted delusions. For someone with superior faculties, someone who has cultivated some familiarity, by keeping their three doors under control and uniting them, all appearances, sounds, thoughts, and sensations are the expression of the true nature of phenomena, or they do not waver from that state.

Even if this is not possible, at least do not get lost to the influence of delusion, and with study, contemplation, and meditation, focus your mind one-pointedly in a virtuous direction, so that you pass the time solely with the experience of the Dharma. This is called 'sealing the appearances of the day.'

Gathering the Key Points of the Senses at Dusk

'Dusk' is to be understood as evening, when darkness falls, known as the 'gloom of dusk', and is taught to be the period from when darkness begins to fall until it is too dark to recognise someone. This period was taught by our Teacher, the Blessed One, to be a time to tame demons. Therefore in order for us, his students, to have good luck with the

Dharma, for our practice to be free from obstructions, and so we are not affected by obstructive spirits and other harm, if we meditate at dusk on protection circles, dedicate red burnt offerings, and give away our body in Chod practice, then the benefits are limitless.

Placing What is Knowable into the Vase at Midnight

When going to bed at night, Dharma practitioners have a correct position in which to sleep. Especially, practitioners of Dzogchen sleep with their head pointing north, facing towards the west, with their right side to the ground, right hand held to the chest, and left hand placed on the thigh. This is the manner in which the Blessed One passed into nirvana, the sleeping posture of a lion.

At that time, what is the method of placing what is knowable into the vase? The consciousness of what is knowable of the six senses turns inwards at the time of night, and we fall asleep. The nature of sleep is indeterminate, so we need to guide it towards the direction of virtue by the strength of our intent. If sleep can be transformed, just as all needs and wishes are fulfilled within the good vase, virtue knows no end and increases. In this way, time spent in sleep does not go to waste, or get squandered and lost, but can be transformed into practice. For this reason, this practice is called 'placing what is knowable in the vase at midnight'.

During the day, visualise your root lama at the crown of your head. When it is time to sleep, visualise your lama passing down the path of the central channel to rest at the level of your heart, in its centre, upon an eight-petalled lotus. Merge your mind inseparably with his. As you fall asleep, the eight lotus petals fold closed and, in a sphere of five-coloured lights your lama grows smaller and smaller, becoming inseparable from the indestructible essence of the heart. You should fall asleep concentrating on this.

How is this beneficial? The purpose of this is to allow the delusion of dreams to arise as luminosity. When visualising the lama in the centre of your heart, the symbol of the nature of samsara is the eight-petalled lotus, as the nature of the eight avenues of consciousness is pure wisdom. Upon this are the symbols of the utterly pure white and red constituents, the sun and moon cushions, upon which resides the nature of your root lama in the appearance of the Great Vajradhara of Oddiyana.

If, having received guidance for the Pure Realm of Great Bliss, you are one of those practising the four causes for being reborn in Sukhavati, then visualise the form of Amitabha. Merging your mind inseparably with his, receive the four empowerments, and together with recollection of the Buddha, you should rest in the luminosity yoga of sleep. Similar instruction is found in *Engaging in Bodhisattva Conduct*:

> As the Lord lay down in nirvana,
> Lie down in the preferred direction.
> From the outset be vigilant
> And determine to rise promptly.

Making Wisdom Luminous at Dawn

Likewise, a so-called 'Dharma practitioner' cannot sleep like a yak, and needs to get up when it is necessary to do so. Generally, when the actions of daily activities can be scheduled at regular times, then all the activities of Dharma conduct become continuous, and this is of great benefit. To this end, when it is time for us to get out of bed at dawn, no later than five or five thirty, in the sky in front of us, visualise the nature of our root lama in the form of the Great Vajradhara of Oddiyana, surrounded by a retinue of many heroes and dakinis. In their hands are hand drums or small wooden drums and bells, so consider that the melody of the mantric sounds they play resounds out to rouse us from sleep.

Then, just as we visualised during guru yoga the previous night, still unseparated from a state of luminosity, sit up and assume the key points of the seven-fold posture of Vairochana. What is this? Legs are in the full lotus position or, if you cannot manage that, sit in a comfortable cross-legged position. Rest both your hands on your knees. Keep your back straight. Touch your tongue to the palate. Keep your lips and teeth slightly apart, so between them the movement of breath is slow and natural. Your neck is slightly bent forward. With eyes straight and evenly balanced between open and closed, stare without a reference point into the space in front of you.

What does 'without a reference point' mean? When we look with our eyes, various sights arise before them. Not focussing on any of these is called 'without a reference point'. When we sit like this, if our body is straight, the channels are straight. If the channels are straight, the wind energies are straight, and so on. There are many special positive qualities and necessities associated with this posture.

At this stage, we should expel the stale wind in nine rounds of breathing. For males, from the left nostril the wind energy of desire is exhaled appearing dirty red. The wind energy of aversion is exhaled from the right nostril, dirty-greyish in appearance. Exhaled from both nostrils, the wind energy of delusion is smoky-black in appearance. Thinking these have gone, we expel the stale wind. For females, right and left are reversed. Having finished expelling the stale wind in nine rounds, take a brief rest. Having rested your awareness, remain until your mind is a clear and suitable vessel for meditative concentration.

At this point, we should bless the wind energy. With the breath relaxed, when we breathe in, we need to visualise the syllable OM with its sound and shape, white in colour. As this wind energy remains inside, visualise its sound and shape as a red syllable AH. When breathing out, visualise both sound and form in the shape of a blue HONG. These three syllables of vajra recitation of white OM, red AH, and sky-blue HONG should be recited twenty-one times or more, depending on time.

At this juncture it is time to bless the speech. Once again, the start of the blessing of the speech begins with the seeds of the three Buddha bodies:

OM AH HONG

Then, according to the recital text:

> Fire from a RAM syllable burns my tongue faculty
> Into a three-pronged vajra of red light,
> Which cradles the *Essence of Interdependence* surrounded by the ALI KALI.
> From this pearl-like string of syllables,
> Light emanates, pleasing the buddhas and bodhisattvas with offerings.
> Re-converging, obscurations of speech are purified, and
> All blessings and accomplishments of vajra speech are attained.

The root of all obscurations accumulated through the mode of speech is the verbal expression of this oral faculty. In terms of engaging in the ten non-virtuous harmful actions by means of the body, this necessitates taking life, stealing, or engaging in sexual impurity or misconduct, and so forth. However, to encourage yourself or others to accumulate non-virtuous karma is a non-virtuous action of the speech. What is more, the speech faculty is the source of the four: lying, divisive speech, harsh words, and gossip. Likewise, based on covetousness, ill-will, and wrong views, it is by means of the speech faculty that others are misguided.

To summarise, when it says:

> Fire from a RAM syllable burns my tongue faculty.

This indicates the door of all negativity, the speech faculty, in the centre of which is a red capital syllable RAM. RAM is the essence of fire, as well

Goodness of the Middle – The Meaning of the Text

as the nature of the great wisdom of the speech of all the buddhas. The fire which comes from this burns non-virtue in the body, together with its basis:

> Into a three-pronged vajra of red light.

To visualise this in detail: From a non-perceptual state, within your throat, from a red SHI syllable, a vajra of red light emerges which represents discriminating wisdom, with a perceptible but not palpable form – non-dual appearance-emptiness. The three-pronged vajra lies flat, the hollow interior of its spherical centre represents inseparable expanse and rigpa:

> Which cradles the *Essence of Interdependence*, surrounded by the ALI KALI syllables.

The vowel syllables of wisdom are ALI, and red in colour. The syllables of illuminating method are KALI, and white in colour. Both method and wisdom ALI KALI are coiled around each other like a snake. Surrounding this are the syllables of non-dual method and wisdom, the *Essence of Interdependence* mantra, like pure lapis in colour, encircling it.

> From this pearl-like string of syllables...

There are those who explain the pearl-like string as being entirely white in colour. However, if we understand that the three: ALI, KALI, and the *Essence of Interdependence* mantra, have the three colours of white, red, and sky-blue, and that they represent the non-duality of method and wisdom, then there are those who explain the example of the 'pearl-like string' to be a shining and luminously clear string of syllables.

In short, whichever it is, the text continues:

> Light emanates, pleasing the buddhas and bodhisattvas with offerings.

From all of those syllables, light rays of the three colours: white, red, and sky blue, emanate. From the tip of each ray of light, an offering goddess emanates myriad offering substances beyond measure. From each of their heart centres, light rays beyond measure emanate, like the offering clouds of Samantabhadra – incalculable, inconceivable, immeasurable by the mind, and inexhaustible. With this kind of offering substances, offerings are made to the buddhas and bodhisattvas of the ten directions, and all the buddhas and bodhisattvas are pleased and gladdened by the offerings.

> Re-converging, obscurations of speech are purified.

All these light rays re-converge and purify lies, divisive speech, and so on – all the obscurations accumulated through the doorway of speech.

> All blessings and accomplishments of vajra speech (of all the victorious ones) are attained.

The nature of vajra speech is beyond expression, the nada sound of the nature of the expanse, taking the form of the sixty aspects of Brahma-like voice. This is the blessing. 'Accomplishment', or 'siddha' consists of the eight common accomplishments, and the supreme accomplishments, united with the nature of the seven aspects of union, to swiftly attain the level of Vajradhara. Consider you attain all these accomplishments.

Then we need to recite the vowels and consonants, and the *Essence of Interdependence* seven times each.

Part One, The Prayer to Invoke the Lama

Invoking the Outer Lama

At this stage, the root text reads:

One, the Prayer to Invoke the Mind of the Glorious Lama.

Here, part one, is the prayer to invoke the lama as the basis for training the mind, and also, relying upon that basis, the methods to train the mind. As the basis for training the mind, there are the outer and the inner lamas. First is invocation of the outer lama:

O lama, heed me! O lama, heed me! O lama, heed me o!

With great longing, we call out three times. The addition of a terminative sound 'o' on the third 'O lama, heed me!' is taught to mean that at that moment we should call the supreme lama with a loud and clear voice of strong longing faith, one that is melodious and extended.

Why is it necessary to call to the lama three times? At the time of reciting the first 'O lama, heed me!' recall that the mind of the lama is non-dual with the enlightened mind expanse of all the buddhas, unity of all the buddhas. The Three Roots are embodied in the lama. He or she is the dharmakaya lord embodiment of the three buddha bodies, so we recite 'heed me'. The meaning of this is, 'Look on me with compassion', or 'Hold me in your compassion'.

When saying the second 'O lama, heed me!' we need to recall that the speech of the lama incorporates the embodiment of the holy Dharma, the embodiment of yidam, and the embodiment of the sambhogakaya. Think, 'Glorious protector, holy lama, it is you who heeds all!' When we recite 'O lama, heed me o!' for the third time, recollect that the lama incorporates the embodiment of the spiritual community, the dakinis, and the nirmanakaya. Think, 'Splendorous holy lama, it is you who heeds all!' with strength of devotion and longing, so tears well up in our eyes, and with such faith that our hairs stand on end.

Following that:

**From the blossoming lotus of devotion at the centre of my heart,
Arise gracious lama, my sole refuge!
Tormented by karma and fierce afflictive emotions,
To protect me from this misfortune,**

Reside as the ornament of my crown chakra of great bliss.

Calling 'O lama, heed me!' three times, the compassion of our lama is aroused.

From the blossoming lotus of devotion at the centre of my heart...

As we visualised the previous night when going to sleep, the eight petals of the lotus in the centre of our heart now gradually open. From within the expanse of the blossoming petals of the pure ground of the eight modes of consciousness, with enthusiastic, longing, and confident faith, we call:

Arise gracious lama, my sole refuge!

While invoking him with the words of the recital, we need to recollect the following meaning: 'In this and all future lives, I have no other hope or refuge – only you; you are the single embodiment of all refuges. Teacher of the excellent path to total liberation, gracious holy root lama, arise!' Reciting this, we need to visualise that the lama in our heart centre travels up the central channel, to reside as the ornament of our crown chakra of great bliss.

Tormented by karma and fierce afflictive emotions.

The cause of our torment is non-virtuous actions. These actions are motivated by fierce afflictive emotions, which generate the result of the suffering of the three realms of samsara, full of torment and pain.

To protect me from this misfortune...

Not possessing the good fortune to practise the holy Dharma, negative karma befalls us, so in order to protect us from the poisonous ocean of karma, afflictive emotions, and suffering:

Reside as the ornament of my crown chakra of great bliss.

Upon the crown chakra of great bliss, in the centre of myriad lotuses of ten-thousand blossoming petals, upon the red and yellow pollen beds, are sun and moon cushions. Upon these, with a body vivid with the majestic splendour of the marks and signs, with unimpeded vibrant speech of the sounds of Dharma, and with a mind vivid with the mandala of wisdom and compassion, resides the:

> Unity of the threefold refuge, the Great Vajradhara,
> My root lama, embodiment of all buddhas.
> Never separating, residing upon my crown
> Continuously throughout the three times, bless me!

By praying for him to remain continuously as the ornament on our crown without separation, we should visualise that he resides there.

Invoking the Inner Lama

The invocation for the inner lama or spiritual teacher is indicated by this line:

Arousing all mindfulness and attentiveness, I pray!

Who or what is the inner lama? The inner lama is both mindfulness and attentiveness in our mindstream, which we need to give rise to. When mindfulness, attentiveness, and carefulness have been lost from our mindstream, then our stream of consciousness is unruly, and it can be said 'There's not a brain in our head'. Chattering unconsidered nonsense, an unruly person is worse than an animal. Bad conduct totally lacks the three positive qualities of mindfulness, attentiveness, and carefulness. It is not unreasonable to suggest that such a person is mad. If our mind is not under our own control, then what are we if not mad?

In this case, the term for thinking 'this is appropriate, this isn't appropriate', not forgetting which things are to be cultivated and which avoided, is 'mindfulness'.

As for 'attentiveness', it is awareness of the meaning of all objects of knowledge, without mixing up words and their meanings. In particular, it is awareness of the cause and result of attaining the high status of gods and humans, and awareness of the proper accomplishing cause and result of the ultimate excellence of the level of liberation and omniscience. In short, the source of all the splendour of the four categories of Dharma, wealth, desirable qualities, and liberation, is attentiveness.

Also, from this explanation of mindfulness and attentiveness, we need to understand that in addition, 'carefulness' has been implicitly taught. It is difficult for us samsaric beings to be careful enough to prevent any desirable situation from deteriorating, or to stop undesirable events from occurring, so we often fall into great suffering. Therefore, from today on, we must be careful to exercise the utmost prudence. This is called 'carefulness'.

In this way, mindfulness is the main practice of the holy Dharma. From *Letter to a Friend*:

> My Lord, the Buddha emphasised mindfulness
> Of the body as the only way to progress.
> Focus and guard it well, for all Dharma
> Is destroyed by loss of mindfulness.

Attentiveness is the source of everything excellent. As Nagarjuna states in his *Hundred Wisdoms*:

> Awareness is the great source of
> Teachings, pursuits, pleasures, and liberation.
> Therefore, starting with respect,
> Maintain it, up to and including wisdom.

Also, carefulness is the root of all virtuous Dharma. From the *Moon Lamp Sutra*:

> However much is spoken of the Dharma,
> Discipline, listening, generosity, and likewise patience,
> The root of it all is carefulness, therefore
> The One Gone to Bliss taught, 'Attain it!'

Furthermore, from *Engaging in Bodhisattva Conduct*:

> Carrying a jar full of mustard oil
> Under the scrutiny of a swordsman,
> In fear of death if any gets spilt,
> Likewise a practitioner should concentrate.

A long time ago there was a fierce king. The fierce king ordered a guilty prisoner to be brought before him, whereby vat of oil which was full to the brim was balanced upon the prisoner's head. Then many red-faced executioners, armed with long swords, were brought in. The king said to the prisoner, 'Holding this vat of oil on your head, make a full circuit of the city. If one drop of oil spills from the container onto the ground, these executioners will immediately cut off your head without any argument. If you come back without spilling any oil, I will not execute you, I'll set you free!'

Having said this, the king ordered many singers to surround the prisoner on all sides and sing many songs. He ordered many dancers to perform beautiful dances. With guitars and all kinds of musical instruments, playing all sorts of melodies, they were sent off together. However, the prisoner was very sinful and very attached to his cherished life, so thinking 'My head is going to be cut off!' he knew the only demarcation between dying and living was merely the steadiness of his steps. Except for the stability of his gaze, there was nothing separating him from death.

Concentrating his vision intensely, as if on the tip of a hair, the prisoner was extremely careful. As sweat dripped from his brow, he was in extreme fear of death, and so had no desire whatsoever to listen to the melodious songs, or watch the beautiful dancing. With mindfulness, attentiveness, and carefulness, he moved forward, concentrating only on how to prevent the oil spilling from the vat. In this way, he finally managed to complete the circuit without spilling one drop of oil.

The king asked him, 'When you were walking around the city, there was singing and dancing on all sides. Was the singing melodious? Was the dancing beautiful?' The prisoner replied, 'I heard nothing, I saw nothing. However, if I could have spilled a little oil and not been killed, then as I did so, of course I could have enjoyed a little of those songs and dances!'

Similarly, if we take negative steps into faults and downfalls, the life vein of liberation will be severed, and we will fall down to negative rebirths in the lower realms. Also, as there is no certainty to the lifespan of beings, then who knows when the Lord of Death will arrive? If he is standing beside us searching with desire for our life-force, if we are continually careless, and so in our distraction engage in only negative actions, then like a prisoner being held by the law, the three realms of samsara are our prison. This inescapable prison of karma is certainly much worse than living in the dungeon of a king.

This being the case, the root of all wrong doing comes down to a lack of mindful attentiveness, so knowing this, always relying on mindful attentiveness and carefulness is the root of positive qualities. Maintaining a basis that does not allow negative conduct to arise is extremely important.

The above concludes the teaching regarding the basis for mind training, invoking the lama.

The Common Outer Preliminaries

Relying upon invoking the lama as the basis for mind training, what follows is the actual teaching on the methods how to train the mind. For this there are six subdivisions:

1) Difficulty of finding the freedoms and endowments.
2) The impermanence of life.
3) Karmic cause and effect.
4) The defects of samsara.

These are the four mind changers. In addition, there are:

5) The benefits of liberation.
6) How to follow a spiritual teacher.

These are the six guidance sections of the common outer preliminaries. By wishing to attain the level of ever-lasting bliss of perfect enlightenment, someone who truly wants to practise the Dharma effectively must first start with the methods to turn the mind away from fixation on this life. These methods are the meditations on the difficulties of finding the freedoms and advantages, and the impermanence of life. Then the methods to turn the mind away from attraction to any future lives in samsara, the topics of karmic cause and effect and the defects of samsara, need to be contemplated. If these four do not grow in your mindstream, even liberation from the suffering of samsara on the path of the Foundational Vehicles of shravakas and pratyekabuddhas, is not accomplishable, not to mention attainment of the level of perfect buddhahood by means of the Mahayana Dharma.

If training the mind in the four mind changers enables someone to turn their mind away from samsara, he or she will have become unlike ordinary people, having developed a distinguished noble intent. People on the lower path want themselves to be liberated from samsaric suffering. Alternatively, those on the path of the Mahayana, can arrive at the levels which are able to accomplish benefit for both themselves and others, and establish all mother-like sentient beings on the path of perfect buddhahood.

Whichever path of the higher or lower vehicles you consider suitable to enter, you can do so. Whichever path of the three types of enlightenment you enter, you should attain the result. If you aspire to enter a particular path, first consider the benefits of that particular level of liberation. Therefore the benefits of liberation are taught, so we can know their positive qualities.

The necessity to turn our mind away from samsara is understood by means of the four mind changers. If liberation is attained, there is happiness and pleasure, but if you think that just an intellectual understanding of the benefits of liberation is enough, it is not. For example, knowing the great suffering of being in prison, and merely knowing that if you get out, it will be nice, is of no use; you actually need to get out. Moreover, if you are not able to get out of prison by your own exertions, you need to rely on someone else who is able.

Similarly, travelling on the path of liberation, we need to rely on an expert guide to lead us on the path, someone who has excellent qualities and experience, and who knows how to lead. For this reason, it is impossible to accomplish liberation without relying on a spiritual teacher. What is more, up to now you have not met with a good spiritual teacher, so there is still no end to the suffering of samsara. The reason you are experiencing samsaric suffering is because you have not met with a spiritual teacher to guide you on the path.

Your father may guide you on the worldly path, your mother may teach you good habits, and relatives may treat you well, however, you and everyone else are wandering down a mistaken path, and so experience only suffering. At the time of death, in all previous and future generations, every single one of us carries a load of negative actions the size of the king of mountains. The consequence of this is that there is nowhere else for us to go except down the path of future lives.

In terms of relying on a spiritual teacher, there are three stages to the method: the beginning, the middle, and the end. At first, we need to examine the lama, otherwise, like an old dog who gobbles up any old scraps it finds, I am not sure it is suitable to rely on all who wear fancy robes. What is more, if someone has not managed to achieve something themselves, they cannot use it to benefit others. Better than that, you need to find and follow a spiritual teacher with the qualities of teaching and realisation. However hard you must work, this will form the foundation of this and future lives, for both ourselves and others, and determine whether we will accomplish or fail in this most meaningful of tasks. Therefore, at the beginning it is important not to make a mistake following a lama.

For example, according to the Tibetan calendar, if it rains on the first day of the month, then for the whole of that month there will not be a clear day. Likewise, if you make a mistake following a lama, it is worse than having a poisonous snake enter your house. Like a malevolent gongpo spirit entering your home, not only will it bring suffering into your current life, but a succession of many lives will be blighted by suffering.

However, it is not enough merely to find a good lama, who is without faults, like a precious jewel. In the middle you need to be skilful in following such a learned spiritual teacher. Without becoming disillusioned or discouraged, study the Dharma and practise its enlightened intent, for among all the activities of this life, it is crucial to hold following the lama as being of the upmost importance.

Following this, in the end you need to be skilful at training in the realisation and conduct of the lama. If a skilful student comes to depend on a skilful lama, most important is to adopt the enlightened qualities of the lama's mindstream. Even if these qualities are not adopted exactly, as if taken from a tsatsa mould, then at least, like woollen cloth seeped in dye, the hue of the student's mindstream needs to have improved a little. Such is the teaching on how to follow a spiritual teacher.

1) DIFFICULTIES OF FINDING THE FREEDOMS AND ENDOWMENTS

THE NATURE OF FREEDOM

Now we come to the actual teaching on the text, which gives instructions on the first of the four mind changers: the difficulty of finding the freedoms and endowments. This is the first of the common outer preliminaries. The way that the freedoms and endowments are difficult to find has two sections:

- The common general reflection.
- The unique particular reflection.

Of these, first the common, general reflection has also several subsections:

- Reflection on the nature of freedom.
- Reflection on the particular endowments related to the Dharma.
- Reflection on examples of the difficulty of finding the freedoms and endowments.
- Reflection on numerical comparisons, and so on.

First of these is the reflection on the nature of freedom:

> I am not in the realms of hell, hungry ghosts, animals,
> Long-life gods, the uncivilised, or those with wrong views,
> In a place where a buddha has not come, or with impaired faculties;
> At this time I have gained freedom from these eight unfree states.

The opposite of the eight unfree states is explained to be the eight freedoms, so therefore if you are not experiencing the eight unfree states then consequently your situation is one with the eight freedoms. If you are born in the eight unfree states, your energy and capability to practise the Dharma is weak, therefore you are not free to do so. So, what is the nature of this un-freedom?

> I am not in the realms of hell, hungry ghosts, animals.

In this rebirth we were not born in hell. In terms of hell there are the sixteen hot and cold hell realms, and the ephemeral and surrounding hell realms, making eighteen. Similarly for the hungry ghosts, there are the two divisions of those who move through space and those who live collectively. For animals also there are those that live scattered, those that live in the depths, and so on. We are free from these three lower realms having attained the freedom of the higher realms.

> Long-life gods, the uncivilised, or those with wrong views.

If you think, 'Aren't the god realms comfortable?' Generally speaking, all gods are subsumed within the three realms – desire, form, and formless – and therefore experience suffering. In particular, for instance in the upper levels of the three realms, time is exhausted in a state without any concepts whatsoever. The god's lifespans are long, but in a state that cannot be said to be anything specific, their lifespans are exhausted, and then they experience the suffering of death and the suffering of falling down to the lower realms. Therefore, the three lower realms and the long-life gods are the four non-human states of non-freedom.

'Uncivilised' refers to a place to which Buddhism has not spread, where virtue and non-virtue are not distinguished, and people do not believe in cause and effect. These are people of a borderland country without Dharma. 'Those with wrong views' are aliens to the Buddha Dharma who take refuge in a different teacher. They are active non-Buddhists, or share the same ideas as non-Buddhists. They would not know faith even if the Buddha flew in the sky before them. They would not know compassion even if they saw a sentient being disembowelled in front of them. Their countries do have religion, but in actual fact, we should say they hold wrong views.

> In a place where a buddha has not come.

If you are born in a place where a buddha has not come, in a dark kalpa, not only is the mere name of the Three Jewels never heard, but in that rebirth you do not even know the difference between virtue and non-virtue.

> Or with impaired faculties.

All those with impaired faculties are different from the average person whose faculties are complete, and they are at a disadvantage when it comes to practising the Dharma. In particular, if someone is severely handicapped their cognitive faculties are compromised and their minds do not function properly, so they lack the good fortune to be able to understand the meaning of Dharma teachings and contemplate them. These latter states are the four human states of non-freedom.

At this time I have gained freedom from these eight unfree states.

Implicit in the preceding teaching of the eight unfree states – the four non-human states of non-freedom, and the four human states of non-freedom – is the understanding of gaining the eight freedoms from these.

The Endowments of Dharma

Five Personal Endowments

Of the ten endowments, which consist of the five personal endowments and the five circumstantial endowments, first to be addressed are the five personal endowments, which are taught in two and a half lines:

> **I am human with complete faculties and born in a central land.**
> **My way of life is not corrupt and I have faith in the Buddhist teachings;**
> **These five personal endowments are complete.**

If we cannot gain a human body, we cannot encounter the Dharma. For example, the people on the northern continent of Uttarakuru are human; however, they cannot take the vows of individual liberation. Therefore at this time, of all the people born on the three continents, the Buddha appeared to those on the southern continent of Jambudvipa, and taught the Dharma.

I am human with complete faculties and born in a central land.

Therefore, being born in a place where the Buddha's teachings have spread, and attaining a human body, is the first advantage of the basis of a human body. Alternatively, if one is born as a human, but without complete faculties, this would become a hindrance to Dharma. This time we are free of these problems, the second advantage of complete faculties.

Also we are 'born in a central land'. If we were born in an outlying region without Dharma, we would certainly not meet with it. This time we have the advantage of being born in a central region of Dharma, which is the third advantage of place. In addition:

> My way of life is not corrupt.

Initially, if we attempt to feign faith in the Dharma and enter the door of the teachings, but later, under the influence of wrong views and so on, engage solely in non-virtue and turn our backs on Dharma, then this is called having a 'corrupt way of life'. Therefore, not falling into this kind of corrupt way of life and being inspired towards virtue is the fourth advantage, the special advantage of intent.

> I have faith in the Buddhist teachings.

The object of faith, the field of offering, is the teachings of the Buddha and those who uphold it. Without faith in these, one's mind does not turn to the Dharma, but that is not the case here. This time, the advantage of having faith turns our mind towards the Dharma. These five advantages, with reference to ourselves, need to be complete, so they are called the 'five personal fortunate endowments'.

FIVE CIRCUMSTANTIAL ENDOWMENTS

Second, are the five circumstantial endowments:

> **A buddha has appeared,**
> **He taught the Dharma, it remains, and I have embraced it;**
> **I have been accepted by a spiritual teacher: the five circumstantial endowments.**

These two and a half lines teach the five circumstantial endowments, of which first is:

> A buddha has appeared.

If we are not born in a 'bright kalpa' when a buddha has appeared in this world, the mere name 'Dharma' is never heard, not to mention any understanding of its meaning. This time we have met with the fortune of a buddha appearing, so firstly, the advantage of the excellent teacher is complete.

> He taught the Dharma, it remains.

If a buddha appeared in the world but did not teach the Dharma, then Buddhism would not have become established, but this time the Buddha has taught the teachings in the three successive turnings of the wheel of

Difficulties of Finding the Freedoms and Endowments

Dharma, so secondly the advantage of the Dharma is complete. However, if he taught the Dharma but the teachings had subsequently disappeared, then that would be the same as being born in a 'dark kalpa'. However, currently the time that the Dharma will remain has not come to an end, which is the third advantage of time of the Dharma.

> I have embraced it.

If we do not embrace the Dharma then it is of no benefit, so embracing the Dharma is the fourth advantage of circumstantial fortune.

> I have been accepted by a spiritual teacher: the five circumstantial endowments.

You may embrace the Dharma, but when you are unable to follow a spiritual teacher to guide you on the path, then being accepted by one is meaningless. If you are not accepted by a spiritual teacher, you may know all the Dharma terms, but it is of no use. When you do not embrace the lama's direct instructions, the summarised meaning of the lama's oral instructions, it is just the same as dying of thirst on the banks of a vast pure lake; in a land of Dharma, one is left empty handed with no Dharma.

To be accepted by a holy spiritual teacher, and to follow his or her oral instructions, are the other circumstances that need to be relied on and complete, therefore they are called the 'five circumstantial endowments'. Thus the five personal endowments and the five circumstantial endowments comprise the ten endowments.

Again from the root text:

> **Although I possess all of these,**
> **Through various uncertain circumstances this life will become relinquished,**
> **And I will move onto another realm of existence.**
> **O Guru Rinpoche, heed me! Turn my mind towards Dharma!**
> **Omniscient master, do not let me stray onto wrong or inferior paths!**
> **Compassionate lama, who is one with them, heed me!**

This first line refers to what we have just discussed – the eight freedoms and ten endowments – all eighteen:

> Although I possess all of these...

Even if we possess these, or have attained the basis of a precious human body, it is still possible that:

> Through various uncertain circumstances this life will become relinquished.

Lord Nagarjuna said:

> This life has many dangers, more impermanent
> Than windblown bubbles in a stream.
> Having fallen asleep breathing in and out,
> It's amazing we wake up at all.

As Nagarjuna states, there are many causes of death. What is more, when we die, where we die, how we die, and so on, are all uncertain. So at the time when this 'life will become relinquished', the compositional factors of this life will cease, and at the time of death:

> I will move onto another realm of existence.

The appearances of the living world fade and in that very moment we are separated from this life. It is time to go to an unfamiliar place without any companions. This will not be this current realm of existence; it is taught it will be another, different realm that we will move into, so what will we do if this new realm is hell? We also do not know if it will be the realms of pretas or animals. We do not know which it may be, each is worse than the last, but still we have to go. Even if we go to a higher realm, our body will be impermanent like this current one, and then as those perceptions fade, think that at some stage it is inevitable we will be led away by the messengers of hell. So, with inconceivable suffering of pure terror, pray:

> O Guru Rinpoche, heed me! Turn my mind towards Dharma!

If we are concerned about the difficulty of finding the current freedoms and endowments once again, without any certainty to this current lifespan, compounded by the fear of going to the lower realms when we die, we must remember: what is certain now is that we know for sure we will die, but we also know at least how to recite the mani mantra. Therefore, we must not lose our mind, as in the past, to the ultimately negative influences of bad habits. Cry, 'Turn my mind towards the Dharma, sole treasure, omniscient great guru Padmasambhava! Do not let me stray onto any wrong or inferior paths!'

DIFFICULTIES OF FINDING THE FREEDOMS AND ENDOWMENTS

First we must enter the path of liberation, and rely on the oral instructions and direct instructions of our lama, as a patient would listen to the words of an expert physician in order to cure a disease. However, for practitioners there are paths that stray, erroneous paths, and the possibility of losing the path – all manner and number of defiles. If we fall under their influence, we will be swept away by obstructing conditions, and come under negative influences. One of these paths of straying is the inferior path of selfishness. A second is straying into meditation that causes rebirth as a long-life god. Because of these and other potential pitfalls, we must pray:

> Omniscient master, lord of Dharma, do not let me stray onto
>   wrong or inferior paths!
> Compassionate lama, who is one with them, heed me!

Here, we pray to the emanation of all buddhas of the three times, the Lake-born Vajra Guru Rinpoche, and the second Garab Dorje of Tibet – chariot of the great secret doctrine, omniscient lord of Dharma – Longchenpa. At one with these two masters, in the single expanse of enlightened mind, is our gracious root lama to whom we pray 'Heed me!'

By reading these words, try to recall their meaning, and turn your mind towards the Dharma. Also, in order not to succumb to straying from the path, make prayers with aspiration to fully complete the path of Dharma. The following few sections of teaching all follow the same pattern in this regard.

Above completes the main teaching on the difficulties of finding the freedoms and endowments; reflecting on the freedoms and, in particular, reflecting on the endowments of Dharma.

EXAMPLES OF THE DIFFICULTY OF FINDING THE FREEDOMS AND ENDOWMENTS

Reflecting on examples of the difficulty of finding the freedoms and endowments is taught in two half verses:

> **If I do not use this current human life meaningfully,**
> **In the future I will not find such a basis for attaining**
>   **liberation.**
> **Once the merit for this congenial existence is exhausted,**
> **After death I will wander as a miserable being in the lower**
>   **realms.**
> **Not knowing virtue from non-virtue, I will not hear the**
>   **sound of Dharma,**
> **Nor meet a spiritual teacher, what a terrible disaster!**

This time, because of previously accumulated merit, we have attained this basis with the freedoms and endowments. What is more, through practising the authentic Dharma which benefits everyone, ourselves and others, the freedoms and endowments have meaning and do not go to waste. But if this is not the case:

> If I do not use this current human life meaningfully,
> In the future I will not find such a basis for attaining liberation.

In the future or in the next life, an authentic basis for attaining liberation – a physical body with complete supporting circumstances, like this one – will be difficult to find. Now, for this one time that we have found this precious human body, so difficult to find, it would be a tremendous loss to use it as an agent of samsara; we cannot afford to use it to 'buy' suffering.

> Once the merit for this congenial existence is exhausted...

This time, having gained the fortunate basis of a human body, we have gained something of great value. If we do not strive through endeavour in the Dharma to attain long-lasting permanent happiness, then the merit that we previously accumulated will become exhausted and spent, so that:

> After death I will wander as a miserable being in the lower realms.

This means going down to the lower realms of hell. It signifies going to the miserable existence of pretas, and the fall to the animal realm. Why will we go to the lower realms? If we do not use this current human life meaningfully, and accumulate non-virtue, the fully ripened result of this in the future is to go to the lower realms. There is nowhere else for us to go. An unmistaken cause brings about an unmistaken result. We will talk more about this below, in the section on karmic cause and effect.

> Not knowing virtue from non-virtue, I will not hear the sound of Dharma.

When we have fallen down and taken rebirth in the lower realms, we will not know the nature of virtue and non-virtue, not to mention any understanding of the holy Dharma. We will not even hear the sound of holy Dharma when we fall down into the unfortunate lower states.

Difficulties of Finding the Freedoms and Endowments

In another situation, we may attain something like a fortunate rebirth in a mere human form, but one that is not complete:

Nor meet a spiritual teacher, what a terrible disaster!

We will not meet with a spiritual teacher, and will not know how to search for one. If we do not meet with a lama, we will not learn how to achieve liberation, so of course this is a terrible disaster. Although we may have a human body, we will be no different from an animal. Not knowing how to attain everlasting happiness is tragic. It is tragic, but if we have taken the erroneous form of an animal or the like, there is nothing to be done; we will be an ignorant and deluded animal. Even if this is not the case now, and we are currently in a place that has the Dharma, if we still do not know how to practise, and do everything except actually taking in the Dharma, then this is an even greater disaster.

This completes the reflection on examples of the difficulty of finding the freedoms and endowments.

Numerical Comparisons

Now we will reflect on the numerical comparisons. This is taught in one verse:

> **Just thinking about the numbers and varieties of sentient beings,**
> **To obtain a human body is barely possible.**
> **Seeing people without Dharma engaging in non-virtue,**
> **Those who act in accordance with Dharma are as rare as stars in daylight.**

Just thinking about the numbers and varieties of sentient beings...

If we think about how many mere sentient beings there are and compare that number to those who have attained a human body complete with the freedoms and endowments, then we understand:

To obtain a human body is barely possible.

The attainment of a human body is clearly only just barely possible. Generally, it is difficult to attain a human body, and in addition, it is difficult to have the complete freedoms and endowments; we could almost say it never happens.

This very slim possibility is taught through the following example: If hell beings are as numerous as stars at night, then pretas are as numerous as stars in daylight. And if the number of pretas is as numerous as stars at night, animals are as numerous as stars in daylight. If animals are as numerous as stars at night, then those with a fortunate physical basis are only as numerous as stars in daylight. Moreover, to get some perspective on the sheer number of sentient beings, if we could only count the amount of microscopic organisms living inside and on the surface of a human body, or if we look through a microscope inside one drop of spittle, only then will we know how many countless microscopic organisms are present there.

> Seeing people without Dharma engaging in non-virtue...

Having attained a human body, with the five faculties complete, if people go down the paths of distraction, and are only inclined to this world and striving for the trifling pursuits of this life, then this makes it difficult for anyone to turn to the Dharma. If they do not make the shift towards the Dharma, then they will have no idea of what it teaches, and for that lifetime no feeling for Dharma will arise. In this case, for people without Dharma, all they do and all they think is nothing but non-virtue. The sun of holy Dharma may have arisen in that place, but above the head of a person without the karmic connection, nothing but darkness gathers – just a mere human form engaging in non-virtue.

This 'mere human existence' refers to someone who has merely gained a human body. So whatever their appearance, be it of a householder or even a monastic, they are equally without the Dharma. In short, those who only engage in non-virtuous activities and do not turn towards Dharma, are taught to be called 'mere human existence'. In a mixture of virtue and non-virtue, someone who is mostly inclined towards virtue, connects with the Buddha Dharma, and is motivated by it, can be considered to have a 'special human existence'.

> Those who act in accordance with Dharma are as rare as stars in daylight.

Entering the door of Dharma, those who practise Dharma properly, and establish others onto the path of virtue, have conduct that benefits others in accordance with the Dharma. This kind of human existence is a precious human existence, and in this way such people accomplish benefit for both themselves and others, now and in the future. But this kind of person is as rare as a star in daylight. Considering this, if you are complete in all these qualities, then it is fitting for you to meditate on rejoicing. If you are not complete in these qualities, strive to complete them and pray:

O Guru Rinpoche, heed me! Turn my mind towards Dharma!

Pray also that your multifarious mind, which is not yet inclined to virtue, now becomes turned to the Dharma. In reliance on Guru Rinpoche, pray: 'Think of me!'

Omniscient master, do not let me stray onto wrong or inferior paths!

Having embarked on the path of Dharma, until attaining the ultimate result, pray that you do not come under the influence of straying, loss, or error. Pray you have the means to find the genuine path, without wandering onto an inferior path in an inferior direction: 'Omniscient master, Dharma lord, think of me!'

Compassionate lama, who is one with them, heed me!

Inseparable and non-dual with these two masters, the very embodiment of the wisdom, compassion, and power of the mind of all the buddhas, pray to your gracious root lama: 'Think of me!'

This completes the common, general reflections on the difficulty of finding the freedoms and endowments. Tomorrow we will discuss the teaching on the unique, particular reflections.

Someone who is termed a worldly person is often smallminded and short-sighted. Such people are both easily influenced and likely to be fickle. Whatever circumstances they meet with, they are easily led astray, so whether considering ourselves or others, the mind of an ordinary person is like that. For example, while sitting in an assembly hall receiving teachings, we think they should practise the Dharma, but when we arrive back in town, full of excitement and trouble, we sink into the mud of attachment and aversion, and those teachings of yesterday are nowhere to be found.

Unless someone is exceptional, generally speaking that is what most of us are like. It is for this reason that when the Noble Ones look upon us, we appear to them as silly children, so they say we are 'ordinary childish people'. A child is easily amused and also easily upset, quick to laugh and cry, so because they are immature they react to everything without consideration. In the same way, as long as someone remains an ordinary person, of course they cannot transcend their ordinary character.

However, we may be ordinary people, but still, who does not wish to avoid experiencing any suffering? Who does not wish to avoid terrible suffering in any future lives? The way to make this possible is to find a method to jump far from the realm of ordinary beings, onto a path of liberation which extends all the way to everlasting bliss. For this method to work, we must be like a child who listens to a thoughtful adult. If a grownup teaches a child positive habits, not only will the thoughtless child become thoughtful, but ultimately they can benefit others and reach a standard which enables them to teach the path to others.

In this way, we are all ordinary beings, just like thoughtless children. If others say to us, 'You're great! You're fantastic!' we are delighted, and happily reply, 'Aren't you divine!' But, when someone criticises us behind our back, not only do we become upset, but even if the person who criticised us is divine, we look for a way to demonise them. In this way people really are ridiculous. So if we are like this, what should we do?

We need to rely on someone who has wisdom beyond our own. Those who have wisdom beyond that of ordinary people are the Noble Ones. Who are they? They are the holy masters of the past. But those masters are not here now, so what should we do? They may no longer be with us, but their teachings are. Their holy representatives, physical relics of the dharmakaya, remain for the benefit of later generations of beings; oral instructions with the warmth of the lineage blessings undiminished. But if we have no faith, even if a master is present, it is of no benefit. Is it the same as one ordinary person meeting another ordinary person, just like when we meet each other and chat.

Through practising the oral instructions, we need to grasp the beginning of the path to liberation, but we must have a guide – a spiritual teacher with experience of the path – otherwise there is a danger we will get confused and err onto a wrong path. In our current situation, neither the teacher nor the student possesses the standard of these requirements. However, at the end of the age, if the sound of the Dharma is broadcast, then even if the person doing the teaching is no one special, what they teach is special, so it can still be considered the holy Dharma.

Take the auspicious divine object of a right-spiralling conch: if you examine one, it is just a seashell, but traditionally it is said that if you hear the sound of the conch of Indra, you will not fall down to the lower realms. The person who teaches this is just a human, but whether from the larynx, or resounding from the right-spiralling conch, either way these are both the sound of the holy Dharma.

Moreover, both the development and destruction of the Dharma are dependent upon people. Therefore, in particular, the spread or decline of the Dharma during the degenerate age should be gauged by whether or not the teachings of transmission and realisation reside in people's minds. This opportunity for us to gather together to teach and study the Dharma is no more likely to happen than the example of the blind turtle encountering a yoke floating upon the ocean.

If we consider the average person, they may have attended teachings once or twice. For those who are more motivated, it is probably three or four times. But considering the circumstances of most people here: each year's teaching lasts eight or nine days, and family members need to take it in turns to attend, so one person only gets to hear one day of teaching every year. However, if someone has the appropriate karmic propensity, with even just one teaching a year, it is possible to turn their mind towards virtue and find a good path. As the saying goes: *For a smart child, one indication is enough; for a dark wolf in the hills, one cry is enough.* In this case, one day a year will be prove to be enough, not just for this life but also for the next.

Talking about this, some call the Buddha Dharma the 'science of the east', classifying it as a kind of science. There is nothing wrong with saying that. The scriptures sometimes refer to the holy Dharma as the 'inner science of the three collections'. Some aspects of science accomplish the aims of mundane life, for example, the science of computers and physics. The holy Dharma allows us to accomplish both physical and mental comfort and happiness. What we have in Tibet is the science of the Buddha Dharma, which is supreme among the sciences of the world. I am not sure that there are wish-fulfilling jewels to be found in the ocean, such that, if you pray to them, they grant you anything you desire, but that which does accomplish all we could ever wish for is the holy Dharma.

Moreover, it is this precious mind of bodhicitta that accomplishes all we desire. Having this, we lack nothing, and we will live having accomplished all our longed for goals. But, not knowing how to make bodhicitta our own, not knowing how to pray or keep it pure, there is a danger we will discard it and try to grasp onto something else. As mentioned earlier, this is childish behaviour, like the worst of children, who are completely unaware of what is important. In this case, when we are someone who wishes the best for ourselves, even if we cannot grasp every word each day of this holy Dharma teaching, at least we can gain some understanding. Then, by gathering the accumulations and purifying obscurations, we can become special compared to others. So, in terms of the Dharma, by becoming our own instructor, we can give ourselves encouragement, saying 'I beg you to strive!'

This year, we are studying this detailed teaching on the preliminaries of the *Heart Essence of the Great Expanse*, and as I mentioned earlier, this is the place from which Dzogpa Chenpo has spread. This monastic seat is a main holder of the Dharma lineages of the Mother Heart Essences. Because of this, the real centre of spiritual practice, the essence of practice for everyone, ordained or lay, great or lowly, is this *Heart Essence of the Great Expanse*. Therefore, the collected key points of this recital text, the common and unique preliminaries, together with guru yoga, are indispensable during both the preliminary and main practice stages of Dzogchen. Even just practising this alone, not only can an ordinary person be liberated from the suffering of samsara, but also with this practice we can attain the level of complete enlightenment to benefit both ourselves and others. Moreover, this does not take many lifetimes; if you have determination you can attain it in one lifetime, one body.

In the teachings of the Secret Mantra, there is what is known as the four doors of Secret Mantra transmission:

1) The verbal door of spoken words to clarify the meaning.
2) The secret door of mantra to invoke the samaya.
3) The mental door of samadhi to focus one-pointedly.
4) The display door of mudra to indicate symbols.

These four doors of Secret Mantra transmission need to be complete in a mantric sadhana practice. A Westerner once said, 'Isn't reciting prayers like talking to God?' From a limited perspective, we would not question what they are suggesting, but from a different perspective, the 'god' that they speak about is the creator of the world. It would be contradictory to think that if they please 'him', 'he' will adjust the universe in their favour.

What is more, who knows whether the 'god' they are referring to is a real, existent god or a subjective symbolic deity. But, as the three seats are the nature of deities, the universe and inhabitants are a pure mandala, and appearances arise as a retinue of deities, if we ourselves and others do not establish appropriate terms to explain a subject, how can we ever discuss it? Therefore, 'the verbal door of spoken words to clarify the meaning' refers to the need to consider the meaning of the words while praying or when reciting a sadhana. Even if the intended ripening of the effect of the key points of four doors of Secret Mantra transmission cannot be managed by beginners, when you recite a daily sadhana, try to focus your mind, and at the very least you should recall the meaning of the words when you chant them.

For the people here practising the four causes to be reborn in Sukhavati, what are the four causes? They are the basis, the cause, the support, and the conditioning factors. As we have gathered together a few times for pure realm practice, I am sure you all have them memorised. What is the first cause, the basis? It is visualising the pure realm. This is the same whether reciting the sadhana or reciting the *Aspiration Prayer to be Reborn in the Realm of Great Bliss*. You should continually visualise vividly in your mind the Pure Realm of Sukhavati and its principal buddha Amitabha with his retinue. This is the first cause for being reborn in Sukhavati.

The second cause to be reborn in Sukhavati is gathering the accumulations and purifying obscurations, of which the main and easiest way to do so is the accumulation of the five-hundred thousand recitations of the Dzogchen preliminaries, which we are currently studying – the swift path of the Vajrayana. The key points of gathering and purification are the seven branches, which are also included in this sadhana. How this should be done is the main subject of our teaching this time, so we will come to talk more about it in the next few days.

The third cause to be reborn in Sukhavati is the support, which is arousing the mind of bodhicitta. Having opened the door of faith and established the foundation by taking refuge, we arouse extraordinary bodhicitta. This is also a main part of the five-hundred thousand recitations of the Dzogchen preliminaries, so we will come to discuss this too in the next few days.

The forth cause is the conditioning factors: prayers of aspiration which we need to recite to complete our practice session purely. Of these, I have already recorded and distributed the *Five Heart Essence Prayers of Aspiration*, and also, we are all regularly reciting the *Aspiration of Sukhavati*. In order to achieve our aspirations, it is no use to just speak the words, we need to accumulate the causes of merit. So, in summary, for this kind of aspiration prayer, or any others, if we embrace the entire practice with the three excellent principles – the complete preparation, main part, and conclusion – then regardless of the size of the root of virtue, whatever we achieve, it all becomes the cause to attain the level of enlightenment.

These three excellences come down to the following three points:

1) The basis of the mind of bodhicitta.
2) The view of emptiness.
3) The wisdom that realises selflessness.

Simply speaking, that which completes a hundred things in one action, is the mind of bodhicitta. The mind of bodhicitta needs to be drawn forth by compassion, so if we begin with a good heart, we can become a real Buddhist. If we practise the Dharma, not only will our future rebirths be happy, but by the same merit, this life also will also be long and fortunate, and our prestige, influence, and luck will increase.

Some of you may have had the thought 'Should I see if I can be reborn in Sukhavati, or is it better to make the aspiration prayer of the Glorious Copper-coloured Mountain?' If enough accumulations are gathered and enough obscurations purified, if the key points of practice ripen, and everything is completed with totally pure aspirations, whether you prefer one pure realm over another, you are actually able to choose. Moreover, we should understand from our recitals that Guru Rinpoche is the emanation of Amitabha:

> Emanated from a ray of light from Amitabha's heart, Padmasambhava.

If we are born in Sukhavati, this is the same as being born in the presence of Guru Rinpoche. Alternatively, having been born in the Realm of Great Bliss, everyday limitless buddhas and bodhisattvas of the ten directions appear there. Also, if those in the realms for receiving the great confirmation of liberation miraculously appear in them in the morning, and return to Sukhavati in the afternoon, then this is the same as being born in any one of those pure realms. The one pure realm that ordinary sentient beings can be reborn in is Sukhavati. The abundant array of pleasure and enjoyment of numerous pure realms is also gathered there, in the Pure Realm of Great Bliss, so first we need to strive at the methods to be reborn in Sukhavati. Having been reborn there, not only do we never need to return to wandering in samsara and experience any kind of suffering, but at the time of our subsequent rebirth, we will become enlightened.

In this lifetime, while we have not attained buddhahood, although we may have not erred from our wish to aim for the Pure Realm of Great Bliss, if we begin to lose control to anger, hatred, pride, desire, and so on, and entangle our speech, actions, and behaviour with non-virtue, all the while embracing malice and deception, then we will not arrive in Sukhavati. Therefore, the integration of Dharma into our mindstream is very important. The first way to do this is to engage in prostrations, circumambulations, recitation of mantras, making offerings, and so on, all with a pure mind. This is important, because first we need to gather the accumulation of merit. Following that, we should engage in the methods to complete the accumulation of wisdom. It is exactly these methods to complete the two accumulations, everything that we have been discussing, that are called 'practising the Dharma'.

Teaching Day Two

As the scholar and accomplished master Karma Chagme said:

> Alas, the human body attained this time,
> There is no knowing the past life from whence it came.
> Who knows how long it may remain now?
> And later, there is no direction as to where it may go.
> In this way, heedless of death, we subdue enemies, protect friends,
> And desire to accumulate food and wealth. For this sole reason,
> We do all kinds of wrongful, non-virtuous deeds without end.

This verse begins with the sorrowful expression of lament:

> Alas...

And continues:

> The human body attained this time...

'This time' refers to how infrequently a human body is attained; a few times in a hundred. It demonstrates the extent of the difficulty of this attainment, rare among scarcity.

> There is no knowing the past life from whence it came.

From what kind of past life, from what accumulated karma, does a wandering consciousness in the bardo intermediate state enter into this cage of flesh and blood that we now inhabit? If we think back into the past, we do not know where we came from. However, if we try to deduce an answer through investigation and analysis, if we see a malicious, cruel mind, and look at the way it perseveres in doing negative and wrong actions, we may think 'Could we have come from the hell realms?'

With a nature full of craving and avarice, someone who feels they have nothing despite possessing all they need, someone who tends to prevent their own hopes from coming to fruition, could resemble the rebirth of a preta. In the same way, some people are ignorant of the key points of good or bad behaviour, not knowing what to accept or reject. They do not consider their future even in this life, not to mention the next. If we look at the manner in which some people do not know how to turn their minds towards the Dharma of everlasting bliss, or its benefit for the next life, we see they are somewhat like animals. The way that some people are very jealous and cruel, happy to witness everyone else's misfortune – they could be like demi-gods, and we may sometimes think that those who are joyful and happy with a forbearing nature, are they not a little like gods?

If we consider those who have met with the teachings, those who can hear the sound of Dharma, we may think: 'Have they had a human body and known the Dharma in a past life? At that time, did they accumulate some appropriate merit?' In particular, if they currently have the fortune to follow the Vajrayana Secret Mantra and receive maturing empowerments and liberating guidance, especially at this time when the spread of the teachings is reduced and weakened, could they have gained a human body and followed the Dharma before? Have their prayers of aspiration been accomplished?

In short, we cannot be sure about the details of our past lives before this one, but here we are now, some wanderers gathered together for a few days. All those we call family, loved ones, monastic companions, and friends are really only like visitors at a market, just passing by.

> Who knows how long it may remain now?

From the perspective of the present time, we do not know the length of this lifespan. We age and become stooped, so, as it is said: *Even if a mountain were to move, our eyes could not see it; even if the conch sounds, our ears cannot hear it.* Becoming senile, our bodies decay, and we cry out 'Aaaargh! Now I won't stay here any longer!' This suffering in old age increases until we begin to think that we would rather die than endure it, but still we have to remain until death comes for us. Alternatively, for some there is no time for either happiness or comfort. With flowing hair, thirty even, conch-white teeth, and a longing for life, they die.

Which it will be, we ourselves do not even know. Because we do not know, we maintain the fantasy that we will remain for a long time, deceiving ourselves. Amidst the hustle and bustle, our life ends. Giving no thought to death, we have a few days in which we can carry on, but there is no saying when death will come. We can pretend to ignore the terrible messengers of the Lord of Death, but that does not make them go away.

> And later, there is no direction as to where it may go.

Thinking about the future, where will you go? What focus do you have that you will go somewhere specific? Karmic wind is like a river's course. As it says:

Teaching Day Two

Karmic wind is a fast-flowing river, how can it be reversed?

Channel a river downhill and it will flow; its course will follow sloping ground and narrow valley gorges. Except for that, even if we have the wish to make a river flow uphill, we do not have the power to make it do so. Like this, driven along by karmic winds, when it comes to our departure, we are powerless to prevent entry into the darkness of hell. The fierce storm of our karma chases after us. Terrifying messengers of the Lord of Death come to receive us. When we depart, what control do we have over our destination? We have none. Yet:

In this way, heedless of death, we subdue enemies, protect friends.

We do not understand the need to think about death, or where we will be forced to go when we die. Neither do we know how to make ready beneficial preparations for when the time comes to die. So some people become obsessed by their enemies, and make malicious plans to get the better of them. Others become obsessed by their families and friends, and are happy when all goes well but miserable when things go wrong, attempting to protect them from any misfortune.

We do all kinds of wrongful, non-virtuous deeds without end.

We engage in all sorts of non-virtuous actions, harbour all manner of various improper thoughts and habits of behaviour. We even commit wrongful acts, up to and including the actions with immediate consequence. We are just like a cow kicking up dirt onto its own head. Ultimately there is no alternative except to experience the consequences ourselves – whatever befalls us, wherever we end up. We are deceived in this way by these illusory samsaric activities, ungraspable as ripples on water. However, in the same way as even a mad person will occasionally come to their senses, through the condition of sometimes hearing the holy Dharma, a little warmth of the compassionate blessings of the lama and Precious Jewels may touch our hearts.

The condition of a tiny amount of merit we accumulated previously, may bring slight realisation of the current illusory samsaric suffering that we are experiencing now. Through this, we have the freedom to turn our mind towards the advice for liberation, so we may find a way out. This is the sign of having some merit where there is generally none, and so it is appropriate to think, 'What good fortune!'

As well as remembering this, we also need to see if we can reach the beginning of a spiritual path, otherwise we may once again be swept away by the madness of a delusory path. Since this is so, this time when we are on the verge of grasping the beginning of the path to liberation is crucial; it is certainly not good to waste this opportunity.

Again Master Chagme said:

> By the blessings of being born in Tibet, Land of Snows,
> The six-syllable mantra is recited; however,
> Without empowerment, transmission, or a focus of meditation,
> Mantra sounds have no syllables, like a horse grinding its teeth.
> Such worldly, ordinary people
> Have 'not found the path' or are 'not on the path'.

This Tibetan Land of Snows is not the same as other places, where people are only occupied with the phenomena of this life, with misguided intelligence focused on the mundane. We are not like people of other places, who are experts in technology and manufacturing. We are a Dharma region, where the teachings have spread – the Dharma that aims for a time of everlasting happiness. By the blessings of being born, as we are, in a land of Dharma, from the time we are born, without being taught we learn the six-syllable mani mantra, cradled in our mother's arms.

When it becomes necessary to receive the true blessing, to receive empowerments, oral transmissions, direct instructions, and so forth, if empowerments are not gained, oral transmissions are not received, and we engage in neither meditation nor visualisation, then we are no different from a horse or cow. Such people are mundane human beings, and are known as those who have 'not found the path' or are 'not on the path'.

In this way, we may think we are a Dharma practitioner, and from the age of white-toothed youth until becoming a white-haired senior, we may believe we have practised the occasional teaching. However, in truth we have not approached the true orientation of Dharma. Without exception, we have only arrived among the ranks of those who have just found the path, or have merely seized the beginning of the path. It is clear that if we do not reach upwards in the direction of liberation, there is no alternative place to go other than downwards, in the direction of samsara and the lower realms.

We may accumulate some conducive merit, but it cannot become a factor for liberation from samsara. Regarding this, Master Chagme also said:

> Trust in the Three Jewels from your heart,
> And strive for the treasury of steadfast bodhicitta.

Teaching Day Two

Those who desire liberation must focus one pointedly with faith and devotion, from the depths of their hearts to the object of refuge, the Three Holy Jewels. In addition to this, we should not separate from the steadfast mind of bodhicitta of supreme enlightenment: at the beginning, through the middle, to the end. Do not be slack, but strive with effort!

Bodhicitta upon a foundation of refuge is the main pillar of both Mahayana Sutra and Tantra. At the time we listen to the Dharma, at the beginning, what is it we cannot be without? It is arousal of the mind of supreme bodhicitta.

How do we arouse bodhicitta? We need to free all sentient beings, as infinite as the sky, from all suffering and establish them in the permanent bliss of complete enlightenment. If we wanted to calculate the number of times these beings have been our parents, we would be unable to do so; they have all been our parents many times over. They are the same as us, in that they wish to be free from suffering, and wish to meet with happiness. However, having come under the influence of ignorant unawareness, they experience the suffering of the three realms unceasingly. How pitiful they are!

If we could free them from suffering and bring them happiness, whatever became of ourselves individually, we should disregard it. However, in order to free all of them from the ocean of suffering, we need the power and strength to do so. Without this, we need to rely on others to find the method to achieve this.

So who does have the power and strength? The answer is: the Three Jewels. The root of these is the Buddha, but up to now, since so many nirmanakaya buddhas have appeared in order to tame sentient beings, if I do not arouse bodhicitta that equals the combined arousal of bodhicitta that all those buddhas possessed, I will not succeed. I must liberate those sentient beings that all the buddhas so far were unable to tame. So, to liberate them, in order to arouse bodhicitta that is equal to the combined bodhicitta that all buddhas so far aroused, I must practise enlightened activities just like all of those buddhas.

When they were at the stage of practising on the path, whatever difficulties the buddhas undertook for the sake of the Dharma, I must do the same. I must have even greater fortitude than them, for the sake of the Dharma. Thinking this, when we receive teachings, again use the analogy that you are a sick patient, the Dharma is medicine, your spiritual teacher is a doctor, and practising the Dharma is the way to recovery. With this thought, together with carefully controlled conduct, you should listen to today's teaching.

Reflections on the Difficulty of Finding a Precious Human Rebirth

Eight Unfree Incidental Circumstances

We are currently studying the *Sublime Path to Omniscience, Recital for the Preliminaries of Dzogpa Chenpo Heart Essence of the Great Expanse*, and yesterday was our first day of teaching. Having covered the goodness of the beginning, stating the title and the expression of worship, we have now moved into the two large sections of the goodness in the middle. This consists of two stages: common outer preliminaries and the unique inner preliminaries, of which, we are still on the common outer preliminaries.

Within the six teachings of the common outer preliminaries, the difficulty of finding the freedoms and endowments, the impermanence of life, and so on, we are currently discussing the first: the difficulty of finding the freedoms and endowments. Regarding the manner of the difficulty of finding the freedoms and endowments, yesterday we completed the common, general reflections, and today it is time to consider the unique, particular reflections.

Within this there are also two divisions:

- The eight unfree incidental circumstances.
- The eight unfree states that cut the mind off from Dharma.

First the eight unfree incidental circumstances are explained in the root text in two verses:

> **Although having reached the sanctuary of a precious human body,**
> **A good physical basis with a very unruly mind,**
> **Is not a suitable foundation for attaining liberation.**
> **In particular, gripped by demons or disturbed by the five poisons,**
> **Beset by negative karma or distracted by laziness,**
> **Like a slave under someone else's control, or out of fear, an imitation of Dharma,**
> **Or in ignorance, and so on: these are the eight unfree incidental circumstances.**
> **When these oppositions to Dharma come upon me...**

Difficulty of Finding a Precious Human Rebirth

If we think about the ordinary general way in which it is difficult to find a human body that is complete with the freedoms and endowments, we understand that finding one is limited to the furthest extremes of possibility. If it is only just within the realms of possibility, by the power of previously accumulated merit, if a human body is attained that has the eight freedoms and ten endowments – the eighteen complete – then we really have found a precious wish-fulfilling jewel, having travelled to and arrived at a precious sanctuary. However:

> A good physical basis with a very unruly mind…

A good physical basis, complete with the freedoms and endowments, is an even better physical basis than that possessed by Brahma and Indra, however a good physical basis led by a 'very unruly mind' will only lead to non-virtue and ruin.

Well, you may think, if a good physical basis possesses the eighteen freedoms and endowments and, having faith in the teachings is one of the five personal endowments, then what is an unruly mind like? Generally, someone with an unruly mind may have meagre faith in the teachings, but because their mind is unworkable through strong bad habits, sometimes they may behave well, but on other occasions badly. When they are not consistently good, their unkind, bad behaviour is like that of some kind of Neanderthal, and this causes all kinds of negativity, suffering, bad talk, and harm. Therefore, such an unruly mind:

> Is not a suitable foundation for attaining liberation.

That kind of mindstream, liable to become unworkable, is unsuitable upon the path of liberation as a basis for practising the holy Dharma.

> In particular, gripped by demons or disturbed by the five poisons.

From here the eight unfree incidental circumstances are enumerated. Being incidental, these can be absent one moment, only to appear the next, causing obstruction on the path of liberation. Generally speaking, of the general and specific activities of demons, here 'gripped by demons' refers to being caught by a fiendish spiritual teacher, a teacher with wrong views and conduct. If that happens, at first, even if you were a genuine practitioner with a mind in accord with Dharma, gradually going along with such a person, and being gripped by their unwholesome influence, you will go down a mistaken path, every day opposing the holy Dharma more and leaving it further behind.

Also, there are two kinds of 'demons' – general and specific. The general demons are counted as four:

1) The demon of afflictive emotions.
2) The demon of the aggregates.
3) The demon of the Lord of Death.
4) The demon of Devaputra.

Generated by grasping at self, countless afflictive emotions, coarse and subtle, lead us down a wrong path causing obstructions on the path of liberation. This is called the 'demon of afflictive emotions'. Tightly grasping at the five defiled aggregates as self, we engage in the suffering of samsara thereby obstructing the undefiled path. This is called the 'demon of the aggregates'. Before coming to the conclusion of practice on the path, something that causes obstructions to one's life is called the 'demon of the Lord of Death'. The demonic Lord of Desire, together with his retinue, shoot five arrows of flowers; whoever they hit, whoever has the greatest afflictive emotions, these increase. This is called the 'demon of Devaputra', the fourth of the four general demons.

There are no demons that are not included within these four, however there are many specific subdivisions:

- The demon of attraction and aversion to friends and enemies.
- The demon of malignant spirits that lead one down a wrong path.
- The demon of meritorious excitement.
- The demon of reifying attachment to food, wealth, and so forth.

Of these, here the demon mentioned in 'gripped by demons' refers to the demon of being carried away by demon-like spiritual siblings and practitioners. On the outside, these demons look like they must be a guru, but their inner nature, all their behaviour, is expert at deceiving the minds of others. Particularly these days, people enjoy receiving gifts from the lama more than they have faith to receive teachings, so when they meet with such opportunities they become beguiled by possessions, food, and wealth. If you get close to them, such people are mass of problems, a nexus of hidden flaws. The things they learn and pick up are nothing but faults.

What are the signs that you have been cursed by a 'demon'? The five poisons of afflictive emotions burn even more strongly in your mindstream; you turn towards a wrong path, and are devoid of compassion and bodhicitta. These are the activities of a demon, the signs you have come under a negative influence. In addition, if you experience the suffering of sickness; if many difficult situations appear suddenly and unexpectedly; you find mindfulness deteriorating and ignorance taking over; feeling unhappy for no reason; suddenly consumed by doubt so that you no longer believe in the Dharma; a growing desire for worldly abundance, so attachment is greater than before; lacking in modesty and a sense of shame, and so on; these are the signs you have been cursed by a demon. These afflictions come from your mind, therefore in this way it is the same as being in the clutches of actual demons.

Disturbed by the five poisons.

Attachment, aversion, ignorance, pride, and envy – these are the five poisons of afflictive emotions that can disturb you. Alternatively, the strength of your afflictive emotions can increase. Generally, as human beings, of course we are under the influence of afflictive emotions, however, this is different. When a coarse afflictive emotion becomes evident and you come under its influence, it is taught that it takes sole charge, and you have no control whatsoever. If we come under the influence of these afflictive emotions, it is as if we have ingested poison, which kills the life force of liberation. For this reason, the 'three poisons' or the 'five poisons' are something that kills or destroys, so they have been given the name 'poison'. So, the second of the unfree incidental circumstances are the coarse or disturbing five poisons. Moving on:

Beset by negative karma.

When it becomes time to practise Dharma, or while you are practising, the fully-ripened result of previously accumulated negative karma falls upon you, and an ocean of suffering surges forth and engulfs you. Not understanding the negative karma that you accumulated yourself, now descending upon you, is the fully ripened result of previous actions, it brings despair in the Dharma. This is the third unfree incidental circumstance.

Distracted by laziness.

We wish to practise the Dharma, and would like to make an effort, but our application is weak, so we think 'Not today, I'll do it tomorrow', 'Not right now, sometime in the future...' Having fallen under the influence of procrastination and laziness, time is spent in distraction and we end up with no time left to practise the Dharma. Some people in their distraction do not even realise they are distracted, so the course of these procrastinating 'slow digesters', as they are called, cannot be changed or turned around. Those distracted by laziness come under the influence of procrastinating attachment to unwholesome actions. This is the fourth unfree incidental circumstance.

> Like a slave under someone else's control, or out of fear.

A 'slave to others' is a 'servant'. As it is said: *For the worker who has already earned his money, there may be nothing to do, but they still must look busy.* For example, all those earning wages in an office live like this. In short, the type of person who sells themselves or their time to someone else is called 'a slave under someone else's control'. 'Out of fear' is to escape punishment from the law and so forth, which is for example, the situation some people find themselves in having committed terrible crimes. They may change their appearance with a wig and disguise, but for this kind of person, even if they have the Dharma somewhere deep inside, it is meaningless. That is the sixth unfree incidental circumstance.

> An imitation of Dharma.

Some people are not practitioners but pretend to be, just wearing the robes in order to get some offerings for doing prayer recitals, and from the monastery. *When the layman is hungry, he wants to be a monk, but when the monk is full, he wants to be a layman.* Alternatively, in order to bring gain, honour, and fame, such people rob, do business, gamble, and so on – all kinds of activities. Having done all these things, they then think, 'I don't know about the next life, but for this one, becoming a monk makes it easier to profit'. Consciously doing so, they drink the poison of misappropriating offerings unscrupulously. Those who act like this are included in the seventh of the unfree incidental circumstances.

> Or in ignorance, and so on; these are the eight unfree incidental circumstances.

The type of person who is extremely stupid and confused, who has not even the slightest glimmer of intelligence, may pretend to follow the teachings, but has only a very slim chance of studying, contemplating, and meditating on them. It is taught that included in the 'and so on' of 'ignorance, and so on' are sinful friends, and those who follow a wrong path that is not the Dharma, but something else. In this way, these eight unfree circumstances are not present one moment, but then suddenly appear the next. Having met with them, they prevent you from practising the genuine path to liberation.

When these oppositions to Dharma come upon me...

These are bad conditions that come from your own side, from an inimical companion who does not accord with the Dharma. At that time, if for example, you think you have met with a negative spiritual teacher, you should search for an alternative one with authentic view and conduct, and then firstly examine them properly. Having done so, you should follow them. Then finally, emulate their realisation and conduct.

If the five poisons disturb you, the best thing to do is merge your conceptual patterns with the expanse of the true nature of phenomena, and practise the path of liberation upon arising. At least you need to rely on the correct remedies, up to and including the remedy for desire, which is meditation on unpleasantness, and the remedy for aversion, which is meditation on loving kindness, and so forth. If negative karma befalls you, you need to purify wrongdoings and obscurations by confessing them, and vow to refrain in future. If you fear you will be carried away by lazy distractions, apply diligence. If you have no freedom, because you are subject to someone else's control, you need to *make your own decisions, hold your own lead.* If you think you are following the Dharma out of fear, see if you can develop unfeigned renunciation in your mind. If you feel you are masquerading in a way that is only an imitation of Dharma, try to abandon fixation to this life. If you feel you are stupid, under the sway of ignorance, pray to the Buddha of Wisdom, and so forth. In short, you must have the full accordant conditions to practise Dharma properly.

If this kind of negative circumstances befalls you, pray:

O Guru Rinpoche, heed me! Turn my mind towards Dharma!
Omniscient master, do not let me stray onto wrong or
   inferior paths!
Compassionate lama, you who are one with them, heed me!

'I pray to the sole treasury, essence of the embodiment of all refuges, Orgyen Guru Rinpoche! Turn my mind away from the wrong path and steer it to practice of the holy Dharma, which is beneficial now and in the future, for myself and others.' As the root text says, 'All-knowing lord of Dharma, having strayed, do not let me fall to a lower place! Gracious root lama, who is at one with them, merge my mind with Dharma, hold me in your innermost heart and bless me!'

This completes the teaching on the eight unfree incidental circumstances, the methods to reverse them, together with the prayers and aspirations to invoke enlightened mind.

Eight Unfree States that Cut the Mind Off from Dharma

Now we will look at the eight unfree states that cut the mind off from Dharma, which are taught in one and a half verses:

> **With little weariness for samsara and without the jewel of devotion,**
> **Bound by worldly cravings and with crude conduct,**
> **Not shunning non-virtue, having a corrupt way of life,**
> **Broken vows, and samaya torn to shreds –**
> **These are the eight unfree states that cut the mind off from Dharma.**
> **When these oppositions to Dharma come upon me...**

As it is taught:

> Seeing the faults of samsara but not the slightest weariness,
> Seeing the enlightened qualities of the Holy Ones, but not the slightest faith.

We hear the defects of the lower realms and samsara, but do not know how to be afraid. Not knowing how to be afraid of the suffering of this life or the suffering of the lower realms, and not understanding that suffering is suffering, we are deluded by the perception that takes suffering to be happiness. The mind that is disillusioned with samsara has 'little weariness', no repulsed renunciation of samsara, and no cause to enter the Dharma. This is the first unfree state.

> Without the jewel of devotion.

If we have no faith in the genuine Dharma or a lama, the entrance to the holy Dharma is blocked. Without a door, we cannot enter the path to liberation. Alternatively, faith is the first of the seven noble riches, so without the jewel of faith, we are emptyhanded. This is the second unfree state.

> Bound by worldly cravings.

In general there are five objects of desire, and among those is particular attachment to and craving for wealth, enjoyment, family, friends, and so on. If the bonds of worldly craving are like a rope that binds us tightly, then desirous and attached to the fetters of these desirable qualities, we can never get enough of such things, so we have no time for the Dharma. This is the third unfree state.

> With crude conduct.

This describes the conduct of someone with a bad character who is not fragrant with even the faintest scent of compassion for others, like a gnarled thorn. Even if someone like this met a spiritual guide, it would be difficult for them to change. It is said:

> You can teach someone new qualities, but a bad personality is hard to change.

This is the fourth unfree state.

> Not shunning non-virtue.

Not heedful of non-virtue – negative karma accumulated through the three doors – such a person is not at all concerned about accumulating non-virtue, and is unconscientious. With their three doors totally unpacified, whatever they do, say, or think, is nothing but non-virtuous negative actions. For such negatively inclined people, the water of positive qualities does not accumulate, and they turn their back on the Dharma. This is the fifth unfree state.

> Having a corrupt way of life.

At first someone may pretend to be on the path of Dharma, but gradually they become worse and worse, until they finally fall into a corrupt way of life. Losing mindfulness of how important the Dharma is for the mind, they get enveloped with unwholesome negative conduct, and become someone with bad conduct much worse than that of an ordinary person who has never encountered the Dharma. This is the sixth unfree state.

> Broken vows, and samaya torn to shreds.

This describes someone who, having entered the outer path of individual liberation, and received the vows of the seven types of individual liberation: layman and laywoman, novice monk and novice nun, and so on, then breaches the precepts. The two ritual systems of bodhicitta vows are:
- The System of Profound View.
- The System of Extensive Conduct.

Whichever of these vows is taken, the precepts, if summarised, involves the discipline of maintaining restraint and bringing benefit. If we turn against this system, then ethical discipline breaks down. This is the seventh unfree state.

Having entered the door of the Vajrayana teachings, you may have received many levels of the river of empowerment that matures the mindstream, and the oral instructions that bring liberation, but the sacred commitments of these are to be observed. If you do not protect your samaya, by opposing your lama, Dharma companions, and so on, the outer, inner, and secret samaya will be broken. This is the eighth unfree state.

Of the four distinctions regarding a breakdown in the sacred commitments – violated, broken down, transgressed, and torn – the worst is torn sacred commitments:

> It is said, if samaya is torn, repair it with your life.

That establishes the extent to which it is difficult to restore.

> These are the eight unfree states that cut the mind off from Dharma.

This means that having initially followed the holy Dharma, having passed over the threshold of Dharma of benefit and joy, you subsequently become cut off or separated from the spiritual community. The bright torch of liberation no longer present, having faded in your mindstream, you no longer have the thought to utilise the path, so your mind becomes unworkable.

> When these oppositions to Dharma come upon me...

When these sudden opposing conditions to your practise of Dharma threaten you, or if you think you are going to encounter them, examine your mind, and take a vow for each of the eight, and in this way be vigilant of the unfree states arising. At each practice session, examine your mind and see if they have appeared from somewhere you did not expect. You need to check carefully.

If you think you have too little weariness, you need to take the suffering of samsara upon yourself and generate feelings of weariness. If you think you have no faith or your faith is drifting elsewhere, you should reflect on the enlightened qualities of the masters of the past, and arouse a mind full of faith. If you come under the powerful influence of impatient desire, craving, fixated attachment, and so forth, recognise that there is nothing worse than this, and look upon sensory enjoyments as illusory dreams, so cutting the bonds of fixated attachment. If you get the impression that your conduct is becoming that of someone with a nasty disposition, like a cruel thorny person, you must face yourself and acknowledge your faults. With peacefulness, gentleness, and carefulness, tame your own mind, putting yourself onto the path.

The remedy for an inability to carefully shun unwholesome non-virtuous actions is a strong mind that delights in virtue, as demonstrated in the life stories of the holy masters of the past. Doing so, you must strive in the methods to make yourself more heedful. When you lead a dangerous corrupt way of life, consider there is a risk you may become even worse than the lowest of the low, so arouse great motivation for the holy Dharma. You need to arouse and engage with each individual positive quality in your mindstream. If you think you have transgressed your vows and samaya, by recalling the consequences, practice pure vision towards the Dharma and your lama. Root out your hidden faults from the very depths of your mind. In addition to confession of faults and vowing to refrain, practise appropriately all aspects of what is allowed and avoid all that is prohibited, doing your best as far as is possible, and strive every day in ways to improve.

Thus we pray to the lama and the Three Jewels:

O Guru Rinpoche, heed me! Turn my mind towards Dharma!
Omniscient master, do not let me stray onto wrong or
   inferior paths!
Compassionate lama, you who are one with them, heed me!

To avoid the unfree states that cut the mind off from Dharma, pray: 'O Guru Padmasambhava, hear me! Single treasury of Dharma, turn my mind towards Dharma, and let me be free from obstacles! If I fall under the influence of any one unfree state, help me not to deviate onto a wrong path, a stray path, or a lower path, omniscient lord of Dharma, heed me! Your mind is the nature of wisdom and compassion, at one with Guru Rinpoche and Longchenpa, non-dual with all the victorious ones, my gracious lama, think of me!' So the prayer reads.

This supplement to the recital text was composed by Jigme Trinle Ozer, therefore the line 'Compassionate lama, you who are one with them, heed me!' mainly refers to Omniscient Jigme Lingpa. However, if we direct our devotion to the successor of the lamas of the three lineages: our own root lama who possess the three kindnesses, then the expanse of their enlightened mind is of one taste with those masters, so in this way we pray to our lama. The nature of the embodiment of all the Three

Refuges and the Three Roots is the lama, therefore it is fitting if you pray in this way.

This concludes the teaching on the difficulty of finding the freedoms and endowments, the first of the six sections of the common outer preliminaries. Having finished this teaching session, when it is time to meditate, first begin with taking refuge and generating bodhicitta. At the time of the main meditation on the difficulty of finding the freedoms and endowments, turn your thoughts inward. This physical basis that you have found at this time, complete with the eighteen freedoms and endowments, is so much more wonderful to attain than if a penniless person were to find a wish-fulfilling jewel that grants any wish. A wish-fulfilling jewel that 'grants any wish', only works for mundane desires. But based on this physical basis, with the freedoms and endowments, we can accomplish permanent happiness, something that we have never done from the beginningless time of samsara up to this point, so do not waste it!

We may have the complete eighteen freedoms and endowments, but we must prevent them from becoming obscured by the eight unfree incidental circumstances and the eight unfree states that cut off the mind. When we are totally free of these, we are complete with thirty-four freedoms and endowments, therefore with a joyful heart we should determine the need to accomplish the path of liberation and enlightenment for both ourselves and others. Do not allow this positive basis which has the difficult-to-find freedoms and endowments go to waste. Snatch them away from the thieves of distraction and laziness, and make the vow that you must swiftly gain the result of practising the teachings.

Consider all the freedoms and endowments in analytical meditation. Engage in analysis and investigation again and again, until your mind becomes tired. If thoughts cease to occur on the subject, at that point do not chase after the past, do not welcome the future, and do not follow thoughts of the present. You should remain in this state without modification, and practise settling meditation. If thoughts once again arise and proliferate, return to analytical meditation on the main topic of meditation. This practice of alternation between analytical and settling meditation applies to all of the following practice sessions. Then, at the end of the practice session, you should dedicate the merit for the benefit of all sentient beings.

2) IMPERMANENCE OF LIFE

GENERAL IMPERMANENCE

The second of the common outer preliminaries is the guidance on the impermanence of life. In the extensive teachings on the preliminaries this is explained in six sections:

1) Meditation on impermanence by reflecting on the outer universe.
2) Meditation on impermanence by reflecting on the beings that live in the universe.
3) Meditation on impermanence by reflecting on holy beings.
4) Meditation on impermanence by reflecting on the lords of all beings.
5) Reflection on the uncertainty of the time of death.
6) Reflection on other examples of impermanence.

Here, in the words of the recital:

> **Right now, I am not tormented by sickness or suffering,**
> **Nor enslaved or under the control of others.**
> **At this time of independence and conducive circumstances,**
> **If, in a state of indolence, I waste these freedoms and endowments –**
> **No question of friends, possessions, and family –**
> **Even this body which I hold so dear,**
> **Will be taken from its bed to some desolate spot,**
> **To be torn apart by foxes, vultures, and dogs,**
> **At which time, in the bardo, my fear will be extreme.**

In two verses and one line the teachings on impermanence are given. If we think carefully about its meaning, and 1) consider the outer universe – the four continents, and Mt. Meru, together with the god realms – they are solid and firm and remain for an aeon, yet they are still impermanent. Finally, seven fires and one flood will destroy them all, leaving nothing but dust. In this case, look at us with our feeble bodies, like bees in late autumn, what resilience do we have? Thinking this, we need to arouse sadness in our hearts.

Also, if we reflect on 2) the beings that live in the universe, from the beings at the peak of existence right down to those in the hell of unending torment, having been born, there is not a single one up to now that has escaped from death; it is impossible to escape. In particular, for us humans living in the world, there is no certainty to our lives. In addition, due to the power of the passage of time, it currently happens to be a period of degeneration in human lifespan. Many people die without even considering that their lives might end. In that case, we should focus to avoid falling under the influence of laziness or procrastination, and practise that which is certain to be of benefit at the time of death. Thereby, at that time we will have no regrets, and attain accomplishment by training in the holy Dharma.

If we consider 3) the meditation on impermanence by reflecting on holy beings, in past times there appeared the seven successive buddhas. In this aeon, the fourth guide, Buddha Shakyamuni appeared, together with an inconceivable retinue of arhats and shravakas, to bring benefit to countless beings to be tamed. All had attained the vajra body, but to sentient beings who cling to permanence, they demonstrated the manner of passing into nirvana.

In the same way, there were those who followed afterwards: the Six Ornaments and Two Supreme Ones of India, and the Eighty Mahasiddhas. Also in Tibet, the Abbot, Master, Dharma King, and the Twenty-five Disciples; the Five Sakya Forefathers; Rongzompa and Longchenpa of the Nyingma; from the Kagyu tradition, Marpa, Milarepa, and Gampopa; in terms of the new and old Kadampas, Atisha, Tsongkhapa, and many more learned and accomplished masters appeared. They attained the supreme and ordinary accomplishments, and mastered control over the four elements, with unimpeded sublime perception and miraculous powers. However, in the end they all demonstrated the manner of not transcending the nature of impermanence. Now all that remains are the stories of their liberating lives.

If this is the case for such eminent masters, what stability do our bodies have? The result of negative karma, propelled onwards by the wind of negative circumstances, an unclean corporeal heap brought together by negative habitual propensities, our body is barely a reliable support for the continuum of consciousness. There is no certainty when this body that connects matter and consciousness for a few days, will collapse, or when matter and consciousness will separate, like a bird taking flight from a post.

From the point of view of 4) meditation on impermanence by reflecting on the lords of all beings, these 'lords' are the great gods such as Brahma, whose lifespans are so long they remain for an aeon. These gods and rishis possess sublime strength, wealth, splendour, eloquence, and power, but ultimately they cannot escape from death.

From the *Treasury of Qualities*:

> Even Brahma, Shiva, Ishvara, and the universal monarchs
> Find no way to avoid the Lord of Death.

Looking at ourselves in comparison, our bodies and possessions are like bees in a beehive, even more impermanent and unstable.

Also, 5) reflecting on the uncertainty of the time of death, for us humans living in this world, there is no rule that decrees, 'a lifespan is x years long'. No one is able to predict when we will die, where we will die, the way in which we will die, or the cause of death. Additionally, the conditions that keep us alive are very few, and the conditions that lead to death are many. There are all kinds of things that we think keep us alive, but actually they too may become a cause of death, just as Aryadevi said:

> The conditions that lead to death are numerous,
> Conditions for life are few,
> And they also become a cause of death.

If we reflect on the way we are unaware when death will suddenly arrive, if we die suddenly today, by this time tomorrow who can say that we will not have taken the form of a puny insect? Reflecting on this with conviction – the uncertainty of the time of death, and the unpredictability of where we will be reborn – we need to strive for the essence of the sacred Dharma.

Also, in terms of 6) the way to meditate on other examples of impermanence, from the *Lalitavistara Sutra*:

> Impermanence of the three realms is like autumn clouds,
> The birth and death of beings is like watching a dance,
> A person's life passes like lightning in the sky,
> Like a waterfall on a steep mountain, it is fleeting.

If we reflect on the impermanent nature of the three realms, the three states of existence – beings below ground, on the ground, and above the ground – they are all like a mass of white autumn clouds; for a moment they are beautiful, but immediately the wind blows and they disappear. The outer world, Mt. Meru, and our houses and homes are all impermanent. On a grand scale, there is the waxing and waning of the aeon. On a smaller scale, we observe the impermanence and shifting of the seasons. Subject to and dependent on these are lands, towns, and monasteries. Among people, the position of those in power is impermanent. The wealth of the rich is impermanent. The beauty of youth is impermanent. Influence or riches, nothing is permanent. We can see directly these manifest phenomena.

Our bodies are like bubbles in water, here one moment gone the next. Like an echo, not to be found anywhere, outside, inside, or in between, thoughts of the mind are like a blustering gale, changing moment by moment. In short, everything born has an essence of death. Everything accumulated has the causal condition to become exhausted. Everything compounded has the nature of separation. The exhaustion of life is as swift and fleeting as a flash of lightning in the sky. The advance of death is like a boulder tumbling down a steep mountain, not stopping for a single minute, advancing ever closer.

Suddenly, from somewhere you were not expecting, you come face to face with the Lord of Death. At that time, stripped naked, empty handed, and penniless, you are separated from everything you cannot bear to part with: your relatives and friends, your home and possessions. Like a hair plucked from butter, or a sheep caught in the flock bound for slaughter, you must go alone, swept away without refuge or protection. Think about this for one moment. If you are asleep, you need to wake up immediately. If you are sitting down, you need to stand up. When you are on the road, you need to forgo the remaining journey and stop and stare. If you are doing something, leave it. If you do not turn your thoughts immediately to the one important matter of death, among all idiots you are the most foolish, enveloped in a great spell of forgetfulness. Knowing this, you need to wake up from this sleep of ignorance.

IMPERMANENCE ACCORDING TO THE ROOT TEXT

Now, to reflect on the various modes of impermanence:

> Right now, I am not tormented by sickness or suffering.

This life is impermanent, like a rainbow in the sky; this body is impermanent like a flash of lightning in the sky. However, at the moment we are not being harmed by a debilitating sickness of the vital energy, or the kinds of contagious disease which spread from person to person and cut the continuum of life like an axe. Also we are not tormented by terrible suffering of hunger, thirst, heat, or cold, and so forth.

> Nor enslaved or under the control of others.

We have not been captured by others – powerless, having been deceived by their evil wiles, so we are not under the control of others.

Impermanence of Life

At this time of independence and conducive circumstances.

We ourselves are in charge of both our body and mind, and are able to do what we want; we have our freedom. What is more we have the wish to practise Dharma, and we have a lama to give us teachings. At the time when teachings are given, the three conducive circumstances are also gathered, so at this fortunate time we must undertake Dharma practice, so that when we die we are sure to have no regrets.

In order to do this, Dharma practice depends on our mind; the mind is the foundation. The mind depends on a physical basis that has the complete freedoms and endowments. To explain this in another way, in order to practise the Dharma, we depend on the three doors – the body, speech, and mind. The chief of the three doors is the mind, because the body and speech depend on it. At this time we need to focus the three doors on the path of virtuous activities, and we need to be able to achieve the path.

With regard to the accordant conditions of the outer world and our inner body and mind, if we do meet exactly with a fortuitous moment when all the causes, conditions, and auspicious circumstances to practise the Dharma are assembled, but:

If, in a state of indolence, I waste these freedoms and endowments.

Then, having met with all these conducive circumstances, so difficult to assemble, if we do not know how to value the importance of this crucial opportunity and, through lazy indolence, abandon our vital objective and pursue trifling matters, then we are abandoning the attainment everlasting happiness in favour of the trifling happiness, fame, and comfort of this life. In doing so, we put off the Dharma until tomorrow and the next day, and never get around to practice, so, in this state of indolence, the sum total of our human life ends up as zero. A human body with the freedoms and endowments is difficult to find; it is very meaningful if you do find one. But by squandering it and letting it go to waste, when the messengers of the Lord of Death arrive at your side, there is:

No question of friends, possessions, and family.

The people around us who we rely on, and our wider circle of friends; the valuables and possessions we have worked so hard to accumulate; our relatives and friends, so dearly loved that we cannot bear to be apart from them; all the other people close to our hearts with whom we have a connection; we long to see their faces, and do not wish to be separated from any of them for even a moment.

Even this body which I hold so dear...

This is not to mention that which, up to now, we have never been separated from – our body, which we hold so dear, just as if it were us who had eaten a thousand delicious foods, worn a thousand attractive outfits, and been decorated with a thousand beautiful ornaments. In just a little while, this body will wear the noose of the Lord of Death around its neck. At that time, we may be as lofty as the sky, as fierce as lightning, as rich as a naga, with beauty to challenge the gods, or as pretty as a rainbow, but there is no way to reverse death with any devious methods or cunning plans.

When the movement of breath in and out becomes rapid and gasping, your once radiant complexion vanishes. Staring at the living with dying eyes, your face grows pale, your limbs quiver, and your perception becomes confused. When you breathe out, but no longer inhale again, you have become a 'corpse' – that which strikes loathing and fear into everyone's hearts. At that time you have become this chilling, terrifying thing that:

Will be taken from its bed to some desolate spot.

Depending on the individual customs of a place, at some stage a corpse needs be removed. Then you will be taken out of the warm bed of the living, stripped off and, alone without companions, taken to a charnel ground, or the like:

To be torn apart by foxes, vultures, and dogs.

Then your body becomes food for vultures, wild animals, and worms. At that time, however beautiful your living appearance was, it is of no benefit now. However lovely your hair was, it is now blown away by the wind. Your eyes may have been almond-shaped and beautiful, but now they are plucked out by vultures. Your conch-white teeth are broken and scattered. The brain in your skull gets splattered onto the ground. Your heart is pecked at by crows. Dogs and wild animals consume you as food, turning you into filthy muck, and eventually into nothing.

Some bodies are not thrown out to a charnel ground in this way, but are hidden and cremated, becoming dust to dissolve away. In short, this physical mass will disappear into the expanse of the four elements. Then, all that remains is the guest of the mind's consciousness:

Impermanence of Life

At which time, in the bardo, my fear will be extreme.

In the bardo intermediate state, the four collected aggregates of name have the perception of a body endowed with all sense facilities. But, as you are buffeted about like a feather in the wind, except for a mother's womb and the ground of total liberation, there is no unimpeded, reliable place of refuge to be found. Yet, this is not the only frightening thing about the bardo state: Firstly, there are the four terrifying sounds. These are the four terrifying sounds of earth, water, fire, and wind. The wind of earth makes the sound of a huge mountain moving. The wind of water makes the sound of a huge ocean churning up. The wind of fire makes the sound of a huge forest burning. The wind of wind makes a sound like a fierce hurricane at the end of time.

In addition to that, there are the three dreadful abysses. These are said to be three narrow defiles arising from the three poisons: the steep abyss, the terrifying ravine, and the deep lake of poison. These appear as white brilliance, glowing red, and deep blackness. Also, there are the howls of malevolent wild animals, blizzards, visions of darkness, and other such phenomena. There is no time now to discuss all the terrifying things of the bardo intermediate state.

You may have heard the story of Guru Nyida Osal's younger brother who wandered in the bardo. Let me tell it again today: One of main figures of the lama lineage of the Karma Lingpa *Peaceful and Wrathful Deities*, was Treasure Revealer Guru Nyida Osal Shewa. He would usually stay in retreat in his monastery. One year while he was in retreat, an epidemic spread in the local town and many people died. Among the many dead was Guru Nyida Osal's younger brother, known as Nubo Dorje Gyaltsen, who was thirty-two that year. With him was his young daughter, who also became infected with the disease and died.

Around three months after they had died, one evening as Guru Nyida Osal was staying in solitary retreat, he missed his younger brother deeply and felt very sad, so he focused his wisdom mind on seeing the beings in the intermediate state. In meditative equipoise, he entered into a kind of samadhi that allowed him to go among the beings of the bardo. As he was passing through, the perception of countless bardo beings arose to him. While he looked at them, his own mother, much younger than before, came up to him from out of nowhere. She said to him, 'Dorje Gyaltsen has fallen to a miserable and sorry place.' 'Mother, I have come to see him', said Guru Nyida Osal. The woman continued, 'I have been guarding him from obstructions...' and went on to recount many miserable details, but Guru Nyida Osal said, 'Mother, I have given him points of training and relieved his suffering. It should be of benefit.'

However, his mother replied, 'Poor Dorje Gyaltsen, thinking to take up human form, is still looking to find a good home in which to be reborn, but as yet cannot find one. I have not let him go to a bad place. In particular, I have not let him go to the home of non-virtuous people. Go down that way and you will meet him'.

So, following his mother's directions, he came to a ford in a river and crossed a bridge over to the other side. There he turned back to look, but the lady was nowhere to be seen. Who was she actually? She was Troma Nagmo, the personal yidam deity that Nubo Dorje Gyaltsen practised his entire life, miraculously disguised as his compassionate mother, come to the land of the bardo to protect him. In a state of joy mixed with sadness, Nyida Osal continued onwards. While on a steep path, he suddenly recognised Nubo Dorje Gyaltsen coming towards him, carrying a load of firewood and singing a long sorrowful lament such as would make anyone who heard it sad.

Whatever they do, bardo beings have no body. Without a physical basis or fixed location, they are like dry rhubarb leaves blown about by the wind. So, as a tethering support for his mind, as a material basis to weigh him down, Nubo Dorje Gyaltsen was carrying a load of dry firewood. Seeing his brother wandering around like this, without a base or body, saddened Guru Nyida Osal. Then the two brothers met each other; they stood for a while in silence, unable to speak. Thinking his elder brother was also a mental body of the bardo intermediate state, Nubo Dorje Gyaltsen was not happy to meet him there, but became even more sorrowful.

Finally, Guru Nyida Osal spoke: 'Where have you been all this time? From where did you come today? You are not like the ordinary dead who have never practised Dharma, but perhaps you did not direct your awareness to a pure realm? Or else, why didn't you take rebirth as a god, or with a human physical basis that has the Dharma? What are you doing wandering around like this?'

Nubo replied, 'Wherever a consciousness in the bardo thinks to go, there they are. There is nowhere I have not been... I have had hundreds of thousands of companions, some I recognised, some I did not. At one time I was travelling with one million seven-hundred thousand others, when suddenly we got separated into three groups. Two-thirds of them got sucked down into a huge chasm, while the other third of us was left behind. Those left behind were still terrified, driven by pelting rain and fierce wind, so some fled into the forest. Others escaped into pits in the earth, or cowered in caves, wherever they could find a place to hide. My mother covered me with a cloak so the beating hail, wind, rain, and storms couldn't harm me. Because of that, until now I haven't fallen into a crevasse, but many of my acquaintances have already been sucked into vast chasms. They are certainly now experiencing terrible suffering.' He shivered as he spoke, and his face was fearful and full of despair.

'Also, I recognised a few people from our home region. They were saying "Lama Nyida told us not go to non-virtuous households" so until now we have been wandering around, seeking to find a pure home with a meaningful human rebirth, but we have not found any that are suitable. Because of this, if we wander too long, one day there is a great risk we will be sucked down into a huge chasm. Previously, because I spent time with you, it was surely beneficial. Yet now I am nothing but an unwholesome defiled being, so I must find a place for my consciousness to grasp onto.' Saying this, he began to wander off. 'They seem not to have gone to the three lower realms, but they haven't found a single good place to take rebirth.' Saying this, Nubo Dorje Gyaltsen, driven by the wind of karma, turned away singing a sorrowful song:

> Happy, so happy, the central human land is truly joyful.
> Miserable, so miserable, the bardo defiles are such suffering.
> Brief, so brief, how fleeting a human life!
> Sad, so sad, helplessness is much sorrow.
> Weak, so weak, how feeble I am.

He departed into the disturbing murky darkness, like a feather blown by the wind; beings in the bardo intermediate state do not have the same daytime perception as we do.

Guru Nyida Osal followed after his brother and called his name, 'Wait, I still have something to say!' When he said this, the man's wooden load caught on some jagged stones, and Dorje Gyaltsen paused with a big sigh. The lama caught up with him and said, 'Tell me in detail, who else have you encountered from the same region?' Dorje Gyaltsen replied, 'I have met many, but with some of them, the moment we met we again became separated, without any time to speak. When you are a "powerless bardo being" you do not know where you will go next. With some, I may wander in their company for around a day, and once I wandered together with a group of ten or so who had once received an empowerment from you; we were together for about ten days. One climbed up to the top of a mountain, but I don't know what became of him, happy or miserable. All the others disappeared, one fell, two fell; everyone falls down.

'There is nothing better than the teachings of the *Liberation through Hearing in the Bardo*. While alive, this is something to which you need to accustom your ears and study, not to mention actually practising it. Those who have heard it know how to choose a good or bad place, so in that way they are different; they remain in control. Many of us went along chanting the *Aspiration for the Bardo* prayer, and hundreds of thousands of others were crying and said, "How happy you are, not only do you know how to recite such an important and beneficial prayer, but you get to travel together!" Like this, they made prayers of aspiration.

'I managed to teach the complete *Aspiration for the Bardo* from start to finish to those people. They then said to me, "During the bardo of the dharmata, why didn't you go down the good path of light? Why do you still remain here?" But I was afraid of the sounds, lights, and rays of the bardo of the dharmata and fainted. I was about to recognise the sounds and lights, but in the end I couldn't. I had received introduction to the bardo twice. If I had received it a third time, I could have recognised the nature of the sounds, lights, and rays, and would certainly have become liberated. All this time I've been searching for a place to be reborn with the Dharma.' Saying this, Dorje Gyaltsen again began to sing:

> Rare, so rare, homes with Dharma are so rare.
> Filthy, so filthy, the homes of wicked people are truly unclean.
> Many, so many, womb-entrances to the lower realms are countless.
> Sad, so sad, the defiles of the bardo are only sorrow.

While he sang this heart-saddening, sorrowful lament, he shifted his wooden load and, passing up over a narrow defile, made his way uphill. Again, the lama followed after him. 'Don't lose hope like this. I will do something to alleviate your suffering. Tell this to all the bardo beings: I, Nyida Osal, recite the *Liberation through Hearing in the Bardo* and *Liberation by Wearing* every day. Tell them to come and listen, and lead them over to me.'

Dorje Gyaltsen replied, 'That is so kind to everyone, reciting daily aspirations and dedications for the bardo. Those aspirations will lessen the number of bardo beings as they manage to find good womb-entrances. Other than myself, there are three Tibetan yogis here. Among all the bardo beings, we are the ones with the most power. They are exclusively practitioners of *Liberation through Hearing*. In the human realm I didn't have time to enjoy myself or be happy. I still wish to take rebirth as a human, so I'm waiting for that.'

'Until you have found a pure mother's dwelling place, I will help you not to fall into one of those huge chasms' the lama said. 'However, if you think about it, while in the intermediate state, a "pure dwelling place" is like talking about a wish-fulfilling jewel in the human realm.' This saddened Dorje Gyaltsen, and he wandered off again, singing another sorrowful song:

> Terrifying, so terrifying, those huge chasms are dreadful.
> Sad, so sad, the defiles of the bardo are miserable.

IMPERMANENCE OF LIFE

Heavy, so heavy, this wooden load is backbreaking.

As he took his leave, Guru Nyida Osal was saddened to tears. He chased after him, calling: 'Wait, I've still got something to say to you!' Nubo Dorje Gyaltsen paused for a moment. 'You don't need to be miserable, I've built a palace for the peaceful and wrathful deities, and will dedicate the merit to you. I've requested many spiritual masters and monks to recite the six-syllable mani mantra. I've established a regular gathering to recite the mani mantra without fail. This merit I will also dedicate to you. Not only that, but I myself dedicate all my spiritual practice, all I've ever done, to you. Our mother, and the wife you left behind, are both reciting the mani mantra for your sake, and since you died they have been doing virtuous deeds, both great and small. So you can feel better and relax.

'As your mental body of the bardo goes wherever you want it to, do you want to take a human form that has the Dharma, in a pure household? Or would you prefer to focus with forceful intent and make prayers of aspiration to be reborn in the presence of Orgyen Rinpoche in the Glorious Copper Coloured Mountain? In my opinion, wouldn't it be better to go to among the vidyadharas in the presence of Guru Rinpoche?'

Dorje Gyaltsen replied, 'I only stayed a short time in the human world and wasn't satisfied. Thanks to the kindness of you, my brother, my accumulation of non-virtue is small, but at that time I didn't receive enough Dharma. When I recall this I'm filled with regret. I'm most regretful and sorry that I could only stay with my parents, brothers, and friends, all of you, for such a short time. Now, even if I search, I won't find that again. I couldn't hang onto what I had, and now there's nothing worse than wanting to search for something I've lost. I'm still going to wait, and pray to be reborn into a pure home.' Saying this, tears streamed from his eyes and he slumped down in defeat.

Then Guru Nyida Osal asked, 'Where has your daughter Traharay gone?' 'Last month, in the middle of a large throng of people I bumped into her, just for a moment, but there wasn't a chance to speak, and I don't know where she has gone. I haven't seen her since.' Missing his daughter greatly, Dorje Gyaltsen started to cry again and, singing a sorrowful song, he shouldered his wooden load, and wandered away towards the end of a perilous path.

Again the lama chased after him. 'Stop! Wait a moment! I've got another question for you. Did you not go in front of the Lord of Death?' 'I didn't go in front of the Lord of Death. If you fall down into a huge chasm, that is the time you meet him, but I don't dare go down there. When I come close to a huge chasm I feel unbearable fear and terror. My heart feels like it's going to explode. I am protected by my mother, but were it not for that, others without protectors are powerless and are forced to go. Their faces grow white with terror, and they faint. They leave in shock and with tears in their eyes. No matter if they scream or stay calm, whatever they do, it is of no benefit. Just speaking of it my heart pounds with fear. Aaaargh, I'm absolutely terrified of being taken down!' As Dorje Gyaltsen went to leave, he sang:

> Afraid, so afraid, the chasm's darkness is terrifying.
> Fast, so fast, the red winds of karma are swift.
> Hot, so hot, the fire of karma burns.
> Roaming, always roaming, I wander alone without friends.
> Abandoned, all abandoned, everything is left behind.
> Heavy, so heavy, bad karma, misdeeds, and obscurations are such a weight!

Singing this, he again shifted his wooden load, and wandered off in despair. Again chasing after him, the lama said, 'Don't be miserable like that, I've made strong aspiration prayers for you to find a good place, in the next life for you to meet with the Dharma, and for us brothers to meet again in that life; I continue to make this kind of aspiration prayers. So, don't be sorrowful, you're not alone, all of us in our turn must come here like this. Not only to you, this all-powerful 'death' comes to all beings, so don't despair. Be determined, the Great Lord of Compassion is helping you. You have received the empowerments and have the blessings of the activities of your yidam Troma, so pray to them!'

Hearing this, Dorje Gyaltsen replied, 'You're right, generally the bardo is miserable, so I am lamenting, but aside from that, I'm probably the most comfortable here, and have the most freedom among all the bardo beings. Reciting and burning the seven-rebirth pill and the liberating diagram has not only brought great benefit to me, but has been extremely beneficial to many beings here. What's more, if you make tsatsas with my bonemeal, and again recite and burn the seven-rebirth pill and the liberating diagram, that too will be very beneficial. There is nothing better that these amendments and confessions for hell...' But before he had time to finish what he was saying, like a dry rhubarb leaf blown by the wind, he was swept helplessly away.

If someone like Guru Nyida Osal's brother, a yogi with the Dharma, is that afraid in the bardo and, what is more, has to be so terrified of falling into the huge chasm of hell, then what about us? Having accrued all the conditions to go to hell, can we sit here comfortably accepting the fact? What if, without enough time to blink an eye, or for those perceptions of the bardo to arise, we were reborn in hell, what could we possibly do? If it were possible for us not to be born in hell but, for example like Dorje Gyaltsen's young daughter, who he met only briefly in a crowd of people, if our children and grandchildren, brothers and sisters, mother and father, who we cherish like our own heart's blood, were to disappear, sucked into a vast dark chasm, and were experiencing the suffering of hell right now, then what could we do?

None of these stories is fictional. And, if none of us understand how to think about actually experiencing that kind of suffering, I do not know if we are more wretched than animals, or are we even worse than that? None of those beings in hell are strangers to us; there is not one who has not been our parent. Therefore, having received this teaching, we must take this to heart. Guru Nyida Osal would regularly welcome the guests in Chod practice, offer them burned food offerings, and dedicate tormas without miserliness, keeping everything clean. He would say, 'If with samadhi concentration, special mantras, and in particular a mind of compassion, dedication is made, then it is of great benefit', having himself witnessed the benefits they bring.

Once again, at a later time, Guru Nyida Osal, in a mixture of meditative experience and dream, saw many bardo beings. Walking up to the top of a valley, in a forest on the opposite side of a river, he heard someone chopping wood, and went over to him. There was Nubo Dorje Gyaltsen, still wandering in the bardo, his brow dripping with sweat, struggling to split some cedar wood. 'What are you doing here? You've been looking for a place to live for such a long time, have you still not found one?' 'I did find a place to live, far away from here, but out of longing for you all, I'm staying nearby, in our own region.' 'If that is so, what are you doing splitting this wood?' 'Wherever I go it is always dark, without sun or moon, so I'm chopping wood to light a torch.'

'Aren't you exasperated at not having found a place to be reborn for so long? In the *Liberation through Hearing in the Bardo*, there are many methods to choose a womb-entrance in the bardo of becoming. You've received so many oral instructions – how to avoid choosing an impure samsaric womb-entrance, and transference to the Pure Realm of Celestial Enjoyment – surely you still remember them? Whichever samsaric womb-entrance you choose, it will be bad, so rather you should concentrate with strong desire on one of the buddha's pure realms, the easterly Pure Realm of Great Bliss, and so on, and you will certainly be able to be reborn there. You don't have a material body. Your body here is called a "mental body of habitual tendencies", so it's easy to control. Wherever you focus your intent, there you will be born.

'It's not just you, I, Nyida Osal, am at this moment in a kind of dream, so what you perceive now is called a "dream body of habitual tendencies". I've left my material body in my bed. Both your empty bardo body, and my dream body of delusion within delusion, are empty forms in the same manner. If you don't believe me, see if you can grasp my hands.'

When they went to hold hands, Dorje Gyaltsen's hands became as if they were graspable. Because beings in the bardo have a measure of direct clairvoyance, Dorje Gyaltsen said 'I've got some higher perception, of course we can touch!' 'Understanding a dream to be a dream, if this man has died, can this be true that the living and the dead can not only touch, but hold each other?' Thinking this, as Guru Nyida Osal looked at the man's face again, his brother also stared back at him. After looking at him carefully, Guru Nyida Osal said, 'Now, after this time, I don't know if we will meet again. If this is the last time we will meet, we need to look at each other carefully.'

Then Guru Nyida Osal thought to himself, 'Alas, if from beginningless time, fixation that grasps at true existence arises in the mindstream, in my brother's perception he still hasn't cut the fetters of reification; this fixation on things being real is difficult to destroy.' Dorje Gyaltsen said, 'I have concentrated on the buddha's pure realm, but it is not easy to transfer there. It must be because I have negative karmic obscurations. I don't want to go to the lower realms, and it seems as if I don't have to go there, but because I didn't have enough time in the human realm, rather than going to a pure realm, I'm thinking of trying to obtain a pure human body.' The lama, realising that his brother was unable to appreciate the amazing and arrayed pure buddha realms, but due to his obscurations wanted to obtain a bad body of the degenerate time, said: 'In that case, I'll help you. Let's go together to find you a pure home.' And he led the way as they searched together.

Travelling along, they saw at the top of the valley an empty three-storied house. 'As you haven't yet found a place to live, how about this one?' asked the lama. Dorje Gyaltsen replied, 'There are hundreds and thousands of this kind of house, I don't want to go inside one like this.' 'Aren't there signs of a house over the way? Why don't we go there?' Dorje Gyaltsen replied, 'I've already been over to that door, but it wasn't clean enough, so I went away.'

Moving on again, the lama said, 'How about this for a home? Shall we go inside?' and climbing up the wall behind the house, he got onto the roof. From the skylight in the roof a ladder lead down inside, and the lama descended. 'Come down and we'll look what it's like inside' he said, but Dorje Gyaltsen did not go down, remaining standing on the roof. The lama went down into a loft space, thinking that no one had ever lived in the house. Many of the beams and pillars were on the brink of giving way. As he went downstairs he saw the house was filled with a mire of entrails, intestines, and rotten blood. Feeling disgusted, the lama thought 'Poor brother, it's not right to leave him in a dirty place like this. I need to find him a good clean house' and he went to leave through a small door. From the rooftop Dorje Gyaltsen sang a sorrowful song:

Filthy, so filthy, the home of wicked people is unclean.
Rare, so rare, a good place to live is scarce.
Sad, so sad, the defiles of the bardo are full of sorrow.
Weak, so weak, my karma for freedom is feeble.
Moving on, always moving on, there is no aim to my wandering.

As he sang, Dorje Gyaltsen climbed down the back of the wall and wandered off. Hearing this, the lama thought 'I must go quickly and catch up with him, and while we talk, I'll help him find a good place to live.' However, the doorway was too narrow and he could not pass through. Stuck there, he heard the sound of his brother's singing fading further into the distance. From the doorway, he called 'Dorje Gyaltsen!' several times, but he had disappeared.

Guru Nyida Osal became terribly unhappy, thinking 'My poor brother, meeting him I didn't have time to speak with him properly; it was because of that wicked house. Earlier, when I held his hand I shouldn't have let go, but instead talked to him. Now that he has disappeared, I probably won't meet him in the future. If I do meet him again, I must carefully ask him his story and, by teaching the Dharma, allow him to go somewhere like the Pure Realm of Celestial Enjoyment, or the Pure Realm of Great Bliss. Otherwise, if I don't take him to a good home, it won't be right.' Then, it was as if he woke up from this weary state, and the experience faded away.

Nubo Dorje Gyaltsen was different from others; he had done some former practice, so he was special. In his next life he became a practitioner of the *Liberation through Hearing* cycle of teachings and a holder of the lineage. If even these kind of people, who have some independence, experience so much difficulty finding a good place to take rebirth, then how much more suffering there must be for us ordinary lowly people – powerless and blown to and fro by the winds of karma. It is for this reason the sorrowful experiences of the bardo intermediate state are not something that only happen to other people, never to befall us. What is more, they can suddenly appear after only a short time. Who can say for certain that, before the sun has set this evening, we will not suddenly find ourselves wandering in the bardo? There is not one person, no matter how courageous they are, who can say so with any certainty.

Whatever we are doing, whether we are at home or out, resting or working, think: 'This is my last activity in this world'. In order to generate the concept of impermanence, keep this always in mind and recite it out loud. We should also remind others of impermanence. As it is said:

> Of all contemplations, meditation on impermanence is supreme.
> Of all footprints, the elephant's is supreme.

Of course, out of all contemplations, meditation on impermanence is supreme. If we are never without meditation on impermanence, due urgency develops in our mind. With the whip of diligence encouraging us, it is just the same as having the path of liberation, the supreme pure land of Sukhavati, within our grasp. In this case, when we arrive in the terrifying bardo of death, the single hope and refuge is the holy Dharma alone. Except for this, our parents, siblings, friends, and relatives cannot protect us. Gold and silver, silks, money, horses, yaks, or other valuables – none of these is any help. When we have previously accumulated merit, if it is sufficient to escort us, then that's it! If not, that's it...

But how can we be sure to have such merit? The mass of non-virtue the size of the king of mountains, which we have accumulated through the three doors, is firstly, unceasing, and secondly, never left behind. It is tied around our necks and inseparable from us. When we think in this way, reflecting on this independence that we currently enjoy, if we do not practise the holy sacred Dharma authentically, getting the better of enemies and looking after the interests of family members, is of no use. All of that is just like a weapon you yourself have forged, that inflicts harm upon yourself, nothing more.

Except for the extent they plan ahead, there is no difference between excellent, middling, and lesser people. Therefore, abandon your homeland and embrace the homeless life. Live in caves with wild animals as your friends. Relinquish the need for food, clothing, and conversation, and as in the life stories of the holy masters of the past, it is fitting to have only few aims: View the essence-less activities of samsara in the same way as someone suffering from jaundice receives fatty food. Repulsed just to talk about it, turn your attention inward. If you journey, contemplating the impermanence of the path, walk towards the Dharma. If you sit, contemplating the impermanence of the environment, bring to mind the pure realm. Contemplating the impermanence of food, drink, and possessions, experience the nourishment of samadhi. If you sleep, contemplating the impermanence of sleep, purify delusion into luminosity.

The riches of the wealthy are impermanent, what is beneficial are the seven noble riches. Power and fame are impermanent, so at all times you should maintain a humble position. Cast yourself out from the ranks of humans and take up a place among dogs, then you will find a place among gods. These three: casting out, taking up, and finding, are the path followed by the holy masters of the past. The parent's wealth left as their children's inheritance is the instructions that they bestowed, so we need to engage with them.

As Jey Milarepa taught:

> Afraid of death, I fled to the mountains.
> Meditating again and again on the uncertain time of death,
> I captured the stronghold of the deathless nature.
> Now my fear of death is lost.

If you find the confidence to be ready to die, you can go on to capture the stronghold of the deathless. So, until that happens, you need to meditate on death and impermanence. Similarly, you must practise with the complete preparation, main part, and conclusion, the same as in the first section of teaching.

In this way, as awareness of impermanence grows in your mind:

O Guru Rinpoche, heed me! Turn my mind towards Dharma!
Omniscient master, do not let me stray onto wrong or inferior paths!
Compassionate lama, you who are one with them, heed me!

Pray: 'O Guru Rinpoche, turn my mind towards Dharma! O omniscient master of the Dharma, do not let me stray onto wrong or inferior, crooked paths! Compassionate lama, at one with these two masters, hold me with your compassion. All of you, please think of me!'

3) Karmic Cause and Effect

Negative Actions to be Abandoned

The Three Negative Actions of Body

In this, the third of the common outer preliminaries, the teaching on karmic cause and effect, there are three sections:

1) Negative actions to be abandoned.
2) Positive actions to be adopted.
3) Teaching on the all-determining quality of actions.

In the words of the recital text, karma is described in one single line:

> The results of virtuous and non-virtuous actions will follow after me.

Also, from the *Abhidharmakosha*:

> From karma, multitudes of worlds are born.

Karma gives birth to cyclic existence; it is the result of karma. How is that the case? There is no other being who instigates someone's migration to the places of the higher and lower realms. Also, it is not by luck or chance that beings randomly go to these places. It all comes about entirely through the working of karma, and is the result of karma without exception. From careful investigation into the cause and effect of virtue and non-virtue, we understand the need to abandon unwholesome negative actions, and strive to adopt positive virtuous actions.

Of this, the first thing we need to understand is the ten negative actions to be avoided. The three negative karmic actions of the body are:

1) Taking life.
2) Taking what is not given.
3) Sexual misconduct.

In terms of 1) taking life, the following four factors need to be complete for the full karma to actualise:

- Basis.
- Intent.
- Execution.
- Completion.

First, the basis is the object: a sentient being that is to be killed, a human, an animal, and so on, is identified unmistakenly. Intent is having the wish to kill arise. Execution is engaging in the method of killing. Completion is when their vital functions cease before the victim was due to die naturally.

This is speaking mainly from the perspective of a householder. If you are ordained, in terms of taking life, killing a human is the first of the four downfalls. The second downfall is taking what is not given. Sexual conduct is the third of the four downfalls. The fourth downfall is counted as falsely proclaiming oneself a lama. If any one of these four occurs and is concealed, then in future the vow is unable to be restored. Because such actions send one down to an inferior place, they are known as 'downfalls'.

Here we are mainly focused on speaking for the benefit of householders. The second non-virtue of the body is 2) taking what is not given. There is a slight difference in what is classified as 'stealing' and what is called 'taking what is not given'. Something taken secretly is called 'stealing'. Something taken by force or deception is classified as 'taking what is not given'. 3) Sexual misconduct: this is differentiated by improper place, improper time, types of people who are protected, Dharma reasons for prohibition, and so forth. Also, if one causes others to forsake their vows, this in particular is extremely bad.

THE FOUR NEGATIVE ACTIONS OF SPEECH

The four negative actions of speech are:

1) Lying.
2) Sowing discord.
3) Harsh speech.
4) Idle chatter.

1) Lying is usually done with the desire to deceive someone, so the truth is not spoken. By falsely proclaiming yourself as a lama, saying you have clairvoyance or have attained accomplishments when you have not, you deceive others. The second non-virtue of speech is 2) sowing discord. There is a difference between doing this openly and in secret. Using

subtle, indirect methods to separate those who were previously amicable, is secretly sowing discord. Forcibly dividing people is openly sowing discord. 3) Harsh speech is revealing others' hidden shortcomings. There is a difference here in the hidden flaws of someone's character and hidden flaws in their knowledge. Additionally, even if spoken gently, if words hurt someone's feelings, this is also included as harsh speech. 4) Idle chatter – everything spoken that is irrelevant, or arouses attachment and aversion, is idle chatter.

The above seven negative actions of body and speech are demonstrable obstructing forms, and when they are complete with the basis, intent, execution, and completion, then the karmic actuality will be fulfilled.

The Three Negative Actions of Mind

Lastly are the three negative actions of mind:

1) Covetousness.
2) Malicious thoughts.
3) Wrong views.

Growing desirous of the wealth and possessions of others, you think how nice it would be if these were yours, and how you must find a way to get them. This is 1) covetousness. Having a hostile attitude to someone else, feeling aversion and anger is 2) malicious thoughts. The view that there is no cause and effect, or to hold eternalist and nihilist beliefs, is 3) wrong views. These three actions of mind are grouped as indemonstrable obstructive forms, so they are completed with just the two aspects of basis and intent.

Other Divisions of Karma

> For those who have been helpful and a source of good qualities,
> You disregard them or cause them harm.

Among these, the worst wrongdoing is acting against those who have been helpful to you: to disregard and engage in killing your parents in this life; acting against any source of good qualities: to kill an arhat, or to draw blood from the body of a buddha with harmful intent; or to divide the monastic community. The fully ripened karmic results of these deeds are certain to be experienced ceaselessly, and for a long time – one must take rebirth in the hell of unending torment. Therefore these are called 'actions with boundless retribution'. As suffering is experienced incessantly, so it is called 'boundless'.

In addition there are five actions that come close to the boundless wrong doings. As taught in *Abhidharmakosha*:

> To abuse one's mother, an arhat,
> To kill a bodhisattva who has reached a certain level,
> Or a student, or stealing what has
> Been gathered for the Sangha,
> Comes close to boundless wrong doings.
> The fifth is destroying a stupa.

In terms of the manner in which these wrong doings are committed, they can be done directly by you, yourself, or you can make someone else do them, and then rejoice in their misdeed. Because you are in cahoots with them, then the fully-ripened result is the same. As it is said:

> Because an army, for example, has a single purpose,
> Each solider earns the karma of an agent.

The Results of Actions

The fruit of every non-virtuous action has four effects that ripen:

1) The fully ripened effect.
2) The effect resembling the cause.
3) The conditioning effect.
4) The proliferating effect.

In the case of 1) the fully ripened effect, if any one of the ten non-virtuous actions is done with a motivation of hatred and aversion, then one is reborn in hell. If non-virtuous actions are done under the influence of desire and attachment, then one is reborn as a preta. When non-virtuous actions are done controlled by ignorance, one is reborn as an animal. That is why it is said:

> Attachment will take you to the pretas,
> Aversion throws you into hell,
> Delusion usually sends you among the animals.

Following that is 2) the effect resembling the cause. There are two kinds of these:

Karmic Cause and Effect

- Experiences resembling the cause.
- Actions resembling the cause.

Experiences resembling the cause are as follows: As the power of karmic experiences becomes exhausted, one manages to escape from the lower realms and for once attain a human body, but having taken life in a previous life, life is then short and full of sickness. By taking what is not given, one becomes impoverished, or even if one manages to come by a little wealth, it gets taken by enemies or rivals. By engaging in sexual misconduct, one's partner will be unattractive and becomes hostile. Lying inclines most people to disparage and deceive you. Sowing discord makes those around you quarrelsome and hostile. Harsh speech makes us hear unpleasant sounds all the time, and turns what we say into quarrels. Idle chatter makes others ignore what we say, and we lack self-confidence around others. Covetousness prevents us from achieving anything we wish for, and causes undesirable circumstances to befall us. Malicious thoughts bring many fears and harm. Wrong views perpetuate these harmful beliefs, and our mind will be disturbed by deceit. These are the kinds of results that will occur.

What are the results of actions resembling the cause? It is said:

Action resembling the cause is rebirth with consistent actions.

Once again, having attained a physical basis consistent with the negative actions we have done in the past. If previously we were someone who took life, once more we enjoy killing, and so forth. This means naturally engaging in our previous negative actions.

3) The conditioning effect is said to be your karma which ripens on your environment. For example, by taking life one is reborn in an unpleasant environment with precipices, ravines, and so forth, a hostile and life-threatening place. By taking what is not given, we sow seeds but crops do not grow, so bad famines occur. By engaging in sexual misconduct we are reborn in a disgusting place. Lying brings rebirth in a fearful place, and material insecurity. Sowing discord brings rebirth in an unpleasant environment. Harsh speech brings rebirth in a nasty place with boulders, stones, and full of thorns, with no way to leave, so forcing us to stay there our whole life. Idle chatter prevents whatever work done from yielding any results, and the seasons are untimely and unpredictable. Covetousness brings bad harvests, scorched lands, and worsening times. Malicious thoughts bring rebirth in a hostile and harmful region. Wrong views bring rebirth in an impoverished place without refuge, protectors, or friends.

4) The proliferating effect: If we do not avert the results of the harmful actions we have done with the remedy of confession, and vows to refrain in future, then the karmic results of non-virtue will increase without limits, and we will have to experience ever more results.

Having discussed the negative actions to be avoided along with karmic cause and effect, we move on to:

Positive Actions to be Adopted and their Results

Now, if we think about the ten positive actions that are to be adopted, we do not say that the ten virtuous actions are merely the opposite of the ten negative actions. Why is that? For example, by merely not taking life, the vow to abandon taking life does not fully bind our mindstream to virtue. For this reason, by merely not taking life, it is not the genuine virtue of abandoning taking life. The mind that has firmly abandoned the ten negative actions needs also to have adopted the ten positive actions; not only do we abandon taking life but we must also protect the life of others. Not only do we abandon taking what is not given, but we must also be generous to others. By abandoning sexual misconduct, we keep discipline. Abandoning lying, we speak the truth. Abandon sowing discord, and instead reconcile disputes. Abandon harsh words and speak pleasantly. Abandon idle chatter and have meaningful conversations and recite prayers. Abandon covetousness and have few desires, knowing how to be contented. Abandoning the wish to harm others, meditate on loving compassion and cultivate the desire to benefit others. Abandon wrong views and build conviction in cause and effect, and the classifications of virtue and wrongdoing. Then stabilise in your mindstream the authentic view of the world. By achieving these things, you can become known as a 'special person of the ten virtues'.

By practising these ten virtues, what are the fully ripened results? If we practise the ten positive actions just a little, we will be reborn as a human. If we undertake doing them a medium amount, we can be reborn as a god in the desire realm. Do a great deal of virtuous activities combined with meditative absorption, and we can be reborn in the highest realm of existence.

From the result that resembles the cause, the experiences resembling the cause are as follows: By abandoning taking life, life is long and without sickness. By giving up taking what is not given, wealth and prosperity increase without harm from enemies or thieves. By abandoning sexual misconduct, you will meet with an attractive partner and have few opponents. Give up lying, and everyone is full of praise and love. Abandon sowing discord, and everyone around you will have respect. Give up harsh words, and you will hear only pleasant speech. By abandoning idle chatter, your words are relevant and everyone respects what you say. Give up covetousness, and everything you wish for is accomplished. By abandoning harmful thoughts, you will be free from harm and negativities. Abandoning wrong views, the true view will grow in your mind. These and other positive things will happen.

Having discussed good and bad karma and their effects, we now move on to:

The All-determining Quality of Actions

It is taught:

> The happiness and suffering of beings
> Is all karma, the Buddha taught.
> Multitudes of actions
> Give birth to multitudes of beings
> In diverse forms, who roam and wander.
> The manifestation of karma is vast!

What is the nature of karma? All the happiness and suffering, goodness and badness, of all beings in the three realms of samsara, wherever it comes from, has no other agent except for the strength of positive and negative actions, from which happiness and suffering is produced. Whether positive or negative, karma never breaks down, decays, or disperses. As is taught:

> At the perilous time of departure, O King,
> Wealth, friends, and loved ones cannot follow.
> But wherever beings come from and go to,
> Their karma follows them like a shadow.

Also in the *Sutra of a Hundred Actions*:

> The karma of beings,
> Even after a hundred aeons, is never lost.
> When time and conditions come together,
> Its fruit will ripen.

Negative, non-virtuous actions are not appropriate to do, even for the sake of our parents, khenpos, or masters. No one can mitigate your karmic maturation; it is certain to ripen upon you alone. Whatever action you do, even if it does not ripen immediately, not even a sesame seed's worth goes to waste. Like the example by All-knowing Jigme Lingpa:

> A eagle flies high above the earth, and
> For a while its shadow is nowhere to be seen, but
> Like the meeting and parting of karmic effects and beings,
> When time and conditions come together, they are perfectly apparent.

In distinguishing between positive and negative karma, virtuous and non-virtuous, superficial appearances are not crucial, what is most important is our motivation. If motivation is generated by attachment or aversion – an impure mind – the action may appear to be virtuous, but in actuality it becomes negative. Therefore, separate the bonds of self-interest from your heart's motivation. If you have the intent to benefit others, superficially an action may appear to be unvirtuous, but in truth it will become a positive action. As it says:

> Mind is key, mind is extremely swift,
> The essence of all phenomena comes down to mind.

Also:

> Actions done with attachment, aversion,
> Or ignorance are negative.
> Actions done without attachment, aversion,
> Or ignorance are positive.

Therefore, the distinction between positive and negative actions is made by the motivation in your heart. Also, whether an action is virtuous or non-virtuous, to obsess on it continuously, and to be without any remedy, as well as the difference of the basis of an action: either a beneficial basis or a basis with enlightened qualities – these are the five factors that truly create great karma.

Whether an action is virtuous or non-virtuous, to apply our body and speech continuously, many times is 'continual obsession'. Whether the mind is positive or negative, has afflicted emotions or, for example, faith, the activity of wanting to obsess over an action intensely is this second factor. To be without any remedy is, in the case of a non-virtuous karmic action, not having any remedy to overcome it whatsoever. For example, if there is no medicine to overcome a disease, then the disease will become stronger. To be without any remedy is factor three.

The two kinds of basis, factors four and five, are powerful objects, so whatever virtue or non-virtue you do, from the perspective of the object, the action becomes more or less powerful. The bases of benefit are one's parents, teachers of the Dharma, and so on. The main basis of enlightened qualities is the Three Jewels. It is taught that whatever we do, if positive or negative actions are connected with these five factors, they are significant. So, it is taught:

> The karma that comes from continually obsessing without remedy,
> With a basis that has the chief qualities,
> Virtuous or not, the five factors make it significant.
> Therefore, strive with positive actions.

At this stage in the recital text we read:

The results of virtuous and non-virtuous actions will follow after me.

As explained above, regarding the cause and effect of positive and negative actions, by always developing conviction in karma, do not disregard even the smallest positive virtuous actions but earnestly seize such opportunities. Do no belittle even tiny negative non-virtuous actions thinking they do no harm. They may be minor, but we must renounce them like poison. Whatever karma we create and accumulate, it all has a result, not ripening on anything external like the earth, water, fire, or wind, but ripening solely upon the mind-body aggregates we ourselves hold. Whatever actions we do follow after us, and us alone.

Therefore, there is not a single person who will not need to experience the fully ripened results of their actions. It is not the case that the powerful and rich can do whatever they want without needing to experience the karmic results, while the feeble and poor have to experience the consequences. What is more, those with influence and status have much greater capacity to accumulate negative actions. As it is said:

> Whoever has power has non-virtue.

Except for someone like the ancient manifested Dharma King Songtsen Gampo, who emanated people both to enforce the law and receive punishment, when someone without even the slightest thought of bringing benefit holds power, they amass terrifying amounts of negative karma. In addition, karmic cause and effect is not something only householders need to be vigilant about, while lamas, monks, and nuns do not really need to be concerned. In particular, it is certainly not the case that those who have the title of an important master are able to do whatever they want without needing to experience the karmic results. If even the Bhagavan and Acharya Nagarjuna demonstrated the manner of receiving the remnants of their karma, in the degenerate age, if those who have gained a place on a high throne through various means do not especially avoid generating bad karma, they will certainly follow after the Dark Horse Lama from Tsang, who was reborn in the ephemeral hells because he misused offerings.

Those who claim to have an elevated view, but disrespect cause and effect, have particularly bad negative karma. Such fools with overt pride do not accept any of the enlightened understanding of the Dharma, and say things like: 'There is no karma, no result of actions. Like the nature of the empty sky, there is nothing to see.' But these nihilistic views do not belong in this teaching. This view of Charvakas is the deceptive spell of demons, so it is taught we should not even listen to the sound of their voices. As Arya Nagarjuna said:

> The Pramana, who believe everything exists, go to the higher realms,
> The Nihilists go to the lower realms.

Also:

> With wrong understanding of emptiness,
> The unwise fall to ruin.

Orgyen Rinpoche said in his testament:

> Great King, in my Secret Mantra the view is most important. You must not lose your conduct to the perspective of the view. If you lose it, you will tend towards negative idle chatter that says virtue and non-virtue are empty. Also, you must not lose your view to the perspective of conduct. If you lose it, you will get tied up with objects and characteristics, and at no time will you be liberated. Therefore, your view should be higher than the sky, and your regard for karmic cause and effect finer than flour.

In particular, spiritual masters that look after groups of people – lamas that teach the path to others, khenpos that explain the collections of scriptures, and those with the title of incarnate lama who are not human but buddhas and bodhisattvas, and who take up worldly existence in the form of humans to work for the benefit of sentient beings – all must be especially careful with regard to karmic cause and effect.

What is more, if someone who teaches cause and effect to others does not guard it themselves, they will have to follow whatever path they have taught to their students. When a bodhisattva works for the benefit of beings with the four means of gathering disciples: generosity, pleasing speech, and so forth, there is no need to mention that they must combine it with motivation of uncontrived pure aspiration. Moreover, it is of the greatest importance that we ourselves engage in meaningful conduct that is consistent with the purpose. This is most essential in terms of misappropriation of property. It is very important that each of us does not sully our mindstream with obscurations.

Generally, we take whatever we can from the hands of others, with the motivation of the eight worldly concerns. We are gripped by the mind of selfish interest, and base our actions on all five kinds of wrong livelihood, even tending towards the four downfalls. Following that, without any pure motivation to offer up or give charitably those possessions which belonged to others, we work to pursue the eight worldly concerns to support our relatives and associates. Finally, we sow countless seeds of negative actions, over and over again, so negative karmic actions increase greatly and non-virtue becomes endless. Following such patterns, there is real danger that we will lead not only ourselves, but all those we are connected to, downwards on the path of samsara. Therefore it is imperative to be very careful.

However lowly someone is, from when they are small, a practitioner who ties a yellow belt needs to know how to accomplish at least their own purpose. In this case, as long as we are someone who desires the best for ourselves, we need to know how to practise with the view and conduct integrated into everything we say and do. However elevated our experience and realisation, we must guard cause and effect in minute detail. However, in general, if we need to explain the intricacies of karma and its fully ripened results in detail, we cannot. Only an omniscient fully enlightened buddha is able to do so. It is said:

> One who knows is all-knowing,
> Without omniscience wisdom, one is not.

However, if we follow the distinctions of karma in the words of the One Gone to Bliss, and the commentaries that clarify his intent, it is clear that on the one side, positive actions, both of attitude and behaviour, are virtuous. On the other side, negative actions, both of attitude and behaviour, are unwholesome. What are more difficult to distinguish are actions that mix positive and negative, like having a positive attitude but negative behaviour. On the one side, positive actions generate blissful results of gods and humans, and on the other, negative actions cause experience of the worst suffering of the three lower realms. But, for a mixture of positive and negative actions, if the thought is pure and not entangled with self-interest, it will become virtuous.

There are examples when it was permissible for a bodhisattva to engage in the seven non-virtues of body and speech: one is the case of the greatly compassionate captain who killed the spear-wielding criminal, and another concerns the Brahmin Char'er Karma, who engaged in impure conduct for virtuous reasons. However, positive actions done with a negative attitude are not positive. For example, some people, in order to pursue the eight worldly concerns, may end up engaging in Dharma practice, or building representations of the Three Jewels. This attitude and behaviour of mixed positive and negative, is like a twisted rope of white and black strands. White strands or black strands, whichever karma it becomes, depends chiefly on the good or bad motivation of the mind.

Also, considering the way in which fully ripened karmic results mature, there is karma that is experienced as perceptible phenomena, karma to be experienced after taking rebirth, karma to be experienced in subsequent lives, and so on. Karma that is experienced as perceptible phenomena ripens in this lifetime, and can be exemplified by the way in which the result of a negative action matures, like the country in which everyone got buried alive. Then there was Vajra, who as the result of positive actions, was born the daughter of King Prasenajit. But having accumulated karma of immediate consequence to be experienced after taking rebirth, as soon as she died, she went to the hell of unending torment. Karma which will be experienced in subsequent lives is the result of such actions like killing a person or a horse.

'Karma' as explained above, in general does not decay, fade away, or ever be lost. However it is not eternal. First, at the time the virtue or non-virtue is accumulated, karma is created. Eventually, at the time of exhaustion, through the power of experiencing it, the result becomes exhausted. However, in terms of negative karma, through confession it can be reduced and lose its foundation. If by means of the remedy, confession is made with the complete four powers, negative karma is reduced, and if the mind of bodhicitta is aroused in the mindstream, like the sun illuminating darkness, negative karma becomes naturally purified.

Similarly, virtuous karma can be squandered and depleted. If the four causes for virtuous karma to become exhausted are encountered, then the root of virtue will be extinguished. The four causes that extinguish roots of virtue are as follows:

1) Having done positive actions, to grow regretful.
2) To boast of our deeds to others.

3) Not dedicating merit.
4) Dedicating merit incorrectly.

There are two kinds of virtuous actions:

- Actions that accomplish samsara.
- Actions that lead to nirvana.

Thus not all kinds of virtue are the same. As to which category an action falls into, it depends on our motivation. With a motivation wishing to reach the higher levels of gods and humans, if you practise the ten virtues, the samadhi meditations of the eight thoughts and forms, and so on, these are actions that accomplish samsara's higher realms. This prevents rebirth in the lower realms for the time being, but does not ultimately bring liberation from samsara.

Having the motivation that you yourself wish to be liberated from the six realms of beings and reach the level of liberation, never to fall into suffering again, if you practise the ten virtues and so forth, these are actions that lead to nirvana. However, because this motivation possesses wisdom but not method, it creates karma to attain the middling level of a shravaka, but does not allow one to attain the level of perfect buddhahood. To explain this in another way, except for your own benefit, this does not accomplish benefit for others.

If we follow the Mahayana path focused on attaining full enlightenment for the benefit of others, and strive for the result of omniscience practising the ten virtues, then this is the path of a superior person's actions that leads to nirvana. In this way, we must embrace our practice with the three excellent principles:

- First, the preparation of arousing bodhicitta.
- In the middle, the main part of non-conceptuality.
- Lastly, the excellence of dedication.

We must always practise in this way, never without the three excellent principles.

In all discussions on the detailed classifications of actions and results, in summary we always say it is interdependence: In dependence on a virtuous or unwholesome cause, the result of happiness or suffering comes about. In reliance on one, the other comes about; thus it is called 'interdependence'. For this reason, Lord Nagarjuna teaches:

Except for what arises from interdependence,
There are no other phenomena.

Without the cause of seed planted in a field, there will be no resulting autumn crops to harvest. Likewise, if there is no cause of the five poisons of afflictive emotions, the result of all kinds of suffering have no reason to occur. By practising the cause of the ten virtues, the result will be to attain the level of the gods and humans. Again, this comes about from cause and effect being dependent upon each other, and is called 'interdependence'. In this way, the causes which depend on the paths of the three levels of enlightenment, results in attainment of the three enlightenments, which comes about through the power of interdependence.

If something is truly established, objectively established, established by way of specific characteristics, and so forth, never changing, altering, or being destroyed, but remains the same, then it is impossible to be established as being real by the actions of interdependence. All interdependent, connected phenomena cannot be established as truly existent, and are thus empty. Therefore, Lord Nagarjuna concludes the above by saying:

> For that reason, there are no phenomena
> Which are not empty.

Again, for example: if, due to a cause, a seed does not change or be destroyed, and is established as being something truly existent, solid, permanent, and stable, then it is impossible for the result, the action of the autumn crops, to grow. It has to be that, as long as the seed cannot change, it must remain as it is. However, under the influence of interdependence, by becoming broken down, a result then grows.

Therefore:

> Whatever is in keeping with emptiness,
> For that, everything is possible.

Similarly, wrong views, aversion, and so on, are also apparent, but without any inherent nature. From the aspect of analysing the truth, there is no way to establish any intrinsically-produced truth with regard to these non-virtuous actions. Due to this fact, emptiness can be determined. From the potency of emptiness that is nothing in and of itself, when the unimpeded nature of interdependence arises, then it can be determined as 'arising from emptiness'. For that reason, emptiness and interdependence are like fire and heat, water and wetness, unable to be separated individually. Indivisible emptiness and interdependence is the very nature of the unity of appearance and emptiness. Appearance eliminates the extreme of nihilism. Emptiness eliminates the extreme of absolute existence. So we need to determine fourfold emptiness that falls into neither of the extremes of eternalism or nihilism.

In that case who is the person who accumulates karma? Karma accumulates by the power of deluded conceptions. Non-conceptuality does not accumulate karma. It is said:

> Karma arises from worldly afflicted emotions;
> Karma comes from the mind.
> Mind is accumulated from habitual tendencies,
> Freedom from habitual tendencies is happiness;
> A happy mind is peace.

In short, the four noble truths which establish samsara and nirvana, teach interdependence. Where does interdependence come from? It comes from ultimate truth. How does it come about? From the truth of the primordially pure nature of dharmata, all worldly phenomena of infallible cause and effect appear, like clouds from the sky. Independent of producer and produced, if the two truths of cause and effect, without which nothing arises, are understood to be inseparable, this is called the 'pure view of wisdom'. Also, with 'pure conduct of skilful means', by carefully engaging in the rejecting and adopting of cause and effect, upon the unity of the two fundamental truths, through the unity of the two accumulations of the path, we need to actualise the result of the level of the unity of the two kayas.

That being the case, upon an understanding of the unity of the two truths of emptiness and interdependence, as long as there is dualistic perception – until grasping at the truth of deluded appearances is destroyed – a beginner cannot be without mindfulness, attention, and care regarding which positive actions to adopt and which negative actions to abandon. Mindfulness is like a having a guard on the door, that does not forget what should be adopted and renounced. Examining our thoughts and actions with attention is like having a watchman on the three doors. Additionally, being careful and never forgetting to be conscientious about each aspect of which things to cultivate and avoid, is like a new bride arriving in her husband's household for the first time. So these are the three keepers of your own three doors.

In particular, by examining and investigating your mind, it is of key importance to increase virtuous states of mind, decrease unwholesome states, and turn neutral states of mind into positive ones. If you do not have firm conviction in cause and effect, you do not even arrive in the ranks of a student or patron of Buddhism, not to mention being a suitable recipient of offerings. If you do have this authentic view of the world, then all virtuous qualities naturally come together. Therefore, before practising Dharma it is very important to establish confidence and belief in regard to the topics of cause and effect.

Teaching Day Three

In the words of my incomparable holy master, Lama Jigme Yonden Gonpo:

> O respected friend, the appearances of this life are a dance of clouds;
> They do not have even the slightest reliability.
> Regarding this deceptive essence-less state of affairs,
> If you have a mind, you must certainly be dismayed.

'O respected friend' refers to Dharma friends, or those who will follow after him in the future. My master is addressing us in a kind and pleasant tone, accepting us with mind full of compassion to give us instruction.

The appearances of this life are a dance of clouds.

Our awareness of sensory appearances of the world in this life is likened to the form of clouds in the sky. When clouds amass in the sky, sometimes they make shapes akin to castles and palaces, other times they resemble images of gods and goddesses. Occasionally, they become forms of aquatic or wild animals. White clouds are as pretty as tufts of lamb's wool, but because of sudden movement of winds, they become black angry rain clouds, swirling with red flashes of lightening. At other times, white and red clouds form a canopy of dense rainbow lights, as if a gifted artist had drawn the array of a heavenly landscape.

We can observe these things, but they do not remain. With one blast from a powerful northerly wind they are all swept away, obliterated without a trace. It is for this reason, just like the dance of clouds in the sky, the way our happiness and suffering of the phenomenal world appears, is, as the poem says, without the slightest certainty.

Likewise, the splendour of youth does not endure. Those who were once young have now become frighteningly aged men and women. Similarly, neither does someone who used to be wealthy always remain so, and later on may become penniless. Last year's fierce and powerful ruler has this year fallen into a pit of disgrace. Not only that, but we may be suddenly afflicted by some painful disease and separated from our family, or our parents and relatives, siblings and children, may also pass away. Nothing turns out as we hoped and undesirable circumstances constantly befall us. How numerous are the sufferings and changes of the world!

> They do not have even the slightest reliability.

This recognises and acknowledges that all appearances in the state of samsara are untrustworthy, and without any reliability whatsoever. Although, in general, when people say, 'That's the way life is!' we cannot always accept such sweeping statements, but this is not the case here. You can see for yourself; such things will have happened to you. You are actually experiencing these appearances here and now, the false dance of clouds, within an illusion of sensory confusion. If this is so, this situation is one that we can all recognise.

> Regarding this deceptive essence-less state of affairs...

This refers to the deceptive seductions of desirable things which, upon investigation, have no essence; delusion upon delusion without interruption – the dream of a deep sleep. Concerning this situation:

> If you have a mind, you must certainly be dismayed.

With the exception of non-sentient inanimate matter, anyone with a 'mind' who gives life any thought, should feel despair, fed up with appearances, these transitory worldly phenomena. Now we have to think about this, the poem teaches it is something we 'certainly', or surely, do not want to dwell on.

Continuing, Yonden Gonpo taught the following:

> Whoever – enemy, friend, or someone in between –
> By nature it is difficult to be friendly with the basis of strife:
>   attachment and aversion.
> They speak of helping, but later scold and blame.
> When considering such situations, weariness overwhelms us.

We sentient beings have become human. If we think about all those we see who share the same speech, actions, and behaviour: a few of them are hostile enemies, the ones we get along with are friends, and some are neither good nor bad, indifferent without any positive or negative attributes. There is no one who does not belong to, or is not included within, these three groups. All of these people, whoever or whatever they are, are singularly difficult to get along with. Some are friends we are attached to, others are objects of aversion, some are the basis of ignorant indifference. Whichever of these roles they occupy, they are still the basis of attachment, aversion, and ignorance. Like a culture which causes yoghurt to set, they are solely the basis that causes suffering to develop.

At first we are happy to see our friends and pleased to meet up with them, but as time passes they become irritating, and many a friend can end up becoming an enemy. In the beginning they are not someone we dislike; you get along well, but many do end up becoming rivals. It is the case that, for most enemies in this world, at first they were allies, but finally they became foes. Among all rivals, those with whom we were once familiar, but later fell out with, are the worst. Those who we are indifferent to also do not usually remain in this neutral state. If we get closer, they all bring a mass of problems. This is always the way, because we are all ordinary unenlightened people. If we focus on them, indeed the faults of others make us irritated, but when the situation is reversed, it is us who are a source of irritation to others.

By nature it is difficult to be friendly.

Therefore, it is the nature of ordinary people that the more we spend time together, or grow familiar with each other, the more we become sick of each other. Why is that? It is because someone with faults is a bundle of trouble. For example, if you touch a thorn it is going to prick you, that is nothing to be surprised about. Of course it will prick you, it is a thorn! If you touch it, pricking you is its characteristic, its nature. Similarly, whoever you spend time with, of course you will get sick of them; they are ordinary people. By nature, an ordinary person is difficult to get along with. Why is that? The poem teaches they are:

The basis of strife: attachment and aversion.

People are the basis from which the afflictive emotions of desire form; they are the object from which the afflictive emotions of hatred arise. People are also in an ongoing state of darkness that causes the delusion of ignorance of both of these afflictive emotions together. What is more, having entered into this vast machine of delusion, it is difficult to get out. This is why it is taught we are in a dark and gloomy prison, tormented by the disease of the three poisons.

They speak of helping, but later scold and blame.

With a tenuous positive thought in their minds, hoping to be of benefit, people say, 'Don't do that, do this. If you do that, you'll run into this and that kind of problem.' Alternatively, you may aim to benefit others by giving possessions, food, and money, or you may hope to help others by providing training, education, and so forth. You try your best, yet in return for your help, others only bring you harm. You may praise them, but they disrespect you back. In the same way, there are some foals that, having filled their stomachs, will kick their mother with their hind legs.

This is not one person making some rare trouble, this is the nature of all beings in samsara. For that reason, regarding the general manifest mode of samsara and, in particular, the attitude of people in these bad times, it is appropriate to have a 'weary heart'. This brings about renunciation from samsara, and the stimulus to feel weariness towards attachment and aversion – the inherent expression of delusion.

Again, Yonten Gonpo gave the following instruction:

> My friend, in a secluded cave, abandon busy excitement
> And follow the biographies of holy masters.
> By practising in accordance with the Dharma, be guided by the
>   holy masters.
> Is this not the pinnacle of a thousand joys?

Saying 'my friend', generally, we are all friends of a similar human kind, and in particular we are all Buddhist friends, part of the same religious tradition. Moreover, as we are gathered together in the same Vajrayana empowerment and the same mandala assemblage, he is addressing us specifically: 'you, my Dharma friend', calling on us to abandon the busy excitement of modern life, and in a secluded rocky cave, to train according to the exemplary lives of the holy masters.

If we are ordained, whatever we do, we should have already left home and embraced the monastic life, but having renounced the smaller unit of family life, we also should renounce the larger home of the distracting and busy monastery. We monastics of the degenerate times, if we do not abandon both our smaller home and our larger home, we will end up trying to fulfil both the obligations of the monastery and lay people, which will only result in more busyness. If we are not able to separate ourselves from these, we will not get to follow the lives of the holy masters. This is what is being taught here.

But what should someone living at home do to practise the Dharma? For lay folk, it is not that there is no way to practise the Dharma, or no way to find the path to liberation. For householders, the way to practise the Dharma is to do so alongside worldly commitments. Just as it is said:

> Decorated with ornaments but having Dharma conduct.

Physically you may live at home, committed to a householder's way of life, but mentally, by not chasing after the discursive thoughts of afflictive emotions, inwardly secluded, your mindstream naturally meditates on peaceful concentration. Even if things are very busy, your mind does not fall into bad habits and patterns. Like the example of being born in the middle of a lotus pond, but not being sullied by the muddy water, it is taught it is still possible to train by following the life stories of the holy masters.

Thus a householder living at home, beginning with an authentic view of the world and confident faith in cause and effect, is not without a way to train on the path. What is more, even if we physically stay in a secluded place, if our mind is not freed from the trappings of busy town life, we will be unable to live in perfect solitude. So, how can we follow in the footsteps of the holy lamas? The answer is given:

> By practising in accordance with the Dharma, be guided by the holy masters.

By practising with your mind and conduct in accordance with the holy Dharma, merge the Dharma and your mindstream into one. If someone asks for help with something that contradicts Dharma, politely decline – in this way, we follow the holy masters of the past, and are guided by them.

> Is this not the pinnacle of a thousand joys?

Generally, what we consider as being happy is merely with reference to the physical basis of the higher realms of gods and humans – when sometimes the gross feeling of suffering becomes less, a slight feeling of happiness can arise. However that is not true happiness; it does not go beyond the suffering of conditioned existence.

Well then, what is the pinnacle of a thousand joys? True happiness is ultimate happiness, which is unsullied by suffering. Having become disheartened by the realisation of suffering, by seizing the holy kingdom of the three solitudes, attain the inheritance of the realisation of practice. Cut the karmic continuum of future wandering in samsara. Uphold the responsibility of bodhicitta and pledged vows to liberate all mother-like sentient beings from suffering and, as the successor of the victorious ones of the past, maintain the life force of the Dharma. Be a refuge and protector to those who are weary and suffering, and a place of refuge for those without a defender, to those who have lost hope or confidence. Having entered the good path that pleases the victorious ones, and followed in the footsteps of the holy masters of the past, this is taught to be the pinnacle of a thousand joys.

In particular, for someone who is earnestly seeking the path of Dharma from the bottom of their heart, it is just as Shantideva taught:

> Upon the pleasant mansions of wide rocks,
> Cooled by the sandalwood moonlight,
> Caressed by silent, gentle forest breezes,
> The fortunate roam and contemplate benefit for others.

Also, the Easterly Lord Kalden Gyatso said:

> If you delight in secluded mountains,
> In the swirls of drifting mountain mists,
> There are naturally-occurring rocky caves.
> If you stay in this kind of place, happiness is yours now and forever.

And again:

> If you delight in secluded forests,
> Among the lush forest foliage
> There is a cool house of tree leaves.
> Stay in this kind of place, and joy will increase.

In those places of accomplishment that our holy forefathers have graced and blessed, make friends with the birds and forest animals. Maintain meditative equipoise and concentration. This is truly the pinnacle of a thousand joys.

At first, teaching and listening to the Dharma, our mindstream is untamed and inflexible. Like stiff, crisp leather, it is unworkable and not on the path. To get on the path we need to train the mind. Without beginning with the mind trainings, however much we may train in the other scriptures of Buddha's word, Sutra, or Tantra, not only are they going to be of no benefit to our mindstream, but there is the risk that we will become jaded by Dharma, and so untameable.

Why do we need to train our mind? We need to come to understand that the suffering of samsara is suffering. Not knowing this, we misunderstand joy and misery, and do not apply genuine diligence to the path of liberation. Before we have properly understood this, if the lama teaches the Dharma, we misunderstand it as a catalogue of misery and inevitability. We think that everything we are interested in, all our wishes and desires, are unacceptable, and what is permitted, necessary, and suitable is singularly difficult and unachievable.

If you think like that and the karmic connection is too distant, and especially if you develop wrong views, then at first although you may be on the path of Dharma, it is possible later you could adopt a corrupt way of life. This happens due to not beginning with the mind trainings. If we really examine this from actual experience, this is what a thoughtless, obstinately disobedient child would do. Such actions only hurt themselves. However, if a cognisant adult says 'Don't do that!' at first the child will not like it, but if we observe as time passes, these trainings clearly bring benefit, so one day it is possible they will come to their senses.

Gyalwa Longchenpa stated:

> In summary, all activities of this life
> Are like good food mixed with deadly poison.
> Wholeheartedly abandon them, as in the biographies of holy masters.

Je Rinpoche taught:

> Whoever you associate with, the three poisons and so on –
> All the afflictive emotions – grow like the waxing moon,
> And positivity retreats like dimming constellations.
> Swiftly abandon bad places and become a vagabond.

Obviously, the Buddha's prescribed precepts do not dictate to us exactly what is difficult and undesirable to practise! However, the disease of afflictive emotions in our mindstream is very powerful, so if we let all our actions, activities, and thinking, which are mostly unfit and unsuitable, come under its control, then we are certain to experience samsaric suffering without end. So the way to avert it, like an expert doctor's prescription for curative treatment, is the Buddha's Dharma discipline of prescribed precepts. This shows what constitutes non-virtue, and the great pitfalls of faults and downfalls. It teaches, 'Do not go in that direction, otherwise you will fall into the abyss of wrongdoing; rather go in this direction and you'll be sure to arrive in the city of everlasting joy!' thus showing the path of liberation of sacred comfort and well-being. Samsaric beings, wretched and miserable, have fallen into a sorrowful place, and are about to fall to a place of even more suffering, so there is no alternative but to tell them the method to save themselves and avert disaster.

If we do not know that suffering is suffering, then we do not know that happiness is happiness. Therefore, if we recognise that suffering of the disease of afflictive emotions – attraction, aversion, and ignorance – is suffering, then we can assert the need to do something to reduce it, even just a little. Thinking this, we need to come out from under the bad external influence of these three poisons, and gain a little independence. With this understanding, think: 'If I can limit them a little, then I'm sure to experience the equivalent increase in joy.' In order to accomplish such a meaningful thing, of course we need to go to a little trouble.

In the words of Padampa Sangye:

> For people without determination, buddhahood is rare.
> Accept the hardship, people of Dingri.

Padampa Sangye gave *Eighty Pieces of Advice* to the people of Dingri:

> Now there's no time... When will there be time?
> Time is an escort of the Lord of Death, people of Dingri.

And again:

> Realise now the great and trifling aims of men and women.
> Do not waste your life, people of Dingri!

All good things of this world, all amazing and valuable good actions in their entirety, come from the ripening result of hard work alone. All the conditioned things of phenomenal appearance are the same in this respect. So while we sit here, if we want to attain happiness that, over countless lifetimes up to now, we have never experienced, of course we need to put in a little effort in the direction of the Dharma. But, for those listening to the Dharma without understanding this, it sounds like a distant legend. Like children listening to a tale, they marvel, play, get distracted and confused, so the days and seasons pass...

From the time the Buddha appeared in this world, to those who had the karma and fortune, he taught the instruction to show the path to liberation; the nectar to pacify the disease of suffering, which cannot always be heard. It is so valuable that, to hear just four words of Dharma, bodhisattvas sacrificed their lives. They did that for this very Dharma! But, at the present time, we do not need to search; due to the power of our good fortune, we hold the Dharma in our hands. However, whether you know how to take your share of this fortune depends on you. If you know how to receive it, this is many times better than being given all the wealth and riches of the world, all heaped up together. We should realise that this teaching contains crucial words on the key points of practice.

If someone said to you, 'Today, I'm going to give you all the riches in the world', and actually gave them to you, it would not be of any use to guard you from the inevitability of death. It also would be of no benefit to prevent you falling down to the lower realms after death. Not only that, but it would actually increase the suffering of this life, just as supreme protector Arya Nagarjuna taught:

> My lord, many possessions bring the same measure of suffering,
> Those with few desires are not the same.
> However many heads the superior nagas have,
> From those, come an equal amount of suffering.

If we had all the wealth of the world, in our next life, because of attachment to riches, it would certainly cause us not to be free from the lower realms.

When we listen to the Dharma, we need to listen carefully to each word and each point. By merging the meaning with our mindstream, we can point the finger at our own faults. By confronting our mindstream with the Dharma, we can correct our mistakes. This Dharma is medicine for our mental state, so if we do not apply it to our mindstream, it is like wind whistling past our ears; barely hearing it, there is not going to be any benefit.

If you suddenly catch a wild animal, at first of course it will be startled and struggle to escape. It cannot be blamed, after all, it is an animal of the hills, without any self-control. But gradually, if you train them, wild white-mouthed donkeys get used to being lead. Even fierce wild animals like tigers, leopards, and bears, once they are tamed, respond to human speech, and so go where they are sent and stay where they are put. If this is the case for an animal, then for a person who knows how to communicate and understand meaning, there is no reason why they cannot be trained, become accustomed, and gain understanding. In this way, if someone listens to the Dharma, and thinking that it may contain some truth, pays a little attention, it is natural they are curious about the meaning behind what is being said. That is the feeling when first joining a Dharma gathering, like the first step that needs to be experienced.

Following that, for the second step, it is natural that scepticism arises regarding what is said: 'Virtue brings benefit and wrongdoing carries consequences? Everything arises from karma?' Later on, we also confront more complex dilemmas: 'The root of karmic cause and effect is interdependence. The essence of interdependence is emptiness. So we must realise the truth of inseparable emptiness and interdependence?' Questioning things in this way at first is not called 'wrong views'. We need to find answers to such questions.

In the authentic scriptures and commentaries, there are three hundred and sixty wrong views of non-Buddhists, along with the beliefs of the lower Buddhist philosophical systems. By challenging and defending these with scriptural authority and genuine logic, the answers to doubts have been clarified, determined long ago. When we hear Dharma teachings that are in a similar fashion, and follow a similar pattern of analysis, when the thought, 'This makes sense!' occurs, at that time we come to possess confident and certain faith. When this happens, and we apply effort, not only are we able to accomplish Dharma for our own purpose, but Dharma can also be accomplished for the benefit of others.

In the past, the students of Jetson Milarepa said to him, 'From the outset, you were certainly an extraordinary emanation of buddhas and bodhisattvas'. In response Milarepa said, 'I was not. At first I was just an ordinary person; a really sinful person at that. So, in fear of going to the lower realms because of my wrongdoings, I attained the result of accomplishment. If you are a determined person, whoever you are, if you endeavour and strive in Dharma in a similar way, you can certainly become like me.' Therefore, read the examples of the deeds of holy masters of the past in their life stories. To find answers to your questions, if you refer to the lucid expositions of holy masters and the scriptural works of scholars, there is no going wrong on the path, or erring in your actions.

One more thing: If you do not personally examine others, but listen to everything they say and credulously follow all their suggestions, no good will come of it. If you run after just anyone, thinking everything they say is true, it will bring you nothing but loss, just like the tale of the Brahmin's goat that became a dog. How did the Brahmin's goat become a dog?

A long time ago there was a young Brahmin. He was a non-Buddhist, so was leading a goat off to sacrifice to the gods. A few thieves saw the young Brahmin approaching, leading the goat, so they said to each other, 'We must make a plan to get hold of that goat somehow'. Having discussed how best to do it, the five thieves waited scattered apart on the Brahmin's path.

He first met the nearest thief, who said, 'What bad omens there are to be seen in this world – there's a Brahmin leading a dog!' The Brahmin boy did not say a word, but when he met with the second thief, who again said the same thing, he thought about replying, but did not. Then when he met with the third thief, who said the same thing as the others: 'Look at the Brahmin leading a dog!' The Brahmin did not say anything but looked back at his goat. Thinking, 'It is really a goat!' he continued on in no doubt.

As he met the fourth thief, the thief jeered as before: 'A Brahmin leading a dog!' The Brahmin boy looked carefully at the old goat: 'This is no dog, it's a goat. It's got all the things a dog doesn't have but a goat does, like horns and a beard, and so on.' Thinking this he carried on.

Then when he met the fifth thief, again the thief said 'Ugh, what a terrible omen to see, a Brahman leading a dog along!' When he said this, the Brahmin thought to himself, 'Not one, not two, but five people have all said the same thing. This looks like a goat, but if it's a harm-bringer, or a vicious demon, or something like a ghost that can transform into anything it wants, coming on purpose to eat the sacrifices, then what am I doing leading it there?' Convincing himself that it would certainly bring harm, the Brahmin boy let the goat go, and the thieves seized it, just as they had planned.

If, with that kind of suggestable outlook, you are easily influenced by other people, then that kind of thing is bound to happen. If you are too suggestable and compliant, undesirable things are sure to occur, and at the very least, you will be gradually lead to ruin.

Therefore, having the foundation of the buddha nature, upon the basis of a precious human body, by relying on the condition of a good spiritual teacher, we need the methods of the profound instructions that they possess in order to engage in the holy direct instructions. To receive such teachings, be cognisant at all times that you have liberation within reach, and remember the necessity of the bodhisattva motivation and conduct. Then you need to listen to and study the Dharma.

4) Defects of Samsara

The Suffering of Samsara

In the scheme of the goodness of the beginning, middle, and end, we have already completed the goodness of the beginning of the *Sublime Path to Omniscience*. In the goodness of the middle, which includes the common and unique stages, we are still on the first. Having covered the teachings on 1) the difficulty of finding the freedoms and endowments, 2) the impermanence of life, and 3) karmic cause and effect, today it is time to teach the fourth of the common outer preliminaries: the defects of samsara, which discuss samsaric suffering.

Regarding this, there are two parts that need to be addressed:

- The general reflection on the suffering of samsara.
- The specific reflection on the individual suffering of the beings of the six realms.

These consist of an implicit discussion of the general suffering of samsara, and an explicit teaching on the particular sufferings of the six realms of samsara.

The overall meaning of the three previous steps of the preliminaries we have already covered is as follows: The freedoms and endowments are difficult to find. Is it enough just to have found them? No. If the purpose of this human body with the freedoms and endowments is not achieved, be aware that it is something difficult to find and also easily lost. However, if, when this body falls apart and dies, we become absolutely nothing at all, then we would not need to give it another thought. If there is no such thing as a future life, there is nothing to take into consideration.

Yet after death, we do not become nothing, and we must take rebirth. As soon as we need to take rebirth, there is no other place beyond the realms of samsara for us to go. As that is the case, defiled karmic actions generated by ignorance and afflictive emotions, virtuous and non-virtuous, cause rebirth as one of the six kinds of beings in the three realms of samsara. This continues on, one rebirth after another, in never-ending cycles of suffering. This is why samsara is called 'cyclic existence'.

To give some examples, it is taught samsara is like a potter's wheel, a waterwheel, or a fly trapped in a jar. As for the example of a fly in a jar, if the fly flies to the top, it is still in the jar; if it flies to the bottom, it is still in the jar. Likewise, going to the higher levels, the levels of gods or humans are still samsara. If you are born in the lower levels of the three unfortunate realms, this is still samsara. So, from beginingless time, throughout the three realms of samsara, there is not one kind of rebirth that we have not taken, and there is not one single being, out of all sentient beings, that has not been our father, mother, enemy, or friend. What is more, they have not been our mother or father, enemy or friend, just once or twice. Every single being has been our mother more times than the earth of a vast land can be rolled up into small pellets.

It is taught the number of times we have been beheaded solely because of desire is incalculable, and if the miniscule limbs of all our rebirths as tiny ants were piled up together, the pile would be taller than the king of mountains. If the tears we shed while experiencing suffering were collected, it is taught they would be deeper than an ocean. Being reborn in hell, the amount of molten copper that we have all been forced to drink is more than the four great oceans put together. If this is the case, we will continue to be reborn in samsara, and those who have not grown even slightly disenchanted with cyclic existence, will still have to experience such suffering.

If, with the appropriate virtuous merit, we took a form like Brahma or Indra, Chief of the Gods, we would have abundant wealth and radiance. But in the end, we still could not escape from death, and we could not simply just die; we would again have to experience the wretched suffering of the lower realms.

With this current physical basis, we may seem to be healthy. Our possessions and wealth increase, and we enjoy a little happiness. But, having deceived ourselves for a few months or years, when this result of rebirth in a higher realm is exhausted, we must experience the extreme deprivation and wretchedness of suffering in the lower realms.

Just like when we are dreaming a pleasurable dream, but then wake up during the happiest part, we cannot rely on anything in samsara. Experiencing the meagre result of slight virtue, we may have a moment of happy perception, but when that propelling karma has been exhausted, we are powerless to remain another moment and, in the blink of an eye, once again find ourselves in hell, being boiled alive in molten iron.

By coming to understand the unreliability of samsara and its suffering, by means of this present rebirth, now that we are able to see the beginning of the path, we can become liberated from this ocean of suffering and attain the everlasting happiness of complete buddhahood. We do so by engaging in practice with the complete preparation, main part, and conclusion. This is the main meaning of the general reflection on the suffering of samsara.

Defects of Samsara

Individual Sufferings of the Beings of the Six Realms

Suffering of Hell

The Eight Hot Hells

Following that, we address the specific reflection on the individual suffering of the beings in the six realms, which has six corresponding sections. The root text begins with the teaching on hell:

> **In particular, if I am reborn in the hell realms,**
> **On a ground of burning iron, my head and body will be hacked by weapons,**
> **Dismembered by saws, and crushed by blazing hammers,**
> **Trapped screaming in a door-less iron room,**
> **Impaled on red-hot spikes, boiled in molten metal,**
> **And burned in the hottest fire – the Eight Hot Hells.**

In a verse and a half the suffering of the Eight Hot Hells is taught.

> In particular, if I am reborn in the hell realms...

Beginning with the suffering and grave consequences of hell, first is the teaching on the suffering of the hot hells:

> On a ground of burning iron, my head and body will be hacked by weapons.

This ground of burning iron is the same throughout all the hot hells. In terms of the first realm of hell called 'Reviving', countless hell beings are herded together. Seeing each other, the perception arises as if the murderer of their father had just appeared, and the fire of hatred and anger flares up towards one another. All kinds of karmically-experienced weapons appear in their hands. They strike at each other, engaging in nothing but killing, beheading, chopping, and wounding. In short, someone's head gets cut off and another's body is sliced up; all end up dying on the blades of these weapons. When everyone is dead, a karmic voice sounds from the sky: 'Revive!' and by the power of karma, all revive and attack each other as before. Like this, they suffer endlessly from dying and reviving, again and again. To consider how long this lasts, in human years, they must experience this for tens of millions of years. This is the Reviving Hell, the most lenient of the hells.

Number two is the Black-line Hell. This is taught in:

> Dismembered by saws.

The terrifying agents of the Lord of Death draw black lines on the bodies of hell beings – four, eight, sixteen, thirty two, and so on – from the top of their heads to the tip of their toes. With iron saws, red-hot and covered with sparks, the hell beings are dismembered from head to toe. As soon as they are sliced up, without dying, they again become whole. The beings of hell consider dying to be pleasurable and would be happy to die, except they cannot. As they become whole, again eight or sixteen or so black lines are drawn, and once more they suffer from being chopped up. They must suffer exclusively like this for hundreds of millions of human years.

Generally speaking, the suffering of hell cannot be expressed in a few words, but with this rough description, we should be able to get a general impression. To do so, we need to understand that on the basis of the earlier hells, the suffering of the latter hells is that much greater.

The third region of hell is the Rounding-Up and Crushing:

> Crushed by blazing hammers.

Into huge mortar-like valleys of red-hot blazing iron, countless hell beings are thrown and crushed by huge blazing hammers, like barley being ground up. The mountains on both sides of the valley become the heads of animals and wild beasts: goats, sheep, yaks and so on, that the hell beings killed while they were alive in the human world. These terrifying creatures, with fire blazing from the tips of their horns, butt their heads together, grinding them between their horns. The hell beings die, and then revive again and again in terrible fear, having to experience this for many billions of human years.

Comparing these lifespans to human years, or to a day in the upper realms of the gods, it is difficult to get accurate figures. But having been born there it feels like, whatever one does, one will never become free.

> Trapped screaming in a door-less iron room.

This describes both the fourth and fifth hells, the Howling Hell and the Great Howling Hell. Having entered into a room of blazing iron, a burning cell, at first you have the impression you entered through a door, but this immediately seals itself up, so there is no door. In there you experience suffering, screaming for hundreds of billions of human years. The Great Howling Hell has two of these burning iron rooms, one enclosed within the other. Upon entering the innermost room, both the outer and inner doors are welded shut. Amid flames and billowing black smoke you suffocate in the revolting fumes, burning but not able to die. Screaming out in terror, you continue to experience this suffering for many thousands of billions of years.

In number six, the Heating Hell and number seven, the Intense Heating Hell, it is taught hell beings are:

> Impaled on red-hot spikes, boiled in molten metal.

First, in the Heating Hell, upon spear-like metal pokers with three prongs, naked hell beings are impaled on the spikes, their bodies pierced just like beads threaded on a mala. In the Intense Heating Hell, not only are they impaled from their feet to the crown of their heads on three-prong metal spikes, but they are also wrapped up in sheets of burning metal, molten iron is poured into their mouths, and they are cooked in boiling iron in massive hellish cauldrons, and so forth. They must experience such kind of suffering which, even though we are not bound to experience it right now, it is terrifying just to mention, and which lasts for a number of human years that cannot be counted.

Eight is the Hell of Ultimate Torment, called 'ultimate' because it is not possible to experience suffering any torture worse than this. We do not have words or means to express in human language the suffering that is experienced there.

> Burned in the hottest fire.

This indicates the suffering of Ultimate Torment. Here they enter a burning iron house which is surrounded by the Additional Sixteen Neighbouring Hells.

It is said among all worldly fire, the hottest is fire is produced by sandalwood. Seven times hotter is the aeon-destroying fire at the end of time. Many-times seven-times hotter even than that, is the fire of the Hell of Ultimate Torment. Like this, the fire of hell is 'the hottest fire' which in its extreme heat burns the bodies of the hell beings like lamp wicks, so the flame and the hell beings cannot be distinguished from each other. Only the sound of their screams and cries indicate the presence of hell beings, their bodies and the fire becoming one and indistinguishable. Experiencing all the suffering of the earlier seven hells, as well as many specific sufferings, they must experience this kind of suffering for a life span of an intermediate aeon.

In this way the Eight Hot Hell realms form one group. From the aspect of them being hot, the suffering is generally similar. However, specifically, from each of the upper hells to each of the lower hells, the suffering increases sevenfold. Also, to imagine the sensation of suffering increasing sevenfold in those lower hells is not like being a mere spectator watching a performance. During our practice sessions, we meditate that our bodies are actually experiencing these feelings in reality.

Up to now, what a terrible mistake it has been for us to generate the causes to be reborn in hell. From this day forward, by resolving not to go down that path any more, we must change our state of mind.

The Eight Cold Hells

The second group of hell realms are the Eight Cold Hells, which are taught in the root text in two verses and one line:

> **On snow mountain cliffs and icy ravines,**
> **Fearful places lashed by blizzards,**
> **My vulnerable body, beaten by freezing winds,**
> **Breaks out in blisters and bursts into open wounds.**
> **I let out an endless scream,**
> **Suffering pain that is hard to imagine.**
> **My strength is exhausted, like a sick person on the brink of death.**
> **I let out long gasps, clenching my teeth. My skin cracks,**
> **Flesh is exposed, and it splits yet deeper, in these Eight Cold Hells.**

All these Eight Cold Hells have the same general corresponding terrain and environment: endless snow-covered mountains with lofty ice-capped peaks, and freezing water or frozen icy ground.

> Fearful places lashed by blizzards.

In this kind of treacherous, terrifying place, snow and blizzards continually swirl, and your body gets lashed and frozen.

> My vulnerable body, beaten by freezing winds...

Beaten by the powerful, unbearably cold wind you freeze, and the cold makes you 'vulnerable'. The resulting intense feeling of suffering torments the vulnerable beings there.

At this point, the particular suffering of the cold hells is mentioned:

> Breaks out in blisters and bursts into open wounds.
> I let out an endless scream,
> Suffering pain that is hard to imagine.
> My strength is exhausted, like a sick person on the brink of death.
> I let out long gasps, clenching my teeth. My skin cracks,
> Flesh is exposed, and it splits yet deeper.

In these six lines, the particular sufferings of the cold hells are enumerated. First are the hells of 'Blisters' and 'Bursting Blisters.' The bodies of hell beings are large, but their skin is extremely thin, like that of a new-born baby, so when they encounter hot or cold conditions, the pain and discomfort is particularly great. Also, because of the power of the cold wind, and the fact that their bodies are naked, they become so cold their flesh breaks out in blisters. In addition, as the temperature drops further, these blisters burst, forming open wounds from which blood and pus oozes. This is taught to be the hell of 'Bursting Blisters'.

> I let out an endless scream,
> Suffering pain that is hard to imagine.
> My strength is exhausted like a sick person on the brink of death.
> I let out long gasps...

These lines teach the experiences in both hells of 'Whimpering' and 'Howling'. Suffering from the cold, hell beings cry out constantly; this is called the Hell of Whimpering. In addition, intolerable feelings of extreme suffering are impossible to endure. This is known as 'total exhaustion of vital strength', which is when the life force that keeps the body alive, the vital essence, is lost or exhausted, and the life essence is surrendered. For example, like a sick person on the brink of death who loses the power of speech, these hell beings have no strength in their voices, and no energy to enunciate words, so they let out long howls and moans of suffering. This is the Hell of Howling.

> Clenching my teeth.

This teaches the Hell of Gritted Teeth and the Hell of Splitting like an Utpala flower. Unable to bear the painful feelings of intense cold, the hell beings' teeth chatter and they clench their jaws, becoming unable to make a sound. This is the Hell of Gritted Teeth.

> My skin cracks,
> Flesh is exposed, and it splits yet deeper.

This teaches the hells of Splitting like an Utpala, Splitting like a Lotus, and Splitting like a Great Lotus. In the hell of Splitting like an Utpala, hell being's skin splits in a way that resembles four petals, and turns blue like the blue Utpala flower. Then the red flesh inside the split skin is exposed and that also splits into eight. This is like a red lotus flower, and as such this is called the Hell of Splitting like a Lotus. Growing even colder, hell beings' skin becomes even darker red, and splits into sixteen or thirty-two 'petals', like a great lotus.

In these Eight Cold Hells.

Regarding the lifespan in the cold hells, in the region of the Indian town Kosala, a full measure of grain is called a 'full dre'. Taking a full dre measure of tiny sesame seeds, in the case of the Hell of Blisters – the least severe of the Eight Cold Hells – it is taught that if a single sesame seed is removed every one hundred years, whenever the full dre of seeds becomes emptied, that is the time it takes for the lifespan in the Hell of Blisters to become exhausted. As it states in the *Abhidharmakosa*:

> Remove one seed from a sesame store
> Every hundred years; when emptied,
> That is the lifespan in the Hell of Blisters.
> Subsequent lifespans increase twentyfold.

In this way, every one of us has experienced the unbearable suffering of the cold hells before. Currently, multitudes of mother-like beings are undergoing this suffering. If we do not grasp the path of liberation in this life, then in the future we will certainly have to experience the cold hells again. Keeping this in mind, we need to meditate. This is the discussion on the Eight Hot and Eight Cold Hells.

THE ADDITIONAL SIXTEEN NEIGHBOURING HELLS

Following this is the explanation of the Additional Sixteen Neighbouring Hells and the Ephemeral Hells:

> **Likewise, my feet are slashed open in a plain of razors,**
> **My body is chopped up in a forest of swords,**
> **I sink in a swamp of rotting corpses, and in unfordable hot embers,**

> In the Neighbouring Hells that surround the Hell of Ultimate Torment.
> Also in the changing hells as a door or pillar, stove or rope, and so on,
> Continually used and exploited – the Ephemeral Hells.

As with the limitless suffering experienced in the Hot and Cold Hells discussed above, in each of the four directions surrounding the Hell of Ultimate Torment, there are an 'Additional Sixteen Neighbouring Hells':

1) The pit of burning embers.
2) The swamp of rotting corpses.
3) The plain of weapons.
4) The forest with leaves of swords.

All four of these can be found in each of the four separate directions, making a total of sixteen.

What is the pit of burning embers like? When the power of the karma to experience the Hell of Ultimate Torment has reduced a little and, after a great many years, is finally exhausted, those beings with only slight karma come to escape. Then, the attractive perception arises of a dark and shady hollow in the distance. But, due to a little karma still remaining, as they rush over to it, these beings fall into a pit of burning embers, and suffer from all their flesh and bones being burnt.

Having escaped from that, second is the swamp of rotting corpses. Again, an attractive perception arises of a large river in the distance. Having been cooked in a mass of fire for many great aeons, these beings feel extremely thirsty, so seeing water they are overjoyed. But when they go there to drink, they fall into a swamp of human corpses, horse and dog carcasses, and the like. Not only do these beings sink under the surface, but they are eaten by many maggots with sharp metal-fanged teeth, so they experience fierce pain and suffer terribly.

Again, when these beings have the perception of escaping from there, in the distance they see a vision of a green and pleasant grassland, so they hasten in that direction. But when they arrive there and look around, of course it is not a beautiful green meadow. The entire ground is a plain of steel razors, with each blade point pointing upwards like blades of grass. Arriving there, beings cannot even find an area the size of the palm of their hands where there are no blades. Wherever they place their feet, the sole is sliced open, straight through. When they put a foot down, it is pierced; when they lift it up, it heals. But, as it touches the ground again, once more it gets pierced through. In this way they experience nothing but suffering. That is the Plain of Weapons.

Not only that, but there is the Forest with Leaves of Swords. Again, when beings escape from the previous suffering, the perception arises of a pleasant forest. But when they go there:

> My body is chopped up in a forest of swords.

Of course it is not a beautiful forest. As they come closer, these beings enter into a forest of weapons where the trees have swords for leaves. As the wind moves the sharp-bladed leaves, with each turn their bodies are sliced up and, unable to turn back, they experience the suffering of being sliced apart. Again, each time they are cut up they heal, only to be stabbed again and again. It is taught that, like a trench, these Neighbouring Hells surround the perimeter of the Hell of Ultimate Torment, encircling it in the manner of a palisade.

Also the 'Mountain of Iron Shalmali Trees' is a hill of shalmali trees where those who lose control of their discipline, violate vows, or who engage in sexual misconduct are born. The perception arises that the friend who they previously lusted after is calling to them from the top of the hill. As they go to climb up, the iron leaves of the shalmali trees, all serrated knives, turn to point downwards, slicing through their bodies. But there is no dying, and when they arrive at the top of the hill, of course their friend is not there. Many vultures and other vicious animals peck at them, and pluck out their eyeballs. Again, the perception arises that their lover is calling them from the foot of the hill. As they descend, the sword points of the shalmali trees turn upwards again stabbing, slicing, and severing their heads from their bodies, but still they do not die. When these beings arrive at the foot of the hill, terrifying metal men and women grab them and bite off their heads, their brains dribbling out from their mouths. This is the suffering experienced there.

> Also in the changing hells as a door or pillar, stove or rope, and so on.

These are varying situations; places of uncertain happiness and misery. For example, in the daytime the beings there may be happy but experience suffering at night, with no dependability. Alternatively, beings experience the suffering of being crushed between boulders, trapped inside rocks, frozen rigid in ice, or burning in hot water or fire. In other cases, these beings may have the perception that their bodies take the form of an inanimate object, such as a door, pillar, stove, rope, broom, or pot; objects or implements that are continually put to use. This brings experience of all kinds of discomfort and suffering. For example, if the perception arises that your body is a stove, when a fire is lit in the stove, you suffer a burning torso, and so forth. This represents the kind of hell beings who experience various undetermined sufferings in the Ephemeral Hells.

In this way, there are the Eight Hot Hells and Eight Cold Hells, making sixteen. Added to that are the Ephemeral and Neighbouring Hells, which makes a total of eighteen. We need to meditate that we have actually been born in these places; not as if we were casually watching a performance or listening to a tale. By meditating that we have actually, right now been born in these realms, when an experience of terror is really developed, think: 'Although I have not been born in hell at this moment, I have accumulated much of the complete karma that will cause me to be reborn there, so I sit here having gathered all the conditions.' At this time, when anger comes to mind, turn your thoughts inward: 'If in this current rebirth, just by meditating on the hell realms I feel this terrified, what will I do when I'm actually reborn there?'

Thinking about how you will not be able to bear such suffering, when you pursue their source, the root cause that brings about rebirth there is clearly taught:

> **The cause of these eighteen hells,**
> **Is motivation of intense anger, so when this arises...**

Generally, the three poisons cast us down into the lower realms, and in particular, the karma of anger causes rebirth in hell. In that case, the main propelling cause to throw us into the eighteen realms of hell is anger and aversion. What is more, it is possible we may know the amount of karmic hatred we have accumulated in this lifetime, but that is by no means all of it. How much remains of the karma we have accumulated and not purified from time without beginning? If we look at this in terms of our hopes and fears, at the very least, we do not even wish to experience the suffering of the pain of being pricked by a thorn, or the discomfort of a spark from the fire landing on our skin. However, despite not wanting to experience the result of the karma we have already accumulated, as soon as we take rebirth, we will almost certainly have to experience the suffering of hell.

With this conviction in mind, and in great fear, at this moment we have attained a human body with the freedoms and endowments. We have met with an authentic lama and have managed to receive the profound oral instructions. At this time, when the conditions to accomplish the level of buddhahood have come together, upon hearing the word 'hell', our heart should pound and we should feel terrified. Think over and over: 'I must strive at whatever means necessary to avoid falling down to hell'. With intense regret, confess the non-virtuous actions you have done in the past. We must resolve that in future we will definitely not commit those kinds of bad, unwholesome actions ever again, even if our lives depend on it.

Just as we do not want the suffering of hell, neither do others, but right now there are those who are currently experiencing intense feelings of suffering. Meditate with great compassion for these beings, and also for those who are currently creating powerful unwholesome causes that will certainly send them to hell in the future.

Take the vow to arouse bodhicitta for these confused mother-like sentient beings. Think, 'I will accomplish the capacity to be able to lead all sentient beings out of the torture of the lower realms, and protect them from suffering. I dedicate all the virtues I have accumulated up to now to these poor sentient beings, in order that they may escape from the lower realms. Therefore, I must have the preparation, main part, and conclusion complete every time I practise.'

Because we are ordinary beings, sometimes we can give rise to good motivation, but at other times we do not manage to maintain it. If we find we cannot endure a situation and develop a:

Motivation of intense anger, so when this arises...

At the time when this motivation of intense negative anger comes to arise, we must recall the consequences repeatedly, and rely on the remedy:

O Guru Rinpoche, heed me! Turn my mind towards Dharma!
Omniscient master, do not let me stray onto wrong or
  inferior paths!
Compassionate lama, who is one with them, heed me!

Pray with intense powerful longing: 'At this time, O Guru Rinpoche, do not let my mind be led down a bad, wrong path but turn it towards the Dharma. At first, although my mind was focused on the Dharma, if I do not grasp the key points of the oral instruction to dispel hindrances and get confused, do not let me stray onto any wrong or inferior path, I pray omniscient master! Chariot of the peak of vehicles of the Land of Snows, the Second Victorious One, think of me! Inseparable lama, equal in enlightened qualities of all the buddhas, the one who showed me the true face of the dharmakaya, my gracious lama possessed of the three kindnesses, think of me!' If you pray sincerely, the inheritance of the blessings of the lineage can be attained.

Defects of Samsara

Suffering of the Pretas

Pretas who Live Collectively

Now we come to discussion on the second of the lower realms, the pretas. Of the two types of pretas, there are those who live collectively and those who move through space. Of those who live collectively there are those with outer obscurations, inner obscurations, and specific obscurations, as well as other such specific divisions. Here the root text teaches the general sufferings of pretas:

> **Likewise, in a poor and unpleasant land,**
> **Where even the words 'food', 'drink', or 'possessions' are unheard,**
> **Food and drink cannot be found for months or years.**
> **A preta's body is emaciated and lacks the strength to stand: the three kinds.**

These three and a half lines teach the shared suffering of the pretas.

> Likewise, in a poor and unpleasant land.

Pretas do not need to experience the suffering of hell, but in the preta realm, there is absolutely no wealth or possessions, food or drink, and so forth. Not only is it desolate, but in every direction the land is unpleasant and filled with rocks, stones, thorns, ravines, and so on. In other descriptions, it is a parched and scorching desert, depressing to look upon:

> Where even the words 'food', 'drink', or 'possessions' are unheard.

In this land, not to mention delicious meals or sweet beverages, even the mere whisper of food, drink, or possessions cannot be heard; their very names are not spoken.

> Food and drink cannot be found for months or years. A preta's body...

Not finding any nourishment for months or years, the body of a preta:

> Is emaciated and lacks the strength to stand.

Without nourishment, their flesh is withered, just skin and bones. This withered and emaciated body lacks all strength, so is unable to stand upright. Because they do not even have the strength to stand up, they cannot support their bodies, and yet they cannot die, so continue to experience suffering.

The three kinds.

This indicates the three particular distinctions mentioned above of outer, inner, and specific obscurations of those who live collectively, and secondly also references the kind that move through space.

What are the outer obscurations like? During the three months of summer when the weather is hot, to us moonlight feels cool like falling drops of camphor, but for pretas even this becomes hot and burns them. During the three cold months of winter, the warm touch of the sun feels to them cold and freezing. In this way the seasons of summer and winter are reversed, and they have four opposing experiences.

Also, sometimes, in the distance they see food and water, rivers, fruit trees, and so on, and want to go there, but when pretas move, their limbs cannot support their bodies and it takes them a long time to arrive. When they finally arrive, on the brink of death, the attractive things that were there before have disappeared. If there was a river, it has become a dry stony gully, and the fruit trees have become dry wood, everything having disappeared. If they do see a little food or drink, it is guarded by many armed guards who chase them with their weapons, striking and killing them. They cannot enjoy the things they desire and are unable to experience consuming any food or drink.

Pretas with inner obscurations each have a head the size of the king of mountains, but their mouths are as small as the eye of a needle. Their necks are as slender as a single hair of a horse's tail, their stomachs are as big as a whole land, and each of their limbs is no thicker than a blade of grass. Having taken up this kind of wretched body, even if they were to arrive beside a vast lake to drink, no water could enter the needle-eye of their mouth. Even if a drop went in, nothing could pass into their narrow throats, and the heat of their mouths would evaporate it. Even if a little passed through, their vast stomachs could never be filled. If, by rare chance, a seed-sized drop of water did pass into their stomachs, it would burst into flames, burning their lungs, heart, and innards for a whole night, so that smoke billowed from their noses. This is the kind of suffering pretas experience.

Moreover, they also experience great suffering from not being able to support their vast stomachs, because their arms and legs are thin like blades of grass. Also, pretas suffering from 'specific obscurations' have many parasites living on their bodies, feeding off them. Whenever pretas meet, in anger they fight and strike each other, and if their wounds become ripe with puss, they consume it like food. They experience this and other suffering that is beyond description.

Pretas who Move through Space

The second kind of pretas are those who move through space. These include the kinds of harm-bringing spirits such as tsen, gyalpo, shindre, and mamo. These all pass their lives in delusion and terror. Every seven days, however they died before, they re-experience the suffering of death repeatedly, each time killed by weapons, crashing in cars down rocky mountain gorges, or dying from terrible diseases.

There are stories about some people who can see this kind of preta. One such person would sometimes hear a boat approaching the bank of a large river during the night. He could hear many people talking, the sounds of rowing, and so on, but by the time he imagined the boat to have arrived in the middle of the river, he would hear screams as it capsized and was swept away by the current. This person saw and heard this kind of thing regularly, but it was not seen by ordinary people. Those who drowned are the kinds of beings who do not know that they have died, and so are reborn as the type of preta that moves through space.

Also, there are other pretas of this kind who want to spread to others the disease they previously died from, infecting people and causing harm. Doing this brings them no benefit, and they only ever experience suffering. Some, when they revisit their previous loved ones or relatives, bring harm, causing them to have psychotic episodes, fits, faint, or even to become mute and so forth, thus causing sickness and unwelcome events.

Again, some pretas have a slight karmic clairvoyance, on which they rely to move around; however, they can still get trapped by guards on treacherous paths, and the like. They may also encounter powerful mantrins who strike them with charmed substances. Trapped by mantras, they get crushed in dark and gloomy holes underground for entire aeons, or suffer being expelled to the far side of a huge ocean. Pretas always perceive the seasons in reverse, as all perceptions which arise to them are distorted. In the perceptions of some people, pretas can be seen neither dead nor alive, in the form of dogs or cats and so forth, riding around on foxes or weasels and the like. These are called 'dead-living demons' and are also a kind of preta who moves through space.

For the entirety of their lives, some pretas wish to steal others' splendour, and endanger their well-being, looking to see if they can find food and wealth to steal; their attitude and behaviour are entirely unwholesome. Therefore, as soon as they take their next rebirth, there is no other place for pretas to go except hell.

When we meditate on the topics of the sufferings of the lower realms, we need to take upon ourselves the following four aspects:

1) Place.
2) Physical body.
3) Suffering.
4) Lifespan.

At the moment, when we do not eat for a whole day, or if we even miss one meal, consider how much discomfort we experience. We need to take to heart the experience of suffering hunger and thirst for many years. If we arrived in a place where the mention of food or drink was never even heard, let alone enjoying any regular nourishment or refreshment, and if we had to stay there for many aeons, what would we do?

What kind of cause brings rebirth as a preta?

The cause of their arising is avarice.

The cause of being reborn as a preta is when you possess wealth, but cannot bear to offer it up to the Precious Jewels. You cannot bear to give anything to the tormented beings of the lower realms. At the very worst, you cannot even bear to use your money to buy food or clothing that benefits yourself, and you avoid buying good things to eat or wear, because you believe you will exhaust your resources. The causal resemblance of having taken rebirth as a preta in the past is that you may be physically wealthy, but your mind is impoverished. So it is taught the chief cause of being reborn as a preta is avarice, as well as hindering others' generosity.

Consequently, it is certain that we have accumulated this kind of karma to an unimaginable extent. Therefore we must cultivate diligence in using the methods to ensure that we do not need to be reborn as a preta in future. We should meditate on compassion for those who are now experiencing that kind of suffering, as well as for those who are accumulating the karma to be reborn in the preta realm in future. We must do this with practice that is complete with the three excellent principles: the preparation, main part, and conclusion.

Defects of Samsara

Suffering of Animals

Animals that Live in the Depths

The third of the lower realms is that of the animals, of which there are two types: Animals that live in the depths of the ocean, and those that live scattered apart. From the root text:

**In great fear of being killed and eaten by one another,
Worked and exploited to exhaustion, ignorant of right or wrong,
Oppressed by endless suffering.**

These three lines show the suffering of the animals.

In great fear of being killed and eaten by one another.

This is mainly understood to refer to those animals who live in the depths. The vast oceans are filled with multitudinous varieties of fish, shellfish, and sea creatures with endless different kinds of shapes and sizes. These kinds of sea creatures kill and feed off one another. The larger ones eat the small; the small nibble at the large. In the dark and murky oceans between the continents they cannot even see their limbs extending out in front of themselves. That kind of miserable environment and unfortunate physical form is truly suffering.

Animals the Live Scattered Apart

As for animals that live scattered apart, this is taught by:

In great fear of being killed.

Those living scattered apart are the animals in the human and god realms: birds, forest animals, wild animals, and so on, which also feed on each other. Like hawks that prey on sparrows, and sparrows that prey on insects, the vast majority live on the flesh of others. Also, hunters use all kinds of methods to trap and kill almost every kind of animal. In short, terrified of being killed, the suffering of fearing for their lives is ever present.

Worked and exploited to exhaustion, ignorant of right or wrong.

In the case of animals that are owned by humans, they are castrated, sheered, milked, burdened with heavy loads, and when they cannot move, whipped. Horses have a bit put in their mouth and are kicked in the ribs with spurs. Beaten with a whip, they are forced to travel long distances. In the case of rideable yaks, their noses are pierced and threaded with rope. Elephants are pulled by the ears with a metal hook. Alternatively, when ferocious wild animals are taught to perform for our entertainment, what a miserable time they must have, not to mention the terrible suffering involved in factory farming.

To summarise: all types of animals are ignorant as to what activities need to be adopted and abandoned, so under the influence of this ignorance and stupidity, they are kept under control. If animals were as intelligent as humans, we would not be able to abuse and control those with superior strength or agility. However, because of their ignorance they must experience the suffering of being exploited.

In addition, the lifespan of sentient beings born as animals and other creatures is uncertain. Some live as long as a century, while others live only a day and experience many births and deaths. Those with long lives suffer from having a long life, and those with short lifespans suffer from only living a short time. To summarise all the suffering of the animals:

> Oppressed by endless suffering.

In short, if we consider the suffering endured by the body of just one animal, it is like reflecting on the suffering of the three lower realms experienced all at once. That is what animals endure. Look at the cows and sheep in a slaughter house, or the countless sea creatures that fishmongers kill, every day in every city around the world. They are skinned alive, and stabbed to death in the heart. There are even terrifying stories of creatures being served alive, picked at with chopsticks by compassionless people.

So, in summary, where does the cause to be oppressed by endless suffering come from?

> **The seed of which is stupidity. When I wander in this darkness...**

Generally speaking, less substantial actions motivated by the three poisons bring about rebirth in the animal realm. Middling actions cause rebirth as a preta, and significant actions cast one into hell. In particular, karma accumulated in ignorance causes us to wander in the animal realm. Therefore, since beginingless time, having accumulated tremendous amounts of this kind of karma that will undoubtedly cause us to wander in the animal realm, we must pray:

> **O Guru Rinpoche, heed me! Turn my mind towards Dharma!**
> **Omniscient master, do not let me stray onto wrong or inferior paths!**
> **Compassionate lama, who is one with them, heed me!**

Pray: 'May I know how to confess and purify this kind of karma accumulated in the past, so it is not necessary to experience the fully ripened result. In future, may even the thought to do such things that cause this kind of rebirth, not arise. May I be able to provide refuge to sentient beings propelled by this kind of bad karma who are now experiencing the suffering of an animal, and also similar sentient beings who are currently accumulating such kind of negative karma. So I may be able to turn them around and lead them on the authentic path, I pray O Padmasambhava, Nirmanakaya Guru Rinpoche, turn my mind towards Dharma. Not just considering my own path of liberation, do not let other sentient beings, stray down inferior or wrong paths due to thoughtlessness. Omniscient Dharma lord, think of us! Non-dual, single embodiment of them, O gracious lama, please be my refuge and my anchor!'

The above describes the suffering of the three lower realms. To take all the key points mentioned earlier of place, physical basis, suffering, and lifespan to heart without error is the direct oral instruction. In this way, contemplating the suffering of the lower realms, when you take it upon yourself and your mind becomes profoundly sorrowful, this is called 'weariness'. In addition to this, the thought to escape from this suffering, a mind longing for liberation, arises. When these two come together, this is called 'fundamental renunciation' and the 'attitude of renunciation'. In this way, develop a powerful attitude of renunciation. In accordance with that, undertake confession of the karma connected to the three lower realms, the extent of which has been accumulated since beginingless time, with the complete remedy of the four powers.

In future, whatever happens, vow never to do that kind of action ever again. For all those sentient beings who have currently been born in the lower realms, know that they are your mothers from past lives and recall their kindness. As the thought of wanting to repay their kindness arises, combine it with the following three links:

1) The link of intent that wishes: 'May all these sentient beings be free of the causes and results of suffering.'

2) The link of aspiration that thinks: 'Wouldn't it be wonderful if they did become free!'
3) The link of the vow that affirms: 'I will free them!'

In addition to these, add:

4) The link of prayer which prays: 'Infallible Three Jewels, free all mother-like sentient beings from suffering! Think of us!'

We need to practise by means of these four links. Practising by means of the four links does not just apply to the three lower realms, we need to meditate in this way for all sentient beings of the six realms. In short, for each practice session, the preparation of arousing bodhicitta, the main part of non-conceptuality, and the conclusion of sealing with dedication, are always of great importance.

Suffering of Humans

We need to understand that it is not just the three lower realms that are full of suffering, but implicitly, the three higher realms have no happiness either. The suffering of the human realm, first of the higher realms, is addressed in the Vinaya scriptures:

> Samsara is a mass of suffering:
> The suffering of suffering, of being conditioned,
> And of change – the three. From the eight,
> Humans suffer extremely.

The eight sufferings comprise the three fundamental great sufferings: 1) the suffering of suffering, 2) the suffering of change, and 3) the all-pervasive suffering of being conditioned, which are mentioned above, together with 4) the sufferings of birth, aging, sickness, and death, which are known as the four great streams of suffering, but counted as one here. In addition to these is 5) the suffering of fear of meeting hated enemies, 6) the suffering of fear of losing loved ones, 7) the suffering of encountering what we do not want, and 8) the suffering of not getting what we want.

Of these, 1) the first of the three fundamental sufferings is the suffering of suffering: Before some previous suffering has faded, some later suffering accrues on top of it, so the suffering becomes doubled. For example, in addition to your father dying, your mother also passes away. This does not just happen in the human realm, all realms in samsara have suffering that mounts up.

Defects of Samsara

2) The suffering of change is as follows: The happiness we have now is not dependable and suffering suddenly arises. While feeling happy in the thought that we have a healthy body free of sickness, suddenly we catch a deadly and incurable disease. We have many relatives, and plenty of possessions, but without taking sufficient care, one member of the family travels to another region and does not make it, dying en route. We are feeling calm and relaxed, but then hear some spiteful rumours, and so on. There is no dependability to the happiness, well-being, or renown of samsara. Everything is subject to the suffering of change.

Then there is 3) the all-pervasive suffering of being conditioned. Everything we currently perceive as happiness and do not perceive as suffering is in fact entirely conditioned by the cause of suffering. The wealth we enjoy spending and the things we consider to be sensual pleasures – the food we eat, the clothes we wear, all our possessions, riches, and enjoyments – whichever we think about, there is not one that is not produced from an unwholesome cause. Thus the ultimate result of engaging with samsara is having to experience the suffering of the lower realms. As an example, we do not feel a single hair placed on the palm of our hand but, if it were to go into our eye, it would bring the suffering of discomfort. When looked upon by those spiritually realised, what sentient beings consider to be happiness is actually suffering.

In addition to these is 4) the 'four demonic great rivers of birth, old age, sickness, and death.' The reason for using the term 'river' is because they are ever-flowing; these 'four great rivers' forever torment the realms of samsara. If we consider the suffering of birth, this comes to both mother and child. The suffering is so great, it is as if both mother and child make a journey to hell and back. Orgyen Rinpoche stated:

> Both mother and child take half a step towards the land of the dead.

As for the suffering of old age, most of it only the old themselves know. As it is said:

> Firstly, outwards, the gathering of wrinkles in the skin,
> Secondly, inwards, the lumps and pits of withering flesh and blood,
> Thirdly, what's in-between: stupidity of deafness, blindness, and absent mindedness.

Among the various appearances of suffering and difficulty of this life, we do not know how we will die, or how old we will be when it happens. As the signs of the Lord of Death strike upon the four elements of the body, the body's strength declines and its beautiful radiance is lost. Previously, even those who were not the most handsome of young people were at least not unattractive. But now, even those who believed themselves peerless among a hundred young lads or lasses are aged and wrinkled. If you look at their arms and legs, they are like bent, dried sticks of wood. If they are not hunched over, they are crooked; their eyes cannot see, their ears are deaf. They eat with toothless mouths, but food lacks the flavour it once had. Lying down, sleep does not come. If they doze, their sleep it is full of disturbing dreams, unlike when they were young. Just as their bodies deteriorate, so the strength of their minds weakens. Their minds become unable to judge rationally, and people disregard them.

Becoming excluded from the ranks of the living and falling into the shadows, it is said: *Old people are powerless, old birds have thin feathers. Try and have a conversation, but there is nothing the senile won't say.* When you get to this stage and are tormented by the sufferings of old age, others need not say it; you yourself reach the point where you start praying for death to come quickly.

If we think about the suffering of sickness, there are many different kinds. Some gentle sicknesses gradually take root and, very slowly grasp ever tighter, eventually taking life. Other diseases cause a death wracked by unbearable, agonising pain. No matter how powerful or radiant with health someone is, there is not a single person who will not succumb to sickness and old age. In the case of leprosy or the modern scourge of cancer, even before dying, peoples' experience of suffering is on a par with the agonies of death.

For a person suffering from disease, the pain of sickness is experienced all day and all night, which confuses the two. They fall asleep during the day, but are not allowed to sleep. They want to sleep at night, but cannot fall asleep. Their fronts are dried out, but their backs are damp and rotten. In short, there is no time to talk about or listen to all the suffering that is experienced; only sick people themselves know it all.

To contemplate the suffering of death, of all suffering, this is the one we must truly fear, the one whose name we dare not mention. To see someone experiencing oppressive suffering on the brink of death, even strangers will shed a tear. At that time, as the dying recall the negative actions they have done previously, feelings of both regret and terror arise together. Gasping for breath, as the bardo of death appears before them, when they see their beloved relatives and close friends crying, all those that they will leave behind, their hearts grow cold.

With sorrow almost breaking their hearts, the dying must part from the living. After this day, in the human world, only their names will remain, and as time passes, even those will be forgotten. If the deceased had the Dharma, things are somewhat better. Knowing the Dharma, even if this dying person does not go to a pleasure grove, they will not die with regret. Likewise, those who are left behind will be less anxious for them. But if the dying person was someone wicked, then their fear and suffering is particularly great. As it is taught:

> To see a wicked person dying
> Is a teacher demonstrating karmic cause and effect.

Even before such people die, all their perceptions become terrifying, as if they had already arrived in the three lower realms.

In addition to all the feelings of suffering, at death the physical elements must consolidate. In this way, there is no one who does not need to experience the suffering of birth, aging, sickness, and death. If a new-born child suddenly dies without having the opportunity to grow old, they will not experience the suffering of old age, but whatever the circumstances that bring death, they are certainly not less painful than the sufferings of old age. And there are still those who think death preferable to experiencing the torments of old age.

Besides these, as mentioned earlier, humans in the world have 5) the suffering of meeting hated enemies, at the hands of which not only are our possessions stolen, but our life is vanquished. There is also 6) the suffering of being separated from our loved ones. Those who are unwilling to part from loved ones even for a day or night, become separated forever, never to see each other again. Then there is 7) the suffering of encountering what we do not want, when unwelcome circumstances occur and we suffer. Similarly, 8) the suffering of not getting what we want – unable to get what we want, we long for so many things, but not one is accomplished. *Climb three steps upward, you arrive six paces down*; none of our endeavours go our way.

Suffering of the Demigods

Next, we bring to mind the suffering of the second of the higher realms, the demigods. From *Letter to a Friend*:

> The nature of demigods is to begrudge gods their splendour,
> Thus their mental suffering is great.
> Although intelligent, they have samsaric obscurations,
> So they are blind to the truth.

There are many kinds of demigods, but whichever kind they are, for the most part, propelled by the power of previous non-virtue, their perception of jealously towards other beings is coarse, and greater than that of any other kind of beings. In their own realm, through disputes over land and property, time passes in constant conflict. What is more, as jealousy of the gods' blissful existence increases, they are constantly at war with them. In these battles, the gods are always quickly victorious. If the gods are injured, they have medicinal nectar which heals their wounds immediately, but like humans, the demigods die from whatever injuries they sustain or any diseases they catch. The gods not only possess miraculous powers but, because of the strength of their merit, are as tall as seven average humans. The demigods are not that tall, so they are always at a disadvantage. The gods have nectar that revives the dead, so as long as they are not killed by decapitation or do not catch a life-threating disease, they do not die.

The gods attach wheels of weapons to their elephants' trunks and feed them a concoction which makes them go berserk. When released, these elephants kill hundreds of thousands of demigods at a time. Rolling the bodies down the side of Mt. Meru, the colour of the Seas of Enjoyment turn blood-red for many days. This is what the main regions of the demigods, in the hollows of Mt. Meru, are like. Not only that, but the kinds of demigods who move through the human realm are motivated by jealousy and cruelty, and inflict many kinds of cruel and jealous harm on others. These deeds cause them to experience all kinds of suffering in return. Such are the sufferings of the demigods.

Suffering of the Gods

As for the third of the higher realms, that of the gods, there are three individual god realms: desire, form, and formless, although the suffering they experience when falling to the lower realms is the same. In the case of the gods of the desire realm, they have both the suffering of passing away at death and falling down. *Letter to a Friend* teaches:

> The colour of their bodies becomes unattractive,
> Their cushions become uncomfortable and flower garlands wither,
> Their clothes become stained, and from their bodies
> Sweat appears, that was never there before:
> The five signs that herald death in the higher realms.

These are the five signs that occur when death is imminent for the desire gods. Also, the Abhidharma teaches that the signs of imminent death include: unpleasant sounds being emitted from their clothes and jewellery, decline in their physical radiance, and sweat congealing on their bodies. Usually the gods have sharp minds, but when death is close, their mind rests on one object and they are unable to blink.

Knowing only too well that these signs of imminent death are complete, this knowledge brings the gods great fear and terror. Moreover, all their friends know they are on the brink of death, and regarding them as unclean, do not come near, which causes even more suffering. As the great majority of the gods fall to the lower realms after death, when they realise this with their clairvoyance, they suffer even more, having to experience this suffering of imminent death and downfall for seven days. Seven days as a god, in human terms, is seven or eight hundred years. They must endure the approach of death for all this time, suffering this hell-like experience while they prepare for death and falling to the lower realms.

Although the gods of the form and formless realms do not have any obvious suffering of imminent death, when the propelling karma which sent them to the god realms is exhausted, just like an arrow fired into the sky, when the force of its propulsion is exhausted, there is no other choice but to fall straight down. So these gods also have the suffering of falling into the lower realms. As it is taught:

> Brahma himself, having achieved bliss free from attachment,
> Will become fuel for the fires of the Hell of Ultimate Torment,
> Suffering endlessly; of this be sure.

In this way, wherever in the three realms the six kinds of sentient beings are born, there is nowhere without suffering. Nothing goes beyond the very nature of suffering. Thus, samsara is likened to a pit of fire, an island of demonesses, the edge of a sharp weapon, being swept away by ocean waves, and living in an foul house.

If we live in a fire pit, there is the certainty of experiencing suffering and pain from being burned by the fire. Likewise, when we enter the fire pit of samsara, the fuel of liberation is burnt away and feelings of suffering occur endlessly. If we arrived on an island of demonesses, lured in by the seductions of samsaric pleasure and happiness, the life force of liberation becomes cut off, as if our very lives had ended. If we touch the sharp blade of a weapon, it will cut us. In the same way, it is rare not to be injured by the weapons of samsara. If we are swept away by ocean waves, we cannot see the shore and it is difficult to avoid drowning. Similarly, swept away by the waves of samsara, it is hard to find a way to escape. In a foul house, there are no pleasant smells. Similarly, in the realm of samsara, there is no joy or happiness. What is more, samsara is like a nest of vicious poisonous snakes. If we fall into a nest of poisonous snakes and get poisoned, there is no alternative but death.

The *Application of Mindfulness* teaches:

> Hell beings suffer in hellfire;
> Pretas suffer hunger and thirst;
> Animals suffer from consuming each other;
> Humans suffer short lives;
> Gods suffer from recklessness.
> In samsara, not even a pin tip's worth of
> Happiness is present.

Do not regard the suffering of the six types of beings in samsara as you would watch a performance, at a distance. Carefully bring it all to mind, as if you were actually experiencing it physically. By meditating like this, belief in karmic cause and effect and an unfeigned attitude of renunciation from samsara will start to develop in your mindstream. If this develops, then forgetting about the petty concerns and business of this life, taking pleasure in virtue and shunning non-virtue, will come about spontaneously. At that time, as faith and compassion naturally grow within, whatever worldly abundance you come across, you will not experience even a moment's desire. Like someone suffering from jaundice who is offered deep-fried food, your feelings of revulsion for samsara will only grow.

Je Rinpoche stated:

> Freedoms and endowments are difficult to find, there is no time in life,
> The mind is habituated, so counteract craving for this life.
> Karmic result is unfailing; consider over and over
> The sufferings of samsara, to reverse craving for future lives.
> Accustomed in this way, towards samsaric abundance,
> Not even a moment's desire will develop, and if
> The attitude that strives every day and night for liberation
> Appears, then at that time renunciation is developed.

We need to practise just as these oral instructions teach, and they also indicate the extent to which our renunciation has developed.

In this samsaric realm, from the highest peak of existence down to the lowest Vajra Hell, there is not a single place with the opportunity for happiness or a moment's comfort. The defiled happiness of the higher realms is taught to be akin to the comfort of scratching an itch. When people who suffer from a skin complaint scratch themselves, the perception arises that is it pleasurable, and they cannot stay still without scratching. In truth, the scratching is not pleasurable; to be without itchiness is comfortable.

Defects of Samsara

Do not just leave this teaching saying: 'When the time comes to speak about the suffering of samsara, it's the tradition to say these kinds of things', seemingly having heard the words and understood the meaning. You need to bring these sufferings to mind, and take them on physically, as I have already mentioned before. By recalling the suffering of samsara, give up on the activities of this worldly life, and on that basis, practise the Dharma.

At one point, when Glorious Lord Atisha was due to pass away, one of his students, a yogi, asked him: 'Lord, would it be good if, after you have passed away, I engage solely in meditation?' Atisha replied, 'Within the Dharma, meditation is included'. Thinking that he was not correct, the student asked, 'Well then, should I stay to teach and study?' 'Those are also included within the Dharma' came Atisha's reply. 'What then should I do?' The master said: 'Give up on this life.'

Also, at another time, a monk was circumambulating a temple when he met with Geshe Dromtonpa Gyalway Jungney, who said to him, 'Circumambulation is good, but wouldn't it be better to engage properly with the Dharma?' So the monk thought to himself, 'Better than circumambulating would be to read the Mahayana sutras', and he went to the library and sat in the hall reading sutras in a loud voice. Again Dromtonpa appeared, and said, 'Reading the sutras is good, however wouldn't it be better to really practise some Dharma?' Again the monk had a think: 'In that case, better than reading the sutras, it would be much better to train in meditative concentration' and, leaving his recitations, with eyes half closed, he tried some meditation. But once again, Dromtonpa said to him: 'Meditating is good, but wouldn't you actually prefer to practise some real Dharma?' The monk, not finding any other ways to practise, said to the geshe, 'Whatever I do doesn't seem to be right. If I'm not following the lines of true Dharma, well then, please teach me how I should practise the real Dharma!' Dromtonpa, repeating twice with earnest emphasis, said: 'Give up on this life! Give up on this life!' and said nothing more.

What did Atisha and Dromtonpa mean? Having first given up on this life, if an unfeigned attitude of intense renunciation develops in your mindstream, then upon that, by training in other practices, your Dharma practice will be genuine from its foundation. This is what these masters taught. Dromtonpa was not saying 'reciting the sutras is not Dharma' or 'doing circumambulations and meditating is of no use and has no benefit'. This is not the meaning of what he taught. What he meant is: 'First whole-heartedly give up on this life, then you need to develop an unfeigned attitude of definitive renunciation in your mindstream'. Having done that, if you then practise the teachings with study, contemplation, and meditation in the right order, this is the correct process of the Buddha Dharma. It is like the frame of a ladder, so we need to know the importance and meaning of climbing up, starting from the foundation.

The activities of this life are the real fetters that prevent us from being liberated from mundane samsara. Therefore, it is certainly difficult for anyone except a lama to be the teacher of the method to escape from it. There is no one else who can do so. What is more, this meditation on the suffering of samsara is at first the method to turn our mind towards Dharma. In the middle, it is the method to arouse conviction in cause and effect. When that arises, we can give up on this life, give rise to compassion for sentient beings, and so forth, right up to finally developing the enlightened qualities of the path.

In short, this is the foundation of all positive qualities, therefore, when the Blessed One turned the three successive stages of the wheel of Dharma, he taught the truth of suffering first. So, if in the future, while you are wandering the realms of samsara, you develop the wish to stop experiencing any more suffering, it is very important to dedicate yourself to this one crucial point of practice, complete with the three excellent principles of the preparation, main part, and conclusion.

So far, we have considered the difficulties of finding the freedoms and endowments, the impermanence of life, karmic cause and effect, and the defects of samsara. These comprise the four mind changers. In addition, in our tradition of the lineage of the Omniscient Father and Son, a fifth mind changer is added, to turn us away from selfish considerations, which we must also understand and take to heart.

With our tradition of being diligent in changing our attitude, the real test is to see whether or not a practitioner will arrive at the ultimate destination. If a crop is not harvested, it will be destroyed by the morning frost. Similarly, if someone cannot change their attitude by means of training the mind, even if they are able to teach from memory the five volumes of scriptural teachings, and moreover, look down upon the heads of thousands of monks from their throne, they are not included among the ranks of authentic practitioners.

Teaching Day Four

Not one of the six kinds of wandering beings, who are as numerous as the sky is vast, has not been our parent. Yet they are without refuge, protector, or friend, as if abandoned without companions in the middle of nowhere. How pitiful they are! We must establish all of them in happiness free from suffering. If we establish these beings in the higher realms, at the level of a god or human, for the time being they will not have to experience feelings of gross suffering. A samsaric sentient being who has never attained true bliss, may consider this to be happiness. However, if we think carefully, there is no essence to the happy result of the higher realms of gods and humans, so it is not actually happiness, but a kind of suffering. It is this which we are currently experiencing. So consider carefully: because what we are experiencing is not happiness but suffering, what we speak is also the speech of suffering.

If we talk honestly about our defeats, mistakes, and failures – tales of sickness, pain, death, and exhaustion – all these things we speak of are miserable cries of despair, similar in many ways to the wails and cries of the beings in hell. Indeed, sometimes we do need to moan and cry. Not only that but, even if we attained permanent liberation from samsara with the enlightenment of a shravaka or pratyekabuddha, it is not ultimate nirvana. In that case, resolve that you must establish all mother-like sentient beings at the level of buddhahood, for all time and succession of lifetimes, so they are entirely free from suffering and possess all happiness. We need to listen to the Dharma on the basis of this preliminary consideration.

However, holding this sort of authentic, kind-hearted thought is merely forging the path with expressions and aspirations. In truth this is not sufficient to bring about the result. To establish sentient beings on the level of buddhahood requires strength of mind, but without the capability to do so, how will we establish them there? As the saying goes: *Even though it wants to see, a puppy hasn't opened its eyes; even though it wants to move, a puppy can't stand up.* We are like a brave person who wants to fight but has no arms. At this stage we are all still sentient beings, so not one of us has any capability. Even though we may wish to protect each other, we are powerless to do so, just like the example of two people being swept away by a river, unable to save one another.

At this time we have met with the Buddhist teachings, and we have done so in a time that the holy Dharma has been taught and is widespread. Having met with a teacher of the path, a spiritual teacher, the according conditions of finding the path to liberation, both from our own perspective and a circumstantial perspective, are complete. This is like glimpsing the brightness of the sun between the clouds. In addition to not losing that, we absolutely must have the firm determination that wishes to attain the exhaustion of all flaws, and the endowment of all enlightened qualities of complete buddhahood. Without this, although we may be receiving teachings of Mahayana Sutra and Tantra, we do not even have the right conditions to fulfil the Hinayana, not to mention the Mahayana. In that case, receiving Mahayana teachings and practising them, would not actually be of any benefit.

These days, looking at diverse places throughout the world, there are many people of both eastern and western descent, who have passed half their lives having received teachings of Mahamudra and Dzogchen. However, the mindstreams of the vast majority of these people have not been elevated even slightly, and the perfume of loving kindness is not even vaguely present, having made no change for the better. Not a few such people can be seen. What has happened to them? This situation comes about because such people are without the wish to attain the exhaustion of all flaws and the endowment of all enlightened qualities. So, it is not that the Dharma is not useful, but that such people have not managed to follow it. This unfortunately verifies the teaching that if someone is not a precious golden vessel, but a broken one, the vital essence will leak out.

In this case, so that you and others may attain the level of perfect buddhahood, train your mind with loving compassion, which is the relative attitude of bodhicitta. In addition to this, placing your mind free of elaboration in a state of no-thought, meditate on absolute bodhicitta. There is no alternative method, other than relying on these two.

Arya Nagarjuna taught:

> If you and this world,
> Desire to attain unexcelled enlightenment,
> Its root is the attitude of bodhicitta;
> Steady like the king of mountains,
> Compassion without partiality or limits, and
> Wisdom that is non-dual.

Whatever activities are undertaken, whether they are included within the two tremendous accumulations of merit and wisdom, depends on whether or not they are connected with the three excellent principles, with the basis of arousing bodhicitta. What is more, reciting even a single OM MANI PEDME HONG mantra, if done together with arousing bodhicitta, is a Mahayana practice and will become the cause for attaining perfect buddhahood. But, if practice is done without arousing bodhicitta, even if your recitals total many hundreds of millions, even if it appears you have accumulated great merit by means of wealth, or even if you took to the hills for your whole life on the pretence of meditating, still none of these would be sufficient to become an actual cause for attaining enlightenment, and would be difficult to include among the Dharma of the Mahayana.

Well, how should I arouse bodhicitta in my mindstream? It needs to be aroused in dependence on both love and compassion. To put this in one teaching, it is included within compassion. Compassion is important at all times to accomplish perfect enlightenment, from the beginning to the end. There is no more exalted activity conducive to attaining the ultimate level of buddhahood than non-conceptual compassion working for the benefit of others.

That being the case, as we practise the Dharma of the Mahayana for the benefit of mother-like sentient beings, if we have not reached the shore of liberation, how are others going to be liberated from the ocean of samsara? For that reason, if we want to seize the path to liberation, there is no way not to arouse the precious mind of bodhicitta in our mindstream. If we have it, that is all we need to accomplish enlightenment. Without it, we do not have the means to accomplish enlightenment; it is of such singular importance.

In this case, for us beginners, just starting our search to find the entrance to the path to liberation, what should we do? From the very beginning, authentic absolute bodhicitta does not develop. For that reason, first we need to train in relative bodhicitta. If we train in arousing relative bodhicitta, it will become aroused. When it has been aroused and we become familiar with it, then at one stage, absolute bodhicitta will develop spontaneously. So first, we train in the methods to arouse relative bodhicitta, and we must become familiarised with it through perseverance. For this, the motivation of the vast attitude of bodhicitta has two aspects to focus on:

- Considering sentient beings with compassion.
- Focusing on enlightenment with wisdom.

What is it like to consider sentient beings with compassion? The desire and wish of all beings experiencing suffering in samsara, is happiness. Every single one of them desires happiness, but they do not know how to accomplish the cause of happiness, which is virtue. They do not wish for suffering, however they are habituated solely to create the causes to experience suffering. They do not follow the direction of good habits, which are like flames burning upwards, but instead are swept away by bad habits of karma and negative propensities, which are like a river flowing downstream. There is not one being who has not been our own parent, and not just once or twice; the number of times that each sentient being has been our parent cannot even be compared to the number of atoms in a vast land, but is even more numerous.

This is the spoken truth of the teaching authority, the Victorious One, and also it is the scriptural authority of his followers, many holy masters. Not only that, but it is the perceptual authority of infallible cause and effect of observable phenomena. By the established truth of these three authorities, taking cause and effect as truth, compassion is aroused for sentient beings, who are like blind children abandoned in the middle of nowhere.

If we are someone with deep conviction in cause and effect, then we will not feign compassion or merely repeat things that others have said. If, in front of us, our old mother, or alternatively, a sibling, relative, or friend of this life was being tortured, then there is no way we would not have sympathetic compassion for them. Right now, out of all those in hell, screaming in the flames, there is not one who has not been our own parent. At the time they were our parents, all of them cared for us, their children, with kindness, not in any way different from our current parents. The situation is just the same for other members of our family, friends, and loved ones from our previous life. Even if they are not currently in hell, they may be experiencing the suffering of the pretas, unable to support their heads on their necks, or their bodies with their limbs. Pretas do not even hear a single mention of food to eat, or liquid to drink, for the longest time, yet they keep moving in the hope of finding some filthy substances to eat, or the mere smell of a burnt offering. If this is the case, don't you feel pity? Of course you feel pity.

Alternatively, having taken up the form of an animal, our former parents may have been reborn as one of our livestock, but unknowingly we sent them to slaughter. If later we came to learn of that, how great our regret would be! In this way, all sentient beings are our parents, so knowing they are our parents, our compassion is aroused. This is the aspect called 'considering sentient beings with compassion', but this kind of compassion alone is of no use. Like the good heart of a kind old woman, if words and actions do not bring benefit, just the power of a good heart merely makes aspirations and builds the path with words. Therefore, we are taught to 'focus on enlightenment with wisdom'. Think: 'I must establish all sentient beings in the permanent happiness of perfect enlightenment, without any suffering whatsoever'. This is focusing on enlightenment with wisdom.

In this way, by means of possessing these two aspects, we take the vows of aspiration and engaging. If we are engaging in the conduct of the six perfections in both thought and deed, then we have been able to follow the impeccable ancestry of the bodhisattva children of the victorious ones. Thinking like this, as long as we are cognisant humans, we should have an ultimate goal in life; either we need to accomplish something Dharma related, or we need to accomplish something worldly.

What is more, if we think in terms of the mundane world, the people of the past laboured from the time their teeth were white until their hair was white. Likewise for us – we follow after those gone before, until the days and months of our life are almost all exhausted. For people of all nations and places, the work of the mundane world is never done. Having not accomplished everything we wanted, on our final day we will grow regretful, and most people die with eyes full of tears and hearts full of regret. There is not a single person who, through engaging in worldly activities, has become fully satisfied and completed everything they wanted to accomplish. There has never been anyone.

If this is so, how then is the holy Dharma practised? When we know the way to practise the Dharma, there are real examples of how it was fully accomplished. In the past, there have been a great number of holy masters, learned and righteous, mighty and accomplished, who form the extensive turquoise mane of the snow lion. Among them, some engaged in worldly pursuits while they were young, just like us ordinary people, but at some point, as renunciation grew, they entered the path of Dharma, and in that very lifetime attained the kingdom of accomplishment. There have been many like this. For that reason, it is not a question of whether the Dharma can be accomplished, it is a question of whether you will accomplish it. By practising the Dharma, anyone can accomplish it; every day will see improvement. But if you remain without practice, a stone is not going to soften.

At this time in particular, we have been born in a place with Dharma, and we do not lack either the Dharma or a lama. As we have this real opportunity to enter the door of the holy Dharma, and we are not held back in any way by conditions, if we do not get to a point where we will have no regrets when we die, among the lowly, we are the lowest, belonging to a group who manages neither the Dharma nor worldly activities. What reason is there to fail at both Dharma and worldly activities?

In the case of the best kind of person, they are born with innate intelligence and wisdom of experience, and from that day forward do not mistake the path. In this life and the next, by means of discernment, they have far-sighted perception, and are able to discriminate between good and bad. This kind of person does not err. In the case of a middling person climbing the hill of middle age, they have both experience and weariness. They know how to listen to the counsel of good respectable people, so they can both improve and be shaped. But, if someone is counted among the lowliest kind, they may reach eighty years old and still have no idea. Their autumn years are ending, yet recognition and death come at the same time. At that time, when the last moments of life are slipping through their fingers, it is too late.

Whoever we are, as long as we are human, we need to make a plan, and having made a plan it needs to be successful, otherwise, throughout our lives *in the dreams of the poor they have a yard full of horses*. In reality we will have accomplished nothing. Everything ruled over in an imagined kingdom is meaningless, a mere heavy karmic burden for future lives. Every thought has already been had; none of these thoughts has been any good. So when thoughts are exhausted, the time has come to practise Dharma. Every activity has already been done, but nothing has been achieved, so we come to the point of exhaustion. Better than that would be to purify a little obscuration of body or speech, which is at least achievable. Talking, talking, talking... except during sleep, we are always talking. We talk, but it is of no use, and eventually we are no longer eloquent, so what are we doing still nattering meaninglessly? If only we made an effort to use our speech to recite the occasional mantra.

Still there is not one place we have not rushed off to visit. *None better than the place you hear about; none worse than the place you've visited.* So if someone says 'Let's go!' your heart should become cooler than ice. What thought do we give to who we associate with? Banding together with just about anyone causes heaps of problems; we are all just clumps of hidden flaws. When we look at someone, we can see their flaws, so looking back at ourselves, there is nowhere our own faults can hide either; they must be obvious in the same way. Making a nest to live with those who have nothing but flaws and problems is taught to be like living in a nest of snakes.

Considering such examples, by following the perfect Buddha, blessed, omniscient, and all-seeing, not only can we practise virtue and abandon non-virtue, but we can also accomplish our own purpose. So as a better alternative, why not strive in the methods to seize for ourselves the path of liberation? Although we understand there is no happiness in the realms of samsara, out of our inherent laziness, where does the time of our human life go? If we do not accomplish supreme liberation at the level of buddhahood, but again circle around and around as before, we will never leave samsara. In this case, in order to free all the multitude of sentient beings from the great rivers of suffering, we must pledge: 'However the Buddha himself practised on the path, in that way I must practise, following the Victorious One and the bodhisattvas.'

As Shantideva taught:

> Your happiness and the suffering of others,
> If not completely exchanged,

> Buddhahood is not accomplished,
> And in samsara there is no happiness.

Therefore, we must accomplish buddhahood for the benefit of ourselves and all sentient beings with this vast attitude of bodhicitta motivation. In addition to that, as we receive the Dharma of the Secret Mantra at this time, we must also have what is called the 'vast means of the Secret Mantra motivation': In the presence of pure wisdom, the universe and its contents are an immense array of purity. In the presence of the natural state of the ultimate nature of phenomena, nothing impure has ever existed. In this way, with the intent that sees this, specifically the lamas who speak the Dharma are the forms of buddhas and bodhisattvas, and all Dharma brothers and sisters who receive the teachings are a gathering of fortunate vajra siblings: heroes and dakinis. We need to have the mental conviction that this is the case. In addition to that, we need to listen to the teachings by means of having the conduct to receive Dharma, in the manner set forth in the Sutras, Tantras, and commentaries.

---

5) Benefits of Liberation

Now it is time for us to listen to the teachings on this *Sublime Path to Omniscience, Recital for the Preliminaries of Dzogpa Chenpo Heart Essence of the Great Expanse*. In the goodness of the middle, at the stage of the common outer preliminaries, we have already finished discussing the four mind changers. Now we turn to address 5) the benefits of liberation, and 6) relying on a spiritual teacher.

At the time the Blessed One first turned the wheel of Dharma, foremost was his Dharma teaching on the four noble truths. The first point of the four noble truths is to recognise suffering. Recognising suffering is the teaching on the defects of samsara. Following that, the Buddha taught us to abandon the source of all suffering, which is the teaching on karmic cause and effect. Then he taught us to rely on the path, which combines the two topics of the benefits of liberation and relying on a spiritual teacher. These then culminate in the actualisation of cessation, which includes the path empowerment and guru yoga. This is how the profound points of the four noble truths link to those of the preliminaries.

To illustrate the proper sequence of practice, in the mind training of the four mind changers, the difficulties of finding the freedoms and endowments and the impermanence of life, enable our obsession with the appearances of this life to undergo a reversal of attitude. The defects of samsara and karmic cause and effect enable us to also reverse our attitude towards future happy karmic results of rebirth as gods or humans. Then we need to know that which we are striving towards: liberation, what it is like? What is more, it is not enough just to learn the positive qualities of liberation – we need to arrive there, so we need someone with experience to guide us. If we have found the path but there is no one who can lead us on it, then the blind will be leading the blind, which is ineffectual. For this reason, the following two sections of teaching – the benefits of liberation and relying on a spiritual teacher – are taught in this order.

To speak about the benefits of liberation, first we need to know the real cause for liberation. Liberation relies on the path, and when we define the path, it is founded on the three vows. The nature of the path is the three – view, meditation, and conduct – and the result of the path is the level of the three degrees of enlightenment. Generally speaking, the Victorious Perfect Buddha taught inconceivable numbers of doorways and approaches to the Dharma, but they can all be summarised into the two Greater and Lesser Vehicles. If we further divide the Greater Vehicle, it can be separated into Sutra and Tantra, which are subsumed within the classification of the three vows – the foundation of the path.

What are the three vows?

1) Vows of individual liberation.
2) Bodhisattva vows.
3) Tantric vows.

The essence of the vows of individual liberation is renunciation. The essence of the bodhisattva vows is to benefit others, and the essence of the Vajrayana vows is pure vision. To summarise these three, they all are about taming our own mind. For each of the three vows there are two divisions: what is to be refrained from, and the vows which restrain. In the vows of individual liberation, that to be refrained from is happiness, comfort, and renown of this life. This means not striving for food, clothing, and conversation with the attitude of the eight worldly concerns. For whichever one of the vows of individual liberation which restrain, with a feeling of renunciation, give rise from the depths of your heart to the unfeigned attitude that thinks, 'I must engage in the methods to escape from this samsaric ocean of suffering.' Making this kind of vow is called the 'outer vow of individual liberation'. The four texts of the Vinaya, the two-hundred and fifty Vinaya rules, and the scriptural collections of the shravakas and pratyekabuddhas, are all contained within this.

If we consider the inner bodhisattva vows and their practices, what is to be refrained from? It is the mind of selfish application. If striving for the enlightenment of sublime liberation is not done with the thought to benefit all beings, then you have strayed onto the Lesser Vehicle, and that is the mind of selfish application. The bodhisattva vows which restrain involve the three kinds of discipline of controlling, gathering, and acting on others' behalf, by which means, benefit for all infinite wandering sentient beings is accomplished. This is the training in the difficult actions of the ocean-like bodhisattva conduct. Additionally, this is the intended meaning of all the bodhisattva scriptural collections summarised.

Following that, whichever of the central vows of the Vajrayana we hold, we are bound by sacred samaya commitments, and what is to be refrained from is the deluded experience of dualistic perception. The vows which restrain involve the stages of development and completion, and the stages of maturing empowerment and liberating instruction, which realise the view of samsara and nirvana as inseparable in supreme purity and equalness. Maintaining the foundation of sacred commitments, to fully experience the co-emergent wisdom of bliss and emptiness, is the outline of the intended meaning of the Vajrayana.

In this way, based on the view, meditation, and conduct, in connection with the individual attributes of the three vows, the result of the path: the three degrees of enlightenment of shravaka arhat, pratyekabuddha arhat, and perfect buddhahood, are attained. Also we should realise that there is no contradiction among these teachings; all the scriptural collections of doctrine should appear as instructions to attain enlightenment. So, of the two paths – the worldly path and the transcendent path – by first relying on teachings of the worldly path which bring about accomplishment of the higher realms of gods and humans, we need to work hard in the methods to complete the thirty-four Dharmas of the freedoms and endowments. This is the excellent physical basis which is necessary to accomplish the path of liberation of the three degrees of enlightenment. This is the first step on the ladder.

However, the accordant meritorious roots of virtue to attain this physical basis and a correct view of the world alone are of no benefit. Wherever we are born in samsara we never transcend suffering. So, upon the renunciation that contemplates this, by engaging in practise of the three scriptural collections of the Sutra Dharma, and the three higher trainings of the Dharma of realisation, realise the non-existence of self-identity and the non-existence of a coarse objective self of phenomena. This crosses the second step on the ladder of the shravaka and pratyekabuddha arhats. By grasping the thought of renunciation with a motivation of selfish application, whereby roots of virtue accord with liberation of the Lesser Vehicle, we realise a temporary emptiness. But, as we do not yet possess the attitude of bodhicitta, we cannot fulfil infinite sentient beings' complete desires. Considering this, we need to enter the path of great beings – the third step on the ladder.

The root of all the practices of the bodhisattva is the mind of bodhicitta, so holding it is like attaining an elixir that turns iron into gold, and everything becomes the actual cause to realise enlightenment. Not only does this transform accordant roots of merit into those of Mahayana liberation, but we enter onto the path of Mahayana Secret Mantra, the upper rung on the ladder. This is the path of many methods and little difficulty, which leads to swift happiness – the path we need to enter.

The path of the Mahayana is subdivided into three:

1) The long path – the Vehicle of Characteristics.
2) The short path – Vajrayana.
3) The swift path – Dzogpa Chenpo.

Of these, the long path of the Vehicle of Characteristics entails training for three incalculable aeons on completion, maturation, and cultivation, as well as much difficult practice. Entering onto the short Vajrayana path of maturation and liberation, if we meditate on completion stages with and without constructs, it is taught that in seven, or five, or even three lifetimes, we can attain the stage of unity. On the swift path of Dzogpa Chenpo, by receiving the elaborate, unelaborate, extremely unelaborate, and utterly unelaborate empowerments, and in particular the great empowerment of the expression of rigpa, we then unify our mindstream with the sacred commitments of non-existence, all-pervasiveness, oneness, and spontaneous presence. By practising the paths of primordially pure trekcho and spontaneously present togal, we perfect the progress of the four visions, and in this way, the great body of transference is attained in mere months and years.

Therefore, in this way, we need to find and enter onto the extraordinary path, and in this lifetime and body, attain the level of sublime liberation and enlightenment. Consider that to meet with this kind of excellent Dharma approach is supremely fortunate, and due to the power of previously accumulated merit. Every single one of the higher and lesser paths of the ten virtues, six perfections, four meditative concentrations, four formless concentrations, generation and completion stages, as well as the unity of samadhi and vipashyana, all solely aspire to attain this perfect buddhahood. So, with the wish to attain it, engage in the methods of practice complete with the three excellent characteristics of preparation, main part, and conclusion.

6) How to Follow a Spiritual Teacher

Examining the Lama

The sixth of the common outer preliminaries is the teaching on how to follow a spiritual teacher. Generally, there is not a single story mentioned in any one of the sutras, tantras, transmissions, or direct instructions where someone has attained buddhahood without following a guru. It has never been heard of, or witnessed, that someone working arrogantly or relying on their own initiative, has given rise to true enlightened qualities without following a lama.

Considering this, for most of us, when we encounter a wrong path or something wayward, we have the mental capacity to follow it without much encouragement, knowing instinctively how to engage in bad activities. This being the case, for us to know spontaneously how to become accomplished, and how to engage correctly with an authentic path to liberation when we encounter one, is highly unlikely. We are like a blind dog, who, lost and undecided where it wants to go, has fallen into the middle of a deep pit. So for this reason, in addition to understanding the qualities of liberation, we must find a spiritual teacher who can lead us with experience, on the path to the holy realm of liberation, and then we must follow them. This is explained in the teaching on how to follow a spiritual teacher.

The actual presentation of this in the recital text is written in the manner of a student aspiring to renounce factors that are unconducive to practice:

> Although I am on the path of Dharma, I do not restrain my
>   negative conduct.
> I have entered the door of the Mahayana, yet I have no concern for
>   others.

This is to be understood in the implicit sense that the student has already followed a spiritual teacher. But what does this entail? Following a spiritual teacher needs to be understood by means of four stages:

- Initially, examining a guru.
- In the middle, following the guru.
- In the end, training in the guru's realisation and conduct.
- How to abandon negativities from the student's perspective.

Of these, first we need to consider in terms of the methods to examine a lama and spiritual teacher. Generally speaking, the character of an ordinary person exhibits more than a few childish traits, and a spiritually advanced person behaves like a mature adult. Because ordinary people have childish temperaments, they are ignorant and mindless, like an infant. Children are easy to deceive, and swayed by circumstances, so in the teachings they are compared to kusha grass blown about by the wind. If stalks of kusha grass grow on top of a wall, when the wind blows upwards the grass bends up, when the wind blows downwards the grass is blown down, tossed around in all directions. Similarly, childish ordinary people, both ourselves and others, are small-minded and easy to deceive, gullible and capricious. That being the case, the problem occurs when they meet with deceptive people, unwholesome spiritual guides, because they are easily lead down a wrong path.

For this reason, we need to find a good spiritual master and virtuous friend who can teach an authentic path, and having found one, it is of great importance to follow them faithfully.

All-knowing Jigme Lingpa taught:

> In order to perfect all qualities of training,
> Follow the holy masters.
> Just as in the Malaya forests,
> Even a stray ordinary log
> Becomes fragrant with the moist foliage of sandalwood.
> Likewise, you take after whoever you follow.

In addition to the trainings of the three vows, the subjects of the samayas, and correct rejecting and adopting, in order to come to possess all the enlightened qualities of training completely, we must follow a holy master who possesses them all, and virtuous friends who understand the methods to increase positivity and resist all negativity.

To give an example of why it is necessary to follow them, in Mt. Malaya in India there is a forest full of white sandalwood trees. Ordinary trees do not have this inherent fragrance, but if they are left in this sandalwood forest long enough, droplets of rainwater fall on them from the sandalwood trees, and in this way they too become imbued with the sandalwood fragrance. This teaches that even ordinary trees may become fragrant with the aroma of sandalwood. In the same way, although at first you may have a few positive qualities, it is taught that if you mix with the wrong people and bad friends, their influence will lead you astray. If we take this teaching on board and consider it carefully, we will come to understand that there really is what is known as 'virtue' and 'non-virtue', and if we realise the key instruction of taking up virtue and rejecting non-virtue, we can actually be free from suffering.

The supreme refuge for all lifetimes is the Three Jewels, but without a spiritual teacher, how will we have the understanding not to mistake the path to complete freedom? Our parents have good intentions, but they do not know how to teach the auspicious path. Not knowing this, the little they teach us may, in the end, send us down a completely erroneous path. However untamed and coarse-minded someone is, however fearsome and unsuitable their temper may be, if they follow a real spiritual teacher, who with their enlightening qualities can make a person's mindstream workable, they too can be established on the path.

For example, the Brahmin son Angulimala murdered nine hundred and ninety nine people, and in order to make it a whole thousand, killed his own mother. But when he was about to attack the One Gone to Bliss, he heard the Buddha's holy Dharma and became his follower, and ultimately saw the truth. Likewise, in the Vinaya sutras:

> Like a vine on a Sali tree,
> Those who follow the holy ones,
> Become pervaded by excellent splendour.

Additionally, Sakya Pandita said:

> Following those who are bad makes you bad,
> Having followed them, they harm you in return.
> By following the irrigation water,
> See the fish scattered on the fields.

This teaches that if you maintain bad company and get swept away by irrigation water into the fields, you will become nothing more than a suffocating fish grounded on dry land.

Finding a lama to teach the authentic path of liberation is the goal of many lifetimes, our perpetual objective. It is the root upon which the outcome depends; whether or not we achieve the vast objective for ourselves and every being depends on this. Therefore, first we must be skilled at examining the lama. This examination is based on the criteria of the Victorious One's teachings, and we need to examine scrupulously, just as jewels are examined with a kashukha stone. Otherwise, as it is said:

> Not to examine the lama is like drinking poison.
> Not to examine the student is like jumping off a cliff.

Such examination needs to be done first. Other than that, it is not correct to examine a lama you have already taken as your teacher. In this case, what qualities should such a lama be complete with?

Lord Longchenpa taught:

> Upon the ground of purity of the three vows' permissions and prohibitions,
> A mindstream moist with vast learning and compassion,
> Expert in the oceanic rituals of the scripture collections and secret mantra tantras,
> Rich with the fruit of pristine wisdom of renunciation and realisation;
> By the splendour of the blossoms of the four attractive qualities,
> Fortunate student bees gather to enjoy.

Not only should the lama be extremely knowledgeable on the aspects of abandoning transgressions and adopting what is agreeable – which are to be adopted and rejected on the respective doctrinal paths of the three vows of individual liberation, bodhisattva, and Vajrayana – but also, with unmistaken conduct, the lama needs to be expert in the rituals of all four scriptural collections: Vinaya, the Sutra sections, Abhidharma, and the scriptural collections of vidyadharas. In particular, the lama's mindstream must be liberated, and possess the extraordinary enlightened qualities of the method of great compassion and the wisdom of emptiness, in unity. By the four means of attraction – generosity, pleasing speech, accordant meaning, and meaningful conduct – the lama works for the benefit of sentient beings with the activities of a Buddha. Therefore, it can be said that they embody the enlightened activity of the Buddha, or are the emanation of buddhas and bodhisattvas, which in fact they are.

From the *Sutra of the Great Drum*:

> Do not mourn Ananda,
> Do not lament.
> In future times I will
> Emanate as spiritual teachers
> To benefit you and others.

Because the enlightened actions and activities of the Buddha are inconceivable, when the time has come that sentient beings need to be tamed by the actual form of the Nirmanakaya Buddha, adorned with the marks and signs of buddhahood – the crown protrusion on his head, the wheel of Dharma on the soles of his feet, and so on – one will actually appear to benefit beings. Also, when it is necessary to appear in the manner of a pandita to realised people on the path, a buddha will appear as such to summarise the teachings and compose commentaries on the intended meaning of scriptures, and in that way work for the benefit of beings to be guided.

These days, in this degenerate age, the buddhas emanate as spiritual masters to teach the path and work for the benefit of beings. From the aspect of their essence, their actions are identical to a buddha's. From the aspect of their appearance, they benefit ordinary people who are unable to meet even one buddha or any of the panditas – beings of the end time who have extremely afflicted emotions. In terms of their sincere endeavours, with regard to their great kindness to degenerate beings, they are even kinder then the Buddha.

For this reason it is taught:

> The enlightened qualities of such a protector equal the Buddha's,
> Yet their kindness is a thousand times greater.

In particular, what kind of qualities does a lama who teaches the Vajrayana need? According to Vimalamitra, a lama must have received empowerments of the outer and inner mandalas, have utterly pure vows and sacred commitments, be expert in the meaning of each outer and inner tantric sections, and have trained in the ultimate significance of the approach and accomplishment, together with the activities. From the perspective of realisation, their view needs to be undeluded. In terms of experience, they must be adept in meditation. As far as their conduct is concerned, they should engage in all manner of activities connected to the benefit of others, guiding those to be tamed with compassion. In this way, it is taught a lama should possess these eight enlightened qualities. In addition to those, in our extraordinary tradition of Great Omniscient Longchenpa, a lama needs to be strong with the blessings of the lineage, have great weariness for samsara, and have few worldly activities.

If the lineage has impurities, because the accomplishments of Vajrayana come solely from the sacred commitments, blessings cannot arise. Also, if the lama himself is not assiduous in undertaking the Dharma, there is no use in him saying, 'This is what is traditionally required'. If the lama himself is someone who acts according to the Dharma, according to what he teaches, one of the signs that his mindstream is liberated through realisation is having few worldly activities. When someone has turned their back on the eight worldly concerns, there is no alternative but to have few worldly activities. The sign that a lama can mature the minds of others through compassion is having vast compassion that never tires of benefitting others. Such a person is called a 'spiritual teacher'.

On the contrary, what are the complete characteristics of someone who is not to be followed? All-knowing Jigme Lingpa taught:

> Like the Brahmins, they guard their father's lineage,
> In a pool of fear lest their seat decline.
> The result of study and contemplation is immersing themselves in worldly concerns;
> These teachers of the path are like wooden millstones.

Regarding the line:

> Like the Brahmins, they guard their father's lineage

It is said the Brahmins hold their own caste as most important, so do not allow it to degenerate. What they do to prevent their caste from degenerating is their most important task. So for someone who maintains such a seat, except for placing importance in having the name 'guru' and continuing to be one, they do not consider taming the mindstreams of students or upholding the doctrine as their concern.

> In a pool of fear lest their seat decline.
> The result of study and contemplation is immersing themselves in worldly concerns.

In order that the Brahmins' temples and seats, their residences and households, do not degenerate, the resultant benefit of doing a little study and contemplation is sacrificed for the sake of worldly conceit. Such people may speak of profound and vast doctrines, but in fact they are only involved in business and agriculture, vanquishing opponents, caring for friends, and so on: worldly abundance. These activities are like those of a lowly householder, so their title and their actual actions are unreconciled. A 'wooden millstone' is useless in grinding grain, and as such, these people are of no use to a student's mindstream. Thus Jigme Lingpa teaches it is unsuitable to follow a teacher like this.

What is more, if you do not examine a teacher carefully, there are many potential pitfalls. The result of previous generosity is the amassing of wealth and possessions, and gathering a retinue and students. Not examining a teacher, many fools chase after the famous and put them on a pedestal. Charlatans promote charlatans, so there are many who disturb the holy ranks of Dharma-accordant monastics. Some who get promoted in this way may at first understand reasoning and comprehend the truth of the situation, but by not voicing objection to their elevated status, allow bad habits to increase. Eventually developing an improper attitude, they persuade themselves they are someone important and grow increasingly arrogant. Such charlatans have overt pride, like a frog in a well, and are all too often encountered.

Another kind of false guide has little learning, and disregards vows and sacred commitments. Because of their low mental capacity they have no qualities of inner realisation, but they act as if they have superior behaviour and qualities of abandonment and realisation. Thus the cord of practice that works to benefit others with love and compassion is severed. Such kind of crazy guide can also be encountered.

If you meet with this kind of person, they will lead you off the path and to the lower realms. At the very least, if someone does not have qualities that are superior to your own, then it is taught to be inappropriate to follow them. To follow someone because they are famous is the wrong way to find a lama. This is like, for example, wanting to rest in the cool shade of a tree, you lean against a tree around which a poisonous snake has coiled; there is great danger.

As taught in the *Dhammapada of Close Ones*:

> Following those who are inferior, people become degenerate.
> By following those on the same level, one remains as before.
> Following someone excellent, one comes to attain holiness.
> Therefore, follow someone greater than yourself.

For example, if a student is on the path of accumulation, they should follow a lama who is on the path of application. If the student is on the path of application, the lama should be on the path of seeing. To guide a student on the path of seeing, the lama must absolutely be on the path of meditation, and for a student on the path of meditation, it is taught the lama needs to be one who is omniscient.

For us ordinary beginners, although the lama who leads us on the authentic path does not need to be a bodhisattva who has attained a bhumi level, if they are not on the Mahayana path of accumulation, there is significant danger of erring onto mistaken paths, as outlined above. Avoiding that kind of error, to find an authentic master in this degenerate time, is a tremendous and wonderful find, in this lifetime and forever. As it is said:

> A lama who possesses ultimate enlightened wisdom,
> Is the nature of compassion and wisdom of all buddhas,
> Appearing in human form in the mind of students.
> There is no more excellent root of all accomplishments.

The lama whose mindstream is rich in the enlightened qualities of learning and realisation is expert in the methods to liberate the mindstream of students. A buddha appears in the form of a human in this degenerate time in order to tame like with like, certain with the intent to practise the extensive conduct of the bodhisattva – such a lama is the embodiment of all buddhas combined. For this kind of great being whose mindstream is perfectly pure with the four immeasurables, even if someone were to harm them, having abandoned anger and seeing the characteristics of sentient beings, they would look on that person with compassionate eyes. Whatever beings do, a bodhisattva still brings joy, as Shantideva says in his praise:

> To whoever causes them harm, still they bring joy.
> I take refuge in these wellsprings of joy.

Therefore, upon all those with whom they make a connection, the bodhisattva showers down positive qualities like rain, which are beneficial both temporarily and ultimately. This constitutes part one, being skilled at examining the lama.

Following the Lama

In the middle, how should we follow the lama? Having found a lama who possesses all the above mentioned qualities, this is the stage to begin to follow them. Thinking of them as the embodiment of all the buddhas, with tremendous devotion of the three doors, disregarding difficulties of heat, cold, hunger, thirst, and so forth, and without concern for our own body or life, we need to practise according to their instructions. In addition to not doing even the slightest action that displeases the lama, we should follow them with confident and certain intense faith and devotion, without any weariness.

It is taught:

> The sick rely on a doctor, a visitor relies on their guide,
> Those afraid rely on a companion, merchants rely on their captain,
> A ferryman relies on his boat. Likewise, in fear of the enemies of
> Birth, death, and afflicted emotions, so rely on the lama.

The way to follow a lama, as a sick person relies on a doctor, is taught in the *Sutra Arrayed like a Tree*:

> Fortunate child, form the concept that you are sick.

Form the concept that Dharma is medicine.
Form the concept that diligent practise is treatment for sickness.
Form the concept that your spiritual teacher is an expert doctor.

Similarly, in order for a visitor to arrive at their destination, they rely on an escort, and merchants who go to sea in search of riches rely on a skilled captain. Likewise, driven down the perilous path of birth and death by the enemy of afflictive emotions, think that in order to protect ourselves from the suffering of the lower realms, we need to rely in this way on a spiritual teacher.

As for the student, there are also situations when they are inappropriate, and when they follow a lama, it taints both lama and student. In particular, it is taught that in the context when the lama examines the student, it is extremely important that the student's nature is good. There are also some people of whom it is said:

> Those with bad natures and glib tongues
> Follow the lama as if he was a musk deer.
> Having found the musk of the holy Dharma,
> Overjoyed by the hunt, they throw out their sacred commitments.

Some people are full of ideas and think too much. They are under the impression that they should study everything, but not practising even a single point of what they have studied, they just accumulate a collection of disparate texts. Others are fickle and do not really know the difference between what is Dharma and what is not, so they easily become disheartened. Saying, 'I followed such-and-such a lama, and did this-and-that practice, but not a single blessing came out of it!' they come to despair in the Dharma and the teachings. In addition to this, when a student is in two minds, instructions can be unhelpful and any blessings they once had dissipate.

Generally, there are three ways to enter the Dharma:

1) Entrance by faith.
2) Entrance by desire.
3) Entrance by an undetermined method.

Of these, what is known as the 'entrance by faith' is as follows: Following the lama and the holy Dharma, by understanding the nature of what is followed and the follower, with a motivation of faith together with renunciation, the student engages in genuine study, contemplation, and meditation. This benefits themselves and others, both in the short term and ultimately.

Those who enter the Dharma through desire do so for happiness, well-being, and renown in this life. With a motivation of bad attachment and aversion, they pretend to follow the Dharma and a lama for a while, but such people's minds are not inclined towards contemplation or meditation that brings liberation from samsara. However, still they go looking for empowerments and transmissions, not considering the lama, but more interested in his benefactors. They engage in various actions and activities but, as they do not have the thought to benefit others, their motivation is that of the afflictive emotions, and they engage in tainted study and contemplation. Not only are there people like this, but without any heartfelt faith in the Three Jewels, or any understanding of the practices of generation or completion, they aim only to make their garish shrine objects and ritual articles as shiny and splendid as possible. This kind of person is taught to 'enter by desire', deceiving themselves and others.

There is also a group of people that enter by an undetermined method. Unlike either of the two just mentioned, these people are erratically foolish and rash. Like a monkey's meditation or a parrot's mantras, they cannot determine enough to say if their focus is this or that. Like a stray dog following someone around, they hang around with everyone else, without grasping in the slightest the import of what is called 'to control bad nature with sacred commitments'.

For that reason, of these three ways to enter the Dharma, we must enter by faith. We must have faith and intelligence, learning and compassion, and follow a lama with respect for vows and sacred commitments. Our three doors should be tame and spacious, and we need to be generous, modest, and have pure vision.

The *Sutra Arrayed like a Tree* teaches what is necessary:

> Fortunate child, like the earth, tirelessly bear all burdens for your spiritual teacher. Like a vajra, be unwavering against all harms. Like a good student, never refuse what the lama says. Like an attendant, undertake everything he says. Like a bull whose horns have broken, have no conceit or pride.

When making offerings, among all recipients of offerings, the lama is the most supreme and holy source to accumulate merit. Why is that? The lama is the embodiment of the essence of all the Precious Jewels, the Fourth Precious Jewel, as is taught in *Equalising Buddhahood*:

> Of the Buddha, Dharma, and Sangha,
> The lama is the fourth.

Also, the lama is the chief of all mandalas, as Guru Rinpoche teaches:

> Lama is Buddha, lama is Dharma
> Similarly, lama is Sangha.
> The lama is the agent of all;
> The lama is Glorious Heruka.

How is the meaning of this to be understood? The nature of the Buddha is unchanging; it is the dharmakaya that possesses all supreme aspects, which, without following a lama, is unattainable. In that case:

> If you have wealth, offer it to the Four Precious Jewels.
> Serve and honour them with body and speech;
> None of it will ever go to waste.
> Of the three ways to please, practice is supreme.

First, we should please our lama with material things. The Tathagata told Nanda that when he was born as the son of King Krikri, he paid respect to Buddha Kashyapa with some perfumed balm, so his skin became gold in colour. Also, when he held a parasol over the Buddha's relics, because of the effort of holding the parasol, it is said he became a universal monarch with all the marks. If this is the case, from the point of view of a student who is gathering the accumulations, the merit of pleasing the buddha who appears in the form of a spiritual teacher becomes the cause to complete the accumulation of wisdom, without any going to waste.

In the middle, we need to accomplish pleasing our lama by means of service, with actions of our body and speech. If we are to gain meaningful merit based on this essence-less body, we need to accomplish service of body and speech for our lama. To do that we should sweep and clean, convey messages, follow requests, and so forth. To welcome or send off a lama is taught to bring about attainment of the major and minor marks of enlightenment. If you are physically incapable, still consider that you have offered your body to the lama. By means of these two kinds of service, be receptive to your lama, and so assimilate the vast and profound truths he utters.

In the end, we need to please our lama entirely with the offering of practice. Go to a remote place, a monastic centre praised by holy masters or a place your lama has approved, and settle into practice. Meditate on the pith instructions he taught you; this is the supreme service.

When a steed is released from its fetters, it attains unbridled ease of movement. Likewise, up to now the omniscience of mind has been bound by delusion. When these fetters are released by the lama's direct instructions, and the teachings open the door of complete liberation, your stream of awareness is liberated to pass unhindered. This is the offering of practice, supreme among all the methods that holders of the lama's lineage may use to please him.

Emulating the Lama's Realisation and Conduct

The above concerns the way to follow a lama. Now we discuss the final stage of emulating the lama's realisation and conduct. How do we emulate his realisation and conduct? As it is taught:

> Like swans that swim in perfect pools,
> Or bees that taste the nectar of flowers,
> Always attend to your lama with wonderful conduct.
> By tirelessly heeding his enlightened mind,
> Through faith adopt his enlightened qualities.

As if pouring a vital essence from one authentic vase into another, we need to be able to draw forth the qualities residing in the holy lama's enlightened mindstream into ours. However, rather than claiming, 'I am meditating on the natural state', searching externally for something profound, or seeking to find it by thumbing through a mess of writings, the method we need to transfer the qualities of the lama's enlightened mindstream into our own is to strive with devotion and prayer.

The process of a student following a lama is likened to that of producing a tsatsa from a mould. Just as the shape of the mould, whatever it is, will leave an impression on the surface of the tsatsa, even if the student does not become identical to the lama, like woollen cloth placed in dye, a previously white strip of cloth can now be said to have colour. So, however pale, still a small change of colour needs to occur.

Thus, it is taught:

> In the beginning, skilfully examine the lama.
> In the middle, skilfully follow the lama.
> In the end, skilfully emulate his realisation and conduct.
> Such a student travels the authentic path.

In particular, at the stage of Vajrayana, the essence of the source of refuge, the Three Jewels, the Three Roots, and so on, are all embodied in the lama. In the degenerate age, the lama spiritual teacher, is a buddha appearing in the manner of a human, to us and others with equal fortune. The lama's mind dwells in enlightenment, yet their actions and behaviour accord with those of ordinary people. By skilful means for degenerate beings to be tamed – the likes of us – they come as a protector for the lower realms and samsaric suffering. In their kindness, they admit us through the door of the holy Dharma, open our eyes to authentic mind, and teach without error the path to liberation and omniscience. More gracious than giving us the entire three thousand-fold universe full of gold dust, is to teach us the path of eternal bliss and liberation.

Therefore, we must follow the glorious holy lama, the essence of all the buddhas of the three times, the lord who pervades an ocean of buddha families and mandalas, by means of the three kinds of faith, and strive in the methods to attain their realisation and conduct.

How to Abandon Negativities from the Student's Perspective

The fourth step is the teaching on how to abandon things that are disharmonious from the student's perspective. This is clearly taught in the root text:

> **Although I am on the path of Dharma, I do not restrain my negative conduct.**
> **I have entered the door of the Mahayana, yet have no concern for others.**
> **Although I have received the four empowerments, I do not practise development or completion.**
> **O lama, I pray, free me from this straying path!**

The first line indicates disregard for the vows of individual liberation:

> Although I am on the path of Dharma, I do not restrain my negative conduct.

Having entered the holy Dharma path to tame our mind, we take the vows of individual liberation; however, lacking unfeigned renunciation or revulsion for samsara, we do not restrain our negative conduct. Conduct that tends to negativity does not accord with the vows. Defeats, transgressions, and so on, make our mindstreams unsuitable. Without finding a remedy, we fail to control our mindstream, so vows are disregarded.

> I have entered the door of the Mahayana, yet have no concern for others.

This indicates a deterioration of bodhisattva discipline. Again, having entered the door to the Mahayana path and aroused the mind of supreme bodhicitta, we do not train in the four boundless attitudes. In particular, because compassion that knows all wandering beings to be our parents has weakened, we become separated from bodhicitta that earnestly seeks to benefit others.

> Although I have received the four empowerments, I do not
> practise development or completion.

This indicates not maintaining the vows and sacred commitments of the Vajrayana. When we enter into the sacred mandala of Secret Mantra Vajrayana, we receive the four maturing empowerments:

1) The vase empowerment.
2) The secret empowerment.
3) The wisdom empowerment.
4) The precious word empowerment.

But, having received these, we need to meditate on the yoga of the two liberating stages:

- The method stage of development – the pure vision stage of the utter purity of all that appears and exists.
- The wisdom stage of completion – the stage beyond elaboration, non-conceptual non-dual expanse and wisdom.

Having such faults, these incorrect conceptions that we have in our mindstream, we need to invoke the lama's blessings:

> O lama, I pray, free me from this straying path!

Slipping from the excellent holy path, we fall into a bad inferior path, so pray with earnest longing: 'O lama, in your holy compassion, may you swiftly liberate and free me from this kind of straying or wayward path, this unfavourable and dangerous defile, and establish me on the supreme path!'
Again the root text reads:

> Although I have not realised the view, my conduct is crazy.
> My meditation is distracted, yet I obsess on theory and
> pretence.
> Although my conduct is mistaken, I do not consider my own
> faults.
> O lama, I pray, free me from this resistance to Dharma.

The way in which all phenomena abide is unconditioned luminosity primordially just as it is, ultimately beyond elaboration, as clear as the sky. It is not subject to restrictions or extremes, with nothing to be removed or added.

> Although I have not realised the view, my conduct is crazy.

Not realising this truth, the thought activity of conceptual mind that imputes emptiness, holds as supreme a temporal emptiness that falls into extremes. Such people boast with phrases like: 'Everything is evenness!' This is 'not realising the view'. 'Conduct is crazy' refers to such people's careless conduct, like a mad performance, also referred to as 'crude conduct'.

The following two lines teach distracted meditation and mistaken conduct.

> My meditation is distracted, yet I obsess on theory and pretence.

In this situation, neither meditation that determines the view – the wheel of dharmata luminosity free of any coming or going – nor the watchperson's castle of mindfulness of the nature of phenomena, which does not get distracted by anything else, are properly established. Such practitioners are continuously pervaded and distracted by the confusion of ordinary thoughts, but overly confident in their familiar patterns of theoretical empty talk, they rely on those saying, 'There is no difference between distraction and non-distraction'. This is empty talk that has no capacity for truth, so to utter such lofty words is just useless pretence. 'Pretence' is understood as 'meaningless impotent noise', which is taught to be empty dry words that make no sense. This kind of theory and pretence grinds down the essence of experience and blessings into dust, annihilating it.

> Just as a mad elephant does not take a straight path,
> Our conduct is wrong, but we are blind to our faults.

Generally, proper conduct is taught with the examples of a bee searching for its hive, the conduct of detached non-attachment, and so on. There are the twenty one forms of conduct, or the seven distinguished forms of conduct, and so forth. But in this example from the root text, conduct is not like this – it is faulty, the wrong conduct of one whose faults are hidden – improper behaviour through craving, vice, and at worst, engaging in unsuitable actions. Yet, not confessing or vowing to refrain from the faults in our mindstream, not considering the effect of faults as unwholesome behaviour, we are blind, like the eyes of an owl in daylight.

> Oil can soften stiff leather, but cannot soften a butter skin bag.
> Dharma can soften the wicked, but cannot soften those who are resistant.

For people who listen to the Dharma but do not understand it accordingly, it can become the cause of going to the lower realms. Becoming resistant to the Dharma, such people reach a state that Dharma cannot soften them.

> O lama, I pray, free me from this resistance to Dharma.

Therefore we pray, saying: 'May all those who have great hidden faults, be liberated by the holy lama's compassion and be led on the path of the completely authentic tradition with genuine view, meditation, and conduct.'

> **Although I may die tomorrow, I hanker for places, clothing, and wealth.**
> **My youth has long since passed, yet I have no renunciation or weariness for samsara.**
> **Although I have heard few teachings, I pride myself on my knowledge.**
> **O lama, I pray, free me from this ignorance.**

The first of these four lines indicates the failing that contradicts the training in discipline. The second line demonstrates the failing that contradicts the training in samadhi, and the third line shows the failing that contradicts the training in wisdom. It is a prayer to the lama to reverse these factors that contradict the three trainings.

> Although I may die tomorrow, I hanker for places, clothing, and wealth.

Regarding the training in supreme discipline, although you know you may die tomorrow, without a renounced non-attached mind, you are still attached to valuables, possessions, and so forth: home and familiar places, clothing and bedding, gold and silver, horses and yaks, provisions, property, and so on. A greatly attached mind is like a preta.

> My youth has long since passed, yet I have no renunciation or
> weariness for samsara.

Regarding the training of supreme samadhi, without undistracted meditative concentration, the time of youth passes in total distraction; the first half of life is over. Well past your prime, one day you reach old age. Even then, despite encountering the long shadows of late afternoon, without any revulsion or renunciation, or any weariness that sees the faults of suffering, still you lack the thought to avoid wandering in samsara in future. Carefully clutching onto the appearances and activities of this life, you are like a mouse underground, unaware of anything except that which is in front of its nose.

> Although I have heard few teachings, I pride myself on my
> knowledge.

This line is understood in regard to the training in supreme wisdom. Without wisdom that discerns precise analysis of phenomena, you have little learning in the proper study of the Dharma. Although you have no qualities of learning, you are also unaware of your own mindstream and so consider yourself a learned person. Swollen with manifest pride, you are someone with a conceited and arrogant mind-set, like a frog in a well.
In this case:

> O lama, I pray, free me from this ignorance.

Whatever happens, when negative people gain a high status it is bad, because negative people may have learning, but their pride is also great.
Shantideva taught:

> May lowly people attain high rank,
> But those with pride be defeated.

Where does the cause of all these problems come from? It arises from having unwittingly come under the influence of delusion. So, wandering blind in this dark place, pray: 'Liberate me, my only father and holy master, by granting me legs of discipline, a body of samadhi, and eyes of wisdom.'
Again, from the root text:

> **Although I get lost in circumstances, I wish for excitement
> and pilgrimage.**
> **I stay in retreat, yet my mind remains as ridged as wood.**

> **Although I speak of discipline, I have not rid myself of attachment or aversion.**
> **O lama, I pray, free me from these eight worldly concerns.**

Again, each line here teaches the opposites of the three trainings, and includes a prayer for this to be rectified.

> Although I get lost in circumstances, I wish for excitement and pilgrimage.

This is the opposite of training in discipline.

> Appearances are expertly deceptive,
> Mind is gullible;
> Discursive thought is easily seduced by conditions.

Just as this teaches, if your mind loses control to unfortunate circumstances, unaware you are being driven along by them, you no longer rise to join the ranks of spiritual gatherings, but wander downwards into market places and towns. There, you come under the influence of bad company, degenerates with wrong behaviour, and the sensory pleasures of illusory wealth. The word 'excitement' is used here to refer to the experience of many people gathered together, whose minds are habituated to yearning and great attachment, which causes agitation.

When consciousness is dependent on external objects, not understanding the equal taste and fundamental truth-less and illusory nature of joy and suffering, you fixate on things as true, grasping and desiring things as if they were solid. Going on pilgrimage with great excitement to view representations of the Three Jewels in many different regions, you think this is enough Dharma practice.

> I stay in retreat, yet my mind remains as ridged as wood.

This describes the opposite of the training of mind. Your body stays in a remote uninhabited place as if meditating for long periods, but you are unable to cultivate inner or secret solitude. Mind is ignorant of the truth of freedom from self-grasping, and thus still dominated by the power of afflictive emotions. Unsuitable to be worked with, your mind remains ridged like a branch of dry wood.

> Although I speak of discipline, I have not rid myself of attachment or aversion.

This teaches the opposite of the training of wisdom. With an assumed manner of smooth outer behaviour, you deceive the minds of others. Where others can see you, you make your appearance according to the Vinaya and speak of the holy Dharma to tame the mindstream of others. However, in truth, the attachment and aversion of your own mindstream remains unchanged and un-weakened, like the behaviour of a cunning cat.

> O lama, I pray, free me from these eight worldly concerns.

What are the eight worldly concerns? We are delighted when 1) gain, 2) pleasure, 3) fame, and 4) praise come to us, and through attachment, we strive for them. On the opposite side, we despise 5) loss, 6) pain, 7) disgrace, and 8) blame, and loath it when they occur. These eight worldly concerns are what ordinary worldly people strive for; they are the opposite of the path of the holy Dharma. Thus we pray: 'Holy lama, may you free me from these by arousing in my mindstream great equanimity, whereby joy and suffering are of equal taste and there is no unhappiness in anything.'

To summarise the meaning of all of the above:

I pray, swiftly rouse me from this deep slumber.
I pray, quickly release me from this dark dungeon.

With this pair of comparisons, we pray to be freed from samsara to the shore of liberation, thus summarising the meaning of the three preceding verses.

> I pray, swiftly rouse me from this deep slumber.

In short, laid out on the bed of subject-object dualism, in the exhaustion of ignorance, leaning upon the pillow of birth and death, wearing the covers of joy and suffering, oppressed by the deep sleep of self-grasping, we experience dreams of various habitual tendencies – a deep slumber. Thus we pray: 'Since wandering in samsara without beginning, still I have not roused from this sleep. I pray to my lama and the Precious Jewels: teach me the method to awaken swiftly!'

> I pray, quickly release me from this dark dungeon.

Arising from the cause of ignorance, the prison of the three realms of samsara is like a king's dungeon. Within it, held by the afflictive emotions of the five poisons, we are bound by the chains of karma. Beaten by the whip of suffering, this fearsome punishment of multitudinous suffering, so numerous it seems we have experienced it all before, has no beginning or end, just like being imprisoned in a dark dungeon. Thus we request compassion with this intense cry: 'I pray for swift release and the freedom of escape; I pray for swift liberation and to be established at the level of omniscience. Supreme lord, holy lama, think of me! Do not abandon me from your compassionate, protecting gaze!'

The above completes the teaching on how to follow a spiritual master and the six sections of guidance of the common outer preliminaries.

Let us contemplate again today's teaching on the benefits of liberation and how to follow a spiritual teacher, as revision and a reminder. Previously we discussed the four mind changers, the difficulties of finding the freedoms and endowments, and so on, which counter attraction to each of the higher and lower realms of samsara, hopefully turning our mind away from samsara entirely.

Having been told: 'This is no good' we need a goal of which it can be said: 'This is better'. Having been told: 'This is undesirable, please avoid it' we need to be informed: 'This is better, aim for this'. This being the case, the reason we do not like the three realms of samsara is because they have suffering. Wherever we are born in samsara, there is nowhere without suffering. In particular, the six types of beings circle around and around, and in this constant cycle, there is no end to the darkness of misery, and the golden sun of happiness never rises. Therefore we must turn our mind away from samsara.

When we look for an alternative place to go, we need to find somewhere without any suffering, where we can be free from suffering forever. When it comes to finding where that is, we learn it is the three levels of enlightenment. In that case, if we arrive at the three levels of enlightenment, how is there no suffering? Of the three, is one any better or worse, more or less comfortable, of greater or lesser benefit to myself and others? As this is the destination of our path, we need to know a little of the three results that need to be attained. What happiness is there in the place to which we escape?

Knowledge of this happiness is called the 'benefits of liberation', which we touched on earlier today. The first of the three levels of enlightenment is that of shravaka arhat, and the second is a pratyekabuddha arhat. Both these are termed liberation of the 'arhats of the Lesser Vehicle'. What is the reason that it is called the Lesser Vehicle?

Not having discarded thoughts that consider their own benefit, practitioners of the Lesser Vehicle do not consider the happiness or suffering of all mother-like sentient beings. Having no thought for others, they strive for themselves, towards their own personal salvation and peace. They do this by studying the three sutra scriptural collections and practising the three trainings of the path, resting in samadhi of thought and form, and meditative equipoise of cessation. By only realising one and a half aspects of selflessness – the emptiness of self, and half of the emptiness of phenomena – based on this manifest realisation, they become liberated, never to wander in samsara in the future.

If they are liberated, they are freed from the realm of samsara, which of course is a special level to attain, but is still lacking compared to the path of the Mahayana. To attain enlightenment, not only is it still necessary to change their attitude by means of the four mind changers, but the attitude of selfish application also needs to be reversed. This is a crucial point of the path that corresponds to Mahayana liberation, and is something not suitable to be without. Moreover, it is taught that if you are reborn in hell it is not a permanent hindrance to attaining enlightenment, but as long as you are not free of selfish application, you will not be able to attain the level of the peace of full enlightenment and perfect buddhahood. Therefore, it is not good for us to select this kind of path to liberation. In the root text, this is what we refer to when we pray:

> Omniscient master, do not let me stray onto wrong or inferior paths!

Although this is called an 'inferior path', when it is necessary to enter onto that path, such practitioners still need to control their mind with renounced discipline, and practise the three trainings. However, if we are given the choice between the three enlightenments of the Greater and Lesser paths, all the qualities of the lower paths are completely included in the greater paths, so obviously it is better to select the path that leads to the level of omniscience and complete buddhahood.

The activities of a buddha are solely for the benefit of sentient beings and nothing else. At that level, all faults are exhausted and all enlightened qualities are present. A buddha possesses all the oceanic qualities of abandonment and realisation, and is endowed with the enlightened qualities of boundless wisdom, love, and power. The three secrets of this ongoing inconceivable adornment of wisdom and enlightened qualities are beyond the scope of ordinary beings' minds to even imagine. But, by means of hearing and contemplating the Buddha's teachings and their commentaries, these benefits of liberation can still be understood to a limited extent.

In addition, we need to understand the causes of attaining the level of liberation. If we understand these, by entering the path of superior beings, we can attain the level of buddhahood. Of course, if we do not practise the Dharma, then we will not accomplish anything. But if we do practise, we need to enter the path of superior beings. When given the choice, why would we not select the easiest and most powerful path over the most difficult and most limited?

The reason we say someone is a 'superior being' is because they have superior strength of mind. What is superior strength of mind? Not fixating thoughts and intentions on selfish, temporary, trifling goals, the 'path of superior beings' concentrates on vast benefit for others – infinite sentient beings without exception. In order to establish these oceanic realms of beings into everlasting happiness at the level of perfect buddhahood, this path is for those who have superior strength of mind.

This being the case, the path of superior beings has the motivation of bodhicitta and roots of virtue which correspond to Mahayana liberation. Within this, it is taught there are also differences between the practices of the long path, the close path, and the swift path. On the long path there are the two accumulations; on the close path there are the stages of generation and completion. On the swift path, according to the guidance of the main practices of Dzogchen, by means of primordially pure trekcho and spontaneously present togal, realisation and experience is perfected swiftly. Conclusion in the Sutra tradition is buddhahood. In the Tantric tradition, it is the unified state of Vajradhara that needs to be accomplished. Such is the understanding from the perspective of the benefits of liberation.

Not knowing that samsaric suffering is suffering means that renunciation of samsara does not arise. Not knowing the positive qualities of liberation means that we do not know how to arouse the intent to seek earnestly for liberation. Thus we have been wandering in the three realms of samsara until now, experiencing suffering. To learn that there is something called 'liberation' is like acquiring eyes when previously we had none. However, in order to actually get there, having entered the path, we need to arrive at that ultimate destination without hindrance. If we do not find a holy spiritual teacher with knowledge of the path to show us, the worldly gods do not know how to teach us this path, the nagas do not know, and neither do our kind parents. Only our lama spiritual teacher has the knowledge to teach us. This is why we learn how to follow a spiritual teacher.

Alongside this, we also need to learn how to associate with virtuous companions and how to reject unwholesome associates. Without learning the methods how to rely on spiritual teachers and reject unwholesome ones, it is difficult to instinctively know how to do so;

there are many potential mistakes and uncertainties regarding false gurus. In particular, the wicked Mara and his entourage have numerous methods to deceive us, and in the case of true practitioners, they are always plotting how to subvert and bring harm. When they sense that sentient beings are being benefitted, the teachings of the Buddha are being spread, or the banner of the forces of good is being raised, then Mara and his minions, which includes those who have been cursed by demons, are filled with jealousy and hatred. As such, all those who cause obstructions to the Dharma or try hamper it, even if they are not a kind of demon, are definitely unwholesome associates.

For this reason, when we examine a spiritual teacher, it is crucial to see if their mindstream is filled with compassion. If they have no compassion, no matter how high their status or great their title, it is hard to say if they are a true spiritual teacher who can teach the path to liberation. However, most important is that we find a spiritual teacher with whom we have a karmic connection. Obviously we are not being instructed to check out all the lamas in the land, and judge if they are good or bad. If this were the case, someone doing such an investigation would need to have realised all the key points of enlightened qualities, and also possess the wisdom eye. Otherwise, how can someone ignorant and blind to the path even begin to judge others?

In that case, if you find a spiritual teacher that you can trust to show you the path to liberation, then that is sufficient. You certainly do not want to disparage others and say they are no good, as Patrul Rinpoche said:

> It is taught there are three you should neither praise nor blame: your own relatives, an unfamiliar lama, and generally no one at all.

And also, as a summary of all of the instructions, he taught:

> At all times, observe yourself without forgetting – this applies to both the Dharma and worldly life. This is the single, extremely profound instruction.

So, alongside examining the spiritual teacher, you need to take a good, thorough look at yourself – the student – to see how good you are. If the qualities of a good student are not fully complete, at least identifying this is one kind of realisation. What is more, you must become your own teacher and instructor. Correct your mind, and put yourself on the right path. When you know how to do this, it is taught:

> The wise do not come under the influence of Mara.

Then, having found a holy spiritual teacher, follow them with the unwavering devotion of 'whatever happens, you know best', completely entrusting yourself to the lama. To accomplish all of his or her instructions is the real cause to attain spiritual accomplishments.

If we want to gather a tremendous accumulation of virtue, complete with the preparation, main part, and conclusion, we need to do so embracing both method and wisdom. If you feel this is going to be a little difficult with your current capabilities, you need to see if you can find ways to combine your efforts with the holy lama's activities, as they engage in the six perfections. For example, if your lama is gathering huge accumulations of merit, you can add your own material support; even small amounts are suitable. Activities of body and speech, whether they are activities of study, contemplation, or meditation, unite them all together. Even if you cannot do anything more than sweep the floor of dust, that is still suitable. From sweeping up, to the vast methods your lama used to complete his accumulations, do whatever you can. In this way, small material offerings and minor endeavours become very effective when they become unified with great accumulations.

How does this work? This is due to the swiftness of the Vajrayana path: if you attend to your lama, serve him, gather the accumulations, and purify obscurations, then this is taught to be effective for the path of accumulation. It is also taught that, by receiving blessings of the lama's oral instructions and practising non-conceptual wisdom, this is the path of connection. In this lifetime, seeing the ultimate truth of the nature of phenomena, is the path of seeing. When this is established, having seen true nature, remaining in a state without anyone meditating on anything, is the path of meditation. Then, realising the ultimate lesson, the actual truth of the way things abide, is the ultimate path. This is what the Buddha taught in the tantras.

If we rely on a spiritual teacher, even if we have accumulated the cause to be reborn in hell in our next life, based on this life now, the negative karma can be all but exhausted into a mere dream. Also, it is taught that if you attend to your lama for just one morning, that benefit can even outshine the benefit of serving many millions of buddhas. In that case, by practising guru yoga, accomplishing service of body and speech for the lama, we complete the accumulation of merit. By merging our mind with his enlightened mind, remaining in meditative equipoise in the nature of phenomena, the accumulation of wisdom is completed. Through these means, the result of completing the two accumulations is the attainment of the two sublime kayas.

If we do not rely on a lama, or we do not know how to follow one, what are the shortcomings? If we do not encounter the oral instructions of the lama, we will grasp on to samsara as being joyful, and will not escape from its defiles of suffering. Being ignorant of the nature of karma and karmic results, except for exclusively tending towards non-virtue, we will not know how to do or think anything to the contrary. Without meeting a lama who has studied extensively, we will not have the opportunity to learn a plethora of knowledge. Although we may pretend to enter the door of holy Dharma, we will really feel that wearing the robes of ordination is some sort of tax, and we will not even reach the beginning of the path to liberation.

In short, due to not following a holy spiritual master, we fall away from all the excellent and positive paths of Dharma. Taken in by the deception of the demon of deluded appearances, we will be lost in total joyless suffering, now and into the future – we will lead ourselves there. In particular, if we not only do not follow a holy master, but criticise sacred objects, then, as it is taught in the *Fifty Verses of Devotion to the Lama*:

> Disparaging the masters,
> The deluded will die from
> Infectious and harmful diseases,
> Demons, plague, and poison.

In this way, if we do not care about our future and do not enter the path of the Vajrayana, we will not attain any spiritual accomplishments. If we do enter the path of the Vajrayana, spiritual accomplishments are swift in coming, however if we make a transgression, the fault is likewise great.

On the Vajrayana path, the most meaningful teachings that can be achieved with little difficulty are called 'direct instructions', but to successfully accomplish these direct instructions, we need to know the methods to do so. If we do not understand the methods how to undertake the graduated techniques and sadhana practices, words of direct instructions alone are of no use. For example, when approaching the six perfections, if we do not rely on the methods to practise the conduct of generosity, and so forth, we cannot realise the goal of the direct instructions, which is the perfection of wisdom.

As it is taught:

> The Buddha taught these auxiliary practices
> All for the sake of wisdom.

What is the meaning of this statement? The true support of all the activities that grasp the entrance to the path of liberation is the positive mind of renunciation. Without renunciation, initially the mind is not turned away from samsara. Because of this, faith and diligence are weak, so whatever teaching we may practise, it does not become the remedy for afflictive emotions, nor does it oppose samsaric activities or cut the root of suffering. If the roots of a poisonous tree are not cut, cutting the branches does not sever the flow of poison. For this reason, if we have no renunciation, we will not have received the vows of individual liberation with any confidence, as I have mentioned many times previously.

Thus, in the common outer preliminaries, the pertaining topics are:

- The arousal of unfeigned renunciation that turns away from samsara.
- The manner in which to earnestly seek liberating freedom from samsara.
- How to examine and follow a holy spiritual master, and following that, emulating his realisation and conduct.

As we recite regularly the root text of the preliminaries, which covers these points, first we should understand the meaning of the words we read. Our second objective is to reflect personally on these points and gain some certainty regarding their meaning. The third objective is to merge these points with our mindstream. We should think: 'What stage am I currently at? From this point on, what is necessary to cut the root of suffering? What is needed to welcome forth a teacher to help bring about happiness in this life and joy in the future? What is needed to benefit other sentient beings, the objects of compassion, who have all been my parents?'

All the Buddha's activities are for the benefit of sentient beings. The entire Dharma that the Buddha taught is aimed solely at establishing sentient beings into happiness. To say this even more directly, it is the method to prevent everyone's suffering, and the method to attain hitherto unprecedented great bliss.

There are multitudinous sentient beings, and none of them thinks the same. Just as medicine is not the same for different illnesses, similarly, the Greater and Lesser Dharma Vehicles were taught to accord with the more or less advanced faculties of all these different people. The Dharma we have met with this time is the Mahayana Dharma path which unifies Sutra and Tantra, so although we have fallen face down into the realm of samsara, fortunately the place we have fallen is soft – we have been born in a place where the Dharma of Sutra and Tantra is taught, and have arrived inside a temple where the Dharma is taught. To summarise the fundamental meaning of what is being said here, it is the thought: 'We want to achieve some benefit', so tighten your belts; what you do not understand you need to learn!

Teaching Day Five

Yesterday and the preceding days, we focused on the mind trainings in connection with the common outer preliminaries. Generally, discussing the Dharma brings benefit to the student's mindstream – the medicine of the Dharma, when relied on by the student, is the cure for the disease of afflictive emotions in the mindstream. That being the case, by training in the mind trainings, we need to turn our mind away from samsara; not only from samsara, but also away from the desire to attain the one-sided quietude of nirvana for our own benefit.

The *Exalted Heap of Jewels Sutra* teaches that Shariputra was to teach the Dharma to five hundred monks, which would have resulted in them attaining arhathood. However before he did so, the bodhisattva Manjushri gave a very profound teaching. Those monks, unable to comprehend its profundity, were scornful and because of that, burst into flames and fell into the hell realms. At this, the Blessed One said:

> Shariputra, because of your Dharma teaching, the monks would have attained arhathood. However, they would not have had the fortune to attain enlightenment. Because of the Dharma Manjushri taught, the monks will be reborn in hell for a time, but when they escape from there, they will actualise complete enlightenment, therefore Manjushri is the one who is skilful in means.

Similarly, in the *Compendium of Dharma Sutra*:

> Even if one were to practise the path of ten virtuous actions for many aeons,
> With aspiration for arhathood and pratyekabuddhahood,
> The occurrence of this mistaken discipline is called 'impaired discipline',
> And is much more serious than the defeating downfalls.

Therefore, with the four mind changers, turn your back on samsara. Alongside abandoning selfish considerations, the need to turn our mind away from one-sided quietude of nirvana is one essential meaning of the mind training. How is adeptness in mind training measured? From the *Seven Points of Mind Training*:

> The entire Dharma is subsumed in one necessity,
> Take yourself as chief witness:
> If you always enjoy a singularly joyful mind

> Even if distracted, then the result has come about.

What is the meaning of all the teachings of the lesser and greater vehicles that the Buddha taught? The one key point is to tame the self-grasping of our mindstreams. What is more, however much we practise the Dharma, however much we meditate on the mind trainings, the main goal is that the attitude of self-cherishing needs to be reduced. If the one who practises Dharma does not remedy self-cherishing, then their practice is meaningless. The root of whether our Dharma practice is classed as authentic, or not, comes down to whether it becomes a remedy for self-cherishing. Therefore, the scale used to evaluate a practitioner is taught to be the extent of their self-grasping.

In addition, if we still wish to ascertain whether or not someone is an authentic practitioner, we are taught:

> Take yourself as chief witness.

If others say of someone: 'They are a genuine practitioner', then from one perspective, as the saying goes: *Heed the talk of a thousand people, or the wisdom eye*. But our minds are hidden, so ordinary worldly people without clairvoyance cannot know another's mind. They are easily satisfied by the various superficial modes of conduct of others with similarly limited minds. The real sign that you are accomplishing the mind trainings properly is if you are consistently unashamed of your own mind; that is most important. Therefore, it is taught that it is unsuitable to trust the talk of others who pass judgement, but take your own mind as its own chief witness. When we do not keep our mind hidden from ourselves, we can become self-purified, and that is ideal.

> Always enjoy a singularly joyful mind.

This teaches that whatever type of unfavourable conditions or suffering befalls us, we should not be afraid or despair. Of course, all sorts of undesirable things do happen, because we are in the three realms of samsara. Otherwise, there would be no point in saying that this place is just like a pit of embers, an isle of demons, or a nest of poisonous snakes. But, whatever fear or suffering arises, we need to be able to allow it to assist our training. At the time when fear and suffering occur, if we face them and practise the Dharma with the mind trainings, then we will come to understand that to examine our own mind is the best training. In this way, remain happy; there is no reason to become worried. It is taught, if we can always maintain this kind of happiness, it is the measure that our mind has become trained.

Teaching Day Five

Also, the meaning of 'practising the Dharma' is to give our own body and mind a new kind of training, whereby we transform what was not good into something good. This means turning something that had no value into something precious. Generally what we term a 'healthy person' should have the mental capacity and optimism to cope with any kind of joy and suffering that may occur. If we live our entire lives happily, that is great. Otherwise, for those whose entire lives are filled with suffering, enveloped in dark misery and unclear states of mind, it is a sign they have no real spiritual foundation. Whether we worship in a temple of Dharma or a worldly temple, or combine both spiritual and temporal activities, we need to be joyful.

Also, acting as if we have something when we do not, of course does not bring any gain, and acting like we have nothing does not make us feel any better either. Rather, children of good parents do not need to feel hopeless or despondent; do not be depressed. In the past, when we experienced bad times and bad fortune, when a family had only five kilos of grain to eat per month, did we not still have a happy outlook? During years of endless struggle under repressive control, folk still remained optimistic. Yet, during these current positive times of good fortune, when we have comfort and plenty, it seems that inside we are full of misery and overflowing with discontent. When we look at one another, it is like enemies confronting each other. Having got full bellies, we have become hostile.

Generally, wandering human beings, whoever they are, are ultimately the same, so we should think of everyone as family and community. With this in mind, we should interact with others based on the four principals of training in virtue:

1) Not to return abuse with abuse.
2) Not to return anger with anger.
3) Not to expose hidden flaws by exposing other's hidden flaws.
4) Not to return a blow for a blow.

Therefore it is taught:

Those who hurt others are not practitioners of virtue.

You may be a householder, but as long as you are a person from Buddhist Tibet, or you have a connection with the Buddhist teachings, then the Dharma guides you both in this life and the next. So we need to be truly happy and radiant with joy. What is more, for young people in the sunshine of the first half of their lives, that season of comfort and happiness is like the three months of summer: do not allow it to be wasted in a state of pointless non-virtuous activity, in bars and gambling dens. When there is free time, it is good to get together with family and friends, to sing and dance to bring happiness into your lives. For the young people, when there is nowhere else to go except for shops and bars, of course there will be some pushing and shoving. Better to do circumambulation around the monastery and temples, and pay homage to the Buddha statues.

As for the old people, do not be morose about mortality, waiting for death. There is no one who, having been born, does not grow old and die. Rather, listen to the liberating biographies of the masters and spiritual songs. For those who can understand them, it is good to read *Karmasataku Sutra*, the *Sutra of the Wise and the Foolish*, the *Father and Son Teachings* of the Kadampa School, and so forth. If you know how to understand them, there are things to be learned from the *Five Chronicles*. Not only that, but it would be great if groups of older people could gather together, and ask those who can read to chant the *Spiritual Songs of Milerepa*, and so on. Reciting *King Gesar's Conquest of Hell* is also very good, and wholly related to the Dharma.

This being the case, the elderly have experienced their share of both the happiness and suffering of this world. If there is satisfaction to be had, this is the time to feel satisfied. If there is weariness to be felt, this is the time to feel weary. What is more, as it is said: *Death comes to all people, like old fur on once courageous tigers*. So, for people of the world, at first their birth is significant, during life the extent of their success is significant, and in the end, the manner of their death is significant. Therefore, if all people are destined to be reborn again, then what is called 'birth and death' is merely the way these events are designated mentally. So, if we wish to stay here, it is comfortable, and every day we remain we can accomplish virtue. If we die, then it is also comfortable; either our destination is a pure land, or alternatively it is appropriate to focus our intent towards a human body with the Dharma. So whatever we do, for a practitioner of the Dharma, there is no unhappiness, there is only joy.

Also, whoever we are: laypeople or monastics, patrons or recipients, it is best to avoid living in small divided groups. Limited sectarianism is not good, as it divides the larger community. With an altruistic intent and understanding, even if we cannot take care of tens of thousands of people, we can surely offer support to a few thousand people with the notion we are all part of the same family. If some members of the larger community are smallminded about many petty issues, again and again, this is bad, and an early sign that things are going to fall apart. Therefore, whether you are a man or woman, old or young, train yourself to be big-hearted; this big-heartedness is the sign of nobleness and great understanding.

Being smallminded and tetchy is characteristic of the faults of a bad nature. So Mipham Rinpoche said:

> This place may be filled with bad nature,
> But if we act nobly,
> In view of this, it is natural that
> We become the better person.

If there are many people with great understanding and big hearts living in one place, then it follows that these are people we can rely on, trust, and place our hope in. When these qualities are present, such a place is a haven we can depend on. Therefore it is taught:

> If you are big-hearted, quarrels are few and you feel happy.
> Do whatever benefits others, and you yourself are joyful.
> Focus on the Three Jewels, and your present and future will be good.
> Accumulate the gathering of merit, and your wishes will be fulfilled.

Additionally, most people like those who are big-hearted and have noble conduct. When the offspring of big-hearted parents are sent out on the path, they usually turn out well. If, in a place there are only those who are mindless and short tempered, then the people who we can trust, or rely on to provide support, are all gone. In a place like that, the happiness of merit cannot catch hold.

If you wish to accumulate wealth, by employing wisdom and discernment, you need to earn it appropriately; to do good business, you must not cheat your associates. At a time when there is a need to earn money, turning to the market outside, you should be successful bringing wealth home. Otherwise, compared to a lifetime spent running around, anxious to accumulate wealth, but burdened by debts and loans, it would be better to stay in a quiet hollow, relaxed and serene, digging for wild sweet potato. When we have money, if a time comes which calls for generosity, we need to be able to give. If you do not manage to be generous, you cannot be sure that later on your wealth will not become a millstone to drag you down.

Therefore, clearly the holy Dharma is something we cannot be without. Without it, there is a great unfilled vacuum in our lives. Although we may have external wealth, we lack inner riches, so for that reason such a person is said to have a 'physical basis of the impoverished', regardless of how much money they have.

Close your eyes, and all that you have now is gone. It is not always useful to leave money to maintain an income for your offspring and relatives. Much better is to leave positive qualities in their mindstreams. These never disappear or become exhausted during times of prosperity or scarcity. That is an inexhaustible wealth. In addition to that, if we can instil in our children a friendly personality, good behaviour, altruistic attitude, and a sense of loyalty, there is hope it can add to the happiness of everyone. In my tale, *Sending Word to the Herd of the 21st Century's Tibetan Youth*, I wrote:

> Meagre possessions of silver and jewels, gathered with sweat,
> Finally become the cause of others' wrong livelihood.
> So spend any extra money on your children's learning,
> And this benefits everyone, yourself and others.

This not only benefits us all, but it brings benefit now and into the future. Whatever happens, good or bad, try to be joyful! As Je Milarepa said:

> Sick, sick, sick! I'm happy to be sick!
> Previously accumulated negative karma becomes exhausted.

In this way, previously accumulated negative karma becomes depleted by undesirable negative conditions. What is more, the training in giving and taking happiness and suffering becomes a support for bodhicitta, so whatever negative circumstances arise, we can integrate them onto the path and rejoice. Make the wish: 'May the misfortune of others fall entirely upon myself! May my misfortune take the place of all the undesirable things which befall all sentient beings.' Thinking this, if you can accept negative circumstances with joy, bad omens become fortunate and negative situations appear as supportive elements; this is a sacred method.

With this sacred method, we have the knowledge how to transform any negative circumstances into good fortune, and negative situations into supportive ones. The fourth line of the above quotation from the *Seven Points of Mind Training* reads:

> Even if distracted, then the result has come about.

For example, for a skilful rider, even if their horse suddenly bolts while they are distracted, they will not fall off. Similarly, although we do not maintain a specific focus on being mindful, it is taught that at one stage, whatever negative situations arise, they do not become obstructions, but can become supportive allies of the mind trainings. So, this is taught to

Teaching Day Five

be the sign of progress. In that case, when we have got to that stage, is there any need to train further? Of course we need to keep training! Except for indicating that the mind trainings are achieving their purpose, it does not mean that we can stop there. Until we achieve enlightenment we still need to make progress!

The Unique Inner Preliminaries

Part Two, Taking Refuge

Having completed all six of the common outer preliminaries, today we move onto the unique inner preliminaries of the *Sublime Path to Omniscience*. The unique inner preliminaries also have six sections:

1) Taking refuge, the foundation stone of all paths.
2) Arousing the mind of supreme bodhicitta, root of the Mahayana path.
3) Meditation and recital of Vajrasattva, to purify adverse circumstances of negative actions and obscurations.
4) Offering of the mandala, to gather the favourable circumstances of the accumulations.
5) The kusali's accumulation of merit, which cuts through the four maras all at once.
6) Guru yoga, the consummate method to realise wisdom in one's mindstream.

Regarding these six practices, both taking refuge and arousing bodhicitta promote gathering of the accumulations and purifying obscurations. The specific method used to purify obscurations is the meditation and recital of Vajrasattva. The mandala offering, and its auxiliary practice of Chod - the kusali's accumulation of merit - are the chief methods to gather the accumulations. These five practices generate the extensive or cooperative conditions to develop absolute innate wisdom in our mindstream. Guru yoga emphasises the key point of devotion, therefore we say it is the direct or swift cause to develop wisdom.

This process is taught in the *Great River of Knowing Sutra*:

> Absolute innate wisdom only comes from
> Achievement of having gathered the accumulations and purified obscurations,
> And through the blessings of a realised lama;
> Know that to rely on any other means is foolish.

A fortunate person enters the path of the Mahayana, and by relying on the special methods of the path of Secret Mantra, realises with ease the profound truth of the way things abide. A person on the path of the Vajrayana who desires to liberate all sentient beings from the ocean of samsara, needs to engage in the practices of the 'four summaries of the Dharma' that the One Gone to Bliss taught. What are the 'four summaries' or the 'four seals which signify the view'?

1) All compounded things are impermanent.
2) All defiled things are suffering.
3) All phenomena are empty and devoid of self.
4) Nirvana is peace.

Someone who engages in the four summaries of the Dharma, with a difficult-to-find physical basis complete with the freedoms and endowments, sees that every part of the universe and its contents is compounded, and therefore impermanent. They also realise that, regardless of good or bad, everything arises from defiled actions, the result of which is the three realms of samsara, so therefore not beyond suffering.

> Absolute innate wisdom only comes from…

Seeing that the nature of the three enlightenments – nirvana together with the path – is cool peace, by following a spiritual teacher to show them the path, such practitioners actualise in their mindstream the way all phenomena abide: the sacred truth of emptiness and no-self, innate wisdom free from all characteristics of elaboration.
The method to do this is taught to be:

> Achievement of having gathered the accumulations and purified obscurations.

This is the achievement of our mindstream, which depends on taking refuge, arousing bodhicitta, and the other unique methods of gathering the accumulations and purifying the obscurations.

> And through the blessings of a realised lama.

By contemplating the manifest realisation of your holy lama who possesses supreme realisation, by means of merging your mind with his enlightened mind, his blessings will enter your heart. This enables you to attain the inheritance of the realisation of the mind transmission. Apart from this, as it is taught:

> Know that to rely on any other means is foolish.

However we depend on various, alternative methods, when we do not have excellent and suitable causes and conditions, how can an appropriate result that accords with our expectations come about? To hope for a result to come about in that way is the deluded thinking of a naive child, so we are told to 'Know that.' But, by depending on the key points of accumulation and purification, emptiness endowed with the most sublime of all attributes, profound inner suchness, can be realised with ease.

Regarding the first method of practice, taking refuge, we are now at the stage of the unique inner preliminaries, but how is taking refuge unique? Isn't taking refuge in the Three Jewels a general feature of Buddhism? Doesn't taking refuge distinguish Buddhists from non-Buddhists? In ordinary terms yes, these are both true. However, here we emphasise a unique way of taking refuge. Generally, of the three capacities of lesser, middling, and great beings, the way which we are about to learn to take refuge is the refuge of great beings. What is more, in terms of both Sutrayana and Vajrayana, this is Vajrayana refuge. Also within Vajrayana, according to the tradition of the peak of the three yogas of the inner Tantras, this is the unique refuge of Ati Yoga.

CLASSIFICATIONS OF TAKING REFUGE

We discuss taking refuge in terms of three topics:

1) Classifications of taking refuge.
2) How to take refuge.
3) The benefits and precepts of taking refuge.

Firstly, what are the classifications of taking refuge? As just mentioned above, these are the three ways of taking refuge for the beings of the three capacities. Thus, fearful and terrified of the suffering of the three lower realms, only aspiring to and yearning for the blissful result of the higher realms of gods and humans, is the refuge of beings of lesser capacity. In a *Lamp for the Path*:

> Those who strive by any means
> For mere samsaric pleasures
> For themselves alone, these beings
> Are rightly called 'lesser'.

The liberation of such beings is merely a temporary escape from the suffering of the lower realms, so this is considered to be a liberation of pointless benefit. In truth, just afraid of the terrors of the lower realms, they focus on the temporary result of the higher realms. So in terms of the period of time, beings of lesser capacity are only taking refuge until they attain the happy result of the higher realms.

Afraid of the suffering of samsara in its entirety, beings of middling capacity strive for peace and happiness for themselves alone, taking refuge out of faith. This path is the Dharma the Buddha taught which begins the vehicle of arhats and pratyekabuddhas. Such beings have awareness of the infinite suffering of existence, so they are superior to those of lesser capacity. They take refuge for as long as they live, and until they ultimately attain the result of an arhat or pratyekabuddha.

Beings of great capacity take refuge in the Three Jewels with great compassion, in order to free infinite samsaric sentient beings from all suffering, and establish them at the level of buddhahood. Therefore, of these three, we need to train in the thought that wishes all sentient beings to attain buddhahood – the refuge of beings of great capacity – which is the entranceway to limitless merit. What is such an attitude like? It involves coming under the influence of vast compassion, and so is correspondingly afraid of personal salvation and the peace that abandons benefiting others. In order to act to put a complete end to the suffering of other sentient beings, we aim to attain the level of buddhahood, until which time we take refuge in the Three Jewels. We take refuge as long as we have not attained the heart of enlightenment, or until we attain the immeasurable wisdom of the Buddha in our mindstream – until we touch the resultant source of refuge which has abandoned all loss, gain, and deception.

The Three Jewels

As we discuss further about taking refuge, whatever we learn about the manner of taking refuge, first it is important to understand the object in which we take refuge: the Three Jewels. Based on the words of the recital text, taking refuge is taught in one verse:

> **In the sugatas of the Three Roots, the true Three Jewels,**
> **In the bodhicitta nature of the channels, energies, and essences,**
> **In the mandala of essence, nature, and compassion,**
> **I take refuge until I realise the heart of enlightenment.**

So, the Three Jewels are the Buddha, the Dharma, and the Sangha. Everyone knows how to list them. However, if we ask for each of them, 'What is the Buddha? What is the Dharma? What is the Sangha?' it can sometimes be hard to find an answer. Although there is no limit to knowable phenomena, and it is impossible for us to know everything, being a Buddhist, and in particular if you are someone who has promised to lead and teach others, if you do not know even the definition of the nature of taking refuge, then that is poor. As all-knowing Jigme Lingpa said:

> However they are disturbed by the three fears,
> The worthy and dependable refuge of the faithful,
> Is the renowned white umbrella of the Three Jewels.
> On entering the teaching, first grasp this.

This teaches that someone, upon first entering the door of the Buddha Dharma, needs to understand the nature of the Three Jewels. But first, what are the three fears?

1) In general, the suffering of samsara.
2) In particular, selfish application.
3) Especially, ordinary deluded fixation.

Fearing these three, we take refuge. Also, there is not a single other place of refuge except for the Three Jewels. But how are they able to provide refuge? It is taught:

> Rejecting other teachers,
> I take refuge in you.
> What is the reason?
> You possess no faults and are perfect in all enlightened qualities.

The buddhas and bhagavans have discarded everything that is to be abandoned, so they themselves have attained a state of fearlessness. They have realised everything there is to be realised, and perfected all enlightened qualities without exception. By the strength of this, they are endowed with both the ability and the expert methods to protect others from danger. In addition, they possess compassion for all without partiality, therefore the Three Jewels are the single suitable refuge.

If the buddhas and bhagavans have the compassion to protect sentient beings, what is the reason that sentient beings are still left in the realms of samsara, experiencing suffering? Although the external factor of the cause for the buddhas to protect sentient beings is complete, the internal factor is not; sentient beings themselves do not have the power to focus their minds one-pointedly in order to take refuge. For this reason, they continue to suffer. If both the outer and inner factors are in accord, the compassion of the Three Jewels is able to lead sentient beings out of the realms of samsara. In this case, the main cause for us to take refuge is to understand the enlightened qualities of the Buddha and his teaching, which is very important in the beginning. To gain this understanding, first we need faith.

Arousing faith and the virtuous Dharma both come about together. Faith is numbered first among the seven noble riches, it is the root of all goodness, and all positive qualities rely on faith, therefore we need to arouse it. In ancient India, there was a learned Brahmin who debated with many Buddhist panditas, but none could defeat him. However, one day he found a volume of Buddhist scriptures in which he read a prophecy about himself that the Buddha had made. This aroused such faith that his negative karma became exhausted and he entered the Buddhist path, becoming the great scholar Asvaghosha.

At the stage of the preliminaries, faith itself is divided into four categories:

1) Inspired faith.
2) Aspiring faith.
3) Confident faith.
4) Irreversible faith.

Of these four, both inspired and aspiring faith are the faith of beginners, and can be affected by circumstances. Only the latter two are the unmistaken goals of our aspirations. For ordinary people, there is something great that opposes faith: after not very long, our life will end and our physical constituents will break down in a charnel ground. The problem is, we are enmeshed in the bonds of karma, and do not expect death to come so swiftly. Even if someone without faith accumulates hundreds of thousands of prayers taking refuge, in truth they are only following ignorance, following desire, and following aversion. So apart from that, they have not been able to take genuine refuge.

THE BUDDHA JEWEL

The first of the Three Jewels in whom we can have faith is the Buddha, who embodies the three buddha bodies:

1) The dharmakaya.
2) The sambhogakaya.
3) The nirmanakaya.

Of these, the dharmakaya is the nature of inseparable expanse and wisdom. It is the very essence of sky-like wisdom, free from absolutely all defilement. Differentiating this, great equalness of pure expanse, the aspect of which makes up the nature of all the kayas, is the svabhavikaya. That which realises the wisdom of consummate abandonment and realisation, the rigpa essence which embodies the thirty-seven factors of enlightenment, is taught to be the jnanadharmakaya. This is taught in the *Ornament of Manifest Realisation*:

> The svabhavikaya of the Buddha
> Is the totally purity of all undefiled phenomena.

And so forth, up to:

> The omniscience of all aspects
> Is called the 'dharmakaya'.

The sambhogakaya is established on the strength of the aspect of samsara – alaya, together with the eight-fold group of consciousnesses, having sunk into the sphere of great equalness of pure expanse – so it is the thousand enlightened qualities of the manifest aspect of the way of abiding of the ground, the nature of the rupakaya endowed with the five certainties of absolute perfection.

What is the nirmanakaya like? He is the guru of beings, the Teacher, the Transcendent Accomplished Victorious One, who, looking with five considerations, was born in this world in the central land, and engaged in the twelve great deeds. Turning the wheel of Dharma, he is the one who engages in nurturing beings to be tamed, fully endowed with omniscient wisdom, loving compassion, and enlightened activities:

In the *Lankavatara Sutra*:

> Abandoning the pure immaculate realm,
> Delightful and called Akanishtha,
> The true Buddha was enlightened there;
> His emanation was enlightened here.

In ancient India there was a non-Buddhist called Nyethung, who followed the Nirgrantha tradition and had no faith in Buddhism. He knew the householder Shrigupta was the head of a wealthy family, so the non-Buddhist sought to lead him astray, saying: 'Outside your door, dig a large hole and fill it with smokeless embers. Cover them first with fine ash, then with fine earth, so it is not obvious. Also, prepare some good food, and mix with it with fast-acting deadly poison. Make preparations in this way, and then call the Buddhists, the Buddha and his followers, to come. Then we will know if he is omniscient or not!' Being easily influenced, the householder Shrigupta was taken in by the non-Buddhist and prepared everything accordingly. When he requested the Buddha and his retinue to visit him, the Buddha acceded, fully aware of his intent, and went to Shrigupta's home the following day.

Arriving outside, as soon as the Buddha stepped upon the embers, the eyes of the blind could see, the deaf could hear, the mad regained their senses, and all those unhappy through suffering achieved happiness. The nature of the embers changed, the flames becoming gardens of lotus flowers. So with the arrival of the Buddha and his retinue, everyone was amazed and developed faith. Both the householder Shrigupta and Nyethung were regretful and confessed.

When the Buddha went inside the house, Shrigupta said, 'I have done many terrible things, heaping evil upon evil, so there is no edible food to offer you. Listening to an evil person, I have laced the feast with poison. I will quickly prepare some alternative, simple food.' But the Buddha responded, 'There is no problem. Serve whatever food you have prepared:

> Attachment, aversion, and ignorance
> Are the three worldly poisons.
> The victorious Buddha possesses no such poison.
> By the truth of enlightenment may poison be vanquished!

Recite this verse three times, adding both the Dharma and the Sangha, and then serve the food; there will not be any problem.' So, just as the Buddha instructed, Shrigupta recited the three verses together and served the food to everyone. The victorious Buddha ate the food serenely – like a peacock consuming deadly poison, not only was he unharmed, but he became even more radiant. With faith, the householder Shrigupta requested Dharma teachings, and in that one session he attained the eye of the Dharma that is flawless and free from defilements.

Another time, there was an extremely elderly householder named Palkye who wanted to become ordained, however the arhats told him, 'You do not have the roots of virtue for liberation through ordination', and not one of them agreed to give him the vows. The arhats were unaware of any root of virtue for the seed of liberation in Palkye's mindstream. However, when the Buddha looked, he was aware that many lifetimes ago when Palkye had taken rebirth as a dog, he was in pursuit of a pig, and it escaped in the direction of a stupa, so both animals made a circumambulation. The Buddha knew that he had that seed of virtue in his mindstream. At the time of his ordination, Palkye was one hundred years old, but he was diligent and attained the level of an arhat, becoming able to fly in the sky.

Thus, the Buddha is fully endowed with omniscient wisdom, loving compassion, and enlightened activities. From the *Seventy Verses on Taking Refuge*:

> In order to awaken from the sleep of ignorance,
> And to develop the mind of wisdom,
> The Buddha blossoms like lotus petals.

To explain a little more, why is the Buddha sometimes called the 'Victorious Accomplished Transcendent One'. Over what is he victorious? What has he accomplished? What has he transcended? The Buddha conquers all the hordes of demons who cause disruption to residing in supreme enlightenment, so he is called 'victorious'. He possesses extraordinary fortune, power, and so forth, so he is 'accomplished'. Also, he transcends all the phenomena of existence – conditioned existence, perpetuation, and so on – or alternatively, he is beyond both extremes of samsara and nirvana, therefore he is called 'transcendent'. So in this way, he is the Victorious Accomplished Transcendent One.

He is also referred to as 'Tathagata', the 'One Gone to Suchness'. 'Suchness' means: however the very nature of reality is taught, other than being just that, it is nothing else. In whichever way the Buddha spoke of suchness, in that same manner he has passed into suchness, therefore he is called the 'One Gone to Suchness'. Another epithet sometimes used to refer to the Buddha is 'arhat' meaning 'foe destroyer'. Such a being has destroyed the enemy hoard of afflictive emotions. Abandoning the two obscurations without exception, arhats maintain the four results of virtuous endeavour, so they are taught to be 'foe destroyers'.

Why is it necessary to refer to a Buddha as 'truly and completely enlightened'? In the *Exalted Hundred-thousand Stanzas* it is taught:

> The afflictive emotions that create continuity of habitual tendencies are totally eliminated in true and complete enlightenment.

Such a Buddha possesses perfect knowledge and perfect virtue – he has 'Gone to Bliss', is 'Knower of the World', the 'Charioteer Taming Beings', and 'Teacher' of all gods and humans. He has completed abandonment and realisation, and epitomises the exhaustion of all flaws and the endowment of all enlightened qualities.

The body of the One Gone to Bliss is adorned with the thirty-two excellent marks and the eighty minor marks. If the accumulated of merit of all sentient beings, all that exists in its entirety, was gathered together, it is taught it would equal the merit of a single pore of the One Gone to Bliss. The entire merit of all his pores combined together is equal to a single minor mark. The entire merit of all the minor marks combined together and multiplied by a hundred, which is already immeasurable, is equal to one of the excellent marks. What is more, it is taught that neither of the two excellent marks – the white ringlet of hair between the eyebrows nor the protuberance on the crown of the head – are included in this. Moreover, the enlightened qualities of each pore on the body of the One Gone to Bliss are unable to be expressed by ordinary beings. Such are the qualities of the body of the Buddha.

What is Buddha speech like? His enlightened speech is the essence of the truth of cessation, and the path that exists as the nature of all the teachings. Turning the wheel of Dharma, Buddha speech is the unmistaken cause to establish sentient beings on the level of enlightenment. It is supreme in every way and embodies the sixty aspects of melodious speech. In his *Praise to the Speech of the One Gone to Bliss*, Patrul Rinpoche wrote:

> A golden bee in the dirty mud;
> A lion king among the wild animals;
> The words that tame beings by any means necessary,
> Come from the speech of the Omniscient One.

Also:

> The blessings of the emanations of enlightened speech are overwhelming.
> The faculties of beings to be tamed, their aspirations, and karmic power,
> For their sake, the speech of the Victorious One is unceasing.
> I pay homage to the miraculous expression of secret speech.

The above describes the nature of the rupakaya, the base which possesses the oceanic enlightened qualities of the marks and signs, and supports the wisdom nature, the essence of enlightened mind.

What is enlightened mind like? Non-referential sky-like purity, the state of omniscient wisdom endowed with all the supreme aspects, is the nature of the dharmakaya Buddha, as mentioned above. The dharmakaya of wisdom realisation is such that it possesses the twenty-one categories of undefiled qualities. Thus, when we take refuge in the Three Jewels, the Buddha is characterised by the three kayas.

Taking Refuge

The Dharma Jewel

Following this is the second precious jewel, the jewel of the Dharma. In general, the term 'Dharma' has ten different definitions, including:

> Dharma is the path of knowledge.

The topics of merit, the path, and nirvana arising in the expressive words of excellent speech, are called the 'Dharma', which is the meaning we need to understand. What is more, these topics are included within the truth of cessation and the truth of the path. The Dharma of the truth of cessation and the Dharma of the truth of the path, explain the nature of the result of liberation and what needs to be done to attain it. Lord Maitreya taught:

> Whatever is freedom from attachment to anything whatsoever,
> Characterised by the two truths, is the Dharma.
> Freedom from attachment itself subsumes
> The truths of cessation and the path.

The Dharma that the Victorious Accomplished Transcendent One spoke includes all of the virtuous scriptures of the first, middle, and final turnings of the wheel of Dharma. It presents the absolute truth, is without affliction or interruption, teaches in detail, is meaningful to behold, and is known individually by the wise. Thus the Dharma of realisation comprises all these crucial points. For this reason, there are two classifications: looking at the meaning of the topic of discussion is called the 'Dharma of realisation', and looking at the words of expression is the 'Dharma of scripture'. Master Vasubandhu taught:

> The holy Dharma of the Teacher is two-fold,
> Incorporating scripture and realisation.

To further classify these two, depending on the subject of expression, they can be divided in terms of the two truths. From the *Root Stanzas on the Middle Way on Wisdom*:

> The Dharma that the buddhas teach
> Is wholly founded on the two truths.

The Dzogchen Path

The two truths explain things in terms of provisional meaning and definitive meaning. Teachings on relative proof contain provisional meaning, and teachings on absolute proof have definitive meaning.

Also, the Dharma can be classified by its different means of expression, known as the twelve branches of excellent speech:

> The Sutra section, melodies, prophesies,
> Verse, aphorisms, narratives,
> Realisation narratives, former events as examples,
> Narratives of former births, extensive teachings,
> Marvels, and teachings in profound doctrines –
> These are the twelve branches of excellent speech.

Additionally, in terms of the remedy, teachings are grouped into the three scriptural collections, which are classified according to the capacity of beings to be tamed, plus the scriptural collection of the vast means of vidyadharas, making four in all. Thus we take refuge in the Precious Jewel of the Dharma.

Those which become the basis for the qualities of realisation are the called the 'grounds', and these in turn are based on five 'paths'. The extensive classification of these grounds and paths is found in the scriptural collection of the bodhisattvas, and in particular, Lord Maitreya's extensive commentary on the meaning of the intent of the Buddha's teachings: *Prajnaparamita's Ornament of Manifest Realisation*, which teaches the stages of hidden meaning and manifest realisation. The scriptures of Nagarjuna and his spiritual sons teach the profound classification of emptiness, especially in the *Five Collections of Middle Way Reasonings*, *Entering the Middle Way* by Illustrious Chandrakirti, and so on.

Similarly, the swift means of the Vajrayana – the grounds and paths of Secret Mantra, the progressions of the four types of vidyadhara, and so on – pertain accordingly to each section of the vidyadhara scriptural collections. These discuss the Precious Jewel of the Dharma which incorporates scripture and realisation; so by knowing the enlightening qualities of the Dharma, the philosophical systems become known, and thereby the characteristics of that which provides refuge from samsara also becomes known.

The Sangha Jewel

The third Precious Jewel is the Sangha. Possessing the eight qualities of intelligence and liberation, the object of taking ultimate refuge is the Mahayana Sangha. Lord Maitreya taught:

Knowledge of things as they are and all that exists,
Is for the sake of seeing authentic wisdom.
The assembly of non-returning bodhisattvas
Possess the eight unexcelled qualities.

The eight qualities of knowledge and liberation are:

1) The quality of knowing things as they are.
2) The quality of knowing things in their extent.
3) The quality of knowing the realisation of inner wisdom.

These become the method for the means to attain the respective paths without obstruction.

4) The quality of liberation from the obscuration of desire which is to be abandoned.
5) The quality of liberation from the obscuration of obstruction.
6) The quality of liberation from the obscuration of inferiority.

In addition to these, the following two are added:

7) The quality of knowing the basis of differentiation.
8) The quality of liberation.

Those endowed with these eight qualities are the Sangha of non-returning arya bodhisattvas. They are the attributes of the Mahayana Sangha. In terms of the arhat and pratyekabuddha Sangha, from the perspective of knowledge and liberation they are inferior, so it is taught they are secondary.

The above teaches the outer and inner Sangha. In our tradition, the term Sangha describes all those who reside on the grounds of the bodhisattva children of the victorious ones. This includes all the dakas, dakinis, Dharma protectors, and guardians who reside on the ground of the vidyadharas, as well as realm-born, mantra-born, and spontaneously present karma and wisdom deities, and all those endowed with samsara-transcending wisdom eyes.

Definition of 'Precious Jewels'

Thus the Buddha, Dharma, and the Sangha are the Three Jewels, but what is the reason for using the term 'Precious Jewels' to refer to them? From the *Uttaratantra*:

> Their occurrence is rare, they are immaculate,
> Possess power, and are the adornment of the world;
> Supreme and unchanging,
> Thus they are the Precious Jewels.

As such, the Three Jewels are permeated by wisdom of knowledge that has no desire or impediment to any objects of knowledge, the likes of which does not exist, and like a wish-fulfilling jewel is rarely occurring. Their loving compassion does not fall into partiality and does not undergo any kind of change, so is without the defilements of disharmonious elements, and therefore 'immaculate'. The Three Jewels 'possess power' so are endowed with great capacity and strength to tame all sentient beings overwhelmed by afflictive emotions. Their enlightened qualities are the 'adornment' of all worlds, inexhaustible, sublime, and vast dharmata suchness. Because this suchness arises as activities that benefit all sentient beings, they are the supreme unchanging nature, thus they are called the rare and supreme 'Precious Jewels'.

As a matter of fact, the teacher of the path to pass beyond suffering, and the ultimate refuge from the suffering of samsara, is the Jewel of the Dharma. What is more, the teacher of the Buddha also needs to be the Dharma.

> The experience of individual self-knowing wisdom;
> I pay homage to the mother of the buddhas of the three times.

The Dharma is the mother of the Buddha. Buddha the Teacher is also the master of the Dharma, as it is taught by no one else, thus these two are like the basis and the based for each other. But, the usual sequence is to place the Buddha first, following by the Dharma, and the subsequent accomplishment of the qualities of those two produces the Sangha, so the Sangha is placed third. Additionally, although the Buddha is named 'teacher', Dharma is the 'path', and the Sangha are 'companions on the path of practice'; in terms of the meaning, the Sangha is the support for the three trainings, so we need to take refuge with this understanding.

From the *Seventy Verses on Taking Refuge*:

> The Buddha, Dharma, and Sangha
> Are refuge for those desiring liberation.

Taking Refuge

How to Take Refuge

There are two kinds of taking refuge: causal taking refuge, and resultant taking refuge. According to our tradition of Secret Mantra, causal and resultant taking refuge are explained as follows: with the wish to gain accomplishment at a future time, taking refuge in the Three Jewels which are perceived as existent in another's mindstream, is causal taking refuge with the desire to attain buddhahood. By means of the paramita vehicle, this requires waiting for the extent of three countless aeons.

Alternatively, the desire for the enlightened qualities and wisdom of the source of refuge to be born in our own mindstream in the future, is resultant taking refuge. This is taking refuge in a way that knows things to be as they really are, and does not require waiting for an extremely long time to pass.

To settle in meditative equipoise in the state of self-arising wisdom that is primordially unborn, is the ultimate resultant taking refuge taught on the Vajrayana path. For this reason, although taking refuge is the foundation stone for all paths of Buddhism, the way we take refuge at this stage is more exalted than other paths, so in this way we can also understand its inclusion in the unique preliminaries.

To speak in terms of the object of refuge, although at the stage of the paramita vehicle the Buddha is the primary refuge, in this stage of unexcelled Vajrayana, the lama takes precedence. For that reason, when we are reciting the four lines of taking refuge, the lama is placed before the Three Jewels:

> I take refuge in the lama.
> I take refuge in the Buddha.
> I take refuge in the Dharma.
> I take refuge in the Sangha.

The lama is named before the Buddha because he is the essence of all three refuges combined. This is because the great wisdom of the lama's mind is none other than, or non-dual with, the mind of all the buddhas. For this reason, the absolute refuge is the Buddha, and ultimately it is the single dharmakaya, as without relying on this, nothing will come about. Therefore the ultimate intent of all Sutra and Tantra comes down to a single point.

The *Uttaratantra* teaches:

> It is to be abandoned because it is misleading;
> They are non-existent because they are subject to disintegration.

> Thus the two aspects of Dharma and the noble assembly
> Are not the permanent refuge.

Also, the Buddha who resides without differentiation from dharmata in the ultimate Akanishtha realm of self-manifestation, abides in body as the Sangha, in speech as the Dharma, and in mind as the Buddha. Thus the nature of the three kayas of the Precious Jewels exists as a single essence. The above quotation from the *Uttaratantra* continues:

> The sole refuge is the Buddha,
> As the Sage is endowed with the dharmakaya;
> Also because that is the ultimate assembly.

From the *Accomplishment of Wisdom*:

> Mind free from purification and accomplishment is Buddha,
> Unchanging and immaculate it is Dharma, and
> With enlightened qualities spontaneously complete, is itself Sangha:
> Thus your own nature of mind is supreme.

In that case, at the stage of taking refuge, refuge is taken symbolically by relying on the liturgy, through rituals of body and speech. Not depending on rituals, meditative equipoise employing or focused on one-pointed concentration in a state of assimilated wisdom, is the ultimate taking of refuge. This is the unmistaken cause of naturally-achieved transcendent refuge.

Benefits of Taking Refuge

Now, in general terms, how much benefit is there to causal taking refuge? Just as we cannot comprehend the extent of space, similarly the extent of the benefit of having taken refuge in the Three Jewels is impossible to measure, and cannot be seen. Likewise, following the Three Jewels, we can understand in the same way it is also difficult to grasp the extent of fully-matured results of non-virtue that have been accumulated:

> Just as the extent of the boundless sky
> Cannot be measured in arm-spans,
> Similarly, following the Three Jewels,
> The extent of qualities and non-virtues cannot be measured.

Generally, if someone takes refuge in the Three Jewels they are considered to be a Buddhist. However, for a student of the Buddhist philosophical system who transforms their mind by it, taking refuge alone does not necessarily determine the difference between being Buddhist or non-Buddhist. However, for a Buddhist patron who has not transformed their mind by Buddhism, taking refuge does determine the difference between the Buddhist and non-Buddhist systems. Therefore, if you have not ever considered that you have taken the vows of refuge, or have never taken refuge from the depths of your heart, then similarly, although you are not a non-Buddhist, you are still included among the ranks of those who are not Buddhist.

My guess is about ten or twenty percent of the world's Buddhist population have not actually taken the refuge vows, and some Tibetans may also make up a large percentage of that group. This is the reason why I give the vows of refuge every day. By understanding the main point of taking refuge, take refuge in the Three Jewels. What is more, if you are someone who has not taken refuge, however many equally meritorious roots of virtue you accomplish, still you have not joined the Buddhist community. Taking refuge is the basis of all the vows, as we have mentioned:

> Anyone can take vows,
> But without taking refuge, you have none.

A place where the qualities of the Three Jewels are not expounded, and even the name of the Three Jewels is not known, is called a 'place of great blindness that the guide has abandoned'. Where the Precious Jewels do not appear is a land in darkness. But, having gone for refuge to the Three Jewels, previously accumulated non-virtue and obscurations are purified. Continue to take refuge, and we also become freed from any future hurt or harm. For all those who rely on the refuge of the Precious Jewels and follow their holy qualities, both samsaric and nirvanic abundance gathers spontaneously. In that case, whatever activity you undertake – anything that includes the Dharma, or at least is not at odds with it – if, at the beginning you make offerings of respectful honour to the Precious Jewels, then you will accomplish your wishes.

For that reason, if everyone here – male and female, from the oldest to the youngest – when you get up in the morning and go to bed at night, recite the prayer for taking refuge once or twice. Similarly, wherever you go or stay, whatever tasks or activities you undertake, by reciting the refuge prayer three times with faith and devotion to the Three Jewels, you will receive their blessings and accomplish your wishes. Things will go well, and ultimately it is certain we will accomplish together the vast objective of liberation from the suffering of samsara.

Refuge Precepts

However, it is not suitable merely to have taken refuge; we need to know the precepts of taking refuge. These are the three precepts of abandonment, the three precepts of engagement, and the three accordant precepts, making nine in all.

First, what are the three precepts of abandonment?

1) Having taken refuge in the Buddha, not taking refuge in worldly gods.
2) Having taken refuge in the Dharma, not harming sentient beings.
3) Having taken refuge in the Sangha, not associating with non-Buddhist friends.

Secondly, the three precepts of engagement are:

1) Having taken refuge in the Buddha, with faith and devotion, seeing all representations of the physical form of the One Gone to Bliss, down to even a broken piece of a tsatsa, as the actual Precious Jewel of the Buddha.
2) Having taken refuge in the Dharma, making offerings, cultivating devotion, and seeing representations of the Dharma, even down to a single letter of the teachings, as the actual Precious Jewel of the Dharma.
3) Having taken refuge in the Sangha, seeing representations of the Sangha, ordained monks and nuns, and even down to a yellow scrap of cloth, as the actual Precious Jewel of the Sangha.

We also need to train in conduct that is in accordance with the Dharma. As such, the three accordant precepts are similar to the above three precepts of engagement. Briefly, the trainings are like this. In short, in this life and future lives, the single repository of our trust and confidence is the Three Jewels. It is taught:

> Here it is possible the ground, sky, and Mt. Meru
> May change places, and the sun and moon fall to the ground,
> Yet it is impossible for the Three Jewels to mislead;
> They are firmly unequivocal, and forever meaningful.

It is possible that a planetary disaster could tilt the globe's axis and the magnetic poles could shift, or even that the moon could collide with the earth, but 'it is impossible for the Three Jewels to mislead'; thus this kind of example is taught. Taking refuge is very important, so the aim of all this talk is in order to place the seed of faith in your mindstream. Some of you may not be familiar with some of these terms, but they are necessary when we teach the Dharma, because just speaking in simple everyday language cannot always express such profound meaning. Step by step, you need to try to develop some understanding and you will learn these terms.

Some modern writers and translators of Dharma books may think they have updated a text and made it easier to understand, but often the result is like tea with only the flavour of the dregs remaining. In the *Supplication in Seven Chapters* it states: 'A sad melody like a child calling out to its parents,' but I heard that someone translated it as 'a puppy calling out to its parents.' This phrase needs to be understood as something melodious, but the howling of a puppy is not necessarily a nice sound! If interpreted incorrectly, the result can sometimes become ridiculous.

Some modern people without faith are known to pass comments implying that spiritual beliefs are only for the simple minded, or that religion is not important. But looking at this from the perspective of even just the terminology of the Buddhist scriptures, which express profound and vast meaning, such baseless assumptions are clearly made in ignorance, especially regarding the authentic words of the Buddha and their commentaries.

Our written language of Tibet is a unified system of defining terminology, specialised in conveying the Buddhist teachings authentically and accurately. For this reason, when you become familiar with the Dharma language of the higher and lesser spiritual approaches, you will reach a high level of understanding. Therefore, attend teachings whenever you can – it has great personal benefit.

TAKING REFUGE ACCORDING TO THE ROOT TEXT

Referencing the root text, the first line of the refuge prayer reads:

> In the sugatas of the Three Roots, the true Three Jewels.

In the method of taking refuge in the tradition of the common spiritual approach, the Buddha endowed with the four kayas and the five wisdoms is the teacher. The Dharma, which is characterised by scripture and realisation, is the path. The Sangha of non-regressing insight and liberation are companions on the path of accomplishment. So, taking refuge in the manner that takes the Three Jewels as escorts on the path, and desiring in the future to accomplish the three in our own mind, is taking refuge in the manner of cause and effect.

The sugatas of the Three Roots.

In the general method of the extraordinary Secret Mantra, the nature of the One Gone to Bliss – consummate abandonment and realisation – is divided into the Three Roots: lama, yidam, and dakini. We offer the three avenues of our being to the root of blessings, the nature of the embodiment of the all the buddhas: our lama. We rely on the yidam, the root of accomplishment that arises from the state of dharmakaya peace as the rupakaya of infinite peaceful and wrathful buddhas. We take the wisdom dakinis, the root of clearing obstructions, in the manner of companions who move with the power of unceasing compassion in the unborn expanse of dharmata. This is the way taking refuge in the Three Roots is taught.

The true Three Jewels.

This is resultant taking refuge, or alternatively it means the sugatas of the Three Roots are none other than the actual Three Jewels.

> In the bodhicitta nature of the channels, energies, and essences,
> In the mandala of essence, nature, and compassion,
> I take refuge until I realise the heart of enlightenment.

Reciting the 'Three Jewels' indicates the outer refuge, the 'Three Roots' indicates the inner refuge, 'nature of the channels, energies, and essences' indicates the secret refuge, and we can understand 'mandala of essence, nature, and compassion' to be the utmost secret refuge of suchness.

We have discussed the meaning of the Three Jewels of the outer refuge in some detail, but what is the inner refuge of the Three Roots like? The lama is the first of the Three Roots. He is the root of blessings revealed from the nature of the essence of the One Gone to Bliss, consummate abandonment and realisation no different from the Three Jewels. All the buddhas of the three times were liberated, and will be liberated, by relying upon the compassion and blessings of the lama. Therefore, it is taught among all meditations, meditation on the lama is supreme, and among all offerings, making offerings to the lama is supreme.

To accomplish practice of the lama, and also to make offerings, depends on devotion. As taught in the *Fifty on the Tantra Class*:

> With unwavering devotion, in six months,
> The level of Vajradhara can be achieved.

Not only that, but in the *Samvarodaya Tantra*:

> By pleasing the lama you will come to attain
> Supreme omniscient wisdom.

As this teaches, whether or not blessings arise depends on your devotion to, and practice of, the lama. All the spiritual teachers who have appeared to teach the path to beings have demonstrated various miraculous manifestations in accordance with the circumstances of the manner of taming beings to be tamed; however their essence is inseparable. For example, just as the moon is a single entity but, moving through its phases, it appears to be different sizes. In fact the one moon does not change.

To illustrate this, according to the root sadhana of *Vidyadhara Yabga* of this lineage, train in the pure perception that sees everything in the universe of appearance and possibilities as the display of the body, speech, and mind of the Great One from Oddiyana. Make supplications and merge your self-knowing awareness inseparably with the enlightened mind of Guru Rinpoche, so appearances, sounds, and awareness arise as deities, mantras, and dharmata. At all times, and on all occasions, the outer container of the world is the palace of the Glorious Copper Coloured Mountain. The world's inner contents of sentient beings are groups of heroes and dakinis. The secret is the state of knowing the emanating and absorbing of mind as self-liberating, just as a bird's flight leaves no trace in the sky. Within this state we make effort to recite the BANZA GURU essence mantra. This is taught to be the essential point of the generation stage, the distillation of the completion stage, the hidden deception of the fundamental way things are, and the knot of the direct instructions.

Therefore, whichever peaceful or wrathful form of the lama guru you visualise, there is no difference, except for the change in appearance of the activities. By changing the appearance of activities, all purposes are accomplished by the four enlightened actions. For example, the remedy to tame male and female noxious spirits, and in particular gyalgong spirits, is the manifestation of the form of the Wrathful Guru. Also for instance, the practice of Wrathful Hayagaru is to tame the nagas, whereby one's body is visualised as the Wrathful Guru, speech as

Hayagriva, and mind as Garuda. These forms that tame are shown merely for the benefit of those to be tamed. In terms of Wrathful Hayagaru, Guru Dorje Drollo is praised as supreme to tame elemental spirits, which is another way in which the appearance of his form changes. Thus, it is also suitable to take the Wrathful Guru as the root deity, Hayagriva as the Lord of the Family, and Garuda in the manner of an adornment.

For the guru in the manner of the vidyadhara accomplisher, when the accomplisher practitioner has reached the essence of what is to be accomplished, what is accomplished itself arises in the form of the accomplisher. In fact, the accomplisher and what is accomplished are not different. For example, if the form of what is to be accomplished is like the heat of the sun's rays, then the manner of the accomplisher is like a crystal jewel. By bringing these two together, this wrathful practice is like magnifying the sun's rays with a crystal to burn the dry grass chaff of malevolent, obstructing, and elemental spirits, and is sharp, swift, and especially exalted.

In terms of the yidam, as for the Gathering of Wrathful Herukas, the eight sadhana practices of Foremost Heruka are united into the one Lord. All the stages for the practice of this mandala are accomplished in connection with the modes of method and wisdom, so the two tremendous accumulations subsumed by the six transcendent perfections are swiftly reconciled. The practitioner unites with the levels of the three vidyadharas of learning and the vidyadharas of the path of no-more learning – the vidyadharas of spontaneous accomplishment endowed with the three kayas and the seven aspects.

Whichever peaceful or wrathful yidam you approach with the four aspects of approach and accomplishment – approach, close approach, accomplishment, and great accomplishment – it is very important not to part from the key points of the direct instructions on the four nails to bind the life-force. When you practise the yidam, invite the countless yidam deities, and meditate that you are the embodiment of all of them. If you meditate that the single yidam embodies all the yidam deities entirely, then it is taught by having a vision of all the deities, accomplishments will come about.

In short, whichever the yidam, in accordance with the methods of taming beings to be tamed, there are manifold displays of enlightened body – peaceful and wrathful, powerful and elaborate – however their essence is entirely subsumed without exception in the single lama. Therefore, in the expanse of wisdom unity, the pervaded object: the mandalas of the yidam, does not transcend the embracing pervader: the Lord of the Family, the lama himself. In this way, we must understand all the mandalas of the yidam to be the manifest display of the lama.

Taking Refuge

Similarly, in terms of the dakini, all of the activity and wisdom dakinis are included within the five families of dakinis. So, for instance Yumka is the Queen of Great Bliss of the Lotus Family of Speech, and Jetsun Arya Tara is the universal empress of all of the Activity Family of Enlightened Activities. Also there are the Lion-faced Dakini, the Secret Wisdom Dakini, the Accomplishment of Sun and Moon Dakini, and so on. There are no others except for these. For that reason, in each revealed treasure, these sadhana cycles appear: the Queen of Great Bliss is for outer accomplishments, the Twenty-one Taras are for inner accomplishments, and the Lion-faced One is for secret accomplishments. This means they are not separate from the mother of the mandala of Avalokiteshvara – the six-syllable mantra – royal mother's vast magical display.

Lady Kharchen from the land of Tibet; Yeshe Tsogyal, Chief of the Dakinis from the land of Oddiyana; All-mighty Queen of Great Bliss from the Glorious Mountain's Palace of Lotus Light; Blazing Blue Light, Queen of the Rakshasas: these are one enlightened form with synonymous names, thus it makes no difference whoever you speak of.

In summary, in the *Glorious Mala* sadhana, when it says:

Ananistha Realm and Khechara Realm...

This refers to Samantabhadri, principal deity of the hundred families of the peaceful and wrathful deities, who dwells in Ananistha dharmadhatu, and to principal deity Vajravarahi, who is the basis of emanation of all the yoginis of the sacred places of Khechara sambhogakaya realm, the emanated enjoyment realms, and so on; and in terms of Tibet, Yeshe Tsogyal who was born in Central Tibet. These are emanations and the basis of emanations, and so apply to the designations of the three kayas. These kinds of inconceivable dakinis of the three places are all subsumed in the lama, the embodiment of the inseparable Three Roots.

What is the definition of 'dakini' or 'sky-farer'? The inner expanse of Dharma or dharmadhatu, transcending elaboration, is the ultimate sky. That expanse is made manifest by the expressivity of the enlightened realisation of dharmata, so the meaning of dakini is to travel to the sky of dharmata, thus 'sky-farer'. Again, there is no 'dakini' besides that subsumed in the lama.

Whichever Three Roots you visualise and practise, at the time of visualising the display of enlightened form, it is manifest yet without inherent nature, luminosity yet without conceptualisation, blissful yet without attachment. Thus endowed with these three characteristics, it is the natural radiance of emptiness. From this unimpeded state of vivid manifestation, whichever recitations and so on, you practice, all are very potent. If you know how to integrate onto the path self-liberated genuine manifestation of the natural radiance of deities and mantras, in a state without any deliberate effort, you will travel the excellent path.

Thus the above discusses the meaning of:

> In the sugatas of the Three Roots, the true Three Jewels...

This is connected with outer and inner refuge. Following this, we recite:

> In the bodhicitta nature of the channels, energies, and essences.

In dependence on the coarse causal channels, essences, and energies, the subtle wisdom channels, essences, and energies are made evident. This is the supreme method of the extraordinary key point of the vajra essence stage of completion, and is taught in terms of three aspects:

1) The channels reside.
2) The energies move.
3) The essences pervade.

First, that which is unchanging resides without movement, so it is taught 'the channels reside'. In the channels, the energies are present in a manner of the support and the supported. The function of the energies is to move and shift, and so are the mount of the consciousness. The entire three realms are formed by the energies, so for that reason it is taught that 'the energies move'. That which depends on both the channels and energies is the 'pervading bodhicitta' – the essences.

In terms of the channels, the 'three channels and five chakras' are well known. The three main channels are the central, rasana, and lalana. The central channel houses the life force. The upper end connects with the crown, where the pure essence obtained from the father resides in the nature of a white HUM syllable. The lower end connects with the secret place, where the red element obtained from the mother resides in the manner of a short AH syllable. The right white rasana channel functions to give rise to the body and essences, and expel and retain blood and waste. The left red lalana channel functions to give rise to the speech and blood, and to remove and retain waste fluid. Here the formation of the channels is described in terms of males; for females the rasana and lalana are arranged in the opposite way.

In terms of the central channel, it can be called the 'middle of the body', located between the rasana and lalana channels in the middle. To speak in terms of the nature of phenomena, as it is free from the extremes of existent and non-existent, it is the nature of non-dual bliss and emptiness, so it is taught to be the 'middle way'. If rasana is left naturally, it is unable to perform any function, like a corpse. If by interdependence the key points are applied, this channel has the nature of bliss, and can experience the characteristics of things, in a way not unlike experiencing the taste of food. Thus it is taught to be called 'rasana' or 'taste'.

If lalana is left naturally, it does not mix with anything else, remaining alone, so it is taught to be 'lalana' or 'alone'. Relying on the direct instructions of the lineage, this channel has the essence of emptiness, and is producer of the experience of the nature of phenomena free of thought. As it does not possess the attributes of conceptualisation, again it is called 'lalana' or 'alone'. In this way, these three channels are the progenitors of all the other channels, so that is the reason in Tibetan their names – 'dbu ma', 'kyang ma', and 'ro ma' – all have the 'ma' letter for 'mother' added.

In reliance on these three channels, if one knows how to apply the key points, and if one is skilled in the activities of the essences, based on rasana the body's karma becomes exhausted; desire for food is cut, and one lives on the nourishment of meditative concentration. Based on lalana, if one is skilled in the key points of the channels, karma of the speech is purified, desire for clothing is cut, and one is warmed by the robes of yogic inner heat. In particular, if one is skilled at applying the key points of the central channel, in its essence the ultimate central channel possesses the nature of empty, transparent light. So, if one is skilled in the key points of its energies, karma of the mind can be exhausted, desire for meditation is purified, and the continuum of dreams is cut. Ultimately, one is able to experience the truth of dharmata luminosity non-residing in the two extremes, so again it is taught to be called 'central'. The three channels are understood like this.

Then there are the 'five chakras', which are generally taught to be:

1) Crown chakra of great bliss.
2) Throat chakra of enjoyment.
3) Dharmachakra at the heart.
4) Navel chakra of emanation.
5) Secret place chakra of sustaining bliss.

In addition to these, two more are added:

6) Liberation juncture chakra of blaze-causing wind.
7) Tri-juncture chakra of blazing fire.

There are also alternative traditions which teach the 'crown protrusion chakra of space', and so on, but at this stage, in the context of Dzogpa

Chenpo, we chiefly apply the key points of four chakra channels. Of these, the crown chakra of great bliss has thirty-two branch channels, the throat chakra of enjoyment has sixty branch channels, the dharmachakra at the heart has eight branch channels, and the navel chakra of emanation has sixty-four branch channels. Additionally, surrounding them, they each have seventy-two thousand smaller channels, and so on. In summary, all areas of the body are connected by a network of channels.

Secondly, regarding the energies that move, within the seventy-two thousand channels, the individual movement of the energies comes about. This is defined by means of two divisions: large movements and small movements. For a healthy person over the period of one day, twenty-four hours, the breath moves twenty-one thousand six hundred times. This is the energy of large movements. As for small movements, this is the movement of the energies together with the eighty-four thousand principal afflictive emotions of discursive thoughts. This is not the energy or wind that moves from the mouth or nose, this is the energy moving within the pulsing blood vessels, which is the basis of thoughts and wisdom. It is also taught that in the chakra of enjoyment, there are one-hundred and twenty-one thousand energies of small movement, all of which move. However, in terms of the main functions, there are the five principal energies:

1) Life-holding energy.
2) Fire-equalising energy.
3) Pervading energy.
4) Upward-moving energy.
5) Downward-clearing energy.

Of these, the life-holding energy maintains the life force at the heart centre. The fire-equalising energy brings warmth and digests food in the navel centre. The pervading energy resides throughout the body and functions to regulate it. The upward-moving energy resides in the upper body and powers the inhalation and exhalation of breath. The downward-clearing energy resides in the lower body and powers movement and expulsion of waste. Other than that, there is much to say about the specific details of the energies: the five outer elements, five inner elements, and so forth. However, to group these together into three categories, there are male, female, and gender neutral energies:

- The male energy moves from the right nostril.
- The female energy moves from the left nostril.
- The gender neutral energy moves equally from the two.

It is taught in the guidance instructions that if one trains the energies – chiefly the male energy for men, the female energy for women, and the gender neutral energy for both sexes – it is easy for the five wisdom energies to arise. Regarding this, there are many key points of instruction, such as relying on the upward-moving energy and the downward-clearing energy together in the key points of the three places. This requires the upper wind energy to be pressed down, the lower wind energy to be gathered, and the middle wind energy to be retained. Or alternatively, there is expelling the wind energy like an arrow, drawing the wind energy like a bow, and retaining the wind energy like a vase, and so forth. However, this is not the occasion to explain them in any further detail.

In summary, there are two types of energy:

1) Karmic energy.
2) Wisdom energy.

As the karmic energy is purified, wisdom energy gathers in the expanse, at which time the uncommon level of enlightenment and resultant enlightened qualities are attained.

Thirdly, the essences are called the 'arrayed bodhicitta'. Of the two major essence elements – white and red – the white element is the nature of the moon, a HUM syllable at the crown, and the red element is the nature of the sun, an AH syllable at the secret place. From here they flow, traversing the paths of the rasana and lalana. From these two, in individual channels which directly spread into the common branch channels, these two reside as the very nature of heroes and Vajrayogini, whereby at the stage of meditation on peace and bliss yoga, they accept offerings of bliss and emptiness.

As the channels, energies, and essences have the nature of support and supported, to reach the essential point of the channels, the key point of the body is most important. To reach the essential point of the energies, yantra is most important. To reach the key point of the essences, diligence is very important. In this way, by relying on the key points of the channels, energies, and essences, in the central channel, when the twenty-one knots of the rasana and lalana are untied two-by-two, each one of the ten grounds is traversed. Moreover, it is taught, when the final twenty-one channels are released at the supreme peak level of the crown prominence, Vajradhara is accomplished.

All-knowing Jigme Lingpa taught:

> Thus the body is the basis of great wisdom.
> Even in samsara, the way essence resides

> Becomes neither impaired nor inferior.
> Bodhicitta ultimate and unchanging
> Pervades it, just like oil in sesame.

When we recite in the root text, 'In the bodhicitta nature of the channels, energies, and essences', with regard to bodhicitta, the Dzogchen Mind Section refers to it as 'bodhicitta' or 'enlightened mind'. In the context of the Space Section and elsewhere, it is referred to as 'dharmadhatu', and in the Direct Instruction Section it is taught to be 'self-arising wisdom'. All of these have the same meaning.

According to the meaning of the above quote from All-knowing Jigme Lingpa, when he says 'bodhicitta ultimate and unchanging', the nature of mind itself – vast pervading luminosity – pervades all sentient beings, from an insect on a blade of grass upwards. For this reason, even in the context of samsara, it does not change from our very essence. It is buddha nature, sublime mind, luminosity wisdom. Therefore, this is the object of secret refuge. Thus, the root text teaches the meaning of taking refuge in the basis of the channels, energies, and essences – vast wisdom that resides in the body – rigpa bodhicitta.

Regarding the meaning of:

> In the mandala of essence, nature, and compassion,
> I take refuge until I realise the heart of enlightenment.

This refers to rigpa bodhicitta, vast wisdom that resides in the body primordially free of change, arising, and ceasing. To grasp the characteristics of this, to express a fraction of its wisdom nature in words, we say it exhibits three attributes:

1) Empty essence.
2) Luminosity nature.
3) Unobstructed compassion.

These three are complete in the one rigpa wisdom. However to speak generally, there is something called 'emptiness endowed with rigpa essence'. This is rigpa before is has arisen from the ground, the essence of emptiness. As its expressive radiance shines, luminous radiance of inner luminosity shines. This, not lost upon the expressivity of dualistic perception, is luminosity endowed with rigpa essence, the luminosity nature. This, lost upon expressivity needs to be called 'unobstructed compassion', however this can be explained in more detail. Rigpa compassion is actually non-grasping, but all the ways in which it arises as rays of light are called the 'compassionate expressivity of rigpa'.

Accompanied by the grasping aspect of discursive thoughts, and arising upon an object, is taught to be called 'outer luminosity'. Not arising upon an object is 'inner luminosity'. But, except for these mere placeholders mentioned as an aside, this is not the time to discuss some of the hidden meaning of the main practice.

This nature of rigpa emptiness, primordially pure wisdom, spontaneously uncompounded undifferentiated ground and result, is unobstructed freedom from grasping, the ultimate mandala of great inseparability of the three attributes. To accomplish this in our mindstream, it is taught we 'take refuge' in the manner of a recitation, until a time when we attain supreme enlightenment. This is taught to be the ultimate undeceiving vajra refuge of the fundamental nature.

How to Visualise the Field of Merit

We have discussed the outer, inner, and secret refuge, together with the supremely secret vajra refuge of the fundamental nature. Now, in connection with refuge, we need to visualise the refuge field of merit. Generally, when we practise the Dharma, we need to engage in sessions of practice, and each session needs to have the following three stages:

1) Preliminaries.
2) Main practice.
3) Conclusion.

Moreover, the preliminaries of each session need to have the following four complete:

1) Adjusting the key points of physical posture.
2) Adjusting the key points of the speech.
3) Adjusting the key points of the mind.
4) Prayers.

In terms of a session of refuge practice, at the stage of the main practice, we visualise the refuge field of merit and, following the words of the recital text, recall their meaning. The conclusion is then sealed by completely pure dedication and prayers of aspiration. Each time we engage in a practice session, these three stages are necessary.

Among all the bodhisattva activities of completion, maturation, and cultivation, visualising the field of merit is connected with the cultivation of a pure realm. The way to visualise is as follows: this place where we dwell is not an ordinary impure place, here the entire ground is chequered with various jewelled patterns. Visualise that it is smooth without hills or valleys, mounds or troughs, or any unevenness. Directly in front of us, situated a short distance away, is the five-branched trunk of the wish-fulfilling tree. It is composed of all sorts of precious materials, with an abundance of leaves, flowers, and fruit, and adorned with hanging jewels, bells, and golden latticework. Visualise that the branches extend out to the ten directions, filling the entire space of the sky in its immensity.

In the middle of the five branches is the central branch, upon which are huge lions – one each in the four cardinal directions and four in the intermediate directions, making eight. With their hind legs they are standing on the central branch, and facing forwards, using both their front legs and their heads, they raise aloft a throne. Upon this precious throne rests a lotus flower of multitudinous colours – white, yellow, red, green, blue, and so on – with sun and moon cushions, the same size as the lotus flower's pollen bed, stacked upon it. Upon this, we need to visualise the form of the buddha, which in essence is the embodiment of all the buddhas of the three times – our own kind root lama. In appearance, he is the Vajradhara of Oddiyana together with his consort. Meditate that he is facing you.

The Great Master from Oddiyana has a white complexion with a red tinge, one face, two arms, and he is sitting with his right leg in the posture of a revelling king. His right hand holds a five-pronged vajra held aloft towards the sky. His left hand is in meditation mudra, and in it rests a skull cup together with an ornamented life vase, filled with deathless wisdom nectar. He is wearing robes of the King of Zahor: a brocade cloak, long-sleeved gown, and so on, over which he wears a red Dharma robe with golden designs. Upon his head is the lotus crown which liberates on sight. Visualise him in union with his consort, white Tsogyal, who is holding a skull cup and curved blade. This visualisation is not of a material appearance, so we should meditate on an empty form, a mass of light, with a life force of wisdom. Indeed, we recite 'a body of light with an essence of wisdom', so we should visualise like that.

In the space above Guru Rinpoche's crown, visualise the lamas of the Dzogchen lineage one above another, the throne of the upper one almost touching the head of the one below, as if in layers. Above all of them, visualise dharmakaya Samantabhadra with a blue complexion. The consort of blue-bodied dharmakaya Samantabhadra is Samantabhadri, who is light blue in colour. Both are naked, cross-legged, with both hands in the mudra of meditation. Male and female archetypes in union, they are radiant with the major and minor marks. Below them is sambhogakaya Vajrasattva, his complexion beautifully white, sitting cross-legged, holding a vajra and bell, and in union with his consort. Visualise both of them adorned with the sambhogakaya ornaments.

Below them is nirmanakaya Garab Dorje, radiantly white in colour. His legs are crossed, and in his hands he holds a vajra and bell at his heart, in the crossed mudra position. Visualise him in the customary attire of a monastic. Below him is Master Manjushrimitra, orange in colour, with the accoutrements of Heruka. Visualise he is holding in his right hand a damaru drum, and in his left a skull cup. Below him is Guru Shri Singha, white in colour with a 'dark complexion', as is taught in the texts. Visualise he has the accoutrements of Heruka, his right hand points skyward in the threatening pointer mudra, and his left holds a skull cup full of nectar. Below him is the learned Jnanasutra, who is white with a reddish tinge. His legs are crossed, and his hands are in the meditation mudra, upon which he holds a scripture. Visualise him as having the attire of a monastic, and the hat of a pandita upon his head.

Below him, we visualise the Great Pandita Vimalamitra as yellowish-green in colour. His legs are crossed, and his hands are in the meditation posture, upon which he holds a skull cup full with wisdom nectar of immortality. He wears the robes of a monk, and on his head is the hat of a pandita. Below him, visualise Padmasambhava of Oddiyana in the attire of the King of Zahor, as described above. On his right is the Dharma King Trisong Deutsen, on his left is the Great Translator Vairochana, and in front is the Dakini Yeshe Tsogyal. These are the three: lord, subject, and partner. Visualise like this.

Below them, visualise All-knowing Longchen Rabjam, fair and radiant, sitting cross-legged. His hands are placed in the manner of Dzogchen taking ease in the nature of mind. He wears monk's attire and the hat of a pandita. Below him is Vidyadhara Jigme Lingpa, white with a reddish tinge, cross-legged, and wearing the white robes of a mantrin. His hair is tied in a topknot ornamented with a volume of scripture. His right hand is in the mudra of supreme generosity, and his left hand is stretched out on the cushion beside his hip. Below him are our own lineage lamas: Jigme Gyalwe Nyugu in customary monk's attire, Migyur Namkhi Dorje, Orgyen Tenzin Norbu, and Dharma Lord Shenpen Nunwa.

Below them, visualise Jigme Yonten Gonpo with a white complexion tinged with red and a moustache, as he really was, in the saffron robes of an ordained monk. He is cross-legged, with both hands in the posture of taking ease in the nature of mind. Below him, visualise whichever lamas from whom you yourself have received direct instructions, teachings, and guidance, and whoever you have a karmic connection with. In this way, surrounding the visualised lamas of the lineage, are the panditas and siddhas of India, and the Tibetan lamas of the new and old schools with which you have a Dharma connection. They, in turn, are surrounded by an inconceivable gathering of yidam deities of the four classes of tantra, heroes, and dakinis. Meditate on the field of merit like this.

In particular, in this lineage of the Heart Essence of the Great Expanse, the chief yidam is the gathering of Herukas, with a retinue of blood-drinkers of the four families. We should chiefly visualise the hosts of deities that are associated with the main outer, inner, and secret practices: Hayagriva Enjoying the Three Realms, Yama Lord of Death Overwhelming with Splendour, Kilaya Overwhelming with Splendour the Mara Hordes, Vishuddha Unity of the Buddhas, and the Dakini Queen of Great Bliss. These days, the field of merit of our lineage is illustrated like that.

On the front branch of the wish-fulfilling tree is the unequalled teacher, Lord of the Shakyas, surrounded by the buddhas of the ten directions and three times, all of them nirmanakayas in the attire of pure conduct. Their bodies are white, yellow, red, green, and blue, and they radiate lights and rays. Upon the right branch, are the bodhisattva lords of the three families, chief of the eight main bodhisattvas of the bodhisattva Arya Sangha, who are variously coloured and surround them. Visualise them adorned with the thirteen ornaments of the sambhogakaya, and in a standing posture with their feet together.

On the left branch, we need to visualise chiefly the Supreme Pair of Shravakas, surrounded by the Arya Sangha of shravakas and pratyekabuddhas. They are all white in colour and wear the three Dharma robes. In their hands they hold a khahhira staff and alms bowl, and are in a standing position. Following this, on the rear branch of the tree is the Jewel of the Dharma in the form of the scriptures of excellent speech, stacked up within a latticework of light, with their titles facing towards us. On top, are the six hundred and forty thousand volumes of the Dzogpa Chenpo tantras, resounding continuously the intrinsic sound of the ALI KALI, and so on.

Between these branches are the wisdom and karmically-established glorious protectors, protectors of the Dharma, and guardians in general, specifically the chief guardians of the Heart Essence lineage: Ekajati, Rahula, and Vajrasadhu. All males face outwards, acting to prevent all outer opposing conditions from coming in. All females face inwards, to prevent inner accomplishments from getting out. In this way, visualise all the objects of refuge present as guiding leaders, showing tremendous compassion towards us with the three enlightened qualities of wisdom, loving kindness, and power.

We stand upon the surface of the ground, together with our parents, as well as both enemies and obstacle makers, chief among all sentient beings together. With hands together and great devotion of the three doors, think 'From now until attaining enlightenment, my lama and the Precious Jewels, heed me! I am depending on you all, and offer myself to you. I have no other refuge or hope except you! Whatever happens, success or failure, happiness or misery, good or bad, positive or negative, you know best!' Usually, whenever we recite the refuge prayer, we should do so three times with this kind of feeling.

Thus, with fierce devotion from the depth of our heart, recite:

> In the sugatas of the Three Roots, the true Three Jewels,
> In the bodhicitta nature of the channels, energies, and essences,
> In the mandala of essence, nature, and compassion,
> I take refuge until I realise the heart of enlightenment.

In this way we need to accumulate one-hundred thousand recitations of taking refuge. When it comes to finish a practice session, on the basis of our devotion, rays of light shine from the bodies of the gathered deities of the object of refuge. These touch us and all sentient beings who, like a hundred birds startled by a slingshot, dissolve into the object of refuge. They in turn dissolve into the central unity of all three refuges, the lama. Our lama then melts into light, and we rest in meditative equipoise, dharmakaya beyond elaboration – indescribable, inconceivable, and inexpressible – in a state of primordial abiding, free from proliferation and subsiding of ordinary discursive thoughts. This is the refuge of the ultimate abiding nature.

Then, arising from this meditative equipoise, in post meditation, visualise the field of merit as before. Not separating from this state, we dedicate chiefly the merit of this practice session, as well as all our gathered merit and that of others, for the benefit of sky-like sentient beings:

> By this merit, may I swiftly
> Come to achieve all Three Jewels,
> So that not even one wandering being remains;
> May they be established on their level.

Thus, we ornament the end of our practice session with this dedication and aspiration. At all times and in all situations, in a state that is never without mindfulness, alertness, and carefulness, we must never separate from the vivid perception of the gathered deities of refuge. For an ordinary person to awaken to buddhahood, although they may not know much, to practise the recital text of the preliminaries together with guru yoga is enough. Whatever the case, the practice and benefits of taking refuge are as discussed above.

We listen to Dharma teachings in order to receive blessings of the lineage and to gain unmistaken understanding of their meaning. But, having heard them, if we just return home without giving them any consideration or importance in our lives, then this does not achieve the purpose. That would be leaving the teachings in the teaching hall. In order to avoid this happening, we should take this scripture of the recital text as a foundation, and see if we can understand the meaning behind the words. When we do come to some understanding, then we need to apply that to our mindstream. By doing so, if you feel that the ways in which you relate to renunciation and accept the teachings have improved, and thus you gain some benefit, then the purpose of receiving teachings has been achieved.

The above teaches the meaning of the four lines of taking refuge:

> In the sugatas of the Three Roots, the true Three Jewels,
> In the bodhicitta nature of the channels, energies, and essences,
> In the mandala of essence, nature, and compassion,
> I take refuge until I realise the heart of enlightenment.

Teaching Day Six

In order to establish all mother-like sentient beings, as infinite as space, in everlasting bliss at the level of complete buddhahood, we need to listen to the holy and profound Dharma and practise its meaning appropriately. Do not let practice become lost under the influence of the demons of procrastination or laziness. When we do not compete with the Lord of Death to see who can act the most swiftly, then we are bound to succumb to his deception. Up to now he has deceived many. How many who thought they were both young and beautiful, have been snatched away without any time for happiness? How many who wished for power and riches, before having time to amass them, were carried off to the charnel ground? There is no powerful force who can command us not to go, and no one can be found to listen to our insignificant and humble pleas.

Without abandoning the teachings in favour of Dharma-platitudes, we need to practise the authentic Dharma. Not leaving it to next year, but doing so this year; not putting it off to tomorrow, but practising today. Even today, between morning and afternoon, we must embrace the morning, otherwise when we look back at our lives, how many years will have been wasted? At New Year we celebrate, happy and delighted, but in truth another year of our lives has ended, so it might be more fitting to be miserable and sad. Not knowing if death will come that year, many begin a new year with celebration, but before the year is out they have moved on.

If someone with clairvoyance were to witness this, it would appear ridiculous. For someone with certainty in the fundamental illusory nature of impermanence, observing this situation, whoever they saw would become an object of pity and compassion. Moreover, it is taught that the measure of the extent to which someone has developed immeasurable compassion, is that whenever they see sentient beings, they shed tears. However, even for the likes of us who have not developed compassion, if we really think about it, the suffering that befalls even just one person is heart-breaking. For example, the suffering that a parent feels when their child dies, or their own physical suffering of pain, disease, and the suffering of death. This is without even mentioning other tormented living creatures.

What we call 'death' is like falling down a steep crevasse of inner mental suffering. Those we cherish in our hearts, who we leave behind, also experience the attached mental suffering of the living. Without the Dharma of death, when beings journey in the bardo they will experience suffering without refuge or protector. To think of them, to whoever sees them, they are the object of pity and compassion. Although there is no way to take away the suffering of others, if there was, and my own death could be substituted for theirs, then why not make mine useful? Anyway I need to die at some point. This kind of meagre renunciation sometimes arises in my heart.

Therefore, whichever samsaric being we observe, ourselves or others, each one is more unhappy than the next, experiencing only misery; all are objects of compassion. However, since we are born as humans in Tibet, this land of Dharma, whatever our circumstances, we are not like those born in an uncivilised place. And we should not be the same; we are those destined to be tamed by Arya Avalokiteshvara. From the time we were small, nestling in our mother's lap, we learned how to say 'mama' and 'mani' at the same time. Of course we are those chiefly to be tamed by Avalokiteshvara: if we look to our origins, to the source of our flesh and blood, having descended from the Great Father Old Monkey King, can we not say that we are included within the lineage family of Avalokiteshvara?

However, looking at the way in which our jealously and anger is extremely fierce, the way our pride and attachment is as strong as it could be, it is permissible to say that we take after Mother Rock Ogress. Yet our ancestors had compassion for sentient beings, were wise, and far-sighted. Unlike us, who pass the days and seasons pursuing pointless activities, they did not waste their valuable human lives for the sake of something trivial. Undertaking hardship and disregarding all exhaustion, they brought the holy Dharma, which has the happiness of sentient beings at its root, here to our homeland.

The founding of a script and culture, the precious Dharma and the traditional systems that these masters established here, is so valuable and extensive that each individual word and meaning could not be bought, even with gold beyond measure. The masters have left so many scriptures that if someone wanted to read them all once in their lifetime, they could not. Not only is there this scriptural tradition, but there are its traditions of instruction and teaching, including the instructional direct teachings on the way these are to be put into practice. Thus, given that such precious teachings are within our grasp, birth at a time when the Dharma has not disappeared but still remains, is merit heaped upon merit. Even taking rebirth as the ruler of the gods – Indra of a Hundred Sacrifices – one hundred times could not rival this.

In fact, previously we have been reborn as the ruler of the gods many times, but it does not mean that we will no longer need to experience the heat or cold of the hells. As it is said:

> Brahma himself, having achieved bliss free from attachment,

Teaching Day Six

Will become fuel for the fires of the Hell of Ultimate Torment.

Having attained this human physical basis complete with the freedoms and endowments, when we are able to practise some of these profound teachings, we do not need to wander in samsara in the future, but can attain the level of everlasting happiness. Considering this, it is hard to believe our fortune, as the sun of joyfulness rises above our heads and shines down upon us.

However, if we do not recognise our fortune and cannot unravel its meaning, if we reflect on how we do not understand and remain oblivious to the truth, we become ashamed of ourselves and embarrassed in front of the holy ones. Or we are just like a poor person who, unaware their hearth is made of gold, leaves it at home and goes begging for a few scraps of food. In our delusion, we cast aside the most effective methods we have in our possession to accumulate merit and accomplish happiness, both for now and the future, and embrace meaningless exhausting work and miserly insignificant tasks, considering such worthless things as being very important. This is like a Dharma-wheel turning monarch abandoning his status to move into the house of a pauper.

Therefore, take a look at the faults of the negative degenerate time: we have no understanding of ourselves; we do not control our own mindstreams and are rotten with laziness. Looking at the state of our own minds, not knowing when we will have to depart, when we consider preparation and provision for our future lives, that which is most useful and beneficial is the holy Dharma. Except for this, even if we were to circle the globe nine times in our search, we could not find anything better. So look at ourselves: we are forever making preparations just for this life, saying we have no time. Those of you who manage to attend seven or eight days of Dharma teachings are few. Some do not even make time to attend one complete day. A few are never free, and have not come at all. Having no time can certainly be included in one of the eight unfree states.

What is more, if you asked me to teach for an extended time, even I would eventually say I do not have enough time. Therefore, in short, there is nothing more important to work at or achieve than accomplishment of the Dharma. Leaving practice of the genuine Dharma becomes 'leaving the trunk in search of the branches'. By leaving behind the true teachings – the study and practice of the Dharma – its supplementary aspects of religious and secular honour become our way of life, whether they are included in the true Dharma or not. We try to perpetuate these mundane concerns, but they are just worn out attachments to former bygone customs. This produces a meaningless result, just like bathing in unclean waters. Like a Brahmin who protects their father's lineage or a wooden millstone, we just go through the motions. The reason this happens is that, while we understand our actions, we are driven by an irreversibly strong karmic force.

How many have the confidence to assume they still have one hundred years of life remaining, and make great plans for their future, only to die in an unexpected place? Of course we do not know how long we have remaining. How many people of high status take their own lives because of their position? How many wealthy people, while busy saving and earning money, have had their life end? How many children turn against their parents, becoming unprovoked enemies? Thus we wield the hammer, only to suffer the blows ourselves!

In this case, is there any essence to worldly phenomena? For this reason, meditate on impermanence – focus not on words but on meaning. All the things we watch and observe are examples of illusion; all things we hear and encounter are teachers of impermanence; all things we recall and consider become examples of meaninglessness. Although we may achieve great fame and renown, this is not reliable for very long, and disappears like a rainbow. Many of the chief offices of assembly end up empty, becoming footnotes in the tales of history. Many business people lives' earnings end up being squandered by others. Therefore, all worldly pursuits are meaningless; we are deceiving ourselves.

Regardless of what action we undertake, it is rare for us to obtain everything we want. Even if we do manage to achieve one of our goals, at no point will our desire become sated. If we gain one, we always want a hundred; gain a hundred and we want ten thousand. Just like King Mandata, however much he had, his desire grew that much greater. His characteristic was that his desire was insatiable; just as if we were to drink salt water, our thirst would never be quenched. In the same way, concerning worldly activities, there are no examples of working and fully accomplishing everything, or of finishing work with everything complete. Only when activities are relinquished, at that time do they finish. Until then there is no end. Worldly activities are like ripples on water, one following after another. Therefore, now it is time to abandon this never-ending weariness and practise the Dharma.

However, for some people their concern is their family: 'However I end up, that's fine, but those I leave behind, my children and family, they won't survive when I'm not around.' They think their dependents will be completely helpless without them. Your family may say that if you were not around, there is no way they could remain either, as if they would commit suicide, but that is unlikely. The very next day, they are sure to search for a better means of living – that is where your family will turn their thoughts. Thinking we are acting for the benefit of our family, we accumulate mountains of non-virtue, but this has no other place to settle except upon our own heads. There is not a single person who will come to help share the load of our non-virtues. As the fully ripened result of non-virtue, if we must experience the suffering of the lower realms, if we cannot currently bear the pain of even a spark from the fire, how are we to endure unbearable hell-fire?

It is taught:

> Without devotion, to meet the lama in the bardo would be amazing!

At the time we are in the bardo, it is not that deities or lamas have no compassion for us, but from our perspective we do not have the strength of devotion or faith to see them. So, for those without the fortune to be guided, it is hard for the buddhas to appear. If we do not want to swap happiness for suffering, then there is the need to practise the basis for happiness: the Dharma.

It is said:

> When the three: people, dogs, and shoes are of use,
> Many feign holding them dear, but there is no authenticity.

When it comes to thinking that people or dogs are of use, then even if they do not really value them, many pretend to do so. Placing their own selfish desires first, it is not us that they hold dear; such people hold themselves dear. As it is said:

> The deceptive speak pleasingly
> Out of selfish desire, not respect.

In the past, a Tibetan nomad visited a Chinese city and came back saying, 'On my right, strangers called me to eat. Others beckoned me from the left to drink, all of them so friendly, like they were close family friends!' But those shopkeepers did not hold the nomad dear, they held dear the money in his pocket. Having arrived at this degenerate time, when people do not have anything to gain, no one holds anything dear. Old people, old horses, and old dogs receive nothing but disparagement. They are considered to be nothing more than excess baggage, like a toothless old dog left behind in a nomad's abandoned campsite. In this case, do not place much hope in anyone; your hopes will become dashed. There is no better hope than the Dharma. So, with the textual tradition of scholars to answer our questions, and the instructional teachings of the lama, our understanding and familiarity will get better and better.

When we touch the pulse of the key points, then the benefit becomes increasingly strong.

Until now we have been lost, because there has not been someone strong beside us to pull us up. If suddenly the terrifying hell realms were to appear in front of us, it is certain there will be no one beside us to protect us. Thinking 'What can I do?' if we, ourselves, do not practise the Dharma which is so beneficial, if up to now there has been no one who knows how to pull us up by the hands, from where are they going to suddenly appear?

Similarly, however much we comply with our friends' wishes, at no point do they become satisfied. They may appear contented at first, but there is no way to satisfy them all the time. Very quickly they act as if they are happy and content, but it is difficult to be close with cunning people. Forget about trying to become familiar with these people of the degenerate age, it is hard enough to be familiar with oneself. Either seduced by sense pleasures, or when encountering fear, panic, and terror, very few people are able to rest in mind and remain calm.

Therefore, abandon the distraction of trying to create harmony with others; we need to practise the Dharma. If deluded people see the teachings, which are of vast benefit to all beings, with their own eyes and still do not understand, there is danger that the enduring goal of all our lifetimes will be destroyed. Therefore, even if your community and monastery are falling apart, you need to leave them and practise the Dharma.

In conclusion, from the past up to now, take a summary of your life: in all that you have thought and done, what can be used on the path of your next life? Have you done anything that is beneficial for both yourself and others, for both now and the future? It is time to engage in the most essential of essentials: the divine Dharma. This needs to be done early; later is too late.

Part Three, Arousing Bodhicitta

Now it is time to study the *Sublime Path to Omniscience, Liturgy for the Preliminaries of Dzogpa Chenpo Heart Essence of the Great Expanse*. Yesterday and the preceding days, having covered the goodness of the beginning, the introduction, we are now on the goodness of the middle, the meaning of the text, which includes the common outer preliminaries and the unique inner preliminaries. We have covered the first of these, and now we are on the second, the inner preliminaries, which include: 1) the guidance on the foundation of all the paths – taking refuge, 2) the Mahayana arousing of supreme bodhicitta, 3) purification of adverse circumstances, negativities, and obscurations – the visualisation and recitation of Vajrasattva, 4) gathering the accumulation of favourable conditions – the mandala offering, 5) cutting off the four maras all at once – the kusali's accumulation, and, reaching the conclusion of the path of action, 6) the wisdom of realisation in one's mindstream – guru yoga.

Of these six, we have already covered the first guidance on taking refuge, and now it is time for the second topic of arousing bodhicitta. In the root text this is taught in one stanza:

HO! Due to myriad appearances, illusory like the moon's reflection,
Beings wander in samsara in a chain of lives;
So they may rest in the expanse of self-knowing luminosity,
From the state of the four immeasurables, I arouse bodhicitta.

This begins with 'HO!' which is an expression of amazement. What is amazing? Explained in relation to the two truths, with regard to conventional truth, the aspiration to establish all sentient beings in unexcelled enlightenment is 'amazing'. With regard to ultimate truth, our self-knowing awareness is primordially at one with pure luminosity. This too is amazing, so we lead with this expression of amazement.

Following that, the first two lines of the stanza refer to unliberated samsaric beings and that which they are to be liberated from: samsara, both its cause and effect. The latter two lines refer to what they are to be liberated to: total enlightenment, both its cause and result. To relate this to our current state, these external phenomena – myriad appearances of illusory delusional manifestations – are taught to be liberated in the ground of undeluded vast dharmadhatu, in the nature of spontaneously accomplished luminosity rigpa. So, the methods and stages how ultimate bodhicitta is aroused in our mindstream, can be understood in this one teaching. We can also say that it speaks in terms of both the object of focus and the form this takes in our mind.

What is the object of focus? To explain this in very clear terms:

> Due to myriad appearances, illusory like the moon's reflection,
> Beings wander in samsara in a chain of lives.

This teaches that all beings of samsara, from beginingless time until now, have already accumulated a great deal of all kinds of karma. Also, conceptual processes of mind fixate upon a plethora of objects which, despite having no true existence, through dualistic fixation have been seized upon as having existence, like perceiving a striped rope to be a snake. What is more, not only in truth is there no snake where the rope is, but the nature of the rope itself consists of a collection of strands of thread. Those again, are nothing more than an arrangement of atoms.

In this way, under the powerful influence of previous habitual tendencies, while not existing, appearances of reflections manifest unceasingly, appearing like a baseless illusion, and are perceived as various kinds of happiness and misery. All these false appearances of our mind arise according to karma, and produce individual accordant perceptions. A single object, such as water, is perceived as burning embers and molten iron by the beings in hell. The pretas perceive water as pus, blood, and sooty sludge. Animals perceive it simply as something to consume. Humans perceive it as water that can quench thirst, and gods imbibe it as nectar. All perceive water in a different way, but in terms of the object, none of these can be established as truth.

Also, in the context of mind, similarly perceptions cannot be established as truth, so the mind chases back and forth after appearances. For this reason, the example given for appearances is the moon's reflection in water. The clear reflection of the moon in the sky arising in a pool of water cannot be established as truth with respect to either the object or the mind. Although they are not established, all these appearances of deceptive false phenomena – various patterns that appear through the power of the interdependence of cause and effect – are the deluded grasped-grasping of this mind, and are perceived for as long as mind remains, until the fictitious source of these illusions collapses. Under the influence of the all-pervasive origin of cause and effect, through the cause of delusion, by the power of accumulated karma, the result is the manner in which the unending suffering of the three realms of samsara is experienced in a 'chain of lives'.

A 'chain of lives' is taught to be one life following another, without end. All realms of samsara, higher and lower, are chained together one after another uninterruptedly, like for example, a fly trapped in a vase, or a burning torch whirling in a circle. This teaches, like a water wheel, there is nowhere in samsara, higher or lower, where we have not wandered or circled around, in nothing but suffering, without even a moment's permanence or reliability. So, all types of migratory sentient beings who wander ever onwards, are those who are to be freed from samsaric causality. Thus, the first two lines of the stanza indicate the aspect of the relative way things appear.

Without separating from the method of vast love and compassion for all unrealised sentient beings, by means of aspiring to arouse bodhicitta and actually engaging in arousing bodhicitta, the method that brings about liberation – generation of the cause to realise the genuine way things are, the genuine wisdom of bodhicitta itself – is taught in the third line of the stanza:

> So they may rest in the expanse of self-knowing luminosity...

This is rigpa, which resides with us primordially – the heart essence of enlightenment, luminosity wisdom free from transition or change, non-dual with the epitome of the nature of dharmadhatu devoid of all characteristics of elaboration – which is actualised.

All of the six kinds of sentient beings of the three realms are exhausted and weary under the influence of myriad suffering from beginingless time until now. For them to be entirely freed from the causes and results of suffering created by the grasped-grasping of delusional thought, they are to be united with the inexhaustible enlightened qualities of abandonment and realisation, freedom and maturation – wisdom that is omniscient in every aspect at the level of perfect buddhahood – where they may finally find relief from weariness in rest. This is compared to offering a good room and a comfortable bed to a visitor who is worn out, weary and exhausted, having travelled a long way. As such, this is taught to be 'so' or 'for the sake of' relieving all weariness, in the rest of everlasting happiness.

> From the state of the four immeasurables, I arouse bodhicitta.

This final line teaches the method and the means to engage in bringing about this result. From this point, this unique nature of the arousal of bodhicitta is the resultant vehicle, especially exalted above the causal vehicle. Moreover from there, it connects to the view of the secret direct instruction section of Dzogpa Chenpo. Thus all the teachings of the ground, path, and result are summarised and taught in these three lines of text.

The key points – from the basis and the way beings are deluded, to its pervasiveness, and ultimately up to the state of liberation – are summarised by Saraha:

> The single mind-essence is the seed of everything,
> From which existence and nirvana proliferate.

If the single fundamental mind – self-knowing awareness luminosity, which throughout eternity has never altered – is not recognised, it is the basis of delusion, but by recognising it and attaining stability, we will be liberated. However, the assertion that these two stages – earlier and later, the basis and the result – are the same, is refuted by Great All-knowing Longchenpa: if the two, the basis of delusion and the basis of liberation, are maintained to be the same, then it brings the problem that the sentient beings of the three realms will have already been liberated many times.

What is it like when one arrives at the state of liberation? Genuine innate luminosity nature free from delusion is like removing tarnish from gold, or extracting the poison from mercury. Upon genuine nature, and upon turning away from the shifting array of delusional grasped-grasping, when this stronghold is seized, there is no returning back into delusion. Due to this particular feature, it is supremely exalted.

Well then, is the expressive power of the ground display of delusion's myriad appearances, illusory like the moon's reflection, which is said to be utterly pure from the beginning and original purity of primordial freedom, the same as or different from ground luminosity? It cannot be said that they are the same. It is not said that this mind energy that engages in grasping at the manifestations of the ground is not deluded. It is deluded. Delusion is not luminosity. However there is not any delusion that has discarded luminosity. In that case, when gold and sand are mixed together, if the gold does not clearly stand out, then it is unapparent; however the gold retains the aspect of its inherent qualities. Likewise, based on this, at the time of wandering in the samsaric chain of lives and delusion, still we have never been separate from innate mind luminosity, which is taught to be 'self-knowing awareness'.

Therefore, having found what is known by the term 'wisdom that abides within from the very beginning', the ultimate resultant stage of this word 'to rest' is being able to gain relaxation in the state of our inner nature, whereby the very identity of undifferentiated ground and result free of all characteristics of dualistic phenomena – the abiding nature of true wisdom, the inexpressible, inconceivable, and ineffable mode of presence – is determined conclusively. In this way, in the primordially pure nature of rigpa, clinging and fixating thoughts do not come forth.

Arousing Bodhicitta

However, all gross thoughts which arise from its dynamic energy and display, arise as ordinary clinging and fixation, whereby, on account of this, formative karma, and sentient beings and their environments – all the delusional appearances of the six types of beings – come forth. So this is included in the ground.

The unique method to rest in the expanse of self-knowing luminosity, and arouse the bodhicitta of supreme enlightenment from the state of the four immeasurables, is taught in relation to the stage of mind of ordinary beings to be tamed. Thus, the arousal of bodhicitta is the entrance to the path of great beings and limitless merit. It is the single unmistaken cause of all good things – current benefit and ultimate bliss.

The Buddha taught in the sutras:

> Wherever beings exist, there is sustenance.
> Wherever there is bodhicitta, there is the Buddha.

Enlightenment itself is born from precious bodhicitta; this is taught in *Introduction to the Middle Way*:

> Shravakas and pratyekabuddhas are born from the Lord of Sages,
> Buddhas are born from bodhisattvas. Moreover,
> Compassionate mind, non-dual mind, and
> Bodhicitta are the causes of the children of the Victorious One.

Where does bodhicitta come from? The above quotation continues:

> Wherever compassion exists, there is bodhicitta.

Therefore, in this way, the precious mind of bodhicitta that is brought forth by compassion is the authentic path that all the victorious ones of the three times have travelled. There is no way for the bodhisattva children of the victorious ones to not train in it. The excellent basis for training, the sole means for benefit, bliss, and all good things for unlimited sentient beings, is the training in bodhicitta.

What then, is this training in bodhicitta like? We can gain a rough understanding based on the following seven topics:

a) The lineage of bodhicitta.
b) The benefits of arousing bodhicitta.
c) The essential meaning of arousing bodhicitta.
d) The definition of 'bodhisattva'.
e) Classifications of bodhicitta.
f) Taking the bodhisattva precepts.
g) The bodhisattva precepts.

The Lineage of Bodhicitta

Topic a), what is the source of the lineage? Previously, at the time the Blessed One took birth as the Brahmin Gyatso Dul, in the presence of Tathagata Vaishravana, he developed determination focused on supreme enlightenment for the sake of all unfortunate sentient beings. Accordingly, he determined to gather the accumulations over three countless aeons. The governing condition for the wisdom dharmakaya is the accumulation of wisdom, and the extraordinary governing condition for the rupakaya is gathering the vast accumulation of merit. By means of the bodhisattva's ocean-like skilful methods in conduct, the vast accumulations are swiftly reconciled; so although we refer to an extremely long period of time – three countless aeons, and so forth – we do not need to confine our thinking to the necessity of completing these amounts unequivocally, counting one by one. For example, by killing the evil spear-holder, the greatly compassionate captain completed many aeons of the accumulations. Also, it is said that the great accumulations that are gathered in many aeons on the seven impure bhumis, are gathered in a single moment on the three pure bhumis.

With this kind of ocean-like activities of perfecting, maturing, and purifying, it was time for the Buddha-to-be's previous bodhicitta aspirations to ripen. He descended from the Pure Realm of Tushita and, having completed the eight deeds up to attaining enlightenment, at the time when human lifespan was one hundred years, the Buddha became completely enlightened at Bodhigaya, the centre of Jambudvipa. For the three kinds of beings to be tamed, he turned the wheel of Dharma in three stages. He prophesied the establishment of incalculable bodhisattva children of the Victorious One in great enlightenment. He also established the continuity of the teachings and prophesied the regents of the Victorious One, the holders of the teachings. These Two Supreme Bodhisattvas, and others, undertook transmission of the teachings until it appears, from our perspective, that they demonstrated passing into nirvana. Thus the original source of this bodhicitta lineage can be traced back to the Blessed One himself.

The chief student of the children of the victorious ones was Manjushri, who accepted as his disciples Arya Nagarjuna and Shantideva. Master of the Tenth Bhumi, the Undefeatable Regent Maitreya, accepted Arya Asanga as his disciple. As it is said:

> View is the Middle Way, conduct is the six perfections.
> Of the grounds and paths, the chief degree of progress in samadhi,
> Is thus taught in those respective scriptures.

Arousing Bodhicitta

Based on the writings of these three masters, the classifications of two or three profound and extensive systems of the bodhicitta lineage came about: the System of the Profound View and the System of Extensive Conduct. Then, who gathered these traditions into one without exception, like all rivers flowing into the sea? They were gathered by the enlightened mind-vase of the All-knowing Lord of Dharma Longchenpa, whose coming was prophesied by the Victorious One. How was he prophesied? From the Sha Temple in Central Tibet, the One Gone to Bliss and the Undefeatable Regent Maitreya confirmed the prophecy that, in the future, Longchenpa would be enlightened as the Sugata Merupradipadhvaja. This is also prophesied in the *Penetration of Sound* root tantra and many other tantras. From that time until now, with regard to both the long and close lineages, the bodhicitta lineage has not been broken. Thus the source of the lineage can be traced back in this way, so this is the first topic – relating the source of the lineage.

The Benefits of Arousing Bodhicitta

For topic b), the benefits of arousing bodhicitta, there are five classifications, summarised conveniently in the following verse:

> Name, meaning, and place are transformed; a remedy for wrongdoing.
> Virtuous results increase further; the door to the lower realms is closed.
> Omniscient perfect buddhahood is attained.

For the first benefit of arousing bodhicitta, how do name, meaning, and place transform? If, in the mindstreams of ordinary sentient beings like us, bodhicitta becomes aroused, based on the mindstream in which it was aroused, the name bodhisattva is given, not only in name but also in meaning:

> The moment bodhicitta is aroused,
> Those wandering wearily in the prison of samsara,
> Become referred to as 'children of the Ones Gone to Bliss'
> And worldly gods and humans pay homage.

As this states, although such beings are still samsaric sentient beings, yet it is suitable that they become the object of homage from worldly gods and human beings, and are considered kin to the children of the Ones Gone to Bliss and the victorious ones.

The second benefit of arousing bodhicitta is the manner in which wrongdoings are remedied. When bodhicitta is aroused, all fully ripened karma that is certain to be experienced is overwhelmed by brilliance, and minor unwholesome karma that is not certain to be experienced, becomes as if pulled up from the root. An example of overwhelming by brilliance is when the light from the sun outshines the light from stars. An example of drawing out from the chest is like thin grass stalks meeting with the fire at the end of time, or the sun melting frost.

As it is said:

> Even after committing the extremes of terrible wrongdoing,
> By relying on courageous bodhicitta, instantly one becomes free.
> Why do the ignorant not rely on this?
> This bodhicitta, like the fire at the end of time,
> Consumes the wrongdoings of the wicked in an instant.

It can also be explained that, depending on the greater or lesser strength of bodhicitta, then the strength to purify negative karma is proportionally greater or lesser. To be more precise, we can understand that bodhicitta is not merely a general experience. As long as we do not forget bodhicitta, then we will not go to the lower realms, and so forth.

The third benefit of arousing bodhicitta is that virtuous results increase further. The way virtuous results increase further is taught in *Engaging in Bodhisattva Conduct*:

> Any other virtue is like the plantain tree,
> Which, shedding its fruit, wanes away.
> But the paradise tree of bodhicitta is everlasting;
> Having born fruit, it does not decay but flourishes.

The result of aspiring bodhicitta arising continuously, again and again, is like a tree in an orchard bearing fruit. More precisely, it is taught:

> To arouse bodhicitta is not most important, most important is for it to arise.

This is to be understood as bodhicitta having already arisen in one's mindstream. With engaging bodhicitta, if the excellent cause of merit itself increases further, then there is no need to mention that the result will increase. Having aroused engaging bodhicitta, for the great unfailing bodhisattva, even during periods of carelessness or sleep, the two accumulations of merit and wisdom continue to increase further. As it is said:

> From that time on, for the sake of liberation,
> For the limitless realm of sentient beings,
> From the moment of genuinely adopting this attitude
> With irreversible conviction,
> Merit arises uninterruptedly,
> Even while asleep, or heedless.

The fourth benefit of arousing bodhicitta is the manner in which the door to the lower realms is shut. For someone who has given rise to bodhicitta, if they temporarily come under the sway of careless weakness, because karmic ripening is undeceiving, they may be reborn in the negative states of the lower realms. But even if they have to go to the hell realms, by the power of their bodhicitta, the brief time it takes for a silken ball to bounce is sufficient.

The fifth benefit of arousing bodhicitta is the manner in which bodhicitta becomes the cause to attain omniscient, perfect buddhahood. Which is the single path that all past, present, and future victorious ones, together with their spiritual offspring, travel? It is this precious and supreme path of bodhicitta. If someone becomes separated from this path, it is impossible that they will attain the wisdom of omniscience. So, when naturally present potential, which is like the status of a king – the aspect that has the potential to become enlightened, and which achieves of the level of perfect buddhahood – and the bodhicitta nature to be developed, come together, it is like a seed with water, manure, heat, and moisture. Thereby, enlightened qualities increase more and more, and in this way they become the abundant crops of abandonment and realisation of the victorious ones.

As taught in the *Tantra of Vairochana Sambodhi*:

> The omniscient wisdom of Vajrapani is rooted in great compassion.
> It is the consummation of the method which comes from the cause of bodhicitta.

THE MEANING OF AROUSING BODHICITTA

Topic c), what is the essential meaning of arousing bodhicitta?

> Arousing bodhicitta is, for the benefit of others,
> The wish for perfect complete enlightenment.

As this teaches, the focus of bodhicitta has two aspects or two meanings. Through the power of compassion, the limitless realms of beings are the focus and, by the strength of wisdom, complete enlightenment is striven for. So, this is a principal mind endowed with these intentions. In short, it is a mind that desires to attain buddhahood, and is characterised by 'aspiring' and 'engaging', which are exemplified by the wish to go somewhere, and actually going there. In fact, these two are also differentiated by the necessity of engaging in conduct and practice, or not. Here the compassion that is taught is great compassion. This is not to be mistaken for the kind of compassion in the mindstreams of shravakas and pratyekabuddhas, which is not great compassion.

The Definition of 'Bodhisattva'

Topic d) is the definition of 'bodhisattva'. For the sake of attaining complete enlightenment, bodhisattvas train in the difficult conduct of the six paramitas, the four means of gathering disciples, and so on. Regardless of a time span lasting aeons or the limitless extent of beings, bodhisattvas continue without fatigue, wear the armour of fortitude, and engage with a dauntless, heroic nature. It is for this reason that they are known as 'bodhisattvas' or 'Heroes of Enlightenment'.

Classifications of Bodhicitta

Topic e) is classifications of bodhicitta. It is taught that if bodhicitta is differentiated exhaustively, there are innumerable ways of classification. However, in brief, it can be subsumed into seven categories:

First, to summarise bodhicitta into one, it is the essence of emptiness and compassion. Secondly, the two accumulations of merit and wisdom, or alternatively the two truths – conventional and ultimate – can be classified into the two divisions of aspiring and engaging bodhicitta that were mentioned a little earlier. Distinguishing bodhicitta into three aspects is done in terms of the three trainings: the three aspects of bodhicitta possess the three trainings of discipline, concentration, and wisdom.

To distinguish bodhicitta into four aspects, on the paths of accumulation and joining, it is called the 'arousal of bodhicitta with earnest application'. On the seven impure bhumis, it is taught to be the 'arousal of bodhicitta through excellent and pure intent'. On the three pure bhumis, it is the 'arousal of fully mature bodhicitta', and at the level of buddhahood, it is the 'arousal of bodhicitta which abandons all obscurations of great compassion', which makes four.

To distinguish bodhicitta into five aspects, this is done in conjunction with the five paths. At the stage of the path of accumulation, it is the 'beginner's arousal of bodhicitta'. On the path of connection, it is the 'arousal of bodhicitta through undertaking thorough purification'. At the stage of the path of seeing, it is the 'arousal of bodhicitta through seeing the nature of phenomena'. On the path of meditation, it is the 'arousal of bodhicitta through complete liberation', and at the stage of no more learning, it is 'arousal of bodhicitta through totally attaining complete liberation'.

How is bodhicitta distinguished into six aspects? It is done in reference to the six paramitas: generosity, discipline, patience, diligence, concentration, and wisdom, with regard to which, bodhicitta is aroused. The seven divisions are taught in the *Ornament of Manifest Realisation*:

> Earth, gold, the moon, fire,
> Treasure, a mine of jewels, an ocean,
> A vajra, a mountain, medicine, a spiritual teacher,
> And a wish-fulfilling jewel. The moon, a song,
> A king, a treasury, a great path,
> A mount, a fountain; as well
> Melodic sound, a river, clouds.
> These are the twenty-two similes.

In order to create the basis for enlightened qualities, the earnest aspiration for enlightenment and its accompanying mind is like the earth. Similarly, an unchanging attitude is like gold. An altruistic attitude, forever being enhanced, is like the waxing moon. Activities done in order to further enhance bodhicitta are like adding fuel to a great pyre, and so forth. Ultimately, for the sake of the single path to be traversed, the innate flow of total omniscience is like a river, and in order for rain of the dharmakaya to be manifest, it is like a cloud. So, by relating these twenty-two similes and their twenty-two meanings to the corresponding three categories: examples, companions, and phenomena, from the path of accumulation until the tenth bhumi, such distinctions are applied.

Taking the Bodhisattva Precepts

Topic f) is the way to take the bodhisattva precepts. Regarding the way in which the mind of supreme bodhicitta is aroused and the manner in which the precepts are taken, the genuine scriptures teach three methods: 1) taking them in the presence of a spiritual master, 2) visualising the victorious ones and the bodhisattvas with the strength of devotion and taking the precepts and, in a similar way, 3) taking them in front of important and blessed representations of the Three Jewels. However, the tradition is to first take the precepts with a spiritual master, and then later to take them in front of representations of the Three Jewels, and so forth. At first, the spiritual master from whom the vows are taken cannot be just anyone; it goes without saying they must be properly qualified.

With regards to the ritual tradition of taking the bodhisattva precepts, there are the two traditions of the Two Great Chariots: the Tradition of Profound View of the Middle Way School, and the Tradition of Extensive Conduct of the Mind-only School. In terms of the distinction between the two, the earlier understanding is that there are differences in the basis and characteristics of the way in which the bodhisattva precepts are taken. However, the later understanding does not make distinction between the two, so there are two different traditions. According to the early tradition, we need to teach taking the bodhisattva precepts based on three parts: the preliminary, main, and subsequent stages.

The preliminary stage is explained in terms of four distinctive features:

- The first distinctive feature is the spiritual master from whom we receive the vows.
- The second distinctive feature is the instructions on training the mind.
- The third distinctive feature is engagement in the causal accumulations that give birth to the precepts.
- The fourth distinctive feature is the roots of the precepts, the bases.

The first distinctive feature is the spiritual master from whom we receive the vows: they must maintain ethical discipline, be expert in the collection of scriptures of the bodhisattva, and possess many enlightened qualities of a holy being. Initially, we pray to such a master and are accepted by them, and then, having offered a mandala, we pray once more to be given the bodhisattva precepts. These are the distinctive features that need to be done first.

The second distinctive feature is the particular instructions on training the mind. These are:

- Considering the bad effects of all suffering, we arouse weariness for the extreme of samsara.
- Considering repaying the kindness of all mother-like sentient beings, we reject attraction to the extreme of nirvana.
- Considering the enlightened qualities of vast enlightenment, we praise the positive attributes of abandoning the two extremes.

The third distinctive feature, the section of the causal accumulations that give birth to the precepts, is the excellent method of gathering the accumulations. At the stage of arousing bodhicitta, vast offerings are required so, by means of the seven branches of prostration, offering, and so on, a vast gathering of merit needs to be accumulated. It is said that once Atisha, in stunned disbelief, said:

> There is no way for you Tibetans not to have meagre merit!
> Don't you accumulate any merit at all?

Clearly, there is no way to avoid the necessity of accumulating merit, and in particular, at the time of taking the bodhisattva precepts, it is necessary to gather extraordinary accumulations.

The fourth distinctive feature is the roots of the precepts, which are the extraordinary supreme bases:

> The object – the Three Jewels.
> The time – until enlightenment.
> The purposeful action – for perfect enlightenment.

Through the means of possessing these three distinctive features of the extraordinary Mahayana, we need to lay the foundation by taking refuge, and repeat the words of the refuge stanza three times. These are all preliminary practices.

The Main Practice of Arousing Bodhicitta

The main stage involves the main practice, which commences with the three prayers that request the consideration of the buddhas, bodhisattvas, and our lama. With these prayers we rouse their attention, which is based on the threefold taking refuge, as it is taught.

Regarding this, taking both precepts of aspiring and engaging bodhicitta together, is the system of the early tradition. Although there is no need to depend on additional rituals when simply striving for perfect enlightenment for the benefit of others, to ensure the precepts never deteriorate, and to hold them with the second hook of promise, then it is taught that rituals are definitely needed. According to Ngari Panchen's *Ascertaining the Three Vows*, the point when the vows are received is at the end of the third recital.

If I cannot find a qualified person from whom to take the vows, how may I take them myself, through the power of devotion? All the buddhas and bodhisattvas have unobstructed omniscience, and the Great Compassionate One is continuously heedful of limitless beings; so with these as your object, by gathering the accumulation of the seven branches, welcome them before you and, by following the procedure of the main practice, the precepts may be taken.

The subsequent stage has three sections:

i. Arousing great power of joy for the activities of the bodhisattva offspring of the buddhas, we meditate on rejoicing.
ii. Letting the gods, demi-gods, and so on, hear about our meritorious activities, we encourage others to engage in meditating on rejoicing.
iii. Conclude with activities offering thanks to the lama and the Precious Jewels.

Here, as this is the first time I have given this instruction on the liturgy of the preliminaries, I have conveyed the complete categorisation as it is, by means of just the names and terms. This is particularly to create auspicious circumstances, but also, although most beginners are not familiar with the Dharma terminology and may not understand it well, in order to establish positive habitual tendencies and make positive karmic connections. Someone who wishes to learn and contemplate the detailed meaning of the bodhisattva precepts certainly needs to study carefully the great scriptures and, at the very least, each of the twenty vows; it is difficult for the key points of the textual tradition to be determined in just a few words.

THE BODHISATTVA PRECEPTS

Topic g) is the bodhisattva precepts, which need to be explained in terms of two points:

- The means to keep the observances.
- The observances themselves.

It is necessary to keep the observances by never separating from both mindfulness and attentiveness. Without mindfulness, attentiveness, and carefulness, the wish to maintain the observances is taught to be like a courageous person going into battle without armour or weapons. To do so would bring nothing other than to ruin to our lives, in the defiles of the lower realms.

What is 'mindfulness'? Not forgetting the Dharma teachings of study, contemplation, and meditation, we merge them with our mindstream. In particular, it involves skilfully training in and studying all the bodhicitta precepts so we do not forget them. To recall them regularly, over and over again, is called 'mindfulness'.

What is 'attentiveness'? In all our daily activities, at all times and in all circumstances, consider: 'What am I doing? Are my thoughts, memories, and activities, virtuous or unwholesome?' Investigate and scrutinise yourself, what you are doing and what you are thinking. You need to investigate if you have made any impairment to the promise you made to engage in the conduct of the bodhisattvas. In short, attentiveness is observing and keeping watch on our own mindstream.

This is the teaching on the precepts of the bodhisattvas, and the methods to maintain the observances.

The Precepts of Refraining, Gathering, and Benefitting

Discipline of Refraining from Wrongdoing

We rely on the above methods to maintain the observances, but what are the actual observances? To sum up all the precepts of the bodhisattvas, they are summarised into the three disciplines:

a) Discipline of refraining from wrongdoing.
b) Discipline of gathering virtue.
c) Discipline of benefitting sentient beings.

Regarding a) the discipline of refraining from wrongdoing, this involves guarding against the root downfalls, as well as their branches. According to the perspective of the *Great Secret Expert in Methods Sutra*, the root downfalls are taught as one. According to the teachings in the *Bodhisattva Stages*, there are four. Following the *Essence of Space Sutra*, there is also the system of explanation of eighteen root downfalls.

How are the root downfalls taught as one? By not letting go of aspiring bodhicitta, but maintaining it for the sake of limitless sentient beings all to attain enlightenment, we aspire to accomplish a wealth of virtue and abandon unwholesome actions. Not separating from the attitude of the three excellent principles, and accomplishing a wealth of virtue, all training is gathered into one. This is easy to understand, succinct, profound in significance, and reaches the highest degree.

Discussed in fourfold terms, the root downfalls involve coming under the influence of the four afflictive emotions:

1) Avarice.
2) Attachment.
3) Anger.
4) Ignorance.

Influenced by avarice, Dharma and wealth are not given to others. Under the power of attachment, we praise ourselves and disparage others. Swayed by anger, we attack others and refuse to accept our own guilt. Under the power of ignorance, we reject the authentic Dharma, teaching a false doctrine that is not the authentic Dharma, or that does not accord with the Dharma.

To discuss the root downfalls in terms of eighteen, there are five that can easily occur to a bodhisattva king, and five that can easily occur to a minister, making ten. For ordinary people there are eight that can easily occur, making eighteen in all. These range...

> From stealing the property of the Precious Jewels and abandoning the Dharma, to
> Committing the five deeds with immediate retribution, and the five wrong views; those for a king.

This and other such verses are taught in the sutras, tantras, and aspiration prayers, and are easy to memorise. Not coming under the influence of these root downfalls, we need to maintain the training in the appropriate manner. If we fall under the sway of the four causes of downfalls, and one or two of the bodhisattva precepts become weakened, then we must immediately correct this. For a person of superior faculties, the way to bring about correction is to rest in the nature of the view which realises emptiness; understand how, except for mere mental designation, negative actions and downfalls have no self-nature. This is taught to be the supreme purification through regret and confession.

For a person of middling faculties, they need to pray to the deities of the awareness mantras. How can this be done? During the day, take the vows of mending and purification, and pray to Bodhisattva Akashagarbha and invoke his mindstream. At dawn, in order to purify our downfalls, having gone to sleep praying to the emanations displayed in our dreams, emanations of arya bodhisattvas will reverse our downfalls. If indications in our dreams did not occur, at day break, send a message of prayer as the day dawns. It is taught that if we confess our downfalls, they will become purified.

Beings of inferior faculties need to make confession by means of the complete four remedial powers, according to the meditation and recitation of Vajrasattva, which we will discuss below. The four remedial powers are:

- The power of remorse for negative actions.
- The power of support.

- The power of thorough application of the antidote.
- The power of resolve.

What is more, in the midst of a gathering of the bodhisattva sangha, you can actually announce your errors: 'I did this kind of transgression. I made this kind of mistake...' confessing and vowing to refrain. We also need to make confession by reciting the *Sutra of the Three Heaps*, and other such texts. Regarding the confession of bodhicitta downfalls in the *Sutra of the Three Heaps*, the three heaps are understood to be:

- Confession.
- Rejoicing.
- Dedication.

This enumerates the root downfalls, together with the methods for confession. The extension of this is that, with investigation and analysis, at all times and in all regards, from the bottom of our hearts, we must absolutely refrain from doing any actions that bring harm to any sentient being, either momentarily or in the long-term. This is the discipline of refraining from wrongdoing.

DISCIPLINE OF GATHERING VIRTUE

Next, b) is the discipline of gathering virtue, which mainly involves the two precepts of aspiration and engagement. Considering the precepts of aspiration, there are five:

> Do not abandon sentient beings and recall the benefits,
> Gather the accumulations and strive at training in bodhicitta.
> To adopt and reject the positive and negative eight doctrines is
>   aspiring bodhicitta.

First of the five precepts of aspiration, 'not to abandon sentient beings', is as follows: if you give rise to the mind that pledges not to engage in benefit and abandon harm for a single being of any of the five types of sentient beings, then this severs aspiring bodhicitta from the root. Because we are all sentient beings, we have not abandoned afflictive emotions, but although anger may initially arise, ultimately, by making aspirations with a kind heart, we must not deviate from the thought 'I, myself will accomplish benefit for all sentient beings.'

Second of the five precepts of aspiration is to 'recall the benefits' of arousing bodhicitta. To check the details of this, recall the meaning of the *Avatamsaka Sutra*. For a more lengthy explanation, recall the meaning of the first chapter of *Engaging in Bodhisattva Conduct*, or for a brief reminder, consult the verses of *Maitreya's Aspiration*. In short, all benefit and happiness in samsara and nirvana appear through the power of bodhicitta. Never forgetting this, we need to develop certain recollection of its benefits.

Third of the five precepts of aspiration is 'gathering the accumulations', which develops the strength of bodhicitta, thus we need to train in gathering the two accumulations of merit and wisdom. We do this by means of the 'seven branches' of prostration, offering, and so on, together with the positive collection of meritorious things of the ten Dharma activities – composing texts, making offerings, and so forth. Embrace the full extent of our accumulations with the non-referential view.

Fourth of the five precepts of aspiration, 'striving at training in bodhicitta', has three subdivisions:

1) Training in the causes of bodhicitta.
2) Training in the actual mind of bodhicitta.
3) Training in the precepts of bodhicitta.

1) Training in the causes of bodhicitta is training in the four immeasurables. For this, we focus on the following four in stages:

a) Someone who desires happiness.
b) Someone who is suffering.
c) Someone who has happiness.
d) Someone who has attachment and aversion.

These are connected with the desire to have, the desire to be free, the desire not to be separated, and the desire for pacification. So, such a person has a) the desire to have happiness, b) the desire to be free from suffering, and is c) someone who has happiness and wishes not to be separated from it, and is d) someone who has attachment and aversion and wishes for the pacification of attachment and aversion. Thus we meditate on the four immeasurables:

- Immeasurable love.
- Immeasurable compassion.
- Immeasurable joy.
- Immeasurable equanimity.

These focus on sentient beings, and observe phenomena in a manner that is non-referential. For example, love that focuses on sentient beings, love that observes on phenomena, and love that is non-referential. In this way we follow the same pattern with each of the four immeasurables. This is training in the causes.

2) Training in the actual mind of bodhicitta. We should not think that taking the precepts of bodhicitta once is enough. Although it is all right if you are not able to do it every single day at the six times, but now and then, regardless of the extended or summarised ritual, we should repeat the vows and take them over again.

3) Training in the precepts of bodhicitta involves equalising and exchanging self for others, which includes the following three:

1. Equalising self with others.
2. Exchanging self for others.
3. Cherishing others more than self.

1. Equalising self with others is as follows: as all sentient beings without exception are the same in their wish for happiness, and their wish to avoid suffering, so naturally it is not appropriate for us not to consider benefitting others. This is the thought to benefit others in the same way as we wish benefit for ourselves, striving to accomplish benefit and abandon harm.

2. Exchanging self for others, think as follows: 'My happiness and causes of happiness, whatever virtue I have, I give it all to all wandering sentient beings, in the same way as I would take the clothes from my own back, and wrap them around others. The suffering and causes of suffering of all other wandering sentient beings, all the non-virtue that they have accumulated – I take it all upon myself.' Exchanging self for others reverses our usual mind-set, so we cherish others instead of ourselves.

3. Cherishing others more than self is as follows: profoundly rejecting the attitude and motivation that desires happiness for ourselves, using our own body and all our possessions, think we must solely accomplish benefit for and bring happiness to the lives of all beings. This is engaging in the extensive conduct of the bodhisattva children of the victorious ones.

Fifth of the five precepts of aspiration is 'adopting and rejecting the positive and negative eight doctrines'. What are these?

> Abandon the four negative doctrines. Their opposite
> Is the four positive doctrines, so practise constantly.

We need to adopt the four positive doctrines and abandon the four negative doctrines. These are the unmistaken cause to recollect supreme bodhicitta without forgetting, in this and all future lives.

The four negative doctrines to be abandoned are:

1. Deceiving those worthy of praise.
2. Developing regret where there should be none.
3. Denigrating the holy masters.
4. Engaging in deception of wandering sentient beings.

The four positive doctrines which we should strive for are:

1. Not knowingly speaking falsely.
2. Engaging in methods to establish all beings in the supreme vehicle.
3. Respecting the bodhisattva children of the victorious ones.
4. Being honest and teaching the truth to all.

This completes the precepts of aspiration. Now we come to the second stage, which is the explanation of the engaging precepts. These are chiefly the practice of the six perfections, which of course are:

i. Generosity.
ii. Discipline.
iii. Patience.
iv. Diligence.
v. Concentration.
vi. Wisdom.

These six need to be practised by means of: the nature that possesses the four special attributes, the manner of practice which is accomplished with the four qualities, by abandoning the seven attachments, and embraced by the three excellent principles. So, by thorough, gradual training, we need to see if we can achieve to put the engaging precepts into practice, without which there is no other way to progress.

Discipline of Benefitting Sentient Beings

Regarding c) the discipline of benefitting sentient beings, there are many categories, but to summarise them, they are all included in the four means of gathering disciples. These are:

1) Generosity.
2) Pleasing speech.
3) Accordant with meaning.
4) Meaningful conduct.

With generosity, gather disciples; but they must be gathered without the slightest desire for greatness, fame, or any motivation of the eight worldly concerns. 'Pleasing speech' does not mean uttering empty praise or flattery. It is the need to teach the sacred Dharma in a way that is eloquent and pleasant-sounding to the ears of others. Meaningful conduct is engaging in practice according to the holy Dharma. 'Accordant with meaning' refers to having complete accord between what is taught and what is practised, so you yourself are also studying these excellent qualities of sacred Dharma. By practising in this way, from initially gaining the benefit of present swift improvement, and freedom from all harm and suffering, we gain the far-reaching benefit of the actualisation of the enlightened qualities of abandonment and realisation of the five paths and ten levels. Ultimately we will attain the level of omniscient complete enlightenment.

This serves as a mere pointer to the bodhisattva training, conduct, and practices, like a name tag on a medicine bag, mentioned only in outline. From the vastness and profoundness of bodhicitta, to the view, meditation, conduct, result, and so on, there is much I have not managed to speak about or finish describing, like someone who cannot speak their own mother tongue, or someone who knows how to explain something but cannot match it in practice. However, for someone who desires liberation and enters the path of the Mahayana, for someone who practises the Dharma in an appropriate manner, one teaching is sufficient, and that is bodhicitta. So, by training in it, we need to achieve benefit for both ourselves and others. Without engaging with bodhicitta, nor arousing it in our mindstream, no one benefits. For that reason, it is not enough merely to arouse bodhicitta in our mindstream. It is absolutely necessary for it to take root there. Having become established, we need to train appropriately in the precepts of aspiration and engagement.

However, in terms of the scriptural tradition, we may think it is already difficult enough just to understand the details in theory, not to mention actually guarding the vows in practice. This is particularly true for someone who has never done any study or contemplation based on the textual tradition – they cannot be blamed, there are many classifications and divisions. But for those who appreciate complexity, this topic can be taught in extensive detail, and for those who like succinctness, it can also be taught with concise meaning and summarised instruction on the key points.

As we mentioned earlier, if the measures to guard against the root downfalls are unified, they can be summarised into one point: by considering attaining enlightenment for the sake of all limitless wandering sentient beings, we undertake practice of the virtuous accumulations and abandon unwholesomeness, never separating from the three excellent principles. This is taught to include the entire cultivation of the virtuous accumulations. But to understand the many distinctions and enumerations is, of course, important if we want to train in the bodhisattva precepts and conduct. First we need to understand the areas in which we need to train, and the things to be adopted and rejected, as they are all very important. However, in terms of a beginner, among the priorities, first to find the entranceway to arousing bodhicitta is of the greatest importance.

THE PRECEPTS OF ASPIRING BODHICITTA

THE FOUR IMMEASURABLES

Of all the divisions of bodhicitta mentioned above, in terms of the essential meaning, there are two types of bodhicitta: relative and ultimate. It is taught that genuine ultimate bodhicitta is aroused through the strength of meditation. So, without depending on such a method, it is difficult for us beginners to achieve the outcome and arouse bodhicitta in our mindstream. As it is said:

> Ultimate innate wisdom can only come from
> The accomplishment of gathered merit and purified obscurations,
> And the blessings of a realised lama.
> Understand that to rely on any other means is foolish.

Therefore, having taken the vows of relative bodhicitta, which incorporate both aspects of aspiring and engaging, we beginners need to see if we can train properly in the precepts of aspiration and engagement. Of these, first the precepts of aspiration are taught, which are based on striving to accumulate merit and training in bodhicitta. For the first of these, the methods to accumulate merit – the mandala, the seven branches, and so on – are detailed below.

For the training in bodhicitta, we train in its cause, which depends on the four immeasurables. In our case, we have not yet aroused bodhicitta in our mindstream, so whether or not it develops, and if it happens that it does develop and does not decline, only then will we definitely seize the path to liberation. Otherwise, we will not have come close to the path to liberation. For that reason, we are doing practice, and first we need to strive in the mind trainings of the four immeasurables. Other than that, listening to a talk on the mere intellectual meaning of the four immeasurables, and then leaving it, is of no benefit. Therefore we must ensure the four immeasurables definitely flourish in our mindstream.

Generally, we contemplate the meaning of what we are taught, and then meditate on the meaning of what we contemplated. By doing both contemplation and meditation, study brings about liberation of our mindstream, which is the general method to make progress. Especially, if we wish to engage in the essence of practice training, even if we have heard only a single word of Dharma, when our main consideration is to bring about some improvement in our practice, something beneficial for the mind, then for us to merely speak about a topic is not adequate. To actually train the mind we need to meditate, and if we meditate, we need to meditate on the causal four immeasurables.

Immeasurable Equanimity

When we enumerate the four immeasurables, they are counted in this order: love, compassion, joy, and then equanimity. However, when we meditate, if we do not begin by meditating on equanimity, it is taught there is a risk that love, compassion, and joy will become biased. When we meditate on equanimity in formal sessions of practice, first the object of focus is sentient beings, and we should hold them in our mind with the perception of immeasurable equanimity. Later, at the end of the session, we need to rest in the state of the non-referential view.

First, we undertake the preliminaries of the practice session correctly, by turning within and reflecting: 'In my current situation I am extremely biased to the side of my friends, my parents, relatives, and so on, and harbour a hostile attitude to my foes and their associates. However, I am under the control of delusion, and I recognise that I am deluded. This fault arises from failing to examine my attachments to those on my own side, and my aversion to others. If I consider things carefully, in a previous life, my enemies have been my relations, and my family members have been my enemies, innumerable times. What is more, if I were to come to some sort of agreement with them, it is possible my current enemies could bring me some benefit as friends.'

What is more, there can be no certainty about the friendly status of family members, as some children have been known to betray their parents. When friends become enemies, they are often worse than the enemies we already have, so if we really think about it, friends can be more harmful than enemies. Without mentioning the influence of a loved one who we deeply cherish, even if some misfortune happens to a friend or relative, suffering arises in our own mind that destroys our current happiness. This causes hindrance and obstruction to our accomplishment of merit, and could even throw us into the lower realms. What greater harm could there be?

As there exists this unpredictability whereby enemies can become friends and friends can become enemies, by establishing the perception that all sentient beings are our parents and children, we should reject and abandon the harmful mind-set of devotion to our family and hatred for our enemies. We should consider them all as equally deserving of benefit. The example given for this is a sage, who invites guests to a feast: when a sage invites guests to his home there is no partiality, everyone is served equally.

When we meditate on immeasurable equanimity, start with one or two sentient beings, and gradually extend this to include all sentient beings under the sun. Meditate until the understanding grows that there is no difference between them and your parents of this lifetime. In this way, we meditate with the investigation and analysis of focused-based analytical meditation. At the time when our mind becomes tired and does not wish to give rise to any more thoughts, stop following after the past, cease welcoming the future, and do not continue the movement of current thoughts. Without modifying anything, remain in that state for as long as you can. This is the samadhi of equanimity. When the mind wishes to resume thinking, engage in analysis as before, alternating between analytical meditation and resting meditation. Through this, develop proficiency in non-referential equanimity. By developing certainty in empty interdependent equanimity without origination or cessation, division or exclusion, this unmodified resting is the supreme method to develop vipashyana.

Between practice sessions, we need to consider the following four links:

1) With the link of aspiration, think: 'May I be free of attachment and aversion to those sentient beings to whom I am attached and averse!'
2) With the link of wishing, think: 'Wouldn't it be wonderful to be free!'
3) With the link of commitment, think: 'I will free myself!'
4) With the link of prayer, think: 'May this come about! Heed me, my precious lama and the Three Jewels!'

Arousing Bodhicitta

Immeasurable Love

Second is the meditation on immeasurable love: immeasurable love focuses on all sentient beings, with love like parents have for their children. Whatever they do, do not lose this loving attitude towards them, and bear any mistreatment. 'Wouldn't it be wonderful if all sentient beings had happiness and the causes of happiness! Whatever happens I will bring such benefit to them!' Make this single wish, wanting to do only that, without any other thoughts.

In terms of our conduct of body and speech, when we see sentient beings, look upon them with smiling eyes, call to them with pleasant speech, and embrace them with a loving mind. We need to think that we will accomplish whatever they most wish for, whatever they get joy from, and all actions that bring them benefit.

When we meditate on this, we begin with our mother of this life and gradually enter into meditation on all sentient beings, which is the full focus. This takes the form of the following aspiration: 'May all beings, in this and all future lives, have the three causes of happiness: faith, renunciation, and bodhicitta. How good it would be if they had these! I am going to enable them to have these causes of happiness! In order for them to possess them, I pray to the Three Jewels. May they enjoy the fruition of happiness – the exalted status of gods and humans – until they reach truly excellent, complete enlightenment! It would be wonderful if they had this! I shall make it so they do!'

Praying to the Three Jewels, alternate between analytical and resting meditating. Strive for the benefit of all sentient beings under the sun, no different from our parents of this life, in methods for their happiness and comfort. We need to meditate until, for example, the attitude and conduct of a mother bird feeding her chick comes about. In non-referential post meditation, between all practice sessions, maintain loving actions of body, speech, and mind. With your body, abandon causing harm to sentient beings. With your speech, do not use harsh words, slander, and so on. In your mind, think only of methods for sentient beings to be happy and comfortable. Do not just think this, but apply it to our body and speech, so we actually accomplish such things.

Immeasurable Compassion

Third is the meditation on immeasurable compassion. The object of compassion generally is all sentient beings living in the three realms of samsara. In particular, at this stage of practice, we need to train by placing our focus on the intense feelings of suffering that beings experience in samsara. Again, it is alright to begin by meditating on our own mother of this life, or alternatively we can also meditate on someone like a prisoner in jail, who is being led away to face death by an executioner. Livestock that are about to be slaughtered are also a suitable focus for meditation. Alternatively, we can meditate on a sick person on the brink of death, as they breathe in and out. Think, for this kind of suffering sentient being, 'Wouldn't it be wonderful if they could be free of this suffering!' Meditate until you feel intense overwhelming compassion, and your eyes fill with tears.

Gradually from there, focus on sentient beings in the lower realms who are currently suffering, then extend your focus to all sentient beings. The cause for beings of samsara to experience this suffering is their unwholesome actions, and yet now, still so many are carelessly engaging in unwholesome actions, creating further causes to experience suffering. Meditate on compassion for all of them.

Wherever space pervades, sentient beings pervade; wherever sentient beings pervade, negative karma and suffering pervades. So, solely engaging in negative actions and suffering, all these sentient beings are truly worthy of our compassion. Think, 'Wouldn't it be wonderful if all of them, the six types of beings, were free of all their individual karmic perceptions, suffering, and habituations, and attained everlasting bliss at the level of perfect buddhahood!' Meditate from the bottom of your heart, with the feeling of longing that a mother without any arms feels when her child is swept away by a river. Finally, we need to rest in a non-referential state of meditative equipoise.

Compassion is the real root of the Dharma, both of Mahayana Sutra and the Vajrayana. Therefore, if someone has no compassion and harbours thoughts and actions that harm sentient beings, they betray the Buddha, disgrace the Dharma, and shame the Sangha, casting themselves and others into the hell realms. So, a Buddhist needs to be completely pure, and have the wish to engage in actions which benefit self and others. Therefore, always take a low seat, wear simple clothes, and do whatever is of benefit to all sentient beings, as often as is necessary. It is taught that if both love and compassion have definitely developed in our mindstream, then even if we do not engage in great recitals of the teachings, spiritual practice, or any direct benefit to sentient beings, this is still enough.

In between practice sessions, do not for one moment be without a compassionate mind. We need to cherish the ongoing aspiration to alleviate the suffering of sentient beings, and actually practise engaging in achieving benefit and happiness for all beings. As is taught in the *Compendium of Dharma Sutra*:

Desiring to attain enlightenment, do not train in many teachings; train in a single teaching. Which is that? It is great compassion. Whoever has great compassion has the entire Buddha Dharma in the palm of their hand.

In this way, there is no more exalted Dharma than compassion to purify negativities and obscurations. All sentient beings in samsara experience limitless suffering. The cause for such suffering to arise comes about through the power of engaging in unwholesome actions. Thinking: 'Wouldn't it be wonderful for them all to be free from both the causes and results of suffering. May they be free! I will free them! I pray, free them, my kind lama and the Precious Jewels, heed me!' Thus alternate between analytical and resting meditation. Between practice sessions, arouse compassion for all the sentient beings you see. It is taught that when you see a sentient being and consider their suffering, if tears well up in your eyes, that is the measure of your training in compassion.

Immeasurable Joy

Following this, we meditate on the fourth immeasurable: joy. What is the object of focus this time? Those in the higher realms have all pleasure and happiness, power and fame, with physical comfort and mental happiness. Their happiness is perfect, and this is the subject of our aspirations, so they are the object of focus here. The form this takes in our mind is as follows: not only should we not feel any jealousy or envy towards beings of the higher realms, but we should wish that they receive even better and more abundant comfort, joy, and pleasure – all the splendour of the higher realms. Without any outer, inner, temporary or lasting harm, wish for them to be endowed with great wisdom, and so on – all the positive qualities of samsara and nirvana.

When you meditate like this, first focus on your kind mother of this life. Recognise that she is your mother, recall her kindness, and wish to repay her kindness, meditating with love that wishes her to be happy, and compassion that wishes her to be free of suffering. Then, for however much property, possessions, food, clothes, and wealth your mother accumulates, be all the more happy, without any jealously or ill-will. By means of this attitude, next focus on someone you are indifferent to, and then progress on to someone you dislike. Gradually expand your focus to all sentient beings. Without separating from this thought, think: 'Their little comfort and happiness is the result of virtue. Wouldn't it be wonderful if that increased and they were never without happiness, the fruit of wholesome actions! May they never be without it! I will make sure they are never without it! Heed me, my lama and the Three Jewels; may beings never be without happiness!'

Whichever of the four immeasurables you meditate on, for the three-fold sphere of agent, action, and subject, elicit certainty that appearances have no self-nature. Between practice sessions, if you see happy sentient beings, meditate on joy without any jealousy or ill-will. Especially for enemies who have harmed you, and all who are the object of jealously, completely rid yourself of the bad attitude that cannot bear the abundant wealth of others. For all ways they have happiness, be especially joyful. As an example, it is taught we need to be like a camel who, having lost its calf, finds it again. It is said a camel is especially loving to its calves, so having lost one if it finds it again, it is joyful unlike any other animal. Likewise, if similar joy arises when other sentient beings are experiencing happiness, this is the measure of our training in immeasurable joy.

For all of these practice sessions we need to have the three-fold preparation, main part, and conclusion complete. In particular, at the end of practice sessions, if we do not want our mind to scatter, rest in meditative equipoise in a non-referential state. Having become familiar with shamatha, connected with the immeasurables and their samadhi, you will become a suitable vessel to develop vipashyana.

To summarise all of this, it is exemplified by a kind heart. All four immeasurables are included within a kind heart. In this case, even if you do not know how to explain a lot with words, leaving behind bad attitudes, and living your life by practicing a kind heart is enough. Je Rinpoche taught:

> If intentions are good, the grounds and paths are also good.
> If intentions are bad, the grounds and paths are also bad.
> Everything depends on one's intentions,
> So always strive for good intentions.

These four lines were repeated regularly by Patrul Rinpoche, who said, 'This is not the repetitive talk of simple men, it really focuses on what is important!' and it is said he would repeat it one hundred and eight times, counting on his mala. If we understand this, and hold others with a kind heart, a good result will also come to ripen for ourselves, so please engage in having a good heart for everyone without fail.

It is taught:

> For the main precepts of aspiration and engagement,
> The precept of aspiration is meditation on the four immeasurables.

Above is the section of the four immeasurables, describing them in a little detail.

The Precepts of Engaging Bodhicitta

It is taught:

> For the precepts of engagement, practise the six perfections.

We mentioned this earlier, but for the first of the six perfections, in terms of generosity, there are three kinds:

1) Generosity of material things.
2) Generosity of protection against fear.
3) Generosity of Dharma.

For the first of these, the generosity of material things, there are three levels: giving, great giving, and extreme giving. For the sake of all sentient beings, giving valuables without attachment, is giving. Giving a horse or elephant, son or daughter, and so on, generously letting go completely, is great giving. Giving your own head, limbs, and so on, is extreme giving. Protecting the lives of sentient beings is 2) the generosity of protection against fear, and teaching the Dharma to establish those deluded onto the path, is 3) the generosity of Dharma. These are the perfection of generosity.

Abandoning and restraining all negative conduct and unwholesomeness like poison, and practising all merit you can, in order to bring benefit to other sentient beings, is the perfection of discipline. Bearing hardship for the sake of Dharma, enduring other's mistreatment, and not fearing the profound truth of reality – these are the perfection of patience. Overcoming laziness that causes the freedoms and endowments to be squandered and go to waste, enthusiastically striving and engaging in the ten Dharma activities and the ten perfections, is the perfection of diligence.

Abandoning distractions and their causes, go to a remote forest or sacred monastic seat, and assume the seven-point posture of Vairochana. Resting in a state of mind not thinking or grasping at anything whatsoever, is the perfection of concentration. Seeing all perceptions of the five sense objects that appear as they do, as apparent yet non-existent – the eight metaphors of illusoriness – look at the nature of the mind which perceives. The thinking which holds unceasingly apparent objects to be objects, subsides in the sky-like state of the empty luminosity true nature of phenomena. Resting in this is the perfection of wisdom.

Regarding these, the three perfections of generosity, discipline, and patience complete the accumulation of merit. Concentration and wisdom complete the accumulation of wisdom, and diligence assists in both. In this way, the six perfections are subsumed within emptiness, the essence of which is compassion, and so it is the root of the Mahayana Dharma, both Sutra and Tantra.

What is the Dharma that is certainly enough on its own, but without which, all means are entirely lost? Having aroused supreme bodhicitta that is drawn forth by compassion, it is meditation on emptiness. If emptiness is realised, then the strength of compassion comes naturally. It is no good without it, and there is no way to separate the two, like fire and heat. At that stage, from the strength of the realisation of emptiness, genuine bodhicitta grows in our mind and we gradually progress higher, so that the level of spontaneously accomplished perfect buddhahood of the twofold purpose is accomplished with ease.

Bodhicitta has limitless benefits: it protects against the suffering of samsara and the lower realms; it is more exalted than the spiritual approaches of the shravakas and pratyekabuddhas; its roots of merit do not become exhausted but increase; it achieves vast merit; it is successor to the legacy of the Buddha; it accomplishes immense benefit for others, and so on and so forth. Therefore, from the bottom of our heart we need to train in arousing bodhicitta, with the three excellent principles of the preparation, main part, and conclusion, complete.

Teaching Day Seven

As Je Lama Mipham Jampal Gyatso said:

> Beings wander in the sorrowful desert of existence,
> Yet the Supreme Sage does not extract them with his hand;
> He taught the path to liberation for all beings to rely on,
> So make effort to adopt the precious means of Dharma.

Sentient beings are roaming in the three realms of samsaric existence. What are these realms like? A 'sorrowful desert' has no grass or water, a place where even birds and wild animals do not gather or dwell, not to mention humans. It is a vast plain of hot sand, so large in size that you cannot identify the cardinal directions, let alone attempt to traverse its distant boundaries. In such a place, there is no food to eat, nothing to wear, and no one for these poor wandering beings to ask, 'What should I do?'

> Yet the Supreme Sage does not extract them with his hand.

The Sage and the Blessed Ones first aroused bodhicitta for the benefit of sentient beings. Subsequently, again for the sake of sentient beings, they gathered the two ocean-like accumulations through many countless great aeons. They engaged in completion of the accumulations, maturation of their mindstreams, and purification, whereby eventually they actualised complete buddhahood. However, there is not a single enlightened activity of the victorious ones that is not for the benefit of other sentient beings. Every fully enlightened buddha has exhausted all flaws and possesses all enlightened qualities. They have abandoned all that is to be abandoned without exception, and perfected all there is to be realised without exception. Their enlightened qualities of strength and power, wisdom, kindness, and spiritual power are thoroughly complete. Having totally vanquished the faults of the four maras, they are endowed with all excellent enlightened qualities. As such, the enlightened qualities of even a single pore on the body of a buddha are beyond description.

Conversely, the fully ripened result of the karma accumulated by wandering sentient beings individually is the multitudinous suffering of samsara which they experience. Yet, the Lord of Sages cannot relieve that suffering by taking it away with his hand, pulling sentient beings straight out with some kind of frenzied force. There is no way to extract them.

Again, this is taught:

> The Sages cannot wash away sins with water,
> Nor can they remove the suffering of beings with their hands.

In that case, what can we do?

> He taught the path to liberation for all beings to rely on.

The nine types of wandering being depend on the teachings of the Sage to find the path to liberation. Teaching the path to liberation to all types of sentient being, they need to rely on this activity of enlightened speech in order to enter onto the path. Thus their liberation depends on this. The above continues:

> Although he cannot transfer his realisation to others,
> By teaching peaceful, ultimate nature, they become liberated.

The One Gone to Bliss teaches the Dharma to tame beings in any way necessary. For sentient beings of lesser aptitude and lower potential, he taught the path of inferior scope. For those who are a little more capable, with middling aptitude, he taught the Dharma of attaining the level of shravakas and pratyekabuddhas. Furthermore, to those of greater aptitude who are suitable for the Great Vehicle, he taught the Dharma of the Mahayana. For those of excellent aptitude and high acumen, he taught the Dharma of the Secret Mantra. To those with the very highest acumen, he taught the pinnacle spiritual approach, the Dharma exalted beyond all others. Through these means, he engages in liberating all unliberated, samsaric sentient beings from the ocean of suffering.

From Patrul Rinpoche's *Praise to the Speech of the One Gone to Bliss, the Great White Lotus*:

> The precious collections of the Sage's excellent words of teaching,
> The excellent commentary scriptures elucidating his words;
> There is no other agent of the liberating path –
> The teachings of the Supreme Sage are the 'True Victorious One'.

It is for this reason, in the above quote from Mipham Rinpoche, he said that for sentient beings wandering in the sorrowful desert of existence to be free from inexhaustible suffering, if they wish to attain genuine liberation, the Buddha taught the Dharma with the activity of his enlightened speech, to protect all beings.

So make effort to adopt the precious means of Dharma.

Even if we were to actually meet the Buddha, there would be nothing more beneficial for him to teach; this is the profound secret of his enlightened speech. As noted in the above quotation from Patrul Rinpoche, we have all the words of the Sage's excellent teaching in the guise of the scriptures – the precious collections of scriptures, and the subsequent commentaries which explain the enlightened intent of his teaching. Therefore, this is like having the Victorious One actually present; we do not need any other agent of the liberating path. Secondly, in the degenerate age, those emanating as masters who teach the Dharma, correctly teach the entire meaning of the Buddha's enlightened intent.

If we have these teachings, not only should we adopt this precious means of Dharma through effort, but it is taught there is no other way for us to escape from the suffering of samsara. It is not like we can be picked out like chaff from barley, or propelled up to a pure realm like a stone shot from a catapult. We cannot say the buddhas have no compassionate blessing for incredibly numerous, suffering sentient beings. If that was possible, of course they would have already rescued us all, without exception. Avalokiteshvara vowed to Amitabha that he would dredge samsara from its very depths, but when he looked from the peak of Mt. Potala, he saw what looked like even more samsaric sentient beings than before. For this reason, if sentient beings themselves do not practise accordingly the path that the Buddha taught, even if the Victorious One actually appeared, he would be powerless.

In that case, as Lama Mipham said, if we ourselves can extract the essence of the beneficial spiritual instructions into our own experience, then it is as if they had been taught directly and especially to us, as if the Buddha had actually seen our own particular situation. Stuck in beginningless samsara until now, forever undergoing suffering without ever any escape, it is suitable to compare this experience to an endless desert, or a dry, sorrowful plain. Not only that, but is not this suffering that continues through both birth and death exactly like floundering in an endless ocean of poison, swimming and drowning, swimming and drowning, without any escape? Will we ever escape? We are close to the door to liberation, born in the presence of the Sage's teaching. We hear the sound of the holy Dharma, but if we still cannot make sense of it, this is like:

> The suffering of having established that a castle has an entrance,
>   but not knowing where it is.

We have heard some distant talk of attaining something called 'liberation', of finding something called 'the path to liberation', but we do not know how to open the door to actually enter the path. One reason we are unable to open the door is due to our misfortune at having come under the sway of karma, afflictive emotions, and habitual tendencies. Another reason is we are lost to the influence of negative conditions, so it is like trying to make water flow uphill.

Additionally, we are deceived by the demon of sense-pleasure. Either we cannot rid ourselves of our preoccupation with wealth, or we cannot let go of our concerns with other people. In short, we are like a naughty child who always has a lot to say: 'I didn't get that done because this happened...' Whoever we are, we all have plenty of excuses. While we remain alive, whatever excuses we make, we can still try to maintain them. However, after this life, when the scales of karmic result are weighed in, and we arrive at the weighing ground of virtue and non-virtue, such excuses are useless. That place is not like the land of the living.

We were born in a land where Dharma has spread, and have met the Sangha communities of lamas and monks. If we think about this, it is fortunate. But, if you have fallen under the influence of negative associates and lost faith in the objects of devotion, getting carried away in quarrels and fights, even though you were born in a land of Dharma, not only are you left without a basis for gathering the accumulation of merit, but there is no more powerful basis than the Sangha to accumulate non-virtue. In short, regarding either Dharma or worldly activities, whichever you undertake, the result you achieve comes down to whether or not you understand the correct methods to accomplish things, and whether you are skilful or not.

If we engage in worldly pursuits, what could be better than raising our status above that of others? Yet, however much we engage in worldly pursuits, that is how much greater the divide grows between us and the Dharma. If this was not the case, then what other reason would there be for the Dharma and the mundane not to accord? There would have been no practical purpose for our Teacher King of the Sakyas to relinquish his kingdom. If we do not practise Dharma ourselves, even if our teacher the Buddha appeared, he could not relieve our suffering with a touch of his hand. So it is taught the Buddha is unable to wash away with water the two obscurations of samsaric beings.

We are told: 'Don't jump from the top of this building! If you do, you will fall many stories to certain death.' But if someone does not listen and jumps anyway, there is nothing we can do. Yet, *even the thick-skinned idiot knows which way the wind blows.* Likewise, if we listen to enough teachings and begin to understand, then there is a chance that we can gain some crucial realisation. In this case, reciting taking refuge without knowing what the Three Jewels are is no good. Without a kind heart of compassion, accumulating a few hundred thousand recitations of arousing bodhicitta, except for the mere benefit of reciting, does not fulfil any great purpose. On one hand taking life, on the other hand saving animals' lives; how can this be included in the authentic ten virtues? Still less virtuous is to receive a few Dharma empowerments without knowing their inner meaning or their commitment samaya. If you now suddenly realise that the urge to understand these things has never arisen in your mind, it is time to do a reappraisal of yourself.

From our arrival into the human world up until today, all that time has already passed. All our activities of each year and each month have been entirely meaningless – empty activities and empty thoughts. If these actions and emotions were truly empty, with neither any benefit nor harm, then at least to that extent, everything would be fine. However, all that we have ever done has been unwholesome activities; all that we have ever thought has been unsuitable mental formulations, the fully ripened consequences of which will come to fall upon us, and no one else. But, if we can actually accept this, it is at least the sign of having some merit where there is none.

At this juncture, before we get swept away, powerless, by some terrible karmic wind, just like the helpless sentient beings of the intermediate state, if we can realise this key point and think: 'That isn't the way, this is the way!' then we need not have any regrets; we can really begin to practise the Dharma of happiness for our mind. Whatever others say, don't worry! 'He doesn't know the first thing about Buddhism!' 'Look, she's trying to meditate!' There is nothing some people won't say. What we call 'other sentient beings' are mad. A 'mad' person is someone who is deluded, so what is there to stare at when an idiot runs off in a senseless direction? Rather, if we purify our own mind, then it will become pure, and this is something we need to engage in doing ourselves.

Lama Mipham also taught the following:

> Like springtime at the end of the cold winter months,
> Afterwards, when youth has passed, it is a time of happiness.
> Like a peacock when rainclouds billow,
> Such is the time of death for those who enjoy Dharma practice.

When the three months of cold winter suffering are over, spring arrives.

Afterwards, when youth has passed, it is a time of happiness.

The three months of winter are cold and miserable, but after that, following the arrival of spring, there is summertime. Similarly, for those who practise Dharma, the middle of life is happier than the earlier part, and the latter part of life is happier than the middle. Moreover, it is taught the next life becomes happier still.

Like a peacock when rainclouds billow...

At the time when the clouds in the sky billow and the roar of the southern turquoise dragon resounds, the peacocks on the ground are joyful and dance a joyful dance, spreading the canopy of their tail feathers. Like this:

Such is the time of death for those who enjoy Dharma practice.

For a person who genuinely practises the Dharma, even if at first they are unhappy, they end up becoming more and more happy. So it is taught that the time when a practitioner is truly happy is at the time of their death. Measured in human terms, not having to be afraid at the time of death is as valuable as all the wealth in the world. Knowing how to practise, if you can accomplish it, this current opportunity does not require any payment. So while this opportunity is within our grasp, we should be careful not to waste it, otherwise something very dangerous lies in wait.

We often talk about these things, yet when we have finished talking, the significance gets lost to forgetfulness. While inside the temple for teachings, we have the thought, 'Oh dear, this isn't good! I need to practise real Dharma!' but when we leave the teaching, as we chat about this and that, we get distracted all over again by bad habits, just like a piece of paper tearing easily along a fold. In this way, slipping into one and then two bad habits, eventually we become callous, and fall under the obstructive power of being resistant to Dharma. No one is to blame, we are all samsaric beings, but if we do not give this any consideration, when we meet with the decisive moment, we will not know what to do and our eyes will fill with tears. When we get to the stage of letting out long sighs, both ourselves and our companions will be miserable. In short, the real root of why our Dharma practice has not been successful so far is because we have not managed to give rise to fierce renunciation for samsara from the depth of our hearts.

Regarding this, what we term 'renunciation' includes two aspects. The first aspect needs to think, 'This samsara is like a prison' and become weary of it. The second aspect is the thought that wants to find a way to be free from samsara. Without these two aspects complete, then it is not counted as true renunciation. What is also required, in addition to these two aspects? Faith is still required. As it is taught:

Teaching Day Seven

Without faith, the entrance to Dharma is blocked.

We need sincere faith, conviction, and most important, irreversible devotion towards the Dharma and our lama. Otherwise, to say we have faith only when the lama gives us gifts, or to pretend to receive Dharma teachings while disapproving of a lama in some way is meaningless; there is no basis to such feelings. If this lama were to say something flattering, then you would surely start to like him. Any faith that comes from feelings of 'liking' has no root or long-term value, it is mere attachment.

Someone who practises the Dharma of the Mahayana needs to have compassion. Compassion needs to be complete with two aspects: the thought of compassion for those who are suffering is, of course, compassion, but the thought of wanting to engage in a method to free them from suffering makes it true compassion. Compassion also has several distinctions: there is compassion with reference to sentient beings; compassion that references the Dharma; non-referential compassion, and so on, which need to be developed by traversing the graduated path. In short, as mentioned earlier, if bodhicitta which is evoked by compassion is not aroused, then the door to liberation will never be found. Without it, even if you have remained in dark retreat for nine years and recited many millions of dharani mantras, so long as you do not have a bad motivation, there is of course the benefit of recitation. But except for that, from the aspect of finding the path to liberation, you are still blindly groping around.

In this case, while you have the wish to enter the real door of the path to liberation, for yourself and others, do not forget the three excellent principles. First, when you seat yourself in the Dharma gathering, arouse compassion for sentient beings who have been your mother, equal to the limits of space – all those who are currently experiencing the torment of the three types of suffering. Think: 'I alone must establish all of them in the permanent bliss of unexcelled enlightenment, freeing them from suffering and its causes.' We do this with the two aspects: the aspect of compassion that references sentient beings, and the aspect of wisdom that focuses on enlightenment, by means of the vast attitude of bodhicitta.

Secondly, when listening to the main Dharma teaching, in a state that is free from grasping at empty appearances, focusing on the illusory apparent mode of interdependent arising – the ongoing vast array of purity – we need to concentrate our three doors of body, speech, and mind as one to listen to the Dharma. Free from grasping at the three spheres, conclude with dedication to full enlightenment. In this way, if the preparation, main part, and conclusion are complete, then they are connected with the three excellent principles. Thus, the preparation is arousal of bodhicitta, the main part is non-conceptual, and the conclusion is dedication. So, if these three excellent principles are complete and we listen to the Dharma by this means, it becomes like a single meal that is sufficient for our entire life. Therefore, in order to make it beneficial, we need to listen to the Dharma with a vow affirming our need to apply diligence.

Part Four, Meditation and Recitation of Vajrasattva

The Four Powers

On the *Sublime Path to Omniscience, the Recital for the Preliminaries of Dzogpa Chenpo*, we have already covered the common outer preliminaries, and of the unique inner preliminaries, both taking refuge, and arousing bodhicitta are now complete. So, we are now at the stage to discuss both the meditation and recitation of Lama Vajrasattva to purify adverse conditions, negativities, and obscurations, as well as the teaching on the mandala accumulation of merit.

Meditating on the profound path brings about the birth of extraordinary experience and realisation in one's mindstream, but what are the main adverse conditions that can cut this off? They are negativities, obscurations, and habitual tendencies. However, the Victorious One in his skill and compassion taught many inconceivable methods to purify these negativities, obscurations, and habitual tendencies. Of all these methods, which is the most supreme? It is engaging in the practice of Vajrasattva.

When Glorious Vajrasattva first aroused supreme bodhicitta, he made a prayer of aspiration: 'Just by hearing my name, may all sentient beings be freed from negativities, obscurations, impairments, and broken vows; accumulation of the five inexpiable actions; sacred commitments that have been impaired or broken, and so on! By the power of entering into the presence of Vajrasattva, may those with evil deeds and obscurations have their negativities cleared!' So in this way, by practising the meditation of Lama Vajrasattva in the manner of the jewel which includes all, by means of the remedy complete with the four powers, we need to engage in confession and purification.

What are the remedial four powers?

1) The power of support.
2) The power of disenchantment.
3) The power of resolve.
4) The power of the remedy.

First of these is the power of support. As it is said:

The object to which we confess evil deeds is the power of support.

Generally, the support or object of confession at the stage of individual liberation includes the preceptor, the master, and the Sangha. At the bodhicitta stage, the support for confession is the lama spiritual teacher, together with a spiritual friend with perfectly-observed conduct. At the stage of confessing downfalls, the support is the thirty-five sugatas, and the buddhas of the ten directions according to the *Liberation Sutra*. At the stage of Secret Mantra, the support for confession is the lama and the host of mandala deities. Particularly, at our stage now, the support for confession is Lama Vajrasattva.

For the power of support, we need to know there are two aspects: the outer power of support and the inner power of support. At this stage, the outer power of support is meditation on Lama Vajrasattva. The inner power of support is taking refuge and arousing bodhicitta. In particular, the most important of all the key points is meditation on compassion. The essence of the outer power of support is faith, so it is very important to have such devotion.

Second is the power of disenchantment with wrongdoing, the essence of which is regret. As Bodhisattva Shantideva says:

> Those to be purified are the negativities of the six doors.
> Make them pure with the remedial four purifying powers.

What are the negativities of the six doors which are to be purified?

> Time, motivation, wandering, nature,
> Object, and function: the six.

First of these six are the negativities of the door of time, which we acknowledge in the following way: 'From the time of beginningless samsara until now, all the negativities that I have accumulated, including those in this lifetime, this year, this month, and today.' Or alternatively, we can say: 'When I was this age, I did such and such an action...' and state some examples, or 'I did this kind of inherently negative deed...' This should include all the things that we did ourselves, everything negative that we got others to do, and also include rejoicing in others' wrongdoing, downfalls, and the like. By means of the mind, do not keep them secret. By means of the body, do not conceal or hide them. By means of the speech, openly admit and confess everything. This is taught to be called the 'power of disenchantment' through the door of time.

Second are the negativities of the door of motivation. The conditions causing a certain kind of karma to arise depend on motivation in the mind, so everything that is motivated by afflicted emotions of the three poisons has its origin through the door of motivation. Third, what are called the negativities of 'the door of wandering' are based on the means of accumulation. There is no karmic action that is not accumulated by means of either body, speech, or mind, so all non-virtue is accumulated through these three doors. Fourth, the negativities of the door of nature are of two types: intrinsic wrongdoing of the ten non-virtues, the five inexpiable sins, and so on, which are definite non-virtues for everyone, and secondly transgression of precepts of the outer individual liberation, inner bodhicitta, and Secret Mantra vows of the vidyadharas. If someone who has taken these three vows transgresses, then it is a serious wrongdoing. Fifth, the negativities of the door of object are non-virtues that are accumulated based on the three samsaric realms of existence, and the peace of nirvana. Sixth are the negativities of the door of function. Whatever the non-virtuous action or downfall, the fully ripened result is undesirable experiences, which means suffering in both this and future lives.

Having thus described the negativities of the six doors that are to be purified, the third power is that of resolve. The essence of the power of restoration is the attitude of resolve for the future. This is the thought that, even at the cost of our life, we will not do such things in future. Fourth is the power of thorough application of the remedy. The essence of this is to develop the intent to strive after the Dharma.

VAJRASATTVA PURIFICATION ACCORDING TO THE ROOT TEXT

So, with this general understanding in mind, we need to consider the meaning of the four powers in connection with the root verses of the recital:

> **AH! In my ordinary form, at my crown,**
> **In the centre of a white lotus and moon seat,**
> **From a HONG, arises Guru Vajrasattva,**
> **Radiantly white sambhogakaya,**
> **Holding vajra and bell, and embracing his consort.**
> **I pray, give me refuge; purify my negativities.**

In these one and a half stanzas, the power of support is taught. First we recite 'AH'. Regarding the AH syllable it is said:

> AH is supreme of all syllables.

AH is the source of all syllables, or alternatively, it is the sound that brings forth all syllables, like the basis of all speech. It is the syllable that represents the truth of the unborn nature of phenomena, so it evokes recollection of the meaning of emptiness which is free from arising, ceasing, and dwelling, and is beyond elaboration.

> In my ordinary form, at my crown...

Here, when we refer to 'my', we do not need to discuss the self-identity of the individual, self-identity of phenomena, grasping at self, or any of these factors. This meditation and recitation of Vajrasattva is not the general path of Mahayana Sutra and Tantra, it is the path of generation and completion, connected with the extraordinary Secret Mantra. So when visualising the power of support – the vivid appearance of Vajrasattva – this is the stage at which we describe our physical posture. Therefore, saying 'my' is to be understood as referring to the practitioner, him or herself.

In this context, we should understand that the word 'ordinary' has a specific meaning of 'leaving naturally unaltered'. This refers to you, yourself sitting unaltered, naturally relaxed. 'At my crown' refers to the space an arrow's length above your head.

> In the centre of a white lotus and moon seat.

There upon a white lotus – the symbol of non-attachment to existence – with a thousand spread petals, in the centre of a full moon disc, is a HONG syllable, the symbol of non-attachment to nirvana.

> From a HONG, arises Guru Vajrasattva.

This HONG syllable is a seed mantra that represents vajra mind. Generally, there are three kinds of mantra: unmistaken cause root mantra, visualisation condition mantra, and recitation activity mantra. Of these, this is understood to be visualisation condition mantra.

We visualise the white HONG syllable brilliantly radiant, emanating rays of light. The HONG transforms, and from this transformation arises the essence of the embodiment of all buddhas, our kind root lama, in the form of Glorious Vajrasattva:

> Radiantly white sambhogakaya.

His body is white and radiant, the sign of being untainted by the stains of the two obscurations, and this whiteness is like a snow mountain refulgent with the sun's rays. We should visualise that his body is adorned with the thirteen adornments of the sambhogakaya. These are the five silken garments, and the eight jewelled ornaments. The five silken ornaments are counted as: multi-coloured chevrons, ribbons that tie up his hair, a white silken upper garment with golden threads, a

Meditation and Recitation of Vajrasattva

multi-coloured decorated lower garment, and a short-sleeved shirt. Alternatively, the silken ornaments are sometimes taught to be: chevrons, an upper garment, silken scarves, a sash, and a lower garment. Also, in a few of the new tantras there is a 'garment for offerings', which represents the Brahman's thread. Whichever it is, visualise Vajrasattva as depicted in well-known thangkas, with the five silken garments.

The eight jewelled ornaments are counted as follows: a crown, earrings, and a necklace are three; two armbands make four; a crystal necklace and a long necklace make five; two bracelets make six; his rings make seven, and two anklets take the count to eight.

>Holding vajra and bell.

Beautifully adorned with the thirteen adornments of the sambhogakaya, Vajrasattva has one face and two arms. In his right hand, he holds a vajra of rigpa-emptiness in a manner that points to his heart. This is a five-pointed vajra. In his left hand, he holds a bell of appearance-emptiness by his side, which is understood as being above the hip, below the navel, at the level where we tie a belt.

>And embracing his consort.

His female vajra consort is white in colour. In her right hand is a hooked knife that cuts birth and death from the root, in her left hand she holds a skull cup filled with nectar symbolising the union of great bliss. She embraces her partner in union. Their forms are apparent yet naturally devoid of existence, like a rainbow in the sky, or the reflection in a mirror. Visualise that Vajrasattva sits facing towards you.

>I pray, give me refuge; purify my negativities.

In this way, visualise Vajrasattva as non-dual with your lama, in the manner of the jewel which includes all. His body is the Sangha; his speech the Dharma; his enlightened mind is the embodiment of the indivisibility of space and wisdom, the Buddha. 'Lord, embodiment of the Three Jewels and the Three Roots, with the faith of total trust, to you I take refuge. I pray, purify and clear negative actions and non-virtuous karma and its causes, together with the afflictive emotions and habituations without exception, for myself and all sentient beings, so all is removed with nothing remaining.' Recite this out loud without losing mental focus or intent, and think: 'May all sentient beings in this way be free of karma, afflictive emotions, suffering, and habituations, and attain the level of glorious Vajrasattva!' Do so with both aspiring and engaging bodhicitta. This is the power of support.

Following that:

With fierce regret I admit and confess.

This line teaches the power of disenchantment with wrongdoing. Why do we need to develop a regretful mind? As we discussed above, in connection with that which is to be purified, what is to be confessed are the negativities of the six doors. This refers to everything that has been accumulated by us and all other sentient beings: the ten non-virtues, the five inexpiable sins, the four serious faults, the eight errors, and so on. We have already completed discussion of the ten non-virtues and the five inexpiable sins above. As for the four serious faults, these consist of the four serious errors, the four serious impairments, the four serious disrespects, the four serious denigrations, and so on; there are many divisions. Of these, sitting at the head of a line of learned masters, remaining in front of a fully ordained monk's prostrations, eating the food of a practitioner, and stealing a mantrin's ritual articles, are called the 'four serious errors'.

Similarly, disregarding a worldly oath, impairing the discipline of individual liberation, impairing the training of bodhicitta, and impairing the sacred commitments of Secret Mantra are the four serious impairments. The four serious denigrations are: having come under the influence of ignorance and stupidity, denigrating the body of a buddha; under the influence of pride and self-regard, denigrating the expertise of a learned master; under the influence of jealously and ill will, denigrating words of truth; and under the influence of biased attachment and aversion, engaging in discrimination of the Dharma.

The four serious disrespects are: the serious disrespect of drawing blood, which is one of the five inexpiable sins; the serious disrespect of wrong views, which is one of the ten non-virtues; the serious disrespect of holding bias towards the Dharma of experience; and the serious disrespect of bringing fault to what is ineffable by nature.

The serious disrespect of drawing blood is one of the five inexpiable sins – to draw blood from the body of the sugata. These days the sugata is not actually present, but lamas and spiritual teachers are emanations and representatives of the Buddha, so this includes harming them. Regarding the serious disrespect of wrong views – which is one of the ten non-virtues – to develop wrong views towards the authentic Dharma and the lama is not only a serious fault, but for everyone connected with our speech, actions, and behaviour, this fault becomes contagious.

Regarding the serious disrespect of holding bias towards the Dharma of experience, we can apply a worldly example to the teachings of the One Gone to Bliss: whether we take milk from the top or bottom of a large copper pot, or muscovado from the edge or centre of a round block, there is no difference – wherever we take from, it is the same; from wherever we experience the taste, it is identical. However, under the influence of partiality, and attachment and aversion, we have the perception that some of the Buddha's teachings are better, and hold the notion that others are not as good. Especially, through praising our own tradition and putting down the traditions of others, our own training of taking refuge becomes at fault. This is taught to be akin to committing suicide by throwing ourselves into a chasm of great negative behaviour, all the while with our eyes wide open. Regarding the serious disrespect of bringing fault to what is ineffable by nature, having too much one-sided attachment to emptiness is taught to lead towards wrong views. This covers the four serious faults.

The eight errors are divided into the eight causal errors and the eight resultant errors. Of these, the eight causal errors are:

> Criticising the virtuous, praising the unwholesome,
> Agitating the mind of someone virtuous,
> Hampering the virtuous accumulations of the faithful,
> Abandoning your lama, yidam, or vajra siblings, and
> Separating from the strict mandala.

The eight resultant errors are:

> Wrong views bring rebirth in hell,
> Wrong meditation brings rebirth as a preta,
> Wrong conduct brings rebirth as an animal,
> Wrong activities bring rebirth as a minion of Yama,
> Wrong offering substances cause ignorance to grow,
> Wrong samaya substances cause them to become poison, and
> Wrong mantras become obstructing conditions.

For all these negativities, in summary think: 'I admit transgressing against the holy Dharma, experiencing worldly shame and embarrassment, and so on – all the non-virtuous karma I previously created that I can actually remember, and everything I cannot. I confess all negativities I have accumulated in lifetimes without beginning, with shame, fear, and intense feelings of regret, without hiding or concealing anything. Vajrasattva, please clear and purify all my wrongdoings and obscurations at this very moment!' With these words, pray to your lama and Vajrasattva, who are not separate. This is the power of disenchantment with wrongdoing.

Following this, we recite the root text:

Henceforth, even at the cost of my life, I vow to abstain.

This teaches the power of restraining from misdeeds, or the power of restoration. From Chagme's *Aspiration for Sukhavati*:

> Without the resolve to restrain henceforth, there is no purification;
> So, even if it costs me my life,
> I vow not to engage in further wrongdoing.

Considering that our previous actions were not good, we become very regretful, as if having willingly consumed poison. Additionally, in future, we need to have the determination and vow that, even if someone were to threaten to sever our vibrant life force immediately, we would never commit such actions again. Otherwise, if we merely mouth the words: 'I admit and confess' without feeling heartfelt regret and resolve, then needless to say, the buddhas and bodhisattvas have unimpaired clairvoyance and enlightened knowledge – they know if an ordinary person is feigning. Although making confession in that kind of way, in general, is not an evil act, however it is difficult to gain any benefit or advantage from it.

We must make the resolve not to engage in any kind of wrongdoing or transgression. This is why we need to hold firm with two hooks: the resolve to refrain, and the vow that affirms: even if it costs us our life, we will not do such things in future. Therefore, like 'nailing down a promise', to continuously persevere in this resolve is the power of restraining from misdeeds.

> Upon a full moon in your heart
> Is a HONG syllable, encircled by the mantra.
> Reciting the mantra invokes his mind causing,
> From the point of union of the consorts' blissful enjoyment,
> Nectar, clouds of bodhicitta,
> Like droplets of camphor, to trickle down. By this, may
> Karma and afflictive emotions, the causes of suffering
> For myself, and sentient beings of the three realms –
> Illness, harmful forces, negativities, obscurations, faults,
>   downfalls, and contamination –
> Be purified without trace, I pray.

Meditation and Recitation of Vajrasattva

In two and a half stanzas, together with the hundred-syllable knowledge mantra, the power of thorough application of the remedy is taught.

> Upon a full moon in your heart.

Reciting this, you should visualise in the heart centre of the Vajrasattva masculine and feminine principles in union, the full moon disc symbolising bodhicitta, complete in all aspects or fully expansive, 'the mere size of a flattened mustard seed', as it is clearly described. On top of the moon disc:

> Is a HONG syllable encircled by the mantra.

In the centre of a moon disc shining white and radiant, shaped like a flattened mustard seed, visualise a white HONG syllable, as if drawn by a single hair. Visualise, surrounding the HONG, the hundred mantra syllables of the dharani mantra, encircled around. As for the manner in which the syllables encircle it, beginning with the OM, the mantra syllables are taught to be like horns. Like the horns growing upwards on a yak's head, think the syllables are upright, almost touching one another, and circle around in a clockwise direction.

> Reciting the mantra invokes his mind causing...

Recite the hundred syllables out loud, recalling their meaning as you repeat them in the manner of saying a prayer, so that the mantra recitation itself invokes the enlightened mind of Vajrasattva.

> From the point of union of the consorts' blissful enjoyment.

As we recite the mantra, from the HONG syllable and mantra string in Vajrasattva's heart centre, nectar of compassion-wisdom, like water dripping from melting ice, drips from the point of union of the Vajrasattva consorts' blissful enjoyment of meditative absorption.

> Nectar, clouds of bodhicitta...

This is the nectar of greatly blissful bodhicitta; great clouds of bodhicitta:

> Like droplets of camphor, are caused to trickle down.

The example used for the white element takes the form of the moon, from which cool moonbeams take a form like droplets of camphor trickling down. 'Nectar, clouds of bodhicitta' is understood to signify that they are white in colour, so our entire body fills up like a crystal vase filled with milk. In this way, these greatly blissful bodhicitta clouds of nectar flow into the crown aperture of Brahma of us and all others indivisibly.

> By this, may
> Karma and afflictive emotions, the causes of suffering
> For myself, and sentient beings of the three realms –
> Illness, harmful forces, negativities, obscurations, faults, downfalls, and contamination –
> Be purified without trace, I pray.

We pray not just for ourselves alone, but for all of the six kinds of infinite samsaric sentient beings in the three realms, to purify the negative karma that all have accumulated through the three doors of body, speech, and mind. We also pray to purify the motivation of those actions – the afflictive emotions of attachment, aversion, and ignorance – which become the causes and conditions to bring about the result of suffering, as well as:

> Illness, harmful forces, negativities, obscurations, faults, downfalls, and contamination.

These include all intrinsic negativities, afflictive emotional and cognitive obscurations, together with associated misdeeds of faults and downfalls. 'Contamination' happens when we associate with improper companions with impaired precepts; someone who has contradicted their sacred precepts of the Secret Mantra brings contamination and incidental impairment to others.

Although we do not purposefully act with harmful intent towards the body of our vajra master, *the tassels get dragged behind the rope*, so falling under the power of negative conditions, or otherwise by not examining or analysing properly, we can incidentally fall into transgression of contaminated precepts. What is more, we cannot think: 'I maintain my sacred commitments', because who knows how many numerous faults of contaminating impairment we may have caught from somewhere unknown? As Druptop Orgyenpa said:

> Except for the enemy of contaminating impairment, nothing has ever got the better of me.
> Except for the lama, no friend has ever provided refuge.

So, even if you think you have done something good, it is possible you may have caught some negative contamination. This is something that will happen to you, whoever you may be, and this includes me, myself as well. When this occurs, there is no other course of action for ignorant ordinary beings, apart from remedying impaired and broken commitments through engaging in confession.

> Be purified without trace, I pray.

All these negativities, obscurations, faults, and downfalls, without a single exception, are driven out without obstruction by the flow of nectar from above, appearing in the filthy form of smoky sludge, sooty effluent, and black fumes. Like dust washed away by a flood of water, it all comes oozing out through the pores and both lower doors. Specifically, all diseases and suppuration of wind, bile, and phlegm emerge in the form of rotten blood. All harmful malevolent forces emerge in the form of frogs, snakes, spiders, scorpions, and so on.

The ground beneath you splits open, and in the depths below is Yamaraja, karmic lord of death, and his entourage of all those to whom you owe karmic debts and debts of the flesh. With their mouths, hands and claws held out, they catch the flow, which makes them satisfied and content, and thus clears your karma and debts. Think all your debts of the flesh, negativities, and obscurations are purified as you recite the hundred syllable mantra.

To give a brief explanation of the meaning of the hundred syllable mantra, the first **OM** is the enlightened qualities and activities of body, speech, and mind of all the Ones Gone to Bliss. Alternatively, it is the nature possessing the five wisdoms, so we begin with it. **BANZA SATO SAMAYA** means 'the sacred commitments of Vajrasattva'. **MANUPALAYA** means 'please protect me with those sacred commitments!' **BANZA SATO TENOPA TISHTA** means 'O Vajrasattva, please remain close to me!' **DRIDHO ME BHAVA** means 'I pray, remain forever with me.' **SUTOKHAYO ME BHAVA** means 'be pleased and satisfied.' This is connected with the following mantra: **SUPOKHAYO ME BHAVA** which means 'be extremely pleased with me, so all enriching activity of what is to be accomplished is achieved, and so you may bestow all excellences of lifespan, merit, and so forth!' **ANURAKTO ME BHAVA** means 'I pray, be fond of me, so you remain without leaving.' Because of the power of the connection of the meaning, the mantra is read from beginning to end, so the order is not to be changed.

SARVA SIDDHI MAME PRAYACCHA means 'fully grant me all the accomplishments!' **SARVA KARMA SU TSA ME** means 'I pray, grant me the accomplishments to achieve all the activities.' **TSITTAM SHREYANG**

KURU HONG means 'unite my mind with the definitive goodness of the glorious most supreme enlightened vajra mind.' **HA HA HA HA HO** is taught to be the sound of the compassionate laughter of wisdom vajra. **BHAGAVAN** is the Transcendent Accomplished Conqueror. **SARVA TATAGATA BANZA MA ME MUNTSA** means 'allow me never to be apart from the vajra of all those gone to bliss.' **BANZI BHAVA** means 'unite me with the level of Vajradhara.' **MAHA SAMAYA SATO AH** means 'O great Samaya Sattva embodiment of vajra speech!'

This is how the meaning of the mantra has been translated, but the translation differs slightly between the transmitted teachings and the revealed treasures. Not only that, but there are also slight differences in the way the mantra is recited. However, there are probably good reasons for this, and although there are slight differences, the meaning is identical. From the point of view of the correct way to recite mantras, take for example 'BANZA'. These days some say that the Sanskrit needs to be pronounced 'VAJRA'. However, the holy accomplished vidyadharas of the past gained their accomplishments based on this mantra sound, and this is how they have transmitted it to us. Personally, I do not think there is any point in conforming to what others may prioritise. Although I have not looked into the debate, I think this is worth mentioning.

In addition, generally someone who recites mantras needs to understand a little about them and their basis. In this case, the root cause of mantra is the syllables; they possess a fourfold established nature, and the result is unobstructed capacity. To discuss this further by means of these three aspects, first there are four enumerated divisions of the cause syllables: root syllables that reside in the body; deity syllables of the palace; emanated syllables of miraculous display, and syllables which symbolise sounds. To which group does this mantra belong? It should be counted among the group of syllables which symbolise sounds.

However, thinking about sounds, sounds alone produce no power; all sentient beings make various different sounds and noises. The lion sounds its roar, people talk, yaks make their grunting noises, and so on; these are all sounds. It is also not acceptable just to say 'mantras are Sanskrit'. It is certain that many wrong views have been propagated in the Sanskrit language. We recite the title of the *Extended Biography of Guru Padmasambhava's Succession of Lives* in the language of Oddiyana: 'RUAKSHA SHAKARANA'. However, except for the blessing that this mantra has, what benefit is there to it being the language of Oddiyana? 'Oddiyana' is now known as Afghanistan, where nowadays although the people may still speak the ancient language of Oddiyana, in modern times it is a Muslim region.

For this reason, what we call 'mantra', on the base of causal syllables which symbolise sounds, needs to possess a nature that is established in four ways which need to be complete. On the strength of this, the result of mantra's unobstructed capacity comes about. The fourfold established nature is as follows:

1) Established by the essence of dharmata.
2) Established by the nature of conditioned phenomena.
3) Established by blessings.
4) Established by powerful energy.

Also, concerning the blessing of mantras, there are languages other than Sanskrit that have been transformed into mantras, in particular the scripts of revealed treasures. There is the symbolic script of the dakinis, the script of Dravira, Tibetan script, and so on. For example, in the mantra of the name of Guru Rinpoche: 'BANZA GURU PEMA THOTRENG TSAL', Thotreng Tsal is Tibetan and means 'garland of skulls'. However, when blessed by mantras, all syllables established by the essence of dharmata are established as the essence of the evenness of vast emptiness; naturally established conditioned phenomena are naturally established unmistakenly as extraordinary appearances. Syllables established by blessings are blessed by the name mantras of Guru Rinpoche, nondual with him and the victorious ones of the three times. Syllables established by powerful energy bring about actual observable phenomena, for example medicine and jewels, so all that which is desired comes forth without impediment.

Since the time of the three Tibetan ancestral Buddhist kings, all of the many emanated translators, scholars, and great masters who possessed both learning and accomplishment, engaged in intimate practice of these mantras. They accomplished the power of blessed knowledge mantras, so that they could fly in the sky like birds, swim in the water like fish, consume rock as if it were food, and pass through cliffs unimpeded. If we follow these mantras by which such masters gained accomplishment, I think there is no need to listen to what others say and change the way we recite them.

Chiefly at this stage of the practice, the development stage key points are important, so when we visualise deities, we speak of the eight measures of clarity and steadiness: four measures of clarity and four measures of steadiness. First are the four measures of clarity:

1) Distinct.
2) Alive.
3) Vibrant.
4) Vivid.

Whichever deity we visualise, their manifest qualities – down to the pupils and whites of their eyes – are not blurred, but clearly distinct. Not hazy or indistinct, but having an intensity of awareness, deities are alive. Neither mindless rainbow colours nor material form, we need to embrace our visualisation with wisdom; therefore arising with hundreds of enlightened qualities, the deity is vibrantly present. This is not a mere inference of ordinary thought, which speculates 'it is something like that'. We need the deity to arise in actuality, vividly in the clarity of our mind.

What are the four measures of steadiness?

1) Immovable.
2) Unchangeable.
3) Utterly unchangeable.
4) Completely flexible.

Our visualisations should be immovable by the general faults of forgetfulness, laziness, and so on. Unchangeable by the specific faults of intermittent vagueness. Utterly unchangeable all day and night, not being oppressed by thoughts sometimes clear, other times unclear. Proficient and completely flexible, so however we visualise the deity – whether standing or seated, emanating or gathering light rays, and so on – we can do so. Thus we should meditate in this way with the eight measures of clarity and steadiness. If all appearances arise as the mandala of the deity, this is the measure that we have attained stability, and is called 'perception as the mandala of the deity'.

However, as beginners, while we are unable to attain that degree of clarity, we can sometimes think about Vajrasattva's body, his face, hands, and so on. Sometimes we can focus on the way he is ornamented, sometimes train in the falling nectar, and at other times think about feelings of regret and confession. Gradually, we should strive until all these visualisations appear simultaneously.

Whichever it is, when it is time to bring your practice session to a close, consider your body as having the nature of light, clear within and without. Visualise in the centre of your body the central channel with the four characteristics, as discussed previously. Extending from that are the four chakras, like the extended ribs of an umbrella.

As is taught, the sixty-four branch channels of the navel chakra of emanation face upwards, the eight branch channels of the dharma chakra of the heart face downwards, the sixteen branch channels of the throat chakra of enjoyment face upwards, and the thirty-two branch channels of the crown chakra of great bliss face downwards. As before, the rain of nectar flows into these channels, so that the four chakras and the whole body, inside and out, overflows with white nectar. We should think we attain the four empowerments, and the four obscurations are purified. As the wisdom of the four joys becomes aroused in our mindstream, both our body and mind become intoxicated with undefiled bliss, whereby the level of the four kayas is established in our mindstream.

Following this, the root text reads:

> **Protector, in ignorance and delusion**
> **I have transgressed and corrupted my samaya.**
> **Guru protector, grant me refuge!**
> **Lord vajra holder,**
> **Embodiment of great compassion,**
> **Chief of all beings, in you I take refuge.**

After which we recite:

> **I admit and confess all corruptions of the root and branch samayas towards enlightened body, speech, and mind. I pray, cleanse and purify my entire accumulation of impurities: negative actions, obscurations, faults, and downfalls.**

Having offered these remorseful and regretful words of confession, the recital text continues:

> **Vajrasattva is gladdened, and with a smil**ing countenance **grants his blessing, saying 'Child of the family, all your negative actions, obscurations, faults, and downfalls are purified.'** Whereby the Vajrasattva masculine and feminine principles in union **melt into light and dissolve into me. By this** condition, my body becomes a sphere of white light marked with a HONG syllable, and I **too** instantly **become Vajrasattva, apparent yet empty, like a reflection in a mirror.**
>
> **Manifest at my heart is a HONG life-syllable, surrounded by the four syllables, from which light rays emanate. Whereby the three realms, including the container and its contents, become enlightened in the nature of the support and supported of the five families of Vajrasattva.**

Reciting this, visualise yourself as Vajrasattva. In his heart centre as before is a moon disc, like a flattened mustard seed, in the centre of which is a sky-blue HONG seed syllable of enlightened mind. In front of that is a white OM, to its right is a yellow BANZA, behind is a red SA, and to its left is a green TO. We should visualise clearly that the four syllables are facing inwards.

What is the meaning of the five syllables 'OM BANZA SATO HONG'? OM is the sambhogakaya that possesses the five kayas and five wisdoms. BANZA means 'vajra' or 'indivisible'. As expanse and wisdom are indivisible, it symbolises dharmakaya. SATO represents the courageous bodhisattva, the nirmanakaya. HONG is the syllable that symbolises the secret enlightened mind of the One Gone to Bliss, and has the meaning of invoking and attaining accomplishments. Therefore, it is taught the meaning of this mantra is 'Consider me with your enlightened mind of evenness, non-dual bodhicitta that subsumes all Dharma!'

OM BANZA SATO HONG

By reciting this many times, from the five syllables, rays of white, yellow, red, green, and blue light emanate upwards. These light rays multiply hundreds and thousands of times, and on the tip of each ray of light countless offerings emanate. These are offered to the victorious ones and their bodhisattva children who dwell in the boundless immense pure realms of the ten directions. Our accumulations are completed and our obscurations are purified. All compassion and blessings appear in the form of multi-coloured rays of light and dissolve into us, by which we attain the supreme and ordinary accomplishments. This creates the auspicious circumstances for the dharmakaya which benefits oneself.

Again, from the five syllables, light rays of the five colours emanate downwards, shining upon all the six kinds of sentient beings of the three realms. All the negativities, obscurations, suffering, and habituations in each one of their mindstreams are totally cleansed and purified, like the sun rising in the darkness. The entire external vessel of the universe becomes the Pure Realm of Manifest Joy. All sentient beings become the five families of Vajrasattva; all perceptions become enlightened forms and temples; all that resounds becomes the sound of BANZA SATO, and all thoughts become the nature of enlightened mind. It is taught that, fulfilling the two benefits by emanation and absorption, conceptual obscurations are purified. This creates the auspicious circumstances for the rupakaya which benefits others.

Following this, when it is time to complete the practice session, all the enlightened forms and pure realms that we have been visualising, gradually dissolve into light. This light merges into us, then from the outside, we also gradually dissolve into light and merge into the OM syllable at our heart centre. OM dissolves into BANZA, BANZA dissolves into SA, SA dissolves into TO. TO first dissolves into the hook at the foot of the HONG. The hook at the foot then dissolves into the small RA. The small RA dissolves into the body of the HA. The body of the HA dissolves into the crescent moon at the top. The crescent moon gradually dissolves into the bindu, which then dissolves upwards towards the nada. The nada finally vanishes like a rainbow, and we need to rest for a moment in meditative equipoise, in state of non-conceptuality free from elaboration.

Once again, in post meditation, the universe and its beings vividly manifest as the pure realm of Vajrasattva. We then need to adorn the end of the practice session with the following prayers of dedication and aspiration:

> **With this merit, may I swiftly**
> **Achieve Vajrasattva realisation, by which**
> **All beings without exception**
> **Are established on that level.**
>
> **Vajrasattva, whatever your enlightened form is like,**
> **Your retinue, lifespan, and pure realm,**
> **Your supreme and major marks, however they are,**
> **May I, myself and others, attain just the same.**

In this way, if we practise daily meditation on Vajrasattva, and recite the hundred syllable mantra twenty-one times each day, this is like not letting a debt incur interest. So by blessing a lapse, there will be no additional increase in negative karma. Also, it is taught in the *Ornament of the Essence* that if we recite one hundred thousand hundred syllable mantras, all downfalls will become purified. In this way, at this stage of the visualisation and recitation of Vajrasattva, if we meditate that Vajrasattva is at our crown, inseparable in nature from our root lama, this is guru yoga in the manner of the jewel which includes all.

What is more, visualising ourselves as Vajrasattva is the development stage. Visualising the chakra channels, and purifying them with the shower of nectar, is the completion stage with signs. It is also taught that visualising all illness, harmful forces, negativities, and obscurations entering the mouth of the Lord of Death is the most supreme longevity practice and dispelling of obstacles. Finally, resting in meditative equipoise in a state of non-conceptuality free from elaboration is also taught to be the completion stage without signs.

It is important to practise all these essential aspects – the complete key points of visualisation – diligently without getting distracted. For those who are accumulating the five hundred thousand recitations of the preliminaries, having already covered the two hundred thousand recitations of taking refuge and arousing bodhicitta, the way to practise the meditation and recitation of Vajrasattva, to accumulate the one hundred thousand recitations of the one hundred syllable mantra, is taught like this.

Part Five, The Mandala Offering

How and Why to Offer the Mandala

Fourth of the unique inner preliminaries is the practice of offering the mandala, to accumulate the merit of accordant conditions. If you think: 'Isn't it acceptable just to purify adverse conditions, wrongdoing, and obscurations?' It is not enough! We still need to accumulate merit of accordant conditions. If the two accumulations of merit and wisdom are not complete, there is no way to attain buddhahood with the twofold purity.

During the stage of the causal vehicle of characteristics, having first completed many countless aeons of both accumulation and purification, subsequently on the path of seeing, the true nature of phenomena needs to be seen. Similarly, on the swift path of the Vajrayana, although there are numerous unique methods which facilitate this, they all require gathering the accumulations and purifying the obscurations. Likewise, the profound realisation of emptiness endowed with all supreme qualities, also depends on the two accumulations. Therefore, as it is taught in the *Compendium of Dharma Sutra*:

> As long as the two accumulations are not complete,
> There is no realisation of sublime emptiness.

Generally, the bodhisattva children of the victorious ones have ocean-like conduct of completion, maturation, and cultivation, but summarised together they are included within the six perfections. What is more, these are included within the two accumulations: the manifest accumulation of merit, and the non-manifest accumulation of wisdom. The first five of the six perfections, from generosity to concentration, are the aspects of method and conduct, and the sixth perfection of wisdom is the accumulation of wisdom. Alternatively, the three former perfections are the accumulation of merit, the latter two are the accumulation of wisdom. Diligence is taught to be the ally of them all.

Whichever it is, in the essence of originally pure buddhahood, all the enlightened qualities of the three bodies of the victorious ones are all originally completely present without searching. However, without depending on the conditions of the two accumulations of the path, they cannot be actualised. To give an example, the light of the sun is intrinsically present, however it cannot be seen if obscured by clouds. The way to be rid of the clouds is for the wind to blow, so the wind is needed to disperse the clouds. But, except for being the cause by which the clouds are cleared, of course the wind is not the genuine productive cause for the sunshine. Whether or not there are clouds, the nature of the sun does not change.

Likewise, if the two accumulations are not gathered, the resulting two kayas are not attained. Due to this, the cause of the producer and the produced is not apparent, but it is explained by labelling the name of the cause on the condition. In short, from arhat and pratyekabuddha to great complete enlightenment, such result is not attained without depending on gathering the two accumulations. However, not everything we refer to as the 'two accumulations' is this same; the two accumulations of arhats, pratyekabuddhas, and bodhisattvas are not the same. How are they not the same? In terms of the causes of intent, the focuses of practice, and the results attained, the differences between all three of them are extremely great. Similarly, regarding the key points of the path of Sutra and Tantra, there is a great difference in the way the two accumulations are gathered. Since that is so, you may think that all Secret Mantra must be the same, but that is also incorrect. Regarding the three sections of outer Vajrayana tantras, all the yogas with signs are the manifest accumulation of merit, and all the yogas without signs are the non-manifest accumulation of wisdom.

In terms of the three sections of inner tantra, Maha, Anu, and Atiyoga are also not the same. It is taught that all the Mahayoga method stages of development are the manifest accumulation of merit, and the wisdom stages of completion are the non-manifest accumulation of wisdom. In Anuyoga, all the main activities to bind the channels, energies, and essences, and the subsequent arising of the illusory forms of deities, are the manifest accumulation of merit. Subsequently, the outcome that results from that method – the four degrees of joy that evoke wisdom – needs to be counted as the non-manifest accumulation of wisdom.

At the stage of Atiyoga, in terms of trekcho, the essence of wisdom which is emptiness is the accumulation of wisdom, and the nature of wisdom which is luminosity is the accumulation of merit. Alternatively, to speak in terms of the unity of primordial purity and spontaneous accomplishment, the spontaneously accomplished four visions are the accumulation of merit, and trekcho realisation of primordial purity is considered the accumulation of wisdom. These are listed in terms of their importance, as causes to bring about final attainment of the two kayas. Whichever it is, if one is not spiritually advanced, a genuine path is difficult to accomplish. However, we beginners need to manage to practise in accordance with the unity of the two accumulations.

What can we understand from this? On the path of both Sutra and Tantra, the accumulations may be gathered on the basis of many things, and the methods by which they can be gathered take many forms. All of these, without exception, are methods of gathering the accumulations. This is the essence of each individual path; all are ways to gather the accumulations. What is more, all methods of gathering the accumulations are included within the single practice which we are about to study. Also, it is easy to do, very effective, includes many methods, and is convenient to put into practice; thus it is an exceptional path. What is this exceptional path? It is this method of offering the mandala.

To engage in gathering the accumulations and purifying the obscurations by this means, we need to offer the mandala with the complete six perfections. How do we do so? It is said:

> Cow urine and dung are generosity,
> Doing the cleansing is discipline,
> Removing creatures is patience,
> Working hard is diligence,
> One-pointed mind is concentration,
> Grasping the layout is wisdom.

This teaches that when we offer the mandala, we should offer it by means of the complete six perfections. As for the offering materials, it is taught they should be chosen according to our financial means: a mandala of precious substances is best, second best is a mandala made of a pure material, and at the very least stone, wood, and so forth, may be offered upon a smooth base. Here we mention 'best, second best, at least' so, if your financial means and circumstances make it possible, then it is taught not to be too miserly, and make the offering with jewels and so forth. However, this does not mean that a yogi who maintains the ascetic life of a kusali without attachment, wandering with the forest animals, by arranging heaps upon a stone with an utterly pure visualisation, cannot offer the best kind of mandala.

The mandala that we offer by pouring grains and precious substances upon a base, and arranging the iron mountains, is offered in order to form a basis for visualising the variegated display of the trikaya pure realm. As a reminder to not forget something, some traditional people tie a thread around one of their fingers. Like that, this offering is done in order to remind us. When we make the mandala offering, the actions we do with our hands are not the most important thing. Most important is to bring to mind the entire display of the trikaya pure realm and, together with immeasurable and boundless emanations, offer that. That is the most crucial key point. Regarding the trikaya pure realms it is taught:

> Its mode of appearance is the nirmanakaya mandala.
> Its mode of abiding is the sambhogakaya mandala.
> Its pervasiveness is the dharmakaya mandala.

When we offer the mandala, there are two distinctions: the accomplishment mandala, and the offering mandala. The accomplishment mandala is the object to which we make offering – the accumulation field for taking refuge, which is the basis for our visualisation. All the arranged heaps need to be visualised in the form of the gathering of deities of the field of refuge, whom we request to reside in the centre of the offerings. If two mandalas are not convenient, it is in order to visualise the accumulation field in your mind. It is also in order to offer the mandala in front of an extraordinary basis. If this is in your usual living room or meditation room, if you are not a true renunciate, you should acquire a statue of our teacher the Buddha. For the representation of his speech, we should have copies of the Great Perfection tantras, or alternatively a copy of the *Compendium of Dharma Sutra*, and the root text of the *Essence of Secrets*. As representation of enlightened mind, a blessed stupa of the sugata also needs to be complete. These should all be placed upon your shrine. In front of these, we need to arrange clean offerings, with a pure mind. Again, most importantly, if our mind is pure, all will be clean. Generally, cleaning our living room is the practice that precedes all practice sessions and, in particular, having displayed representations of enlightened body, speech, and mind, offerings that are arranged need to be clean.

The Trikaya Mandala

For the offering mandala, in front of us we have already arranged the three actual representations of buddha body, speech, and mind. Visualised in the space above that are the essence of the three kayas, the accumulation field of the Victorious One and his children, the bodhisattvas. Visualising all this we recite the root text:

> **OM AH HONG**
> **A realm of a billion third-order thousand-fold worlds,**
> **Filled with the seven precious things and the wealth of gods and humans,**
> **Together with my body and possessions; by offering them entirely,**
> **May I attain the authority to turn the wheel of Dharma.**

Mandala Offering

In this one stanza the nirmanakaya mandala of the mode of appearance is taught. We recite the three syllables 'OM AH HONG'. They are the seeds of the buddha bodies, so they lead the words which offer this mandala of the pure realm of the three buddha bodies.

> A realm of a billion third-order thousand-fold worlds.

This is taught to be in a pure realm of a billion third-order great thousand-fold world systems, together with the four continents, Mt. Meru, and the heavenly realms. 'Third-order thousand-fold' does not mean three thousand. The four continents, Mt. Meru, and the heavenly realms, together with the sun and moon, are taught to be a first-order, base level thousand-fold world system. Similarly, one thousand to the power of two of these form a second-order, middling thousand-fold world system. One thousand to the power of three of these form a third-order, great thousand-fold world system. For each of these, there are a billion pure realms. These are the realms to be tamed by one nirmanakaya buddha.

> Filled with the seven precious things and the wealth of gods and humans.

This refers to the seven precious things belonging to a universal monarch: a precious wheel, a precious jewel, and so on; the eight auspicious symbolic possessions, and so forth. Bring to mind a collection filled with the artefacts and wealth of gods and humans. Offer an actual wealth of offerings in accordance with your means, whatever is excellent and fine, and also imagine all the attractive things we can – owned and ownerless – and visualise them as well. In addition to that, offer your own body, all your wealth and merit, joy and happiness – all of the possessions you enjoy, without even the slightest attachment – offer everything in its entirety to the gathering of your lama and the nirmanakaya deities.

> Together with my body and possessions; by offering them entirely,
> May I attain the authority to turn the wheel of Dharma.

This is offering your body, possessions, and so on. In short, offer everything that you cherish and hold dear, all that is attractive without exception, with the prayer of aspiration: 'May I attain the holy authority of a natural nirmanakaya Dharma king, to lead all wandering sentient beings onto the path of liberation and omniscience, with the holy wheel of Dharma.' This is the common mandala of the nirmanakaya, or the nirmanakaya mandala of the way things appear.

Second is the extraordinary mandala of the sambhogakaya, or in the Dharma terminology of our tradition, this is also taught to be called the 'sambhogakaya mandala of the way things are'.

> The greatly blissful Akanishtha Realm of Dense Array,
> Endowed with fivefold certainty, the assemblage of the five families –
> Inconceivable clouds of desirable offerings –
> With this offering, may I enjoy the sambhogakaya realm.

The Akanishtha Realm of Dense Array is in space above the previous nirmanakaya pure realm, and is called 'the greatly blissful pinnacle realm', however this is not the pinnacle of existence: 'In the utterly pure Densely Arrayed pure realm, within an immeasurable mansion of precious wisdom, is the assemblage of the five families endowed with fivefold certainty.' The five certainties are:

1) The certain place is the Densely Arrayed.
2) The certain teachers are the buddhas of the five families.
3) The certain retinue is bodhisattvas of the tenth bhumi.
4) The certain Dharma is the Mahayana.
5) The certain time is the continuous cycle of eternity.

Like this, the mandala assemblage of the five families is endowed with fivefold certainty, in an unimaginably arrayed realm and celestial abode.

> Inconceivable clouds of desirable offerings –
> With this offering, may I enjoy the sambhogakaya realm.

These are inexhaustible clouds of offerings – desirable offerings of beauty, song, and dance, offered by innumerable emanated goddesses – fully adorned manifold clouds of all things desirable, limitless and boundless. Think: 'By offering this well, may I enjoy the spontaneously accomplished pure realm of the sambhogakaya.' This is the extraordinary mandala of the sambhogakaya, and can also be called the 'sambhogakaya mandala of the way things are'.

Third is the special mandala of the dharmakaya, or in the Dharma terminology of our tradition it is also taught to be called the 'all-pervasive dharmakaya mandala'.

> Utter purity of appearance and existence, the youthful vase body,
> Adorned with unceasing compassion, the play of dharmata,

Mandala Offering

**A realm completely purified of grasping to kayas and bindus.
With this offering, may I enjoy the dharmakaya realm.**

This is in the space above the previously mentioned sambhogakaya pure realm, a primordial utter purity of all substantial appearance and existence. The basis of the way the expanse and inner lucidity of the youthful vase body abides, unborn and beyond concepts, is:

> Adorned with unceasing compassion, the play of dharmata.

This outwardly luminous radiance of unceasing compassion – the four manifestations of luminosity and so forth, whatever arises, together with the thought patterns of expressivity – all self-arise as the adornment of the play of utterly pure dharmata.

> In this way, all phenomena of myriad appearances
> Are the ornament of space, arising in the nature of the kaya.

As this teaches, this is a primordially self-arising realm:

> A realm completely purified of grasping to kayas and bindus.
> With this offering, may I enjoy the dharmakaya realm.

This is a pure realm completely purified of any grasping, such as fixation on the empty form of kayas and bindus as substantial entities, arranged in the manner of a heap. By offering this without dualistic grasping, primordially free basic abiding nature, determined with the non-dual view just as it is, we pray: 'May I enjoy the wholly positive dharmakaya pure realm, the original basic space!' Visualising this is the all-pervasive dharmakaya mandala, or the special mandala of the dharmakaya.

Of all the methods to gather the accumulations, the most supreme method is this offering of the mandala. If you accumulate other compounded merit, for example by distributing offerings and serving tea to the Sangha, commissioning thankas and building representations of the buddhas, giving oil for lamps, and so on, it is taught that for all objects of material offering and objects of generosity, it is difficult not to mix them with the three defilements. Firstly, when working for the initial funds to make an offering, it is difficult to not to get mixed up with the defilement of non-virtue and wrong livelihood. In the middle, during the main activity, it is rare to not defile it with complaints about how difficult it is, using unpleasant language. Even after finishing, it is difficult to not mix with the defilement of avarice, thinking: 'I spent too much time and money'. Therefore, although these other accumulations of merit are good, it is difficult not to mix them with defilements.

This offering of the mandala is a special method that, just by using our hands, we can gather great accumulations of merit. Therefore, with the single harmonious enlightened intent of all Sutra and Tantra, new and old schools, this is the unexcelled, indisputably renowned method to accumulate merit. When this is connected with the recital text, it is the mandala of the three kayas, from which nothing is excluded. Moreover, this can also be discussed based on understanding of the outer, inner, and secret mandalas:

Offering the mandala forms a support for visualisation of the four continents and Mt. Meru, together with the wealth of gods and humans, emanated thousands of millions of times and offered up. By the means of bringing to mind all the offering substances in the immense pure buddha realms which are equal to the number of atoms in the universe, if we offer all this to the buddhas of the ten directions, together with their bodhisattva children and their students, then the merit is the same as having actually offered it all. This is the outer mandala.

As for the inner mandala, visualising in the space in front of you the gathered deities of the Three Roots, your body acts as a mandala: your four limbs are the four continents, your spine is Mt. Meru, your skin is the mighty golden base, your central channel is the wish-granting tree, and your heart is the wish-fulfilling jewel. Think that your flesh, blood, and bones, together with your organs, are countless desirable objects of gods and humans, and are suitable to be offered. Such is the inner mandala.

Considering your mind to be a wish-fulfilling jewel, make offerings continuously to the gathered deities of your lama, the three kayas, and Three Roots: mind-emanated offerings of undefiled wisdom of great bliss in the form of the offering clouds of Samantabhadra – totally inexhaustible vast clouds of offerings, offered for the ongoing continuum of eternity. This is the secret mandala. If we make offerings in this way, while also maintaining the state of meditative equipoise, as long as we do not get confused and stray from the undistracted, uncontrived state of rigpa, then the special accumulation of ultimate wisdom is also completed. Tilopa taught:

> My child Naropa, never part from the two accumulations,
> They are the wheels of your chariot.

Also the learned and accomplished Karma Chagme taught:

> If your measure of accumulations is full,

Mandala Offering

Realisation will grow strongly,
Wisdom will increase powerfully, and
Your Dharma-accordant wishes will be accomplished.

When we come to finish the mandala practice session, finally the assembled gathering merges into us, and we need to settle into equipoise in a state of non-conceptualisation of the three spheres.

In this way, of the five hundred thousand practices of the preliminaries, we have now covered taking refuge, arousing bodhicitta, the hundred syllable mantra, and this, the mandala offering, completes the fourth practice.

Part Six, Gathering the Accumulation of the Kusali

The Significance of Chod

Following the teaching on the mandala, and an extension of that practice, is gathering the accumulation of the kusali – the Chod giving of the body. On some occasions, this section is also taught as a supplementary practice and can be included in a different section. Here, this method to gather the accumulations is done by arranging our own body as the heaps of a mandala, which cuts the four maras in one fell swoop.

As taught in Machik Labdron's oral tradition:

> Establish the four immeasurables in your mindstream,
> Merge reference-less rigpa with the expanse.
> Transform your owner-less physical mass into food;
> Rest in equipoise in the state beyond words.

In this 'Chod' or 'Cutting', what is it that we cut? We should cut away the four maras into the expanse:

> The substantial mara, the insubstantial mara,
> The mara of pleasure, the mara of pride;
> These are included in the mara of pride.

As this teaches, the four maras come down to the root of the pride of inner grasping at a self. Just as when the roots of a tree are cut, the branches and leaves are also automatically severed, that which is to be cut is the mara of proud self-grasping. That which does the cutting is the wisdom that realises selflessness free of elaboration. The way this cuts is by establishing reality, the way things really are, as sky-like, unembellished, beyond description, conception, and expression – the great dharmakaya mother, nature of the perfection of wisdom. This is what is called 'Chod'.

Chod Accumulation According to the Root Text

In the recital, first 'P'ET!' is spoken. The meaning of this is the combination of the letter of gathering method 'PA', and the letter of wisdom that cuts 'TA', to form the syllable 'P'ET'. This gathers sentient beings by the power of the method of great compassion, and cuts the self-grasping in the mindstream of ourselves and others with the profound wisdom of emptiness. To make our mindstream workable, with the bodhicitta unity of emptiness and compassion – the essence of which is the four immeasurables – we utter 'P'ET!'

With this, visualise in the middle of your heart centre, the essence of your mind's consciousness, Machik Troma Nagmo. Her body is dark-blue in colour. In her right hand she holds aloft a hooked knife, and in her left hand she holds a skull cup full of blood to her heart. Behind her right ear is the head of a squealing black pig. Meditate that she has the attire of a wrathful deity and is swaying in the dancing pose.

As you recite 'P'ET!' you need to think that she travels the path of the central channel, exits far out from the crown aperture of Brahma, and your body becomes a corpse. It is taught that if you have really mastered the meditation, or the visualisation of the essence of your mind as Troma Nagmo, then it is also suitable for your consciousness to move into space from the outset, and in that same moment give rise to Troma. Otherwise, first visualise Troma Nagmo, and then that she travels upwards. Either way is fine. Then follow the words of the recital:

> **By losing attachment to my treasured body, I conquer the god Mara.**
> **Through the aperture of Brahma, my consciousness is ejected into space.**
> **Mara Lord of Death is conquered; I become the Wrathful Yogini.**
> **With a hooked knife in her right hand, conquering the demon of afflictive emotions,**
> **She slices off my skull, conquering the demon of the form aggregates.**
> **Her left hand holds the skull cup in the manner of an action performer,**
> **Placing it on a hearth of human skulls – the three kayas.**
> **Inside, my corpse, which fills the third-order thousand-fold world,**
> **Is melted into nectar by a short AH and a HUM syllable,**
> **Purified, multiplied, and transformed by the power of the three syllables.**

This body of ours is the basis of self-grasping. All the fixating concepts which grasp with treasured attachment to our body are abandoned from the root.

> By losing attachment to my treasured body, I conquer the god Mara.

So, as the cause of harm is no longer being produced, the condition of the harmer, the mara of Devaputra, is defeated naturally.

> Through the aperture of Brahma, my consciousness is ejected into space.

Your consciousness – awareness without reference point – arrives in the expanse of space via the crown aperture of Brahma, or the door of the great channel, and your awareness and space merge inseparably. Thus you are freed from the extreme of permanence.

> Mara Lord of Death is conquered; I become the Wrathful Yogini.

Arising, ceasing, and dwelling disperse like clouds in the sky, so Mara Lord of Death is automatically conquered, and you are freed from the extreme of nihilism. Your awareness is vividly apparent in the form of Troma and, in that instant, your body becomes a corpse and collapses to the ground. Visualise that your corpse is fat and greasy, and fills the extent of the third-order thousand-fold world system.

> With a hooked knife in her right hand, conquering the demon of afflictive emotions....

In Troma's right hand she holds a hooked knife, which symbolises the wisdom of realisation of the true way things exist. This conquers the mass of thoughts – attachment, aversion, and ignorance – afflictive emotions that have no self-nature.

> She slices off my skull, conquering the demon of the form aggregates.

Without any grasping or attachment to the basis illustrated by the aggregates of the physical form – the aggregates of the four names – Troma slices off the skull of the corpse and the demon of the aggregates is conquered.

> Her left hand holds the skull cup in the manner of an action performer.

In Troma's left hand she holds the bhandha, or skull cup, in the manner of an action performer. At this stage there is no need to think about putting the skull cup you visualised previously to one side, and picking up this one you just sliced off. Visualise that your sliced-off skull cup, itself non-dual with Troma's symbolic implement, is placed with its forehead facing towards you in the manner of an action performer, upon three human skulls. These serve as hearth stones, equal in size to Mt. Meru.

> Inside, my corpse, which fills the third-order thousand-fold world...

With the hooked knife in your right hand, pick the corpse straight up, and place it in the skull cup. This corpse, which fills the third-order thousand-fold world, transforms into food for all those who are the object for offerings.

> Is melted into nectar by a short AH and a HUM syllable.

Below the skull cup is a red short AH syllable with the nature of fire. What we call a 'short AH' is the lower half triangle of a capital AH letter with its point facing upwards (Λ). From the presence of this short AH, fire flares up, heating the skull cup. The corpse inside melts and bubbles to the boil, and everything unclean: pollution and dirt, pus and blood, and so on, boils over in the form of froth and scum. Visualise that this flows into the mouth of Yama the Lord of Death.

Above the skull cup is an upside-down white HUM syllable, with a nature of nectar. As the steam rises, it touches the HUM syllable heating it up, whereby a flow of nectar drips down from its crown. This merges non-dual with the nectar in the skull cup. Finally we need to think that the HUM syllable also overflows with light and melts, merging inseparably into the nectar.

> Purified, multiplied, and transformed by the power of the three syllables.

By the blessing and power of the three syllables of the three kayas and three vajras, the nectar is transformed into everything desirable, and blessed as offering substances. OM purifies all the imperfections of colour, smell, taste, and so on. AH multiplies it many times. HONG transforms it into all varieties of offering substances and objects, whatever is desired. Visualise that it becomes immaculate nectar of wisdom, with a nature that gives rise to everything desirable.

OM AH HONG

Reciting these three syllables, you need to visualise and repeat them until you can no longer maintain the entire visualisation. Then, as you visualise all of the offering substances, in the space in front of you, upon a precious throne piled with silken cushions, is your gracious root lama. At this time visualise his body as deep maroon in colour, with the accoutrements of Heruka. He has one face, two arms, and three eyes. In his right hand he holds a golden vajra at his heart centre, in a pointing manner. In his left hand, upon the mudra of meditative equipoise, he holds a skull cup full of the wisdom nectar of immortality. In the crook of his left arm he holds a khatvanga, and his body is ornamented with a tiger-skin skirt and the six bone ornaments. His head is ornamented with the five dried skulls, and his two legs rest in the posture of a revelling king. This is the lama with the accoutrements of Heruka.

In the space above him are the lineage lamas. In the middle is the gathering of yidams and dakinis. In the space level with the skull cup is the gathering of Dharma protectors and guardians established through karma, together with regional deities and owners of the locale, all present. On the ground below are the principal guests, the obstructing gek spirits and karmic creditors, among all the six kinds of sentient beings of the three realms. Visualise them like dust billowing in the sun's rays.

At this stage, saying 'P'ET!' dualistic grasped-grasping is directly cut through, impelled by its sound.

> **The sacred bond with the upper guest recipients of offering is fulfilled,**
> **Completing the accumulations, whereby the supreme and common attainments are achieved.**
> **The samsaric guests below are pleased, clearing karmic debts.**
> **In particular, the malicious and obstructive ones are satisfied.**

This teaches the white distribution.

> The sacred bond with the upper guest recipients of offering is fulfilled.

There are two upper guest recipients of offering: the guests of reverence – the Three Jewels, and the guests of qualities – the protectors. It is taught that your root lama, the lamas of the lineage, and the entire gathering of buddhas and bodhisattvas, partake of the distilled nectar essence with hollow vajra tongues. All the gathered yidam deities of the four and six tantra sections partake of the nectar with tongues in the form of each of their symbolic implements, and it is taught the gathered heroes and dakinis, together with the Dharma protectors and guardians, partake with tongues of hollow sunbeams. In this way, consider all the guests are served and partake of the distilled essence, whereby they are filled with delight.

> Completing the accumulations, whereby the supreme and common attainments are achieved.

Thereby, your two accumulations of merit and wisdom are completed. Consider that the two obscurations of afflictive emotions and obscuration to the knowable are purified. All corruption of the sacred commitments is cleared, whereby think that you attain the two accomplishments, supreme and common. The minds of the dakinis, together with the Dharma protectors and guardians, are filled with delight, whereby all opposing conditions and obstructions to accomplishing the holy Dharma of enlightenment are cleared, and all according circumstances and goodness develops and increases.

> The samsaric guests below are pleased, clearing karmic debts.

Then, still visualised as Troma, you scatter nectar from the skull cup in your left hand, so nectar falls like rain, covering all places in the three realms of samsara. With this nectar, the lower guests invited out of compassion – those of the three realms of samsara who have become guests – and:

> In particular, the malicious and obstructive ones are satisfied.

In particular, visualise that the obstructing gek spirits, the guests who are karmic creditors, become satisfied. Of the various distributions: the white distribution, the red distribution, the variegated distribution, and so on, this is taught to be the white distribution. Generally, the Chod offering of the body teaches both the white distribution and variegated distributions.

> **Illnesses, negative forces, and obstacles are pacified into the expanse.**

This line teaches both variegated distributions. Again, from the steam of the boiling nectar, inconceivable clouds of offerings of flowers, incense, lamps, fragrant water, and so on, radiate forth and are offered to the upper guests. For you, yourself and all other sentient beings, the accumulations are completed and obscurations purified. For all the lower guests, anything they desire falls like rain bringing them enjoyment, so that karmic debts are returned, debts repaid, flesh debts purged, and all illnesses, negative forces, and unwholesome deeds and obscurations are purified. All of the guests are satisfied and appeased. The six kinds of beings are freed from all their individual karmic perceptions and suffering, as well as habituations. Think that all males are established at the level of Avalokiteshvara, all females are established at the level of Jetsun Tara, and the three realms are dredged from the depths, so not even the name 'samsara' remains. This is taught to be the variegated distribution. By this, all obstructions to accomplishing enlightenment of the holy Dharma are pacified into the expanse of evenness.

Adverse circumstances and clinging to self are smashed to dust.

Adverse circumstances appear as friends, and grasping at a self – the root of all karma and afflictive emotions – is removed from its place and smashed, as if into atoms and dust.

Finally, all offerings and objects of offering without exception...

Finally, at the stage of bringing the practice session to a close, all the activity of offering, the offerings of nectar and so forth, yourself, the practitioner who is doing the offering, and the objects of offering, the upper and lower guests, without exception...

...are the basic nature of uncontrived Great Perfection AH!

This is unborn basic nature not established as any essence whatsoever, free of all elaboration – a nature of ceaseless distinct appearances thoroughly complete, non-dwelling vast evenness of rigpa fully pervaded by compassion – a spontaneously accomplished way of abiding in the genuine uncontrived expanse. Saying this 'AH!' we enter into a non-referential state of meditative equipoise.

Generally, this practice called 'Chod' means to cut self-grasping, the root of ignorant deluded perceptions. As it is said:

> Wandering in eerie places and mountain hermitages is outer Chod;
> Forsaking your body as food is inner Chod;
> Cutting the single root completely is true Chod.
> I am a yogi with these three Chods!

This teaches that if you possess these three, you have the name 'yogi'. What is more, if you do not cut the root of self-grasping from deep within yourself, when demons arise in your perception, if you perceive them to be external, there will not be just one but many. This is just as the Ogress of the Rock said to Jetsun Milarepa, who replied:

> If you do not know demons are the root of mind,
> If you take a demon to be a demon, it will be harmful.
> If you know a demon to be your mind, you will be free.
> If you realise a demon to be empty, it will be cut.

Also:

> This apparent manifestation of malevolent male and female yakshas,
> When unrealised are demons,
> Making trouble and causing obstacles.
> If you realise it, demons are deities,
> And all accomplishments arise from them.

Therefore, without parting from bodhicitta of love and compassion, and by cutting the root of your self-cherishing and self-grasping, all that which is to be cut and that which does the cutting, pervades into the expanse of the single true nature. Thus you actualise the full expression of consummate actual cutting, which is the ultimate Chod.

Teaching Day Eight

We ordinary beings, stricken with the disease of afflictive emotions, held captive by the demon of ignorance, and under the control of delusion, are helpless without any strength of mind. What we are most familiar with and used to experiencing, are mental processes that are unsuitable. Motivated by the negative perpetuation of these habitual tendencies, we tend towards negative habits. We do not know how to travel the authentic path on our own, under our own power, and we are unlikely to have the karmic connection to be introduced to someone to guide us. The mind of the foolish person on a wrong path is like water flowing wherever it is channelled; it is easy for water to flow downhill. Similarly, if there is a guide who leads us downwards, naturally it is easy to speed in that direction. As it is said: *when your actions go downhill, bad conditions occur without being summoned.*

Turning upwards, there are those who can guide us to enter the authentic path that delights the Victorious One, but it is difficult to have the good judgement and fortune we need to follow their direction. The reason for this is that we do not possess any excellent or noble habitual tendencies. When we unintelligent samsaric sentient beings teach the Dharma to each other, we start by saying, 'We must practise the Dharma with the thought of benefitting all sentient beings as infinite as space.' The one who says this has it well-rehearsed, and to those listening, it is all too familiar. However, when it actually comes down to it, when we want to put the Dharma into practise, benefit for others is put aside, yet we still do not understand how to benefit ourselves. At that time, if both the one who is speaking and those who are listening are at that point, if we have no actual Dharma practice, to pretend we do is futile. Still, no one believes our pretence. As long as the perception of this life has not faded, anyone can say anything to anyone, but we are walking on a razor's edge. Who knows which will arrive sooner, tomorrow or the next life? Guru Rinpoche taught:

> Life is impermanent like autumn clouds,
> Our family and friends are like shoppers at a market place.

When we arrive at the place where true and false, cause and effect, are weighed out, it will become clearly understood what was just empty pretence. Like wandering consciousnesses in the bardo, we meet only briefly, once in a hundred times. Now that we have met with this opportunity to speak about important matters concerning both our present and our future, clearly there is no time for meaningless chat.

As this is the case, from the opening Sanskrit title, when we practise the Dharma of the Mahayana, we need the complete three excellent principles connected with the preparation, main part, and conclusion. If these are not complete, our practice does not join the ranks of the Mahayana Dharma. Other than not entering the path of the Mahayana Dharma in the first place, as soon as we wish to do so, our practice absolutely must be connected with the three excellent principles. Without these, it is taught we will not attain the level of buddhahood; we will not achieve the enduring goal of all successive lifetimes of ourselves and others.

Except for merely repeating the words 'all sentient beings are my parents', in fact, leaving aside insects, horses, yaks, and so on, we cannot even keep in mind the idea that our friends in town, our neighbours, and so on – humans like ourselves – are the same as our parents of this lifetime. Unable to think in this way, we lack the compassion that focuses on sentient beings. When this is the case, there is no need to mention great compassion, no need to mention middling compassion, we do not have even a little compassion. Except for concern and fondness for our own blood relatives and offspring, to tell the truth, we have no compassion at all. This feeling is merely a mind of cherishing, connected with attachment and aversion. No need to mention humans, this is something that wild tigers and mountain wolves also exhibit. There is nothing amazing about it.

If someone here was wretched and sick, an old abandoned person with no relatives or clan, unable to die but unable to live, or if there was an impoverished and fearful orphan, left without a guardian and tormented by suffering; if, towards such a person our compassion were aroused, then that would deserve to be called 'compassion'. This is the sign that there is a seed of compassion in our mindstream. However, if such a wretched person had previously accumulated some negative karma, the result of which had ripened in this way here and now, the full maturation of this karma upon their physical basis in this world is actually a powerful purification. For them, it is possible they could wait until the result of their negative karma became exhausted. However, how many of us have ever considered that we continue to accumulate new karmic causes, and we will inevitably need to experience their full ripening?

What we are currently experiencing is not that bad; compared to the suffering of the lower realms, the hells and the pretas and so forth, this cannot even be called 'suffering'. For the fully ripened result of the karma that we accumulate from taking just one life, how much suffering in hell would we have to experience? How long would we have to experience it? With the passing of many great aeons of time, even if this was sufficient time for such karma to be exhausted by the power of experience, even if we were to gain a human body at some point, through the influence of causal resemblance, it would be necessary to repay the karma of taking life with our own life five hundred times over. The karma of taking what is not given, sexual misconduct, lying, divisive talk, harsh words, gossip, covetousness, malicious thoughts, and so on, cannot begin to be counted. Yet these are still not the most terrible wrongdoings. Those who accumulate the karma of immediate consequence, and those who develop wrong views towards the Dharma and their lama, will need to take rebirth in the hell of unending torment, as if they had been earmarked for slaughter. What can they do? Considering this, there is no way not to arouse concern and compassion for all the sentient beings we see around us. Truthfully, they really do deserve our compassion.

We self-centred ordinary beings really are like children, and what is more, among many children, we are the thoughtless ones. We behave badly without the slightest shame, and are interested only in ourselves. Some of our kind parents who gave us life are still with us, but through age the four elements of their bodies have become frail and their physical strength is weakened. Their mental powers are impaired so, like the late afternoon sun on the crest of a hill, they sit as if waiting for death. There are those, now gone down the great path of the next life, who while on the brink of death, gazed at the living with the eyes of the dead, saddened by the sight of those they were leaving behind. Oblivious to their current state of happiness or sadness, as each year passes we forget them more and more.

If we talk sincerely about our own individual shortcomings and improprieties in life, we really are worse than some animals. As we discussed at the stage of the four immeasurables, if camels lose their offspring, or their calf dies, they grieve for the rest of their lives, and die in such sadness. Also, when a crane's partner is killed, year upon year, it grieves alone. These are animals, so except for grieving, they do not know how to practise the Dharma that would bring benefit. However, sometimes I think our behaviour is worse than such animals. We understand that if we practise the holy divine Dharma it is beneficial for both ourselves and others, and we know that we can only receive Dharma teachings rarely, yet still we forsake them in favour of petty household tasks.

Think of your parents or your children, brothers, sisters, or friends who have died, all of those for whom your heart still aches. For most of them, their passing occurred in the context of negative habitual tendencies. It is also difficult to form a good aspiration when you are at the point of death. Now, there is nowhere else for them to go except to the three realms, the abodes of the six types of beings, where they experience suffering. Having just now been reborn in hell, if they hope and yearn for those of us who are still alive, would it not be wrong if we did not also turn our thoughts occasionally towards them?

If their unwholesome actions were not too serious and they had embraced virtuous companions, and especially if they had seized the path that a holy spiritual teacher taught them to avoid being reborn in the lower realms, it is possible they may have gained another human rebirth. However, if when they were on this side of life, they were badly confused by the joy and sadness of attachment and aversion that thinks only in terms of us and them, enemies and friends, then even if they have gained a human body, by the karma of retribution it is likely they have been born in the household of those they did not like. If we also dislike that family's offspring, then how can we ultimately distinguish the difference between friend and foe? In truth, we are not much different from ignorant, impulsive wild people living in the jungle.

We probably know our parents, and it is likely we know or knew our grandmother and grandfather. But I imagine there are probably lots of people who have never given much thought to who their great-grandmothers and fathers were, except for perhaps their names, not to mention knowing anything about the generations that came before them. Thinking about it, our bodies were formed from their flesh and blood, so how are they different from our own parents? If we trace back all the way to the infinite beginning of samsara, in truth all those beings are the same as our relatives in this life. Thinking in this way, there is nothing we cannot understand about the truth that all sentient beings are our parents.

Therefore, we need to see if we can arouse impartial love and compassion for all sentient beings. If there is already a little love and compassion in our mindstream, allow this to increase; we need to train in fostering this until it becomes great compassion. Without compassion we cannot practise the Dharma, just as without barley there is no way to mill tsampa. The degree to which someone is or is not a Buddhist is witnessed by whether or not they have faith and compassion. If you notice the benefit of increased faith and compassion, then there has been benefit in receiving teachings. From the aspect of faith and compassion, if there has not been even a slight increase then, like firing an unfledged wooden arrow into a forest, which leaves no trace of where it went or where it struck, there has been no aim or target for receiving teachings. Not only will we not become liberated for many lifetimes, but there is no way to guarantee we will not take lower rebirths.

Here the 'faith' I am talking about does not mean you should have faith in me. The important thing is having confident faith in cause and effect, which is called 'the authentic world view'. Having confident faith in cause and effect, if we do not separate ourselves from love and compassion, which are like moisture, and sow the seed of bodhicitta, then a small green shoot will spring up. At that time, under the influence of faith and compassion, renunciation grows with revulsion of samsara. Not for self-benefit, but for the benefit of others, by not separating from bodhicitta, the authentic view becomes born in our mindstream. Thus, passing through the stages of the grounds and paths, we can attain the level of complete buddhahood.

Whenever we gather together, I am always talking about this; it is so important! From the lama high up on the throne, down to the old grandmothers and grandfathers in the community, see if you can seize the path to liberation! Seize the path to liberation! When you come to seize the entrance to the path of liberation, whatever happens, you will be fine. When bodhicitta is aroused in your mindstream, if it does not decrease or get forgotten, even if, due to karma and conditions, you had to take rebirth in hell, you would not need to suffer for very long. By the power of bodhicitta escape is swift. Regardless of how much negativity you may have accumulated, when you embrace bodhicitta, the darkness of a thousand years is illuminated in an instant by a single lamp.

On the contrary, without the attitude of renunciation, without compassion, and without even the slightest hint of the fragrance of bodhicitta, if someone poses majestically on a triple-layered golden throne under a many-layered five-coloured silken umbrella, needless to say their next rebirth will be as a hell being. Even before being reborn in the actual hells, they will have to remain for an extended period in the Ephemeral Hells.

Also, in terms of pursuing an education in the scriptures, even if someone diligently studies all five textual groups of the Buddha's teachings, if this does not liberate their mindstream, there is no benefit. Alternatively, from the perspective of arranging, preparing, and conducting rituals, knowing the metre and melody of recitations, and the movements of ritual dancing alone, no matter how thoroughly, is of no benefit. It is said:

> Monastics become enlightened via the order of arrangement.

This means it is necessary to have confidence in the order of the generation and completion stages, because if we do not actually seize the beginning of the path to liberation, just knowing the physical and vocal actions does not have great benefit; at least this is what I have found to be true personally.

For a while, some young men and women have an opinion of themselves which is higher than the lofty blue sky; they think there is no ageing or decline. But the old grandmothers and grandfathers have travelled that very same path to arrive where they are today. What is more, to get older and experience old age is actually the goal of our aspirations. We say to each other: 'Live long, live a hundred years!' However, some do not survive past the time of youth. Without time for any joy or happiness, the Lord of Death's lasso catches them. Put into an old sack and placed upon three stones, they become a corpse. When the beautiful radiance of their almond eyes is gone, the rows of their thirty conch-white teeth are scattered, wind blows away their hair, and the four elements of the body's flesh and blood vanish, they become food for dogs and vultures. We do not know when people will no longer speak our own names, and the mani mantra will be recited for us. Who knows when this will happen?

Looking around at your companions, you know not everyone is going to die of old age. If there is birth, of course there is death. Where is there a place where people do not die? People are the same in that they all die, but the ways in which they die are not alike. Some, from a young age are devoted to the Dharma. They have naturally few afflictive emotions, great faith in the divine Precious Jewels, and shun non-virtuous actions like poison. If such people understand the key aspects of the true Dharma, for them death is not death, it is flight. Such people truly gain the essence of taking a human body with the freedoms and endowments.

However, others are not like that. The young think they have hundreds and thousands of years to live. Those in a high position think there is no possibility of falling down. Those who are full think they will never become hungry. Having scaled a lofty mountain, some never consider the downward descent. Like throwing a heavy stone into a bottomless lake, in this way when we create the causes for rebirth in hell, at that time our misery and regret is that much greater.

Some old people get to the stage where this life is telling them, 'Leave now, leave now!' and the next life calls, 'Come now, come now!' Although they still remain, there is no feeling of comfort. Their bodies having aged, as the elements degenerate, old people lose the power of the five faculties. Together with the aging of the outer body, their inner mental confidence becomes weaker. Even though they may still have things they used to enjoy, they no longer have the capacity to enjoy them. Like an antiquated object or a worn out machine, they are beset by problems of all kinds. Walking, sitting, lying, or moving, whatever they do is uncomfortable, and they are afflicted by sickness and pain. Although young people do not say it, they often think, 'It would be better without this senile, abandoned old wreck'. At that stage we have no control, experience the contempt of others, and so on... We could speak about the suffering of old age all day and still not be finished.

However, at that time, if you have a focus and basis for your mind to rely on, having embraced the beginning of the path to liberation, then you are happy to be sick and death is a joy. If not, even if someone has recited ten million mani mantras, who knows what may be revealed as arising in their mind at the time of death? Although they may have completed their promised obligation of reciting one or two hundred thousand recitations of the name of Amitabha, was it embraced by correct arousal of bodhicitta, and prayers of dedication and aspiration? Generally speaking, other than training in the four causes to be reborn in the Pure Realm of Great Bliss, other practice is not necessary. Even if someone is an ordinary being, if they practise the four causes, they can arrive in the Pure Land of Great Bliss. However, if the four causes have not been practised correctly, as soon as they close their eyes, it is difficult for Lord Amitabha and the Eight Bodhisattvas to appear before them in welcome.

If that is the case, whoever you are, regardless of age, gender, and whether you are a layperson or ordained, you must strive to see if you can seize an authentic path to liberation. *For those who understand, one word is enough; for a trained horse, one flick of the whip is enough.* When you are not sure if you have embraced the beginning of the path to liberation, regardless of what you may say, you are still running around in confusion. We have been wandering around in beginningless samsara up to now. This life, we have been born in a place where the Dharma has spread, and although the sun has risen over the earth, if we do not open our eyes, from our own perspective, we are still wandering in the same dark gloom.

By practising the path, we are carried by the power of gathering the two accumulations of merit and wisdom. The method to traverse the noble levels and paths of the Mahayana relies on the basis of the unity of the two truths, from which the path of the unity of the two accumulations is practised. The result of this is the level of the unity of the two kayas, which needs to be attained. This being so, the two attitudes of bodhicitta need to be aroused in our mindstream. As Dodrupchen Jigme Tenpe Nyima said:

> Meditate on the root of the path: renunciation and bodhicitta.
> Without the root, how can the branches grow?
> Train in the essence of the path: the essence free from extremes.
> Without the essence, how will the branches grow?
> Find the goal of the path, Dzogchen luminosity;
> Without finding the goal, your path is ephemeral.

To allow the non-conceptual wisdom of ultimate bodhicitta to be aroused in our mindstream, we need to give birth to both relative aspiring bodhicitta and engaging bodhicitta in our mind. The arousal of this kind of aspiring and engaging bodhicitta in our mindstream is divided into the four immeasurable attitudes, and summarised in compassionate love. So, if we speak of this summarised into one point, it is that we should not be separate from a compassionate attitude. For compassion to grow in our mindstream, it depends on having a kind heart. In short, the root of everything comes down to having a kind heart. As it is taught:

> If the intent is good, the levels and paths are also good.
> If the intent is bad, the levels and paths are also bad.
> Everything depends on intentions,
> So always strive for a kind heart.

Sometimes many words are used to make a minor point, but at other times a few words have great meaning, so that is why I repeat this again and again; having a kind heart is extremely important. If all the people of this region received Dharma teachings, and every one of them became kind hearted with a compassionate mind that benefits others, then all of us would become the noble Sangha. At that time, if our inner enemy of afflictive emotions can be tamed from within, external harmful adversaries will automatically be tamed. Even if there were hostile bandits or thieves, there would be no need to be afraid; deities and guardians will protect you. The Dharma protectors guard those who are in harmony with the Dharma, so any harm is automatically repelled.

In this way, if everyone similarly had a kind heart of compassion and an altruistic attitude, this would no longer be the human world, but a heaven; even surpassing a heaven, it would be a pure realm. We visualise this and make prayers of aspiration, with a pure noble intent for this to happen. However, for this to actually manifest is a little difficult. The reason it is difficult is that there is no way to reverse the decline of the degenerate dark age. The 'dark age' is so called because at that time, bad people in all countries repeatedly engage in negative conduct.

> If people engage in negative conduct, then it is called the 'dark age'.

This prophecy has come to pass. To give examples of how this manifests, it is possible that in one family, the mother maintains an attitude of Dharma, however the father's bad personality cannot be improved. Alternatively, although the father understands the key reasons for engaging in virtue and gathering the accumulations, and wishes to do so, other family members drag him down. Some people reach the stage of old age, when the holy Dharma should be the single focus of their faith, however, in the shadow of their children mixing with bad associates, the cause and effect of unwholesome deeds and suffering prevents them from practising. On the other hand, some people have good offspring, who from the start are decent people and recognise virtue and vice, avoid karmic cause and effect, get along with folk, and have faith in the buddhas and lamas. Although some old people are stooped, they are bent in a good way, like the horns of a wild black antelope, or a right-spiralling conch. But there are others whose mindstreams are crooked, like the horn of a miserable old yak which curls into its own eye. Those who cannot differentiate virtue from non-virtue are objects of our compassion. As it is said:

> Show love to the impoverished; have love for those who are horrible.
> Show love to the belligerent; have love for those who are careless.
> Have compassion for those under the control of others;
> Have compassion for those obsessed with what is wrong.

These are truly the unmistaken objects for our compassion. However, for those who are at the stage of not believing in hell unless they are shown it directly, for the time being there is nothing we can do except leave them be. There were some beings whose time to be tamed had not arrived and could not be tamed by the actual One Gone to Bliss, so like us, they were left behind. Therefore, we should arouse the kind of bodhicitta that is not afraid of anything whatsoever: the extent of numerous beings, a time period of many aeons, or conduct that is difficult to perform – so that for the sake of one sentient being, even if we had to journey through hell, we would not retreat. We must make prayers of aspiration to be of benefit to wandering sentient beings. Doing so, regardless of however difficult sentient beings are to tame, however bad their karmic connection, it is certain that samsara will come to an end.

Part Seven, Guru Yoga

Visualising the Accumulation Field

By means of a completely pure mind, embraced with authentic arousal of bodhicitta for all, self and others, the time has come to listen to the *Extraordinary Inner Preliminaries of the Sublime Path to Omniscience, Recital for the Preliminaries of Dzogpa Chenpo Heart Essence of the Great Expanse*. Today is the last section of the extraordinary inner preliminaries, so it is time to teach guru yoga. The ultimate method to actualise the wisdom of realisation in our mindstream, guru yoga needs to be taught in three sections:

1) Visualising the accumulation field.
2) Offering the seven branches.
3) Praying resolutely and accomplishing the nature of the four vajras in our mindstream.

Of these, first is visualising the accumulation field. In the root text:

> **EH MA HO!**
> **My perception is of a spontaneously present realm of vast purity –**
> **The perfectly arrayed Glorious Copper Coloured Mountain, in the centre of which**
> **Is my form basis Vajrayogini,**
> **With one face, two arms, radiant red, holding a knife and skull cup,**
> **Two feet poised astride, three eyes gazing skywards.**

'EH MA HO' is an exclamation of wonderment. What is wondrous? Perceiving all that appears and exists as a realm of vast purity is wondrous. Training in a pure realm is the domain of a strong mind, therefore we need to be certain that all that appears and exists as a realm of vast purity is indeed like that, and give rise to its vivid appearance. Generally, the perceptions of the six kinds of sentient beings are misconceived, deluded perceptions of impure appearances of the universal container and its contents, perceived in confusion. This is the way that individual beings perceive things. In their individual perceptions, a glass of water is different in the way each of the six kinds of being perceives it.

In the perceptions of bodhisattvas who have attained the bhumis, during mere post-meditative awareness, they perceive the interdependence of illusory perception like the illusion of the reflection of the moon in water, and so forth. In the experience of the genuine wisdom of fully evident suchness, all that appears and exists arises as the display of the kayas and wisdom. That being the case, erroneous deluded perception and the interdependence of illusory perception, are both the apparent mode of existence. Genuine wisdom perception is the actual mode.

So, leading with this expression of wonderment, for a beginner the correspondence of appearance and existence cannot actually arise. However, by altering your mind and visualising the pure development stage, the actual mode of existence, the true actuality of the luminosity of the kayas and wisdom, is unfabricated purity. Thus:

> My perception is of a spontaneously present realm of vast purity.

Wherever your perception pervades is the natural, spontaneously present actual state, completely pure. Through the power of this, its apparent mode of appearance, the full extent of all its immensity and boundlessness, is:

> The perfectly arrayed Glorious Copper Coloured Mountain, in the centre of which...

In the centre of the vividness of the palace of the Glorious Copper Coloured Mountain, supreme and perfect in full array with all attributes:

> Is my form basis Vajrayogini.

This is you, yourself as a suitable vessel for empowerment, having the auspicious connection to develop the wisdom of bliss-emptiness, with the extraordinary purpose of being accepted. In essence, this basis is the dakini Yeshe Tsogyal, appearing in the physical form of Jetsun Vajrayogini:

> With one face, two arms, radiant red, holding a knife and skull cup.

Her one face symbolises the single dharmakaya bindu. Her two arms symbolise the integration of method and wisdom. Her body is radiant red, which is the sign of her discerning wisdom completely pure of desire, and protecting with compassion the realms of wandering beings. In her left hand is a hooked knife that cuts the three poisons from the root, held at her side. With her right hand, she holds up a skull cup damaru drum in the expanse of space, which she plays to waken the sleep of ignorance.

Two feet poised astride, three eyes gazing skywards.

Residing neither in samsara nor nirvana, her two feet are poised astride. She has three eyes, which symbolise the three kayas, and gaze longingly at the heart of the lama. Her body is naked, adorned with the six bone ornaments. She is adorned with garlands of white lotuses. You should visualise her as apparent, but insubstantial, like rainbow light. Then follows the main visualisation of the accumulation field:

> **At my crown, upon a blossoming hundred thousand-petalled lotus, sun, and moon,**
> **Is the embodiment of all sources of refuge, my root lama,**
> **Inseparable from the nirmanakaya Lake-born Vajra.**
> **He is youthful with a rosy complexion,**
> **Wears a tunic, Dharma robe, cloak, and cape,**
> **With one face, two arms, seated in the posture of royal ease.**
> **His right hand holds a vajra; his left a skull cup and vase.**
> **Upon his head he wears a petalled lotus hat.**
> **Cradled in his left arm is the supreme consort of bliss-emptiness**
> **Concealed as a three-pronged khatvanga.**
> **He sits in the midst of a mass of light of rainbow rays and spheres.**
> **Surrounding him, in a beautiful lattice of the five lights,**
> **Are the twenty-five emanations, lord and subjects, and**
> **Pandits, siddhas, and vidyadharas of India and Tibet, yidam deities,**
> **Dakinis, Dharma protectors, and the oath-bound, gathered like clouds,**
> **Visible in a state of great equal presence of luminosity emptiness.**

In the upper sky in front of you yourself, visualised as Jetsun Vajra Yogini, is a great lotus flower formed of all kind of precious things, blossoming with a hundred thousand unfurled petals. Upon this, on sun and moon seats equal in size to the pollen bed:

Is the embodiment of all sources of refuge, my root lama.

If you are thinking, 'Why is the lama the essence of the embodiment of all sources of refuge?' The lama's body is the Sangha, his speech is the holy Dharma, his mind is the Buddha. Externally, the Three Jewels are embodied in the lama. Internally, the essence of the Three Roots is also the lama. The root of blessings is the lama. The object signified here is the ultimate lama's enlightened mind of great wisdom, and that which signifies it is the symbol of the lama, the basis of blessings and devotion, whose enlightened form is actually present.

The yidam root of accomplishments is also the lama. If the ultimate nature of the lama's enlightened mind is vast wisdom, then the yidam symbol which has this nature is the immense assembly of the peaceful and wrathful deities, or the display of the vast wisdom of the lama's enlightened mind. The root of enlightened activities is the dakini, and again, similarly this is non-dual with the lama. In the sky of the ultimate nature, the expressivity of compassion arises ceaselessly liberated upon arising, thus he is the sky-farer. The mind of the lama is dharmakaya; his speech is sambhogakaya; his body is the nirmanakaya. His enlightened qualities are the gods of wealth, and his enlightened activities are the Dharma protectors and guardians. Therefore, he is the one who emanates and gathers the oceanic source of refuge, or alternatively, he is the embodiment of the source of refuge treasury of incomparable compassion. He is the glorious root lama.

> Inseparable from the nirmanakaya Lake-born Vajra.

Non-distinct and inseparable from the lama himself, essence of the embodiment of all sources of refuge, is the Lord of Conquerors, Lake-born Vajra, the Great Master from Oddiyana himself. From the Milky Lake in the south-west, not arisen into being from the cause of a father or born from the condition of a mother, he arose in the centre of a lotus, the sudden birth of enlightened awareness. Born from the lake, he is therefore named 'Lake-born'. With the realisation that appearance and existence manifest in the ground, and unwavering from the vajra of ultimate dharmata, he is thus endowed with the miraculous vajra body of a supreme nirmanakaya, prophesied by the Victorious One to be the Second Buddha.

> He is youthful with a rosy complexion.

Through the unity of bliss and emptiness, he is white with a rosy complexion, and has the radiant beauty of an eight year old youth. He:

> Wears a gown, Dharma robe, cloak, and cape.

He is wearing a gown, the symbol of perfecting the Secret Mantrayana, the Dharma robe of the shravakas, and the cloak and cape of a bodhisattva, which are in general distinct items.

> With one face, two arms, seated in the posture of royal ease.

His one face symbolises the single taste of the suchness of all phenomena. His two arms symbolise the connection of method and wisdom. Seated in the posture of royal ease is the sign that, having completed activities for his own benefit, he is now engaged in benefiting others.

> His right hand holds a vajra; his left a skull cup and vase.

Having perfected the enlightened qualities of renunciation and realisation, he holds in his right hand a golden five-pointed vajra, the sign of residing on the level of a vidyadhara of spontaneous presence with the essence of the five kayas of a Buddha. He holds it in the manner of threatening the demons of dualistic perceptions and conceptual patterns. In his left hand, upon the mudra of meditative equipoise, as a sign of accepting those to be tamed with the great siddhi of a vidyadhara with power over life, beyond birth and death, he holds a life-vase filled with the nectar of deathless wisdom with a sprig of the wish-fulfilling tree ornamenting its brim.

> Upon his head he wears a petalled lotus hat.

Guru Rinpoche has a variety of different hats; here he is wearing the Lotus which Liberates upon Seeing, or the Lotus Hat.

> Cradled in his left arm is the supreme consort of bliss-emptiness concealed as a three-pronged khatvanga.

He holds a three-pronged khatvanga trident in a manner which secretly conceals his consort from those with wrong ideas.

> He sits in the midst of a mass of light of rainbow rays and spheres.

He sits in the midst of a mass of light spheres radiating five-coloured rainbow rays.

> Surrounding him, in a beautiful lattice of the five lights...

Around this, surrounding him is a space that arises as a lattice of five-coloured light rays in a checker-board pattern. Inside this beautiful expanse, in the centre of a circle of rainbow light:

> Are the twenty-five emanations, lord and subjects.

These are the manifestations displayed by the buddhas and bodhisattvas: the eight great vidyadharas of India, and the twenty-five emanations, lord and subjects of Tibet. When Guru Rinpoche came to Tibet and turned the Dharma wheel of the Secret Mantra, his fortunate pure entourage – the manifestation of the single mandala of the Secret Mantra – were specifically the three: the lord, the subject, and his partner. The lord was Dharma King Trisong Deutsen, the subject was Great Lotsawa Vairochana, and his partner was Khandro Yeshe Tsogyal. These three were foremost among the twenty-five lord and subjects who attained accomplishment.

> And pandits, siddhas, and vidyadharas of India and Tibet, yidam deities.

In addition, this refers to the pandits who visited India, the source from where the holy Dharma spread, and who travelled to the land of Tibet – those who had unobstructed expertise in the immense fields of knowledge, chiefly in the five fields of learning. Additionally, these are the vidyadharas who attained the supreme and common siddhas, the four types of vidyadharas who attained the supreme accomplishment: ultimate unity at the level of Vajradhara. They also attained the eight common accomplishments, which are enumerated as the sword, eye potion, swift feet, and so on. As for the general etymology of 'vidyadhara', it can be taught that a practitioner of Secret Mantra who 'holds' wisdom or rigpa awareness, however their lama introduced them to it without separation, is called a 'vidyadhara' or 'holder of rigpa awareness'. It is taught that the collection of teachings they practise is called the 'vidyadhara pitaka', as Secret Mantra is categorised as the fourth collection of teachings.

For someone on this path, as they actualise the realisations of the levels and paths, there are four stages. These are classified in terms of the kinds of realisations of the four vidyadharas:

- Fully mature vidyadhara.
- Power over life vidyadhara.
- Great seal vidyadhara.
- Spontaneous presence vidyadhara.

One whose mind itself matures as the form of the deity, but still cannot be liberated from the fully ripened enclosure of the physical body, is taught to be a 'fully mature vidyadhara'. One who has attained the accomplishment of being beyond life and death is a 'power over life vidyadhara'. One who has transformed into the form of a deity of the great seal is a 'great seal vidyadhara', and it is taught that one who has become a regent of the sixth Buddha Vajradhara is a 'spontaneous presence vidyadhara'. 'Yidam deities' refers to the eight yidam sadhana classes for accomplishment, or alternatively the vast array of gathered deities of the mandala.

> Dakinis, Dharma protectors, and the oath-bound, gathered like clouds.

This refers to dakinis established through wisdom and karma, sky-farers and those who travel by strength, who roam the celestial and terrestrial pure realms. The Dharma protectors are those who have vowed to protect the Dharma – having had the seal of the Buddha's teaching placed on their crown, they drink the oath water of the sacred commitments, thus becoming samaya oath-bound guardians, and so forth. In summary, the principal guru and his retinue of gathered deities, together with the oceanic gathering of the Three Roots and oath-bound ones, are present in their entirety, gathered like clouds or like an assembly at a market. Generally, regarding the accumulation field, it is taught that during the stage of taking refuge, the accumulation field is visualised in tiers. At the stage of Vajrasattva purification, it is visualised in the manner of the jewel which includes all, and at this stage of guru yoga it is visualised as a market assembly.

> Visible in a state of great equal presence of luminosity emptiness.

For the visualisation of the accumulation field, its manifestation is luminosity and its essence is emptiness, apparent yet empty like the reflection in a mirror. In actuality, it is the unity of evenness, and its abiding nature is great luminosity, which we should visualise in a state of one single taste. When we visualise the deities of the generation stage, they need to possess the eight measures of clarity and steadiness, which we discussed previously during the meditation and recital of Vajrasattva. However, for the sake of clarity, I will mention them again. The four measures of clarity are: distinct, alive, vibrant, and vivid.

Whichever deity we visualise, their manifest qualities, from the pupils and whites of their eyes, are not blurred but distinct. This is called being 'distinct'. Without separating from the intense clarity of awareness, having an intensity of luminosity and emptiness, is taught to be 'alive'. Visualising deities, they are not like mindless material forms, but are embraced by omniscient wisdom, down to every strand of hair. Thus they are present, arising with clear sensory perception of twelve times one hundred enlightened qualities. This is taught to be called 'vibrant'. Not just an inference of ordinary thought that thinks, 'there are these kinds of forms', or 'they need to be like that', deities are visualised as if directly experienced, brilliant and clear. This is called being 'vivid'.

Then there are the four measures of steadiness: immovable, unchangeable, utterly unchangeable, and completely flexible. This involves being unmoved by external circumstances of forgetfulness and so on, and meditative samadhi remaining unchanged by inner conditions of drowsiness and so forth. Continuously, day and night, not being oppressed by even subtle circumstances or discursive thoughts, is utterly unchangeable clarity. At whatever stage, or however we visualise the form of deities, our visualisation should be flexible regarding physical colours and symbolic implements, emanation and absorption of rays of light, the enlightened deeds of the four activities, and so on. In this way, with these eight measures of clarity and steadiness, we need to strive gradually in visualisation. There is a great necessity for doing so like this.

In addition, by supporting this by practising the direct instruction of the four stakes that bind the life force, there is the need to unite with the levels of the four types of vidyadhara, and so forth. Regarding this, there is a great deal to be said. However, for someone who trains in Secret Mantra, there is no way not to know these things. Moreover, it is not acceptable to be proficient only in vivid presence. Having become adept in vivid presence, the stage of gathering needs to be practised, so at the end of the generation stage, the gathering stage needs to be done.

Whether example luminosity or true luminosity has grown in your mindstream, when the three qualities of final luminosity – the wisdom of the ultimate nature free of elaborations – arises, you may wish to actualise the extraordinary completion stage, the luminosity of the illusory body. Alternatively, having abandoned the ordinary physical basis, you may wish to manifest the unified divine kaya of the stage of training. Or, having abandoned the final mental body of ignorant habitual tendencies, you may wish to actualise the unity of no more learning. Alternatively, if you cannot be liberated in this life, but resting in meditative equipoise in the realisation of luminosity dharmakaya of the first bardo, you may wish to see if you can manifest in the unity of the sambhogakaya, and so forth. Whichever practice you wish to engage in, the gathering of the completion stage is more important than the generation stage.

Guru Yoga

In summary, at this stage we need to visualise that our ordinary perceptions naturally cease in the state of great equal presence of luminosity emptiness, in accordance with the meaning of the words of the recital text.

Invoking Enlightened Mind by means of the Seven Vajra Lines

Having completed the main visualisation of the accumulation field, we recite the seven line prayer to invoke the enlightened mind of Guru Rinpoche. This prayer was spoken simultaneously by many hundreds of thousands of dakinis, so these vajra lines have tremendous blessings.

> **HONG! In the north-west of the land of Oddiyana,**
> **Upon a blossoming lotus flower,**
> **Endowed with wondrous supreme attainments,**
> **Is the renowned Padmasambhava,**
> **Surrounded by a vast retinue of dakinis.**
> **Following you I practise,**
> **So I pray, come to bestow your blessings!**
> **GURU PEMA SIDDHA HONG**

This prayer begins with a 'HONG' syllable, which represents the essence of enlightened mind of all buddhas. Invoking enlightened mind – inseparable space and rigpa, vast infinite pervasiveness – with the symbolic syllable, we call longingly the invitation of Guru Rinpoche, connected with the five aspects of excellence, together with the oceanic gathering of his entourage of heroes and dakinis. Thus visualise you receive blessings with unwavering compassion, like a loving mother embracing her child, as the lead syllable, the vajra of the HONG, naturally resounds.

> In the north-west of the land of Oddiyana, upon a blossoming
> lotus flower.

This teaches the excellence of place. In the north-western region of Oddiyana, where herukas, mamos, and dakinis gather like clouds, upon a pristine sparkling lake pure with clarity, a red flower of the Brahmins grows. Upon this great lotus flower, beautifully in blossom, Guru Rinpoche is:

> Endowed with wondrous supreme attainments.

This teaches the excellence of Dharma. How are his attainments wondrous? His one enlightened form is counted to have eight manifestations. Radiant with the marks and signs of enlightened form, born as prince to the king, he is the Lotus King. Renouncing the kingdom by enlightened means, engaging in the conduct of unattached ascetic discipline and spreading the teachings of the Secret Mantra, he is Nyima Ozer. With desire-less and unobstructed vast enlightened understanding in the knowable fields of study, inseparable from Bodhisattva Manjushri, he is Loden Chokse. Perfecting the enlightened intent of the three scriptural collections and the six sections of tantra, he is Padmasambhava. As the lord who turned the wheel of Dharma like the Victorious One, Lord of Sages come again, he is Guru Shakya Senge.

Moreover, attaining the level of an immortal vidyadhara with power over life, and thereby arising as the master of oceanic mandalas of the Three Roots, he is the Lotus Born Guru. Intimidating with great miraculous power all the malicious antagonist demons and non-Buddhists, he is Guru Senge Dradrok. Travelling to Tibet and spreading the teachings of the Buddha, binding under oath and taming all non-humans and unruly gods and spirits, filling the land with concealed treasures of the teachings wherever he placed his feet, he is Guru Dorje Drolo. Thus his one enlightened form has eight manifestations.

What is more, with his twenty secondary magical manifestations and so forth, engaging in the enlightened activities of the three secrets, he perfected the self-benefit of renunciation and realisation. By this means, through attaining the supreme accomplishment – unity of the realisation that appearance and existence manifest in the ground – he engaged in tremendous benefit for others, with the combined total power, blessing, and capacity of all the victorious ones in one. Thus his complete entire biography is condensed into this one line: 'Endowed with wondrous supreme attainments.'

> [He] is the renowned Padmasambhava.

This teaches the excellence of the teacher. To summarise his titles, he is called the great teacher of Secret Mantra, Mahaguru Padmasambhava. In this way Padmasambhava is renowned throughout not just the billion realms of the worlds of forbearance, but throughout as many universes as there are atoms in the pure realms of worlds that pervade space.

> Surrounded by a vast retinue of dakinis.

This teaches the excellence of the retinue. The entire manifold display of the secret profound mandala of Guru Rinpoche's enlightened body, speech, and mind, in the manner of sun and light rays, arises as the different appearance aspects of the principal and retinues. These are the embodiment of the objects of refuge, the Three Jewels and the Three Roots, surrounded by the numerous entourages of oceanic vidyadharas, heroes, and dakinis. Visualising this, we recite:

Following you I practise.

This implicitly teaches the excellence of the time. How does it teach this? In the timelessness of the three times – the great time of primordial purity – 'like a child following his mother, I, your fortunate devoted child, follow you who have mastery over the dharmakaya kingdom of unwavering enlightened intent. From this time forward, until my mind becomes one taste with the expanse of your enlightened mind, I follow you, so I may become like you and perfect accomplishment.'

So I pray, come to bestow your blessings!

'Through your three secrets, in order to bless my body, speech, and mind I pray with devotion, come to this place!' Thus we invoke Guru Rinpoche's enlightened mind with these melodious words of longing, which unify all of our wishes. The final line is:

GURU PEMA SIDDHA HONG

These Sanskrit syllables combine with Guru Rinpoche's name to invoke accomplishments, in the same way a hundred thousand dakinis invoked him with their symbolic song. Again, this mantra is not recited in other languages; the vajra syllables are repeated directly as they are.

If we translate 'GURU' literally it means 'heavy' – a supreme heaviness of enlightened qualities, and it has the meaning of 'lama'. 'PEMA' is the name of this great master born from a lotus in the centre of a lake, and it chiefly indicates the lotus family of non-attachment. 'SIDDHA' means 'accomplishment', bestowing both the supreme and common accomplishments. 'HONG' is the syllable of the unimaginable secret of enlightened mind, so the whole mantra means: 'Gather within me all the secret profound points with ease!' or 'Hold me in your enlightened mind and send blessings of mind transmission!'

In this way, with these words, from the Glorious Copper Coloured Mountain, we invoke with faith and devotion the Palace of Lotus Light, with its structures and inhabitants. Like pouring water into water, we need to think they actually appear, and dissolve inseparably into the samaya beings which we visualised earlier in the space in front of us.

Offering the Seven Branches

Following this is the offering of the seven branches. Again, it is not sufficient just to have the completely pure desire to accomplish benefit for others. Even if we wish to accomplish benefit for others, without having attained the level of perfect qualities of abandonment and realisation, we cannot. Therefore, the cause to attain that capacity of enlightened qualities, to accomplish tremendous benefit for others, is gathering the accumulations and purifying the obscurations, so this needs to come first. Although there are many methods to gather the accumulations in both the Sutra and Mantra vehicles, the accumulations gathered over many aeons on the Sutra path can be completed in each moment on the Mantra path.

What are the differences between the two paths? The differences are in the field of accumulation and the motivation. At the stage of Secret Mantra, the main object for gathering the accumulations is not held to be the yidam or dakini. The lama is considered the supreme field for gathering the accumulations, thus this is the purity of the field. The purity of the motivation is doing so entirely for the sake of others, attaining in this one life and one body the unified level of Vajradhara. Moreover, the purity of the object is the offerings manifested by deities, mantras, and meditative concentration, which are offered.

Therefore, although there are many methods to gather the accumulations, to summarise them all, they are included in the seven branches. So at this stage, for the sake of accumulating and purifying, the seven branches are taught. To further summarise the seven branches, they are included within three branches: accumulation, purification, and multiplication. The two branches of prostration and confession of wrongdoing are included in the branch of purification. The two branches of rejoicing and dedication can be considered as the branch of multiplication. The remaining three of the seven branches are the branch of gathering the accumulations.

First the remedy for pride, the branch of prostration, is taught:

> **SHI, with my body manifested as many times**
> **As atoms in the universe, I prostrate.**

Here the verse begins with 'SHI'. Generally speaking, the SHI syllable is the unattached speech of the essence of the lotus family, chiefly present in the form of Lama Padmasambhava, so this is to remind us of the trikaya lama. From time to time, this SHI syllable is also the seed syllable for multiplying many times, therefore we begin with it here.

Guru Yoga

With my body manifested as many times as atoms in the universe.

From the heart centre of you, yourself visualised as Vajra Yogini, in your ordinary form, you are multiplied as many times as there are atoms in all the hundreds of thousands of innumerable pure realms, one for every atom in each pure realm.

I prostrate.

Like this, we manifest again and again an inconceivable number of times, and together with all sentient beings, with great devotion of the three doors, we prostrate. Putting our palms together in the three places, we touch the ground with the five principal parts of our body: the palms of our two hands, our two knees, and our forehead, making five. At this stage, we need to prostrate reciting 'I prostrate' together with the visualisation.

As we previously discussed, the 'five-hundred thousand preliminaries' are taught in our tradition to be 1) taking refuge, 2) arousing bodhicitta, 3) meditation and recitation of Vajrasattva purification, and 4) the mandala offering of accumulation. Now, this is the fifth practice of prostrations, connected with the offering of the seven branches. For this fifth practice, if you combine it with the above words of prostration, this is the singular approach of the three doors, which is good. Alternatively, for the sake of convenience, there are also those who do their prostrations while reciting the prayer of taking refuge. There are also those who prostrate in unison with the hundred syllable mantra, so there are many variations. It seems to me that, having got used to it, combining one recitation of the hundred syllable mantra with one full prostration is comfortable, so we can practise in accordance with our individual circumstances.

Prostrations are done in order to bring an end to the conceit of a mindstream that is filled with pride. If we have pride, any qualities we may have are a hateful demon, so whichever of the conduct of the six perfections we engage in – generosity, and so on – this hateful demon does not allow us to go down the authentic path. From the teachings of Patrul Rinpoche:

> You are below the third-order thousand-fold worlds; take a low seat.
> The country is above you; do not have great pride.
> There is no one as bad as you, so have few friends.
> There are no activities both worldly and spiritual; do not say you want such a thing.

Always taking a low seat, we should show respect to all. However, if you are someone with the ordination lineage of training, although it is not appropriate to contend for the head seat with a motivation of pride, if you are a monk or nun, it is also not suitable to have to sit on the lowest seat among your family members. For the sake of respecting the monastic training in other's mindstreams, it is important to consider who is more senior, and for how long they have maintained the precepts. For the sake of respecting the training of your own mindstream, it is appropriate to accept prostrations and respect according to tradition; it is the instruction of our teacher the Buddha that this is necessary.

Second is the remedy for avarice, the branch of making offerings:

> **With offerings actually laid out, and those mentally emanated by the power of samadhi,**
> **I make a symbolic gesture, offering all that appears and exists.**

Offerings actually laid out refers to offering substances that are prepared in accordance with our means and needs. They should be of an appropriate standard, not mixed with any unwholesome attributes, good quality, clean, and attractive. Arrange them well, so they form an attractive support for visualisation. Mentally emanate in the entire extent of the sky, the ground, and the surrounding space, the offering substances of gods and humans: flowers, incense, lights, perfume, and so on, as well as pure lands and temples, places and environments, pleasure gardens and groves. In addition, offer the eight auspicious symbols, the seven attributes of a universal monarch, the eight auspicious substances, the eight or sixteen or thirty-two vajra goddesses, up to many thousands, bedecked with countless offerings of song, dance, music, and so on. Manifest these in a similar way to the offering clouds of the bodhisattva Samantabhadra.

By the power of profound samadhi, offer a symbolic gesture of offerings of the entire phenomenal world, all that appears and exists, including those offerings that are actually laid out and those that are mentally emanated – an ocean of offerings of both the surpassable and the insurpassable. We should aspire to make offerings continuously, as long as it takes until samsara is emptied, to all the recipients of offering: the visualised gathered deities of the accumulation field, and chiefly the victorious ones of the ten directions with their bodhisattva offspring, who are nothing other than the miraculous display of the lama. In particular, these mentally emanated offerings are called the 'mode of arising of the wish-fulfilling jewel of the mind itself', and are taught to be especially exalted.

Third is the remedy for aversion, the branch of confession of wrongdoing.

> **All unvirtuous actions of my three doors**
> **I confess in the state of dharmakaya luminosity.**

'From beginningless samsara until today, those misdeeds and downfalls I remember and those I cannot, done through the three doors of body, speech, and mind, which are to be purified – wrongdoings of the six doors and the activities connected with them, the ten non-virtuous ways of action, the five inexpiable actions, the four serious faults, the eight errors, misappropriation of offerings made to the Three Jewels, and so on – all the unacknowledged karma that I have accumulated without exception, I confess by means of the complete remedial four powers.' The way this is confessed is 'in the state of dharmakaya luminosity.' Confession is made in the sky-like state of the realisation of the dharmakaya luminosity. However confession is made, it is free from confession and confessor, in a state that is not separate from the realisation of the fundamental nature – true meditative equipoise. This is the branch of confession.

Fourth is the remedy for jealously, the branch of rejoicing:

> **Subsumed within the two truths,**
> **I rejoice in all accumulations of virtue.**

All-knowing Jigme Lingpa said:

> From the perspective of objects of comprehension,
> The entire meaning of the eighty-four thousand gates
> Of the Dharma taught by the Victorious One,
> Is the two truths: worldly, relative truth and ultimate.
> Other than these, no third exists.

In the realm of limitless sentient beings, with respect to the methods to tame the three poisons that we have in our mindstream, that which describes them are the three collections of scripture, the knowledge and understanding of which are the three trainings. If we enumerate these scriptures specifically, eighty four thousand gateways to Dharma were taught. However, there is not one that does not depend on either the conventional truth of the way things appear, or the ultimate truth of the way things are. So, a third possibility is negated.

With great joy, from the depth of our hearts, it is taught we 'rejoice' in our own and others' accumulations of virtue. These are likewise included within the two truths: contaminated and not subject to contamination. Moreover, there is a big difference between 'contaminated' and 'not subject to contamination'. To go into a little detail on the meaning of this, it is understood that all the roots of virtue subsumed by conventional truth are contaminated with afflictions, and all roots of virtue subsumed by ultimate truth are not subject to contamination. In terms of the path, all roots of virtue of the paths of accumulation and training are contaminated, and all roots of virtue of the paths of seeing and meditation are established as not subject to contamination.

In terms of the two accumulations, the entire accumulation of referential merit is contaminated, and the accumulation of non-referential wisdom is not subject to contamination. Alternatively, in terms of meditation and post-meditation, the meditative equipoise of an arya being is not subject to contamination, and all roots of merit of their post-meditation are established as contaminated. Aside from that, in terms of the supportive element, all roots of merit embraced by the supportive element of wisdom are not subject to contamination, and all those without its embrace are contaminated. These are the divisions.

Fifth is the remedy for ignorance, the branch of imploring the buddhas to turn the wheel of Dharma. For this branch, in some recital texts there is only this one line: 'I implore you to turn the wheel of Dharma of the three vehicles.' In our tradition, Gyalse Shenpen Tharye bestowed an amendment in the Dharma transmission text:

> **For the three types of beings to be trained,**
> **I implore you to turn the wheel of Dharma of the three vehicles.**

In these two lines, the fifth branch of imploring the buddhas to turn the wheel of Dharma is taught. Three types of beings to be trained are the shravakas, pratyekabuddhas, and bodhisattvas, or alternatively they are beings of lesser, middling, and superior faculties. For the sake of beings to be tamed in the Mahayana – which is divided into Sutra and Mantra, together with the vidyadharas – we implore the buddhas to turn the wheel of Dharma of the three vehicles. We implore those who bear the responsibility of bringing tremendous benefit to others: the buddhas, bodhisattvas, lamas, and spiritual teachers, not to become discouraged by ingratitude or weariness, and not to display a manner that does not teach the Dharma, so that sentient beings may accumulate merit, and so forth.

Guru Yoga

Emanating our body hundreds, thousands, and countless times, we offer golden thousand-spoked wheels, right-spiralling white conchs, and so on. With an utterly pure and superior intent, we request the buddhas to turn the wheel of Dharma of the three vehicles in order for the great drum of the holy Dharma to resound in the world. The three vehicles are as described above, or alternatively, it is also appropriate to divide them threefold according to the classification of the nine vehicles:

The outer vehicles that lead away from the origin of suffering:
- Shravaka
- Pratyekabuddha
- Bodhisattva

The inner vehicles that evoke awareness through ascetic practice:
- Kriya
- Upa
- Yoga

The secret vehicles of overpowering means:
- Maha
- Anu
- Ati

So this is the prayer for the Dharma wheel of the nine stages of vehicles to be turned.

Sixth, the remedy for wrong views is praying for the buddhas not to pass into nirvana, which is taught with:

> **As long as samsara is not empty,**
> **I pray you remain, not passing into nirvana.**

Whether in this realm or in others, we need to pray to those lamas, buddhas, and bodhisattvas who may direct their compassionate minds to other realms, having completed benefitting sentient beings with the fortune to be tamed. We pray to the buddhas who, under the influence of various conditions, may leave those beings who remain unprotected. Just as in the past the layman Tsunda prayed to the Buddha, emanate your body many countless times. Pray that as long as these three realms of samsara are not emptied, until not a single sentient being remains, the buddhas do not pass into nirvana, but remain as sole protectors, refuge, and defenders of the welfare and happiness of all sentient beings. When we accomplish roots of merit that focus on the stable lives of our lamas, these are also counted as part of this sixth branch.

Seventh is the remedy for doubt and indeterminacy, the branch of dedication:

> **All the roots of virtue accumulated in the three times**
> **I dedicate to the cause of supreme enlightenment.**

When dedicating, the witnesses to our dedication are the victorious ones and the bodhisattvas. That which is to be dedicated is all the merit we have accumulated in the three times, all the roots of virtue of the buddhas and bodhisattvas that are not subject to contamination, as well as the contaminated roots of virtue of all sentient beings. By saying 'I dedicate to the cause of supreme enlightenment' we should dedicate with the two aspects or the two purposes complete. In particular, we need to dedicate wisdom focusing on complete enlightenment to the cause for all sentient beings to attain unsurpassable, omniscient, complete enlightenment.

As for the way to do this, however we dedicate, if for a beginner, a genuine dedication without conceptualisation of the three spheres is not possible, we should make some approximation of it. We need to invoke certainty that the appearances of the three spheres are ineffable by nature, or alternatively dedicate with such intent, just as the buddhas and bodhisattvas dedicate. Unless we affirm our intent with dedication and prayers of aspiration, roots of virtue are indeterminate, so we do not know where they will wind up. This completes the seven branches.

Accomplishing the Nature of the Four Vajras

Prayer for the Time to Attain Accomplishment

Next are the prayers to accomplish resolutely the nature of the four vajras in our mindstream. These are taught in three prayers: 1) the prayer for the time to attain accomplishment, 2) the prayer for the time of requesting accomplishments, and 3) the prayer for ultimately mixing inseparably with the expanse of enlightened mind. First, the prayer for the time to attain accomplishment is indicated by the following words:

> **Lord Guru Rinpoche,**
> **You are the glory of compassion and blessing**
> **Of all buddhas combined,**
> **The sole protector of all sentient beings.**
> **My body and possessions, mind and heart,**

Guru Yoga

> I offer to you without reservation.
> From now until I attain enlightenment,
> In all happiness and sorrow, good and bad, highs and lows,
> Great Lord Padmasambhava, heed me!

Our glorious protector, holy lama, is chief of all mandalas, with the complete authority of Heruka. By seeing, hearing, touching, or remembering him, the seed of liberation is sown in our mindstream. Thus he is the fourth Precious Jewel, the agent of the enlightened activities of all the buddhas. From our own perspective, by the blessings of his compassion, he establishes us on the profound path of maturation and liberation in one lifetime, in one body. By forceful means he establishes us on the level of Vajradhara, so his kindness is even more exalted than the Buddha's.

Measured from the perspective of his enlightened qualities, our lama's realisation is as vast as space; his wisdom and compassion are immeasurable like an ocean. His compassion is like a river, constant and powerful. His nature is like Mt. Meru, his mind being steadfast and firm. He is loving towards all wandering beings like a parent, and so on. If we think about each individual aspect of our lama's enlightened qualities, they are unfathomable. In particular, if we pray to him, whatever accomplishments we wish for will come forth effortlessly, just like a wish-fulfilling precious jewel. So, thinking 'I rely on you, place all my hope in you, and accomplish this for you!' with tears of devotion welling up, we pray:

> Lord Guru Rinpoche.

A 'Lord' or 'Jetsun' is akin to a king, one worthy of veneration. Saying, 'Lord of the Dharma Family, Presiding Master of all Mandalas, Mahaguru, Jewel that Fulfils All Wishes' we call to our lama, who is inseparable from Guru Rinpoche.

> You are the glory of compassion and blessing of all buddhas combined.

The lama is the sovereign of all buddhas, the wisdom knowledge of all the buddhas of the ten directions and the three times. He is all their loving compassion, their activities of enlightened action, power of protection, and all blessings and accomplishments unified into one, glorious holy master.

> The sole protector of all sentient beings.

To the lord protector of all sentient beings without exception, to our sole refuge and defender, offer:

> My body and possessions, mind and heart.

This is our cherished body, and the wealth and possessions we own to cater for its needs. It is all things we have, including our accumulated merit and virtue, everything we own great and small of the thoroughly-held three bases, without any hiding, concealing, or keeping secret, and without any deceit or deception:

> I offer to you without reservation.

Without any reservation of attachment whatsoever, offer them to Guru Rinpoche.

> From now until I attain enlightenment,
> In all happiness and sorrow, good and bad, highs and lows,
> Great Lord Padmasambhava, heed me!

Think 'From this time forward, until I attain unsurpassed enlightenment, whatever occurs: happiness, misery, good times or bad, or if physical or mental feelings of joy and comfort arise, heed me! You know best! Whatever bad circumstances occur, from suffering to the adversity of sickness and pain, again heed me! Whether through excellence I meet with glory, or through negativities I encounter disaster, whether I attain status or position, great power or fame, or if through terrible wretchedness, I fall to the lowest depths of suffering and misfortune, I have no refuge or hope other than you. Great lord, embodiment of all the buddhas, powerful lord Padmasambhava, heed me!' Thinking this, recite the words of taking refuge with complete trust and surrender.

Then, the mantra prayer to invoke enlightened mind is the BANZA GURU mantra, which we need to count on our malas as we recite. After each one hundred and eight repetitions of the mantra, we repeat this prayer once more to invoke enlightened mind. As part of guru yoga, we need to complete ten million repetitions of this siddha mantra. During each practice session, however many repetitions of the mantra we make, after completing about two thirds, we need to recite a second prayer to request accomplishments and invoke enlightened mind:

Guru Yoga

Prayer to Request Accomplishments

I have no other hope but you.
Beings of this bad, degenerate time
Drown in a mire of unbearable suffering,
Protect us from this, great guru!
Bestow the four empowerments, blessed one!
Elevate my realisation, compassionate one!
Purify the two obscurations, mighty one!

As we recite the first line 'I have no other hope but you', think: 'This wretched sentient being of these degenerate times has a karmic connection with you, so other than you, your devoted child has no second refuge.'

> Beings of this bad, degenerate time
> Drown in a mire of unbearable suffering.

Now is a bad time, with the five degenerations on the increase. How are the five degenerations increasing? Decline in life force is the degeneration of life span. Decline in the virtue of householders is the degeneration of afflictive emotions. Decline in the virtue of monastics is the degeneration of the view. Decline in enjoyments is the degeneration of the time, and so forth. We degenerate wandering beings with meagre merit have countless kinds of unbearable suffering, terribly difficult to endure. Escaping from one, we cannot get free from another, and we drown in this mire of samsaric suffering.

> Protect us from this, great guru!

'Swiftly protect us from this unbearable intense suffering, Lord Mahaguru!'

> Bestow the four empowerments, blessed one!

The four sublime empowerments that mature the mindstream are the vase, secret, wisdom, and word empowerment. 'Bestow them upon me now to mature my mindstream, blessed one with unimpeded wisdom!'

> Elevate my realisation, compassionate one!

'Elevate and liberate my mindstream with the extraordinary realisation of the true transmission of the profound fundamental nature, loving compassionate one!' To these prayers you can also add invocations for Guru Rinpoche's wisdom, kindness, and power.

Purify the two obscurations, mighty one!

'Purify both obscurations of afflictive emotions and obscuration to the knowable, together with subtle habituations, mighty one with unimpeded power!' This prayer of fulfilment needs to be spoken once between each full mala count of the siddha mantra. Next is:

PRAYER FOR INSEPARABILITY OF MIND AND ENLIGHTENED MIND

At the time when my life comes to an end,
My perception is the realm of Chamara's Glorious Mountain,
In the unified nirmanakaya pure realm.
My form basis, Vajrayogini,
Becomes a sphere of shimmering light,
In great inseparability with
Lord Padmasambhava to become enlightened.
From the miraculous display of bliss and emptiness,
The play of this great wisdom,
For sentient beings of the three realms without exception,
May I appear as a true guide to lead;
Grant me this assurance, Lord Pema.
I pray from the depths of my heart,
Not just merely repeating the words,
Bestow blessings from the expanse of your enlightened mind!
May these aspirations be fulfilled!

Having recited this prayer, again recite the siddha mantra. This prayer is repeated below, where we will discuss its meaning.

At this stage, we accumulate the twelve-syllabled BANZA GURU siddha mantra, which is the life mantra of all vidyadharas, the embodiment of the mind of all buddhas, and the chief mantra of the cloud-like gathering of heroes and dakinis.

OM AH HONG BANZA GURU PEMA SIDDHI HONG

Reciting this, 'OM' is the essence of the nirmanakaya, 'AH' is the essence of the sambhogakaya, and 'HONG' is the essence of the dharmakaya. Thus 'OM AH HONG' embodies the essence of the three kayas, and it is the life mantra that is the single embodiment of the three secrets. 'BANZA' translates directly as 'vajra', which is understood to be the wisdom of inseparable expanse-rigpa, free from transition or change. 'GURU', as mentioned earlier, has the meaning of 'heavy'; heavy with the weight of enlightened qualities which are established in the lama, and understood to be the perfection of unsurpassable abandonment and realisation. 'PEMA' means the lotus flower, which is not tainted by the faults of samsara, and has the power of activity free of obscurations of hindrance, thus possessing spontaneously present, everlasting and all-pervasive enlightened activities. 'SIDDHI' means accomplishment, all supreme and common accomplishments. Saying 'HONG' means 'by the realisation of your enlightened mind bestow upon me all accomplishments.'

This is the extraordinary dharani mantra that requests accomplishments of the secret inconceivable manner of the inexhaustible wheel of adornment of enlightened body, speech, mind, qualities, and activities. My lama would say, 'Having recited one hundred million siddha mantras and being unerring in faith, you need have no doubt that you will be reborn in the presence of Master Pema in the Glorious Copper Coloured Mountain.'

Part Eight, Prayers to the Lamas of the Lineage

Main Prayer to the Lineage

At this stage, in order to develop enthusiastic conviction, we recite the prayer to the lineage, in connection with its history:

E MA HO! In a pure realm without restrictions or extremes,
Is the original Buddha dharmakaya Samantabhadra;
The sambhogakaya, like the display of the moon in water, Vajrasattva.

'E MA HO' indicates the meaning of 'wonderfully marvellous'.

In a pure realm without restrictions or extremes.

In a pure realm which is not limited and does not fall into any extremes whatsoever, free of all extremes of elaboration, an inherently manifest ground without self-nature:

Is the original Buddha dharmakaya Samantabhadra.

On primordial ground in the original beginning time, the primordially enlightened teacher dharmakaya arises as the six special qualities of non-dual expanse and wisdom, in the inward lucidity of the youthful vase body, and is called Samantabhadra or the 'Original Lord'.

The sambhogakaya, like the display of the moon in water, Vajrasattva.

This is the inherently manifest sambhogakaya, and from this, like the reflection of the moon in water, is the outward lucidity of the nature emanation kaya, the manifest expressivity of wisdom, which is naturally blessed by glorious Vajrasattva. This is the mind lineage of the victorious ones.

The nirmanakaya with marks complete, Garab Dorje.

This is the nirmanakaya appearing to tame wandering beings, understood to be the Great Master Garab Dorje, with the marks and signs complete. Master Garab Dorje composed the language of Dzogpa Chenpo in an excellent manner.

> **I pray: bestow blessing and empowerment.**

By saying this we pray to the lamas of the three kayas, so they may 'bestow blessings and profound empowerments upon us'.

> **Shri Singha, treasury of the ultimate Dharma;**
> **Manjushrimitra, sovereign of the nine yanas;**
> **Jnanasutra, great pundit Vimalamitra;**
> **I pray: show us the liberating path.**

The first line refers to the Great Master Vidyadhara Shri Singha, who actualised unembellished supreme realisation and gained mastery over the treasury of all the profound Dharma. He was Garab Dorje's student, as was:

> Manjushrimitra, sovereign of the nine yanas.

Emanation of Arya Manjushritikshna, the great master known as 'Manjushrimitra' actualised the distinct and utterly complete great meaning, and so turned the wheel of the Dharma of the nine yanas, steering all wandering beings upwards.

> Jnanasutra, great pundit Vimalamitra.

This is the great pundit Jnanasutra who attained the supreme accomplishment, and the great pundit Vimalamitra who arose in the rainbow body of great transference. These masters transmitted the lineage from one to the next, which forms the Sign Lineage of Vidyadharas and culminates in the Great Master from Oddiyana. Pray to these great arya vidyadhara lamas, equal to buddhas:

> Show us the liberating path.

This prayer comes from our hearts: 'I pray, please show me the path that liberates my mindstream.'

> **Sole ornament of this world, Padmasambhava,**
> **Supreme true heart children: lord, subject, and partner,**
> **Longchenpa, revealer of oceanic mind treasures;**
> **Jigme Lingpa, entrusted with the dakinis' space treasury;**
> **I pray: bestow attainment of the result – liberation.**

Prayers to the Lamas of the Lineage

In this world, the one friend of the Dharma who spread the teachings of the Buddha in general, and in particular the teachings of the Secret Mantra, is the second Buddha Padmasambhava, and his:

> Supreme true heart children: lord, subject, and partner.

These three supreme heart children, the lord, subject, and his partner gained certainty in the profound direct instructions, thus becoming matured and liberated.

> Longchenpa, revealer of oceanic mind treasures.

This is the venerable Gyalwa Longchenpa Drime Ozer, who naturally unravelled the symbols of the profound ocean of mind treasures, and in the expanse of the exhaustion of phenomena seized the stronghold of the dharmakaya. He is the All-knowing Lord of Dharma, Drime Ozer.

> Jigme Lingpa, entrusted with the dakinis' space treasury.

In three visions of the wisdom body of All-knowing Longchen Rabjam, Jigme Lingpa received transmission of the profound space treasury of the wisdom dakinis. Praying to all of these masters, together with the Great Vidyadhara Jigme Lingpa, we recite:

> I pray: bestow attainment of the result – liberation.

'I pray from my heart to you all, my lamas who are non-dual with the Lord of the Teachings, Garab Dorje, Hero Holder of Secrets – manifestly bestow the ultimate result of liberation free from abandonment and attainment.'

Following this are the additional prayers to the lineage:

Lord of this Dharma, Changchub Dorje, is Jigme Trinle Ozer, and **Siddha Jigme Gyalwe Nyugu** is Dza Trama Lama. **Supreme emanation Mingyur Namkhe Dorje** is the Fourth Dzogchen Rinpoche. **Son of the victorious ones, Shenpen Thaye**, is the First Gemang Tulku. To them **I pray: show me the true face of fundamental nature**. Glorious Heruka, Yeshe Dorje is Dho Khyentse, and we pray **to Orgyen Jigdral Chokyi Wangpo**, Patrul Rinpoche. **Mighty siddha Pema Banza**, is Khenpo Pema Dorje. **To the lake-born guru, Khyentse Wangpo**, Jamyang Khyentse Wangpo, and them all, **I pray: bestow the supreme and ordinary attainments.**

Following this, there are also more additional prayers to the lineage lamas, including Orgyen Tenzin Norbu, Mura Pema Dechen Zangpo, Gonchok Drakpa, Tupwang Tenpe Nyima, and so on. These are important lineage lamas of the Nyingthik, added with faith by devoted later generations of disciples, some of which differ slightly. However, our truly close lineage is transmitted from Mingyur Namkhe Dorje to Orgyen Tenzin Norbu, then to Shenpen Chokyi Nangwa, who passed it to my lama, whose holy name is difficult to express, but to mention it for the sake of clarity, Jigme Dadrin Yonten Gonpo. This is considered the hearing lineage of individuals.

Supplementary Prayers of Aspiration

Aspiration Prayers for Liberation in this Life

Included here are supplementary prayers of aspiration for this life, the bardo intermediate state, and the next life. First are three prayers of aspiration for this life:

> **With the revulsion of true renunciation from samsara,**
> **Relying upon my vajra guru meaningfully, as my eyes;**
> **Through the profound practice of following instructions as given,**
> **Without inconsistent application, but with diligence,**
> **May blessings of enlightened mind be transferred!**

With revulsion that understands the three realms of existence, this samsaric place, to be one of suffering, the uncontrived attitude of true renunciation that wishes to be free from it arises. With that strength:

> What's the use of wanting? All desire is the cause of delusion.
> Look at the way we do not get what we want!
> What's the use of wealth? Our mind is attached to possessions.
> Look at the way all we accumulate is left behind!

So, without desire for anything, through the power of revulsion:

> Relying upon my vajra guru meaningfully, as my eyes.

Our kind lama teaches the stages of maturing empowerments and liberating instructions of the Secret Mantra Vajrayana, meaningful for all those who have a connection. So rely on him, as you do your eyes, with great faith and devotion:

> Through the profound practice of following instructions as given.

Having examined the lama, after you start to follow him, practise whatever is instructed, in the same way as Naropa followed Tilopa, or as Milarepa followed Marpa. In particular, practise the profound points of the Dharma with tremendous application of the three doors without flagging:

> Without inconsistent application, but with diligence.

'Inconsistent' is taught to be sporadic leisureliness, sometimes engaging diligently night and day without a break, while at other times abandoning practice, and so forth – endurance in application that is not steady. After having actually taken vows, we cannot go back on, or abandon our commitments whatever the circumstances, but must remain consistent from the very core of our heart. So with this kind of absolutely firm determination in our hearts:

> May blessings of enlightened mind be transferred!

This teaches 'May the profound enlightened blessing of the ultimate innate wisdom of the lama's mindstream be transferred to mine.' Also:

> **Appearance and existence, samsara and nirvana, are primordially the realm of Akanishta;**
> **Deities, mantras, and dharmakaya the result of purification, perfection, and maturation –**
> **Great Perfection without effort of acceptance or rejection.**
> **The radiance of rigpa transcends mental experiences and conceptual analysis.**
> **May I directly perceive dharmata laid bare!**

By seeing the abiding mode of all phenomena of appearance and existence, samsara and nirvana, as the primordially pure Akanishta dharmadhatu pure realm:

> Deities, mantras, and dharmakaya are the result of purification, perfection, and maturation.

Attachment to appearances is perfected as the enlightened forms of deities. Sounds are purified into mantras. Thoughts are matured into the dharmakaya, so the ultimate result of threefold purification, perfection, and maturation is:

> Great Perfection without effort of acceptance or rejection.

All objects of rejection are purified in non-arising. The remedial attitude of acceptance is also free from reference, transcending active effort – beyond all words, thoughts, and expression – the ineffable boundless rigpa emptiness of Great Perfection.

> The radiance of rigpa transcends mental experiences and conceptual analysis.

The inherent radiance of self-arising rigpa transcends grasping cognition of mental experiences and conceptual analysis which focuses on view and meditation.

> May I directly perceive dharmata laid bare!

This is 'from now until reaching the culmination of liberation of the four visions', so the measure of directly perceiving the inherent radiance of rigpa – the first of the four visions, the profound truth of dharmata – is actualised similitude wisdom settled in the revelation of dharmata. Thus this teaches: 'May I perceive that laid bare!'

> **Utterly liberated from defining thoughts, encompassed in rainbow light,**
> **May visionary experiences of kayas and bindus increase;**
> **May expressivity of rigpa reach fullness as sambhogakaya pure realms;**
> **May enlightenment be attained, the great exhaustion of phenomena and transcendence of mind;**
> **May I gain the eternal stronghold of the youthful vase body!**

Utterly liberated from defining thoughts, in all-encompassing rainbow light, visionary experiences of kayas and bindus increase. This is the increase of visionary experiences.

> May expressivity of rigpa reach fullness as sambhogakaya pure realms.

This is the expressivity of rigpa brought to absolute completeness, whereby experience of the path reaches fullness as the self-manifest sambhogakaya pure realms. This is rigpa reaching fullness.

> May enlightenment be attained, the great exhaustion of phenomena and transcendence of mind.

All appearances of phenomena are exhausted in the unborn expanse of dharmata, so this is transcendence beyond the extremes of mental conceptualisation and analysis – freedom from conceptual assumption itself. This is reaching the level of dharmata exhaustion.

> May I gain the eternal stronghold of the youthful vase body!

The 'youthful vase body' is a special Dharma term from the early translation tradition. Free from birth and death, aging and decline, is it 'youthful'. Not manifest in a manner of outer luminosity, it resides in a manner of deep lucidity. Alternatively, from the aspect that it is inner lucidity of subtle wisdom, then applying a term for the ultimate dharmakaya, it is called the 'vase body'. Actualising this kind of youthful freedom from birth and destruction – purity of freedom from incidental impurities, the abiding nature of the vase body – 'May I gain the eternal stronghold!' Above are the prayers of aspiration in connection with this life.

Aspiration Prayers for Liberation in the Bardo

Following this are the prayers of aspiration for liberation in the bardo intermediate state.

> **If I have not mastered the experience of the ultimate yoga,**
> **And this gross body is not liberated into pristine space,**
> **At the time when the constituents of life fall apart,**
> **May death luminosity dawn as primordially pure dharmakaya!**
> **May the appearances of the bardo be liberated as sambhogakaya!**
> **By completely mastering the paths of trekcho and togal,**
> **May I be liberated, like a child leaping to its mother's lap!**

The 'ultimate yoga' is taught to be Ati Dzogpa Chenpo in which the fully ripened result of the four elements which combine to make the gross form of this body, are transformed into an extremely subtle pristine body.

Therefore, by the power of meditating on trekcho it disperses into minute particles, and by the power of meditating on togal it arises as the body of great transference. However, not mastering the experience of the actual abiding nature of Dzogchen, or if your practice has not developed fully:

> And this gross body is not liberated into pristine space.

If it cannot be liberated in this life as a body of light:

> At the time when the constituents of life fall apart.

When the time comes for us to die, when the constituents of life fall apart at death:

> May death luminosity dawn as primordially pure dharmakaya!

At death, when the primordially pure ground luminosity of the first bardo arises, appearing like a cloudless sky, as it says in *Training in the Realms of the Three Kayas*:

> Clear and unconfined, like an autumn sky,
> Rest in this state of empty lucidity free from obscuring veils.
> At that time, certainty in present primordially pure expanse
>   beyond mind,
> Ordinary mind, open and free,
> Is found, and by the power of this equipoise,
> May I in that instant, seize the stronghold
> Of the primordial expanse of the ground, the secret sphere of
>   inner luminosity,
> Expanse of Samantabhadra's realisation endowed with six special
>   qualities!

This says: 'May I be liberated at that stage.' If we are liberated at that stage, it is considered to be liberation in this lifetime. Again, from this aspiration:

> If I am not liberated in the first bardo,
> The appearances of space dissolve into spontaneously present
>   luminosity,
> And when the eight modes of dissolution arise:
> Sounds, lights, rays, mandala groups, and so forth...

The meaning of this is taught in the line:

> May the appearances of the bardo be liberated as sambhogakaya!

This teaches that by recognising the entirety of the appearances of the bardo of dharmata as mind's own manifestation, 'May I be liberated as sambhogakaya!'

> By completely mastering the paths of trekcho and togal,
> May I be liberated, like a child leaping to its mother's lap!

This teaches: 'By completely mastering the profound practise paths of primordially pure trekcho and spontaneously present togal, may I be liberated in a manner that is non-dual, like a child leaping to its mother's lap!' This is to be understood to imply the six modes of arising, the two gates, the appearances of the eight gates of spontaneously presence and so forth, of the main practice stage. This aspiration for liberation in the bardo combines aspirations for the bardo of dying and the bardo of dharmata.

Aspiration Prayers for Liberation in the Next Life

From here, passing through the bardo of becoming, we are taught the method how to find relief from taking up a subsequent existence.

> **In this great secret luminosity, the supreme pinnacle vehicle,**
> **Buddhahood is not sought elsewhere; the face of the dharmakaya manifests.**
> **If I am not liberated into the primordial state,**
> **By following the supreme path of five practices of buddhahood without meditation,**
> **May I be born in the five natural nirmanakaya realms;**
> **Especially in the Palace of Lotus Light,**
> **Where the Lord of Orgyen, supreme chief of the ocean of vidyadharas,**
> **Celebrates the feast of the great secret Dharma,**
> **May I be born as his most favoured child,**
> **Relieved to become provision for limitless beings!**

In this great secret luminosity supreme vajra essence pinnacle vehicle:

> Buddhahood is not sought elsewhere; the face of the dharmakaya manifests.

Not needing to search for buddhahood elsewhere, the inherently indwelling true face of the dharmakaya manifests – the primordial fundamental nature, the level of Samantabhadra itself.

> If I am not liberated into the primordial state.

If you were unable to journey there, and so were not liberated:

> By following the supreme path of five practices of buddhahood without meditation,
> May I be born in the five natural nirmanakaya realms.

What are the five practices for attaining buddhahood even without meditation? They are: liberation through seeing, liberation through hearing, liberation through taste, and so on, as well as liberation through remembering the phowa transference, the instructions for engaging in the object, the physical points, and so forth. By following this excellent path, the natural nirmanakaya realms are: eastern Manifest Joy, southern Endowed with Glory, western Lotus Mound, northern Accomplishing Highest Action, and central Blazing Mountain, which are the five realms for receiving the great relief of liberation, and:

> Especially in the Palace of Lotus Light.

Especially, in the Glorious Copper Coloured Mountain, the pure realm of the gathering of vidyadharas, in the Palace of Lotus Light:

> Where the Lord of Orgyen, supreme chief of the ocean of vidyadharas,
> Celebrates the feast of the great secret Dharma.

In the place where all those with good fortune are celebrating the feast of the great secret, esoteric and profound, Secret Mantra Vajrayana Dharma of maturation and liberation:

> May I be born as his most favoured child,
> Relieved to become provision for limitless beings!

Born as the most favoured heart child, the chief student of the Great One from Oddiyana, entirely relieved of karma, afflicted emotions, and suffering thus perfects self-benefit. For the benefit of others, 'May I embody or become the glory of provision for the higher rebirths and definite goodness of enlightenment for limitless wandering beings of the three realms!' In this way, for the aspirations for this and the later bardos to be accomplished with ease, we pray:

> **By the blessings of the oceanic victorious vidyadharas,**
> **And the truth of inconceivable dharmata,**
> **With the basis of the freedoms and endowments to perfect, mature, and purify,**
> **Actualising this interdependence, may I attain enlightenment!**

By means of the basis of this physical body with the freedoms and endowments, what are the three: 'perfecting, maturing, and purifying'? They are absolutely perfecting the unlimited enlightened qualities of the Dharma of the One Gone to Bliss, maturing all sentient beings who are to be tamed, and purifying everything completely as a Buddha's pure realm. 'Actualising the profound meaning of interdependence, may I perfect the twofold benefit and attain the level of complete enlightenment.' In this way, uniting the words with their meaning without hypocrisy, we should pray from our hearts with intense devotion and yearning.

Part Nine, Taking the Four Empowerments

Following that, we come to the stage of taking the four empowerments to receive accomplishments.

> **Embodiment of all the victorious ones, venerable lama heed me!**
> **Bestow blessings to dredge samsara from its depths.**

This is recited three times, as is the tradition in this lineage. With intense longing, we should pray exclusively to our lama, inseparable from the Lake-born Vajra, on which basis he thinks of us lovingly. With this in mind we take the four path empowerments. Generally, there are three kinds of what we call 'empowerment':

- Ground empowerment.
- Path empowerment.
- Result empowerment.

At this stage, these are taught to be path empowerments, and if we distinguish the subdivisions there are:

- The ground empowerment of the path.
- The path empowerment of the path.
- The result empowerment of the path.

Here, these are considered to be path empowerments of the path. We take them ourselves in a manner of self-empowerment, and they also serve as tantric mending and purification of vows.

> Then, **from between the eyebrows of the guru, an OM syllable, shining like a crystal, radiates light rays** like moonlight **that enter into my crown. This purifies** that which is to be purified: the three **karmas of the body**, taking life and so forth **and**, as it is the channels that give rise to the body, the **obscurations of the channels**. Of the three vajras, **blessings of vajra body enter me.** Of the four empowerments, **I receive the vase empowerment.** The wisdom of the meaning of the empowerment purifies thought patterns into the web of magical illusion. Wisdom of appearance-emptiness is born in my mindstream. Sight, sound, and awareness is liberated into the continuous state of deities, mantras, and wisdom. Saying '**I become a**

vessel for meditation on **the development stage**' means that, having received the empowerment, we become a suitable vessel for meditating on the path development stage. Of the result of the four vidyadharas, **the seed of a fully mature vidyadhara is sown** in my mindstream. **The fortune to attain the level of nirmanakaya is placed in my mindstream.** Of the ultimate four kayas, the fortune to attain the level of nirmanakaya is placed in my mindstream.

From Guru Rinpoche's throat centre, **from an AH syllable, blazing like a ruby in his throat, light rays** like red lightning **radiate, and enter my throat. This purifies** the four **karmas of speech**, lying and so forth, **and** as it is the energies that give rise to speech, the **obscurations of the energies** are also purified. **Blessings of vajra speech enter me. I receive the secret empowerment.** The meaning of the empowerment – wisdom of luminosity-emptiness – is born in my mindstream. Energies arising, entering, and remaining are transformed into mantras, whereby I **become a vessel for mantra recitation.** Of the four vidyadharas, **the seed of a vidyadhara with power over life is sown** in my mindstream. **The fortune to attain the** ultimate **level of sambhogakaya is placed in my mindstream.**

Once more, **from a sky-blue HONG syllable in his heart centre, light rays**, taught to be like the smoke from a long incense stick, **radiate and enter my heart. This purifies** the three **karmas of the mind,** covetousness and so forth, **and** as it is the essences that give rise to the mind, the **obscurations of the essences. Blessings of vajra mind enter me. I receive the knowledge wisdom empowerment.** Actual wisdom – the wisdom of bliss-emptiness – is born in my mindstream. **I become a vessel for bliss-emptiness candali.** Thought patterns are liberated into a state of bliss-emptiness, thereby **the seed of a Mahamudra vidyadhara is sown** in my mindstream. It is taught **the fortune to attain the** ultimate **level of dharmakaya is placed in my mindstream.**

Again, from the HONG in his heart centre, **a second HONG syllable, like a shooting star, shoots outwards, merging inseparably with my own mind. This purifies alaya karma and obscuration to the knowable.** The basis of the three doors is alaya karma, together with obscurations of alaya consciousness. Grasping at the threefold sphere is obscuration to the knowable – free of all of these, **blessings of vajra wisdom enter me. I receive the ultimate empowerment indicated by words.** The meaning of the empowerment – self-arising wisdom – is born in my mindstream. **I become a vessel for primordially pure Dzogpa Chenpo.** Conceptions that grasp at the three doors as being separate are liberated into dharmata, whereby **the seed of a spontaneously accomplished vidyadhara is sown. The fortune to attain the ultimate result of svabhavikakaya is placed in my mindstream.**

At this stage, Guru Rinpoche's enlightened body, speech, and mind and your three doors, merge in one taste. In this state, we should maintain the self-expression of the view, and strive at praying and reciting the mantra. This is called 'seeing the lama as the natural face of the dharmakaya'. Thus, the seeds of the four vajras exist in our mindstream, connected and established from the very beginning. So, having entered the mandala, in order for the vajra master to awaken them, the ground empowerment brings about their ripening.

At the stage of guru yoga, taking the four empowerments ourselves, independent of other conditions, constitutes the path empowerment. Taking them in this way is important to sow the seeds of the oceanic enlightened qualities of purification, perfection, and maturation. Therefore, we should practise taking this path empowerment regularly, in accordance with the requisite number of mantra repetitions. At the stage of ultimate fruition, receiving the 'empowerment of great light rays' – the empowerment of non-dual profundity and luminosity – and attaining perfect and complete buddhahood, is the result empowerment.

How to Bring the Practice Session to a Close

Through this understanding, when it comes time to bring the practice session to an end, it is the tradition of this lineage to recite once more the following prayer to invoke enlightened mind:

At the time when my life comes to an end, my perception is the realm of Chamara's Glorious Mountain. At the time when life ends, when death befalls us, our entire perception is of the south westerly continent of Chamara, the Glorious Copper Coloured Mountain, **in the unified nirmanakaya pure realm.** In the centre of an emanated pure realm, the unity of appearance-emptiness, **my form basis** is visualised as **Vajrayogini.** This **becomes a sphere of shimmering light**, not a physical body mass of flesh and blood, but a sphere of bright light, **in great inseparability with Lord Padmasambhava, to become enlightened** in self-knowing inseparable great bliss.

> **From the miraculous display of bliss and emptiness,**
> **The play of this great wisdom,**
> **For sentient beings of the three realms without exception,**
> **May I appear as a true guide to lead;**

Grant me this assurance, Lord Padma.

From the unity of unchanging great bliss and emptiness of nature – the natural expression of the miraculous display of the play of non-abiding great wisdom transcending elaboration – for all types of wandering sentient beings that reside in the three realms and the three states of existence, without exception and without leaving any behind, I pray to you my true guide, supreme nirmanakaya, great Lord Padmasambhava: grant me clear assurance to possess power like this, so I may lead them all to the level of liberation and omniscience! Assure me of this!'

I pray from the depths of my heart, not just merely repeating the words.

This prayer is not mere words, but is prayed with intense faith, devotion, and longing from the depths of our heart.

Bestow blessings from the expanse of your enlightened mind! May these aspirations be fulfilled!

In this way, threefold blessings of wisdom, compassion, and power, not subject to contamination, are bestowed from the expanse of enlightened mind. 'I pray, may all these aspirations be fulfilled as wished, in accordance with the Dharma.'

Uniting the recitation and meditation, receive the path empowerments. Having done so, by reciting in this way, with devotion and longing, **again from the heart centre of the lama, a warm red ray of light** burning hot, **suddenly** appears and **shines forth. Just as it touches my heart, myself visualised** from before **as Vajrayogini,** in an instant, **I transform into a sphere of red light** the size of a pea. This is taught to be like a spark flying from a fire with a crackling sound, **which dissolves** and is subsumed **into Guru Rinpoche's heart centre becoming inseparable,** mixing into one taste. **Meditate in equipoise** for as long as this remains, **in a state free from focus, thought, and expression.**

It says in the *Supplication in Seven Chapters*:

> Thus, although appearances, objects of the eye,
> The entire outer universe and its inner contents,
> Are perceived, remain in a state without self-grasping.

Taking the Four Empowerments

Purified of grasped-grasping: the luminosity-emptiness form of deities.
I pray to the lama of self-liberation from attachment.

Thus, that which resounds as objects of the ear,
All sounds perceived as melodious or jarring,
Are audible yet empty; remain in a state free of thought.
Empty sound unborn and unceasing: the speech of the victorious ones.
I pray to the empty sound of the speech of the victorious ones.

Thus, that which stirs as objects of the mind,
Whatever afflictive emotional thoughts of the five poisons arise,
Do not engage in mental fabrication of welcoming or following.
To leave mental stirring in its own place is liberation in the dharmakaya.
I pray to the lama of the self-liberation of rigpa.

As this teaches, whatever appears is the play of the single dharmata, never straying from the expanse of the lama's enlightened mind. Whatever manifestations of the six-fold group that arise – appearances and sounds, seen and heard – do not modify them with mind or corrupt them with grasping. In a state of great transcendence of dualistic mind, undistractedly maintaining the watchman of mindfulness, staying in deliberate non-grasping, is called 'meditating'. Staying unmoved by the winds of sinking, agitation, mental proliferation and re-converging, is shamatha, and the abiding clarity aspect of mind arising free of murkiness is vipashyana.

When entering equipoise in this kind of concentration – united shamatha vipashyana – it is well known in the general tantras that, generally speaking, we establish the foundation with the view, cultivate with meditation, enhance with conduct, and then unite with the ultimate result. However, on the path of natural Great Perfection, resting in the nature of the view of unobstructed transparent rigpa-emptiness, non-dual with the enlightened mind of the lama – the direct experience of extraordinary realisation of blessed mindstream evoked by devotion – is called 'meditation'. All aspects of behaviour that are embraced by this kind of view and meditation, purified from acceptance and rejection, grasping and fixation, is conduct. If the result is resting in the essence of the basic view, primordially liberated dharmata, then in the single expanse of uncontrived natural abiding, the single taste that is the wisdom of all view, meditation, conduct, and result, is the unmistaken excellent path of Great Perfection.

At this stage, by meditating on guru yoga, when realisation of the actual transmission is transferred to our mind, the true face of fundamental nature is seen. What are the signs of seeing this?

The sign of meditation is lack of afflictive emotions.

Therefore, the signs of the birth of extraordinary realisation are love, compassion, and bodhicitta, as well as faith, renunciation, and the birth of the wisdom of full discernment of phenomena. These enlightened qualities occur spontaneously together with the birth of extraordinary realisation, just as the sun has rays of light.

Having arisen from that...

Arising from that meditative equipoise, in post-attainment, visualise all appearances and existence as the manifestation of the lama and, without separating from that state, we need to seal it with excellent prayers of dedication and aspiration. With completely pure devotion and samaya commitments, if you complete the path up to this point, even if you do not meditate on what is called the 'main practice' separately, independent of any other main practice, you will doubtlessly pass on to Chamara's Glorious Mountain. In that pure realm, it is taught you will progress on the path of the four kinds of vidyadharas faster than the coursing of the sun and moon, and arrive at the level of Samantabhadra.

The Goodness of the End – The Conclusion

The above completes a fully detailed, extensive discussion of the goodness of the middle, the meaning of the text. Now, before the conclusion of the author's colophon, there are several prayers of dedication and aspiration, liturgical recitations which were most likely added later as annotations to the main text. Whatever the case, nowadays everyone has memorised this way of reciting, so there must surely be good reason to follow this tradition.

Following guru yoga, it is most suitable to recite the *Aspiration of the Glorious Copper Coloured Mountain*, and the general Heart Essence aspiration prayers, the *Aspiration for Actualising the Words of Truth*, and so forth – whichever are appropriate and you are able to recite, in accordance with your time and circumstances.

The additional liturgical recitations of dedication and aspiration are:

>Glorious root lama, precious one, I pray,
>Dwell on the lotus seat in the heart of myself and others,
>Accept me with your great kindness and
>Grant me attainments of enlightened body, speech, and mind!
>
>Regarding the activities of the glorious lama,
>May I not give rise to wrong views even for a moment, and
>With devotion that sees all he does as positive,
>May the lama's blessing enter my mind!
>
>In all my lives, may I never be apart from
>The genuine lama, and enjoy the glory of the Dharma.
>Perfecting the qualities of the levels and paths,
>May I swiftly attain the level of Vajradhara!

Part Ten, Prayers of Dedication

>Through this merit, may all beings
>Complete the accumulations of merit and wisdom,
>And attain the two holy kayas
>That arise from merit and wisdom.
>
>Whatever merit all beings may possess,
>What they have done, will do, and are doing,

May they all attain the stages of perfection,
Just as Samantabhadra did.

Just as the courageous Manjushri understood,
And Samantabhadra did too,
I train following them all,
And completely dedicate all this merit.

With the dedication all buddhas of the three times
Praise as supreme,
I also dedicate completely all my roots of virtue
For excellent conduct.

Part Eleven, Special Prayers of Aspiration

In all my lives, wherever I am born,
May I have the seven qualities of the higher realms,
Meet with the Dharma as soon as I am born,
And have the freedom to practise correctly!

Also, may I please the holy lama,
And practise Dharma day and night.
By realising the Dharma and achieving its innermost meaning,
May I traverse the ocean of existence in that life.

In samsara, may I fully expound the sacred Dharma,
And never tire of working to benefit others.
Through vast impartial service to others,
May all attain buddhahood together!

Following this is the conclusion, the author's colophon:

This liturgy for the *Preliminaries of Dzogpa Chenpo Heart Essence of the Great Expanse, the Sublime Path to Omniscience*, was written by the great tantric yogi Jigme Trinle Ozer, who was nurtured by the kindness of the Vidyadhara Jigme Lingpa and many other holy masters, and gained determination in the samaya. By this merit, may followers see the lama as a Buddha, by which result, self-aware rigpa, Samantabhadra's own face, becomes apparent, and may they become of ceaseless benefit to oceanic beings and worlds! Sarva mangalam! Virtue!

Concluding Words

The above completes a full teaching of the preliminaries in the manner of practical guidance, based on the *Sublime Path to Omniscience, Recital for the Preliminaries Arranged in Proper Order,* from the set of teachings of Dzogpa Chenpo Heart Essence of the Great Expanse. I hope that all we have heard becomes celebration for the mind, nectar for the heart, a guide for the confused, and a lamp for those who cannot see. I hope we can find a place of rest, so our weary and exhausted minds may recover from the continuous suffering endured from beginningless time until now. May we be consciously heedful of the way the source of all suffering – non-virtuous unwholesome actions – are experienced based on the three doors, and reduce the strength of the mechanism of the hidden disease of self-grasping, the all-pervasive origin of everything, the great demon of ignorance at the root of existence.

With this focus, by relying on the methods to gather the accumulations and purify the obscurations, in addition to suddenly being able to transfer the wisdom realisation of the actual transmission, this profound and precisely effective teaching transforms sentient beings into buddhas. For these reasons, I especially elected to teach this recital text for the preliminaries, with the intent for it to be suitable for the mindstreams of all practitioners, and fitting for both new and old practitioners alike to practise.

Whatever name or title we may have been given, and however our points of view differ, in truth, as a follower of our teacher the Buddha, if we are preceptors who give the vows of individual liberation, bodhisattva, and tantra, then our single thought and core hope is to embrace the holy Dharma – to see if it can be of benefit to sentient beings. There is no other purpose to the activities of the Buddha than to benefit sentient beings, and this responsibility also falls to us who are his followers. In my opinion, being conscientious about this is significant for all of us, both now and in the future.

However, whatever activity we engage in requires the gathering of causes and conditions, so without relying on a combination of interdependent origination, we cannot accomplish any conditioned phenomena. If we cannot bring both right and left hands together, there is no way to join our palms. If the three factors of a drum, a drumstick, and the effort of the human hand do not come together, there is no way to sound a drum. Likewise, the lama teaches the Dharma and students show devotion, but additionally, if they are not encouraged by the whip of diligence, it is difficult for the resulting achievement of practising the Dharma to benefit the student's mindstream. Through relying on the methods of conventional truth to gather the accumulation of composite roots of virtue and purify obscurations, the outcome of realisation of ultimate truth is the uncontrived abiding nature of phenomena. So similarly, to transfer the unity of the two truths free of elaboration – sky-like blessings of the mind transmission – also depends on the student.

I imagine all of us here want to say that we are Buddhist, but honestly, those with the complete characteristics are somewhat rare. However, if you are asked, 'Do you have faith in the Dharma?' of course you should say 'Yes!' In modern times, although a significant percentage of the world's population does not believe in any religion, if we take the people born in Tibet as an example, the great majority of us do have faith in the Three Jewels, and believe in karmic cause and effect. Although everyone, young and old, can say they are Buddhists, it is necessary for those who intentionally come to the teaching hall to receive Dharma teachings to have true faith in Buddhism. However, there are two kinds of people with faith: those who have blind faith, and those who have faith through correct reasoning. The term 'blind faith' is not just a phrase used by those who proclaim nothing spiritual exists, in order to belittle religion. In Buddhist terms, the name for never understanding any specific reasoning can be called 'blind faith'. In the scriptural tradition it also mentions 'faith followers of dull faculties', and 'Dharma followers of sharp faculties'.

To give a simple example, if we think about brewing a pot of tea to quench our thirst, first we draw water, then light a fire, after which we can boil the tea. If the order of these actions is complete, then the purpose is achieved. To take a more significant example, a nomad raising cattle increases his herd of calves for the sake of gaining income from milk and yogurt. Similarly, if a farmer ploughs his field and sows seeds in the spring, there will be crops to harvest in autumn. All these activities have a beginning, middle, and an end. In the same way, when practising the Dharma, we also need to go through the activities from beginning to end. Moreover, Dharma practise is of much greater significance than those worldly activities. In this world, the truly outstanding activity is this pure practise of the holy divine Dharma. Within it, there is benefit for all sentient beings, for every one of us who lives and breathes.

However, while those who practise the Dharma are many, those who accomplish it are rare. To practise, it makes no difference whether you are rich or poor, or have high or low status. The differences appear in how well we know how to practise, and how singularly tenacious we are at practice. If that is the case, it is not necessary for lay men and women to abandon their home and family and immediately retreat into the mountains. Without cutting self-grasping inside, without renunciation growing within our heart, there is no benefit whatsoever in climbing into the mountains, even if we scaled the whole range, just as there is no benefit for the birds and wild animals who spend their entire lives in the mountains.

Therefore, the medicine of the Dharma is the method to overcome the afflictive emotions, which are the disease produced by the five poisons in our mindstream. Therefore, it needs to be practised by ourselves and applied to ourselves. Again and again, make an estimate of the length of your life. If due to a sudden accident, death occurred now, what preparation have you made? Summarise your life's work – in the first half of your life what did you achieve? From now on, what is the best thing to do? Hopefully, something slightly more constructive than the dogs and yaks wandering aimlessly around outside.

The special feature of being a human in general, and additionally being a Buddhist, is having the wisdom and perspective to analyse our current situation. Now the time has come to put this to use as much as possible. For us to come together and have this Dharma talk happens only once or twice in our lifetimes. However, the inner meaning of each word we discuss is lifelong medicine for the mind. It is as if we have gained a universal panacea, a nectar that wipes out a hundred illnesses, which we are able to put to use. This is the enlightened activity of the speech of the Victorious One.

Actually, a great place to put the Dharma into practise is in towns and cities, where excitements abound and attachments and aversions increase. When we encounter enemies, we need to use weapons and armour, so when meeting foes, it is unwise to leave protection behind. Likewise, we need to align the armour of the Dharma with our actual thinking and behaviour in life. Otherwise, when we are about to lose ourselves to the influence of the afflictive emotions – the sickness of attachment, aversion, and ignorance – if at that time we do not know how to apply the medicine of the Dharma, flicking through our mala beads is pointless.

They say, 'People with full stomachs recall the Dharma' however, in our case, it is probably when we are full and happy that we forget about the Dharma. It is even worse when we get carried away by excitement and distractions. We may only remember the Dharma when we feel truly miserable. What is called 'renunciation of the suffering of samsara' is when both feelings of gloom and weariness are combined, and then only the Dharma can give us hope and protection. This is like when a bird gets enveloped in smoke, it develops the desire to fly away.

In short, someone who wishes to be happy and comfortable, both now and in the future, must not be without a kind heart. Of course we have attachment, aversion, and ignorance, we are ordinary samsaric beings. However, when fierce afflictive emotions develop, by relying on their remedy according to our strength of mind, the method to suppress them is to pray to the lama and the Precious Jewels. At all times, before, during, and afterwards, try to think carefully. When afflictive emotions are powerful, at least refrain from doing anything impulsive, then afterwards we will have little regret.

Generally, whatever purpose or activity we engage in, by considering the past and thinking about the future, we should ensure we create no cause for regret. It is said that those who think first are wise, and those who become regretful later are foolish. Without clairvoyance, although we cannot see if all our future plans will turn out as we wish, based on a compassionate beneficial attitude, merge your mindstream with the Dharma and find a way to seize the real path to liberation. There is nothing mistaken about such plans and there is no need to look back. This is a reminder of what I have been talking about for the past eight days, so read the life stories of the holy masters from the past. This is no different from meeting those lamas in person and partaking in the nectar of their speech.

In terms of the Sangha of monks and nuns, you are the foundation of the teachings of the Buddha. You need to guard the five root precepts like your eyes. At this time, the true principle of both the Buddha and his teaching is the holy Dharma of the Vinaya, the subject of which is the training in discipline. Applying it to our mindstream, maintaining the Vinaya with disciplined study and concentration, combined with meditation, is the practise of the path of the three precious higher trainings. This indicates that the teaching of the Buddha is in our mindstream. Therefore, it is taught:

> Following the incomparable Teacher,
> Not contradicting the discipline of the Sage's excellent teaching,
> Having the fortune of the pure conduct of authentic vows,
> Such a person is the enlightened activity of the Victorious One.

The foundation of all positive qualities is pure discipline. With this in our mindstream, even if we have nothing else, we are the object of the offerings of sentient beings and gods. If someone were to take offence, however much they criticised us, it would make no difference. As it is said:

> If a spring does not dry up itself,
> How can it be blocked with earth?

Criticism makes no difference to those with pure discipline, so in a large gathering, those with discipline are manifestly noble. Therefore it is taught:

If someone has discipline, even if they are unlearned and dim,
They have no difficulty arousing samadhi and wisdom.

If discipline is not pure, even if someone has other qualities, they are still immoral. We must have completely pure discipline as the foundation of all positive qualities. If discipline is not pure, it is like leaves fallen from a tree. They may appear attractive for a while but are of no real use. It is taught:

> Without roots, there are no leaves or fruit.
> Therefore, arrange the interdependent connections of the path
>   from the beginning.

In particular, these days, when the true teachings are frail and in decline, to observe one type of discipline for one day still has inconceivable benefit. A sutra I often quote is the *King of Samadhi Sutra*:

> The merit maintaining one type of discipline for one day,
> At a time when the holy Dharma goes into decline,
> When the teachings of the One Gone to Bliss become undermined,
> Is even more especially exalted than
> Venerating billions upon billions of buddhas
> With a pure mind, with food and drink,
> Parasols and banners, rows of oil lamps,
> For as many aeons as there are grains of sand in the Ganges River.

Leaving aside the two hundred and fifty rules of Vinaya, even not to be tainted by the faults and downfalls of the four roots, and the fifth of consuming alcohol, is difficult to observe at this time. Why is this? As taught by Jigme Tenbe Nyima:

> For those who are not perfect the precepts are incredibly difficult
>   to observe,
> And to become holy we must train earnestly.
> Discipline is the most important sign of practice,
> So do not let your own value go to waste!

At this time, when those who possess discipline are as rare as stars in the daytime, even to maintain one or two precepts is that much more valuable. Therefore it is very important for us to keep the Buddha Dharma in our mindstream pure.

Our monastery of Dzogchen is the wellspring of the early translation tradition's Vinaya doctrine of monastic discipline. From the earliest times up to now, this pristine wellspring has remained unsullied to its furthest shores, so it does not need repeating that in non-sectarian monasteries, whichever the monastic tradition, the root training of discipline must be taught above all. It is taught:

> Not wishing to follow the Sage
> Into the city of liberation as a protector of beings,
> The one in robes who serves the home
> In a samsaric town is deceived by demons.

Even if you cannot spend your entire life in study, contemplation, and meditation, except for striving in accordance with your capacity in spiritual practice, it is not appropriate to get waylaid into serving members of your family. If you are a layman or laywoman, encourage harmony within your household; the associations of human life are short. It is pointless to have no happiness while we are alive and mourn when we die. Communities need to live in harmony and get along with each other. Lama Mipham said:

> All people in the land are companions in happiness and sadness.
> There is little point to struggling for gain and success,
> And crucially there are many benefits in having few conflicts.
> Living like this, we are happy and so are our companions.

Whoever you are, do not make long-term plans as if you will live forever. As it is said:

> From the lord on his throne to the beggar holding a stick,
> Everyone born is destined to be taken away as a corpse.
> No one remains, all enter the path of future lives,
> Yet we do not grow weary. Mind is deceived by clinging to permanence.

This teaches that, from the lord who sits on his high throne down to the lowly beggar holding a stick, it is as if everyone comes into this world only to be carried away as a corpse. The last thing we will ever do, the real conclusion of our life's work, is our corpse being thrown into a charnel ground. See if there is any intrinsic meaning to what we have done in our lives, or was it all just for the purpose of being carried off as a corpse at the end?

Concluding Words

Whether you come from the wider community, or whatever the size of your monastery, if someone happens to be better off than you, do not be jealous or hostile. If someone is successful or wealthy, this is the merit of the area and they are an adornment of the people. Being jealous cannot take that away. It is also not acceptable to condemn or have contempt for those who are worse off than you. In life there is much happiness and misery, so we do not know from whom we may one day need to ask a favour. Even if this is not necessary, having contempt for those who are worse off than us is a sign that we are terrible people. You are not appointed as someone who judges the qualities of others. There may be a lot of mean people in the world, but at all times we need to examine our own mindstreams and put ourselves on the right path. Yet it is hard to say that even we ourselves see our own faults.

Examining your inner mindstream, do not be careless and let life go to waste. Within this, all inner meaning is included: the manner in which it is difficult to find a free human basis, the way this is of great benefit if found, the way life has no permanence, the manner in which there are no methods to overcome death. And when we die, there is no other hope or refuge except for the holy Dharma. Sincerely, do not forgo these truths. Aim your attention towards the holy Dharma and an unceasing sun of happiness will rise.

As this is so, for the entire short span of our human lives, practise the Dharma with happiness and joy. There is no need to have the wish to practise the Dharma, but be intimidated that you cannot accomplish it. If faith in the Three Jewels develops for a moment, if an attitude of compassion the size of a sesame seed arises, that is the Dharma. To spend your life with the Dharma is the equivalent of showing gratitude to your kind parents, and this is also a good thing to leave to your descendants. The middle of life is more pleasant than the earlier part of life. The latter part of life is happier than the middle of life. As the darkness of misery finally clears, the next life is happier than this one. Thus there will arise an un-setting sun of these three joys.

As our Dharma teaching of the Tibetan year of the Earth Ox, 2009 comes close to completion with the final dedications, as all composite phenomena are comprised of the four extremes of impermanence, so this phenomenon of our meeting is also impermanent and ends in separation. The All-knowing Lord of Dharma said:

> We wish to stay in our good home
> Forever living there, but separation is certain.
> We wish to stay with family and friends
> Forever in their company, but separation is certain.
> We wish to stay with our good lama

The Dzogchen Path

Forever listening to Dharma, but separation is certain.

Although I am not a good lama, I embraced the lotus feet of our former holy masters of the past who were both learned and accomplished, and cherished the nectar of their enlightened speech. At that time, I was the youngest student and got left behind. Most especially, in the manner of a final testament, the Sixth Dzogchen Rinpoche Jigdral Changchup Dorje entrusted me with the great responsibility of focussing on the future revival of the teachings. During the upheavals of 1959, just one or two days before we were taken to jail in Dege, Dzogchen Rinpoche, together with Great Khenpo Tupten Nyendrak and my precious khenpo and master Yonten Gonpo, bestowed upon me long-life empowerments, one for each of my years. This was just before we were forced to leave Dzogchen. Since granting me those empowerments, I have had the feeling that their remaining life spans were dissolved into mine.

However, in the changing circumstances of flourish and decline, the path of human life passes through much happiness and suffering. This is now a bad time when the five degenerations are increasing. And generally, when the Dharma is profound, evil demons are also powerful. So, wherever we prepare to spread the teachings of the true holy Dharma, whoever is preparing to maintain the unfaltering life force of the teachings of the Victorious One, for them demonic obstructions are likely to begin. Particularly, these teachings of Dzogchen Monastery are easy to spread, but have significant obstructions. Both these factors are unique among others. Either this is due to the geomancy of the land and environment, or the manner in which interdependent circumstances were arranged when the monastery was originally established. Whatever the case, the fact is that our teaching is special in that it spreads easily, but is affected by strong negative obstructions.

Additionally, we met with a period of time when there were no holy masters born, no basis for gathering merit, and no temples standing. But that was not just here in Dzogchen. All around Tibet, whatever amount of the Buddha Dharma that resided in the mindstreams of one or two people remained secret, so no one knew about it. Except for that, there was a time when the Dharma teachings of the Buddha disappeared. Taking our region here as an example, many of those who had both an altruistic attitude and vast wisdom have already departed, one after another. But for all those lamas who passed on, and for all those who still remain, it is not appropriate to abandon their heartfelt wishes to the dust. Holding these aspirations dear, led by the remaining senior lamas and tulkus of Dzogchen Monastery, from the Buddhist teachings to all aspects of work, everyone shouldered their particular burdens, endured all setbacks, and continued onwards. Eventually from 1991 to the present

Concluding Words

day, I believe the doctrine of Dzogchen Monastery, the source of the doctrine of teaching and accomplishment of the Early Translation Nyingma Tradition of Lower Dhokham, and mother of the holy Dharma of Vinaya, has been re-established once more onto its former path.

Everyone is clearly aware of these events and the revival which happened here, and our actions are clear proof. However, whether or not we express what happened clearly, this kind of story and discussion of historical events will become just a tale for people of future generations. When we practise Dharma, impermanence needs to grow in our mindstream, so it is not good to grasp at permanence, hoping and fearing for the future. But we do need to have a plan in order for both the spiritual and worldly not to go into decline, and to remain for a long time. If we need to maintain the teachings for a long time, *the legacy of an influential father should in turn be maintained by his son; the jewellery of a wealthy father should adorn his daughter.* Having passed on the legacy of Dzogchen Monastery's teachings into the hands of the new generation, so long as it does not fall under the influence of obstructing negative influences, I believe the monastery, together with the wider community, has now arrived in a period of happiness.

Personally, I am not a good example, from either a Dharmic or worldly point of view, and I sometimes wonder, have I aroused renunciation for the activities of the phenomenal world, this illusory mechanism of the eight worldly activities, or have I just grown weary of them? But I do pass on the lineage of these transmitted guidance instructions, the nectar of profound instruction that I received in person from our holy masters of the past. When the fortunate time comes for us to be given the inheritance from our fathers, if we grasp the intent to befriend the birds and forest animals in a secluded hermitage away from people, and spend our entire life in retreat, or alternatively, from time to time connect the regional population, ordained and lay alike, with the Dharma in this way, then this is also the activity of the victorious ones.

This time we gathered together for several days and discussed much in connection with the Dharma. In such a large gathering of many thousands of people, that not even the slightest obstructing condition occurred is due to both the strength of the blessing of the Dharma, and all of your good intentions. It is also due to the power of the truth of the enlightened aspirations of our holy masters of the past. Therefore, at this juncture of auspicious aspirations for the unceasing sun of happiness to rise over the heads of everyone, as all things gathered must separate, so for the time being we shall soon depart and go our separate ways. As all of you return to your homes, do so happily and full of joy, with the aspiration that, as we gathered together here in a single group of a single mandala, so we may gather together in a pure land in the future. I wish you all long and healthy lives! May you be protected by the Three Jewels!

Represented by these roots of virtue of teaching and listening to the Dharma, rejoice in the merit of receiving teachings; engaging in sessions of practice; making circumambulations; doing full-length prostrations; cutting out meat from our diets; lighting and donating offering lamps; sponsoring gilding of the Buddha statue; saving animals and ransoming lives; making promises to undertake virtuous activities and abandon unwholesome ones; building important representations of Buddha body, speech, and mind; sweeping and keeping clean the inside and outside of the temple, as well as the surrounding environment; requesting dedications and reading names; helping to pitch tents and prepare bedding for the Great Offering Ceremony for Bodhicitta; washing vegetables, and bringing yogurt and milk. Everyone made a fit example of accumulating merit with a pure and sincere attitude. In particular, this year's patron, the regional community of Dzashug Tridar, all its leaders and members of the community were diligent and devoted followers of the Dharma.

In short, rejoicing in everyone who stepped into this Dharma assembly ground, together with all the roots of virtue that we, ourselves and others have and will accumulate, we dedicate in general to the precious teaching of the Buddha, embodied by scriptures and realisation, to increase and develop ever more, by means of the ongoing principles of both theory and practice. We dedicate to completely fulfil the enlightened intentions of the masters of former generations, holders of the teachings, who have passed away, and to those who currently reside, so their lives may be long and healthy. We dedicate to all communities of gathered Sangha to be harmonious and have pure discipline, so all qualities of the three trainings increase for evermore. In all places on earth, may rainfall be timely, may crops always be abundant and livestock thrive. May all human and animal diseases, and all conflict and fighting cease, in order for all to enjoy the glory and happiness of the golden age.

In particular, we dedicate for the sake of our parents, relatives, and friends of this life, those with whom we have both a good connection and a bad connection; to those who have passed away on this earth; everyone killed in wars, or who died in earthquakes, fires, and floods; to those who died from starvation or disease; to those who died with no Dharma, and to those who died with faith having received teachings. We dedicate chiefly to those who have karmic debts of hope and attachment, to aggressive enemies, harmful obstructing forces, people who have a physical body, ghosts without any physical form, and so on, among all limitless sentient beings, so they may all ultimately attain total omniscience at the level of perfect and complete buddhahood. Until they attain it, may they find an excellent physical basis that possesses the seven qualities of a high rebirth, and have the fortune to practise correctly the Dharma of the Mahayana.

We dedicate however Lord Manjushri, Arya Samantabhadra, and so forth, dedicated, for the sake of all wandering beings. Let us arouse this aspiration of dedication and recite the prayers together:

> By this merit, may beings attain the all-seeing nature,
> Defeat the enemies of wrong-doing,
> And from the turbulent waves of birth, old age, sickness, and death,
> In the ocean of existence, be liberated!
>
> However the Bodhisattva Manjushri attained omniscience,
> Likewise as did Samantabhadra,
> I follow in the example of all of them,
> And dedicate all this merit extremely well.
>
> SHI! The previous Tathagata Shikhinra,
> Mahasiddha Kukuripa of the Noble Land,
> Known as 'Paldan Tangpa' in the Land of Snows,
> I supplicate at the feet of Pema Rinzin.
> May there be auspiciousness for the teachings to remain a long time!
>
> Beautiful sole ornament of the Sage's teaching, Longchenpa,
> Powerful lord of the teachings of theory and practice, Jigme Lingpa;
> May the doctrine of our incomparable lamas be upheld until the end of samsara,
> By teaching, practise, study, contemplation, and meditation.
>
> Crown ornament of millions of glorious learned and accomplished ones,
> Great chariot of the teachings of Sutra and Tantra, scripture and realisation,
> Fearless victorious Nyingma Dzogchenpa!
> May the teachings of Shirasing Buddhist College flourish!

The Dzogchen Path

Like a twinkling star, an oil lamp,
An illusion, a drop of dew, a bubble,
A dream, a flash of lightning, or a cloud;
View all composite phenomena to be like this.

ROOT TEXT

THE ROOT TEXT

THE SUBLIME PATH TO OMNISCIENCE
RECITAL FOR THE PRELIMINARIES OF DZOGPA CHENPO
HEART ESSENCE OF THE GREAT EXPANSE
ARRANGED IN PROPER ORDER

By Dodrupchen Jigme Trinle Ozer

Although primordially enlightened, your unceasing forms tame beings in any way necessary.
You display various miracles, yet are free from aggregates, elements, sense-fields, and dualistic grasped-grasping.
Although appearing in human form, you are actually a buddha, blazing with a thousand light rays of wisdom and compassion.
Not just in this life, you are my refuge forever; I rely on you [Khyentse Ozer], bless me!

Firstly, Blessing the Speech:

OM AH HONG
Fire from a RAM syllable burns my tongue faculty
Into a three-pronged vajra of red light,
Which cradles the *Essence of Interdependence* surrounded by the ALI KALI.
From this pearl-like string of syllables,
Light emanates, pleasing the buddhas and bodhisattvas with offerings.
Re-converging, obscurations of speech are purified, and
All blessings and accomplishments of vajra speech are attained.

A A, I I, U U, RI RI, LI LI, E E, O O, ANG AH

KA KHA GA GHA NGA, DZA TSA ZA ZHA NYA, TA THA DA DHA NA, TA THA DA DHA NA, PA PHA BA BHA MA, YA RA LA WA SHA KA SA HA CHA

YE DHARMA HETU DRABHAVA HETUN TEKAN TATAGATO HYAVADAT TEKANTZAYO NIRODHA EVAM VADI MAHASHRAMANAYE SOHA

Repeat seven times.

The Dzogchen Path

One, Prayer to Invoke the Mind of the Glorious Lama:

O lama, heed me! O lama, heed me! O lama, heed me o!

Call out with intense longing.

From the blossoming lotus of devotion at the centre of my heart,
Arise gracious lama, my sole refuge!
Tormented by karma and fierce afflictive emotions,
To protect me from this misfortune,
Reside as the ornament of my crown chakra of great bliss.
Arousing all mindfulness and attentiveness, I pray!

I am not in the realms of hell, hungry ghosts, animals,
Long-life gods, the uncivilised, or those with wrong views,
In a place where a buddha has not come, or with impaired faculties;
At this time I have gained freedom from these eight unfree states.
I am human with complete faculties and born in a central land.
My way of life is not corrupt and I have faith in the Buddhist teachings;
These five personal endowments are complete. A buddha has appeared,
He taught the Dharma, it remains, and I have embraced it;
I have been accepted by a spiritual teacher: the five circumstantial endowments.
Although I possess all of these,
Through various uncertain circumstances this life will become relinquished,
And I will move onto another realm of existence.
O Guru Rinpoche, heed me! Turn my mind towards Dharma!
Omniscient master, do not let me stray onto wrong or inferior paths!
Compassionate lama, who is one with them, heed me!

If I do not use this current human life meaningfully,
In the future I will not find such a basis for attaining liberation.
Once the merit for this congenial existence is exhausted,
After death I will wander as a miserable being in the lower realms.
Not knowing virtue from non-virtue, I will not hear the sound of Dharma,
Nor meet a spiritual teacher, what a terrible disaster!

Root Text

Just thinking about the numbers and varieties of sentient beings,
To obtain a human body is barely possible.
Seeing people without Dharma engaging in non-virtue,
Those who act in accordance with Dharma are as rare as stars in daylight.
O Guru Rinpoche, heed me! Turn my mind towards Dharma!
Omniscient master, do not let me stray onto wrong or inferior paths!
Compassionate lama, who is one with them, heed me!

Although having reached the sanctuary of a precious human body,
A good physical basis with a very unruly mind,
Is not a suitable foundation for attaining liberation.
In particular, gripped by demons or disturbed by the five poisons,
Beset by negative karma or distracted by laziness,
Like a slave under someone else's control, or out of fear, an imitation of Dharma,
Or in ignorance, and so on: these are the eight unfree incidental circumstances.
When these oppositions to Dharma come upon me,
O Guru Rinpoche, heed me! Turn my mind towards Dharma!
Omniscient master, do not let me stray onto wrong or inferior paths!
Compassionate lama, you who are one with them, heed me!

With little weariness for samsara and without the jewel of devotion,
Bound by worldly cravings and with crude conduct,
Not shunning non-virtue, having a corrupt way of life,
Broken vows, and samaya torn to shreds –
These are the eight unfree states that cut the mind off from Dharma.
When these oppositions to Dharma come upon me,
O Guru Rinpoche, heed me! Turn my mind towards Dharma!
Omniscient master, do not let me stray onto wrong or inferior paths!
Compassionate lama, you who are one with them, heed me!

Right now, I am not tormented by sickness or suffering,
Nor enslaved or under the control of others.
At this time of independence and conducive circumstances,
If, in a state of indolence, I waste these freedoms and endowments –

The Dzogchen Path

No question of friends, possessions, and family –
Even this body which I hold so dear,
Will be taken from its bed to some desolate spot,
To be torn apart by foxes, vultures, and dogs,
At which time, in the bardo, my fear will be extreme.
O Guru Rinpoche, heed me! Turn my mind towards Dharma!
Omniscient master, do not let me stray onto wrong or inferior paths!
Compassionate lama, you who are one with them, heed me!

The results of virtuous and non-virtuous actions will follow after me.
In particular, if I am reborn in the hell realms,
On a ground of burning iron, my head and body will be hacked by weapons,
Dismembered by saws, and crushed by blazing hammers,
Trapped screaming in a door-less iron room,
Impaled on red-hot spikes, boiled in molten metal,
And burned in the hottest fire – the Eight Hot Hells.

On snow mountain cliffs and icy ravines,
Fearful places lashed by blizzards,
My vulnerable body, beaten by freezing winds,
Breaks out in blisters and bursts into open wounds.
I let out an endless scream,
Suffering pain that is hard to imagine.
My strength is exhausted, like a sick person on the brink of death.
I let out long gasps, clenching my teeth. My skin cracks,
Flesh is exposed, and it splits yet deeper, in these Eight Cold Hells.

Likewise, my feet are slashed open in a plain of razors,
My body is chopped up in a forest of swords,
I sink in a swamp of rotting corpses, and in unfordable hot embers,
In the Neighbouring Hells that surround the Hell of Ultimate Torment.
Also in the changing hells as a door or pillar, stove or rope, and so on,
Continually used and exploited – the Ephemeral Hells.

The cause of these eighteen hells,
Is motivation of intense anger, so when this arises,
O Guru Rinpoche, heed me! Turn my mind towards Dharma!

Omniscient master, do not let me stray onto wrong or inferior paths!
Compassionate lama, who is one with them, heed me!

Likewise, in a poor and unpleasant land,
Where even the words 'food', 'drink', or 'possessions' are unheard,
Food and drink cannot be found for months or years.
A preta's body is emaciated and lacks the strength to stand: the three kinds –
The cause of their arising is avarice.

In great fear of being killed and eaten by one another,
Worked and exploited to exhaustion, ignorant of right or wrong,
Oppressed by endless suffering,
The seed of which is stupidity. When I wander in this darkness,
O Guru Rinpoche, heed me! Turn my mind towards Dharma!
Omniscient master, do not let me stray onto wrong or inferior paths!
Compassionate lama, who is one with them, heed me!

Although I am on the path of Dharma, I do not restrain my negative conduct.
I have entered the door of the Mahayana, yet have no concern for others.
Although I have received the four empowerments, I do not practise development or completion.
O lama, I pray, free me from this straying path!

Although I have not realised the view, my conduct is crazy.
My meditation is distracted, yet I obsess on theory and pretence.
Although my conduct is mistaken, I do not consider my own faults.
O lama, I pray, free me from this resistance to Dharma.

Although I may die tomorrow, I hanker for places, clothing, and wealth.
My youth has long since passed, yet I have no renunciation or weariness for samsara.
Although I have heard few teachings, I pride myself on my knowledge.
O lama, I pray, free me from this ignorance.

Although I get lost in circumstances, I wish for excitement and pilgrimage.

> I stay in retreat, yet my mind remains as ridged as wood.
> Although I speak of discipline, I have not rid myself of attachment or aversion.
> O lama, I pray, free me from these eight worldly concerns.
> I pray, swiftly rouse me from this deep slumber.
> I pray, quickly release me from this dark dungeon.

Invoke the compassion of your lama by calling out with great fervour.

Two, Taking Refuge:

> In the sugatas of the Three Roots, the true Three Jewels,
> In the bodhicitta nature of the channels, energies, and essences,
> In the mandala of essence, nature, and compassion,
> I take refuge until I realise the heart of enlightenment.

Repeat three times.

Three, Arousing Bodhicitta:

> HO! Due to myriad appearances, illusory like the moon's reflection,
> Beings wander in samsara in a chain of lives;
> So they may rest in the expanse of self-knowing luminosity,
> From the state of the four immeasurables, I arouse bodhicitta.

Repeat three times.

Four, Meditation and Recitation of Vajrasattva:

> AH! In my ordinary form, at my crown,
> In the centre of a white lotus and moon seat,
> From a HONG, arises Guru Vajrasattva,
> Radiantly white sambhogakaya,
> Holding vajra and bell, and embracing his consort.
> I pray, give me refuge; purify my negativities.
> With fierce regret I admit and confess.
> Henceforth, even at the cost of my life, I vow to abstain.
> Upon a full moon in your heart
> Is a HONG syllable, encircled by the mantra.
> Reciting the mantra invokes his mind causing,
> From the point of union of the consorts' blissful enjoyment,
> Nectar, clouds of bodhicitta,
> Like droplets of camphor, to trickle down. By this, may

Root Text

Karma and afflictive emotions, the causes of suffering
For myself, and sentient beings of the three realms –
Illness, harmful forces, negativities, obscurations, faults, downfalls, and contamination –
Be purified without trace, I pray.

OM BANZA SATO SAMAYA | MANUPALAYA | BANZA SATO TENOPA TISHTA | DRIDHO ME BHAVA | SUTOKHAYO ME BHAVA | SUPOKHAYO ME BHAVA | ANURAKTO ME BHAVA | SARVA SIDDHI MAME PRAYACCHA | SARVA KARMA SU TSA ME | TSITTAM SHREYANG KURU HONG | HA HA HA HA HO | BHAGAVAN | SARVA TATAGATA BANZA MA ME MUNTSA | BANZI BHAVA MAHA SAMAYA SATO AH

Having recited this as much as possible:

Protector, in ignorance and delusion
I have transgressed and corrupted my samaya.
Guru protector, grant me refuge!
Lord vajra holder,
Embodiment of great compassion,
Chief of all beings, in you I take refuge.

I admit and confess all corruptions of the root and branch samayas towards enlightened body, speech, and mind. I pray, cleanse and purify my entire accumulation of impurities: negative actions, obscurations, faults, and downfalls.

Vajrasattva is gladdened, and with a smile grants his blessing, saying 'Child of the family, all your negative actions, obscurations, faults, and downfalls are purified.' They melt into light and dissolve into me. By this, I too become Vajrasattva, apparent yet empty, like a reflection in a mirror. Manifest at my heart is a HONG life-syllable, surrounded by the four syllables, from which light rays emanate. Whereby the three realms, including the container and its contents, become enlightened in the nature of the support and supported of the five families of Vajrasattva.

OM BANZA SATO HONG

Having recited this as much as possible, then enter meditative equipoise.

With this merit, may I swiftly

Achieve Vajrasattva realisation, by which
All beings without exception
Are established on that level.

Vajrasattva, whatever your enlightened form is like,
Your retinue, lifespan, and pure realm,
Your supreme and major marks, however they are,
May I, myself and others, attain just the same.

Five, Mandala Offering:

OM AH HONG
A realm of a billion third-order thousand-fold worlds,
Filled with the seven precious things and the wealth of gods and humans,
Together with my body and possessions; by offering them entirely,
May I attain the authority to turn the wheel of Dharma.

The greatly blissful Akanishtha Realm of Dense Array,
Endowed with fivefold certainty, the assemblage of the five families –
Inconceivable clouds of desirable offerings –
With this offering, may I enjoy the sambhogakaya realm.

Utter purity of appearance and existence, the youthful vase body,
Adorned with unceasing compassion, the play of dharmata,
A realm completely purified of grasping to kayas and bindus.
With this offering, may I enjoy the dharmakaya realm.

Six, the Kusali's Accumulation:

P'ET! By losing attachment to my treasured body, I conquer the god Mara.
Through the aperture of Brahma, my consciousness is ejected into space.
Mara Lord of Death is conquered; I become the Wrathful Yogini.
With a hooked knife in her right hand, conquering the demon of afflictive emotions,
She slices off my skull, conquering the demon of the form aggregates.
Her left hand holds the skull cup in the manner of an action performer,
Placing it on a hearth of human skulls – the three kayas.

Root Text

Inside, my corpse, which fills the third-order thousand-fold world,
Is melted into nectar by a short AH and a HUM syllable,
Purified, multiplied, and transformed by the power of the three syllables.

OM AH HONG

Having recited this as much as possible:

P'ET! The sacred bond with the upper guest recipients of offering is fulfilled,
Completing the accumulations, whereby the supreme and common attainments are achieved.
The samsaric guests below are pleased, clearing karmic debts.
In particular, the malicious and obstructive ones are satisfied.

Illnesses, negative forces, and obstacles are pacified into the expanse.
Adverse circumstances and clinging to self are smashed to dust.
Finally, all offerings and objects of offering without exception
Are the basic nature of uncontrived Great Perfection AH!

Seven, Guru Yoga:

EH MA HO!
My perception is of a spontaneously present realm of vast purity –
The perfectly arrayed Glorious Copper Coloured Mountain, in the centre of which
Is my form basis Vajrayogini,
With one face, two arms, radiant red, holding a knife and skull cup,
Two feet poised astride, three eyes gazing skywards.
At my crown, upon a blossoming hundred thousand-petalled lotus, sun, and moon,
Is the embodiment of all sources of refuge, my root lama,
Inseparable from the nirmanakaya Lake-born Vajra.
He is youthful with a rosy complexion,
Wears a tunic, Dharma robe, cloak, and cape,
With one face, two arms, seated in the posture of royal ease.
His right hand holds a vajra; his left a skull cup and vase.
Upon his head he wears a petalled lotus hat.
Cradled in his left arm is the supreme consort of bliss-emptiness
Concealed as a three-pronged khatvanga.
He sits in the midst of a mass of light of rainbow rays and spheres.

Surrounding him, in a beautiful lattice of the five lights,
Are the twenty-five emanations, lord and subjects, and
Pandits, siddhas, and vidyadharas of India and Tibet, yidam deities,
Dakinis, Dharma protectors, and the oath-bound, gathered like clouds,
Visible in a state of great equal presence of luminosity emptiness.

HONG! In the north-west of the land of Oddiyana,
Upon a blossoming lotus flower,
Endowed with wondrous supreme attainments,
Is the renowned Padmasambhava,
Surrounded by a vast retinue of dakinis.
Following you I practise,
So I pray, come to bestow your blessings!
GURU PEMA SIDDHA HONG

SHI, with my body manifested as many times
As atoms in the universe, I prostrate.
With offerings actually laid out, and those mentally emanated by the power of samadhi,
I make a symbolic gesture, offering all that appears and exists.
All unvirtuous actions of my three doors
I confess in the state of dharmakaya luminosity.
Subsumed within the two truths,
I rejoice in all accumulations of virtue.
For the three types of beings to be trained,
I implore you to turn the wheel of Dharma of the three vehicles.
As long as samsara is not empty,
I pray you remain, not passing into nirvana.
All the roots of virtue accumulated in the three times
I dedicate to the cause of supreme enlightenment.

Lord Guru Rinpoche,
You are the glory of compassion and blessing
Of all buddhas combined,
The sole protector of all sentient beings.
My body and possessions, mind and heart,
I offer to you without reservation.
From now until I attain enlightenment,
In all happiness and sorrow, good and bad, highs and lows,
Great Lord Padmasambhava, heed me!

I have no other hope but you.

Beings of this bad, degenerate time
Drown in a mire of unbearable suffering,
Protect us from this, great guru!
Bestow the four empowerments, blessed one!
Elevate my realisation, compassionate one!
Purify the two obscurations, mighty one!

At the time when my life comes to an end,
My perception is the realm of Chamara's Glorious Mountain,
In the unified nirmanakaya pure realm.
My form basis, Vajrayogini,
Becomes a sphere of shimmering light,
In great inseparability with
Lord Padmasambhava to become enlightened.
From the miraculous display of bliss and emptiness,
The play of this great wisdom,
For sentient beings of the three realms without exception,
May I appear as a true guide to lead;
Grant me this assurance, Lord Pema.
I pray from the depths of my heart,
Not just merely repeating the words,
Bestow blessings from the expanse of your enlightened mind!
May these aspirations be fulfilled!

OM AH HONG BANZA GURU PEMA SIDDHI HONG

Eight, Lineage Prayers:

E MA HO! In a pure realm without restrictions or extremes,
Is the original Buddha dharmakaya Samantabhadra;
The sambhogakaya, like the display of the moon in water,
    Vajrasattva;
The nirmanakaya with marks complete, Garab Dorje;
I pray: bestow blessing and empowerment.

Shri Singha, treasury of the ultimate Dharma;
Manjushrimitra, sovereign of the nine yanas;
Jnanasutra, great pundit Vimalamitra;
I pray: show us the liberating path.

Sole ornament of this world, Padmasambhava,
Supreme true heart children: lord, subject, and partner;
Longchenpa, revealer of oceanic mind treasures;

Jigme Lingpa, entrusted with the dakinis' space treasury;
I pray: bestow attainment of the result – liberation.

Additional Prayers:

> Lord of this Dharma, Changchub Dorje;
> Siddha Jigme Gyalwe Nyugu;
> Supreme emanation Mingyur Namkhe Dorje;
> Son of the victorious ones, Shenpen Thaye;
> I pray: show me the true face of fundamental nature.
>
> Glorious Heruka, Yeshe Dorje;
> To Orgyen Jigdral Chokyi Wangpo;
> Mighty siddha Pema Banza;
> To the lake-born guru, Khyentse Wangpo;
> I pray: bestow the supreme and ordinary attainments.
>
> With the revulsion of true renunciation from samsara,
> Relying upon my vajra guru meaningfully, as my eyes;
> Through the profound practice of following instructions as given,
> Without inconsistent application, but with diligence,
> May blessings of enlightened mind be transferred!
>
> Appearance and existence, samsara and nirvana, are primordially the realm of Akanishta;
> Deities, mantras, and dharmakaya the result of purification, perfection, and maturation –
> Great Perfection without effort of acceptance or rejection.
> The radiance of rigpa transcends mental experiences and conceptual analysis.
> May I directly perceive dharmata laid bare!
>
> Utterly liberated from defining thoughts, encompassed in rainbow light,
> May visionary experiences of kayas and bindus increase;
> May expressivity of rigpa reach fullness as sambhogakaya pure realms;
> May enlightenment be attained, the great exhaustion of phenomena and transcendence of mind;
> May I gain the eternal stronghold of the youthful vase body!
>
> If I have not mastered the experience of the ultimate yoga,
> And this gross body is not liberated into pristine space,

Root Text

At the time when the constituents of life fall apart,
May death luminosity dawn as primordially pure dharmakaya!
May the appearances of the bardo be liberated as sambhogakaya!
By completely mastering the paths of trekcho and togal,
May I be liberated, like a child leaping to its mother's lap!

In this great secret luminosity, the supreme pinnacle vehicle,
Buddhahood is not sought elsewhere; the face of the dharmakaya manifests.
If I am not liberated into the primordial state,
By following the supreme path of five practices of buddhahood without meditation,
May I be born in the five natural nirmanakaya realms;
Especially in the Palace of Lotus Light,
Where the Lord of Orgyen, supreme chief of the ocean of vidyadharas,
Celebrates the feast of the great secret Dharma,
May I be born as his most favoured child,
Relieved to become provision for limitless beings!

By the blessings of the oceanic victorious vidyadharas,
And the truth of inconceivable dharmata,
With the basis of the freedoms and endowments to perfect, mature, and purify,
Actualising this interdependence, may I attain enlightenment!

Pray sincerely from your heart.

Embodiment of all the victorious ones, venerable lama heed me!
Bestow blessings to dredge samsara from its depths.

Repeat three times.

Nine. Taking the Four Empowerments:

From between the eyebrows of the guru, an OM syllable, shining like crystal, radiates light rays that enter my crown. This purifies karma of the body and obscurations of the channels. Blessings of vajra body enter me. I receive the vase empowerment. I become a vessel for the development stage. The seed of a fully mature vidyadhara is sown. The fortune to attain the level of nirmanakaya is placed in my mindstream.

From an AH syllable, blazing like a ruby in his throat, light rays radiate and enter my throat. This purifies karma of speech and obscurations of the energies. Blessings of vajra speech enter me. I receive the secret empowerment. I become a vessel for mantra recitation. The seed of a vidyadhara with power over life is sown. The fortune to attain the level of sambhogakaya is placed in my mindstream.

From a sky-blue HONG syllable in his heart centre, light rays radiate and enter my heart. This purifies karma of the mind and obscurations of the essences. Blessings of vajra mind enter me. I receive the knowledge wisdom empowerment. I become a vessel for bliss-emptiness candali. The seed of a Mahamudra vidyadhara is sown. The fortune to attain the level of dharmakaya is placed in my mindstream.

Again, from the HONG in his heart centre, a second HONG syllable, like a shooting star, shoots outwards, merging inseparably with my own mind. This purifies alaya karma and obscuration to the knowable. Blessings of vajra wisdom enter me. I receive the ultimate empowerment indicated by words. I become a vessel for primordially pure Dzogpa Chenpo. The seed of a spontaneously accomplished vidyadhara is sown. The fortune to attain the ultimate result of svabhavikakaya is placed in my mindstream.

> At the time when my life comes to an end,
> My perception is the realm of Chamara's Glorious Mountain
> In the unified nirmanakaya pure realm.
> My form basis, Vajrayogini,
> Becomes a sphere of shimmering light,
> In great inseparability with
> Lord Padmasambhava, to become enlightened.
> From the miraculous display of bliss and emptiness,
> The play of this great wisdom,
> For sentient beings of the three realms without exception,
> May I appear as a true guide to lead;
> Grant me this assurance, Lord Padma.
> I pray from the depths of my heart,
> Not just merely repeating the words.
> Bestow blessings from the expanse of your enlightened mind!
> May these aspirations be fulfilled!

Uniting the recitation and meditation, receive the path empowerments. Having done so:

Root Text

Again from the heart centre of the lama, a warm red ray of light suddenly shines forth. Just as it touches my heart, myself visualised as Vajrayogini, I transform into a sphere of red light which dissolves into Guru Rinpoche's heart centre becoming inseparable, in one taste.

Meditate in equipoise in a state free from focus, thought, and expression. Having arisen from that:

> Glorious root lama, precious one, I pray,
> Dwell on the lotus seat in the heart of myself and others,
> Accept me with your great kindness and
> Grant me attainments of enlightened body, speech, and mind!
>
> Regarding the activities of the glorious lama,
> May I not give rise to wrong views even for a moment, and
> With devotion that sees all he does as positive,
> May the lama's blessing enter my mind!
>
> In all my lives, may I never be apart from
> The genuine lama, and enjoy the glory of the Dharma.
> Perfecting the qualities of the levels and paths,
> May I swiftly attain the level of Vajradhara!

<u>Ten. Dedication:</u>

> Through this merit, may all beings
> Complete the accumulations of merit and wisdom,
> And attain the two holy kayas
> That arise from merit and wisdom.
>
> Whatever merit all beings may possess,
> What they have done, will do, and are doing,
> May they all attain the stages of perfection,
> Just as Samantabhadra did.
>
> Just as the courageous Manjushri understood,
> And Samantabhadra did too,
> I train following them all,
> And completely dedicate all this merit.
>
> With the dedication all buddhas of the three times
> Praise as supreme,
> I also dedicate completely all my roots of virtue

For excellent conduct.

<u>Eleven. Special Prayers of Aspiration:</u>

In all my lives, wherever I am born,
May I have the seven qualities of the higher realms,
Meet with the Dharma as soon as I am born,
And have the freedom to practise correctly!

Also, may I please the holy lama,
And practise Dharma day and night.
By realising the Dharma and achieving its innermost meaning,
May I traverse the ocean of existence in that life.

In samsara, may I fully expound the sacred Dharma,
And never tire of working to benefit others.
Through vast impartial service to others,
May all attain buddhahood together!

This liturgy for the preliminaries of Dzogpa Chenpo Heart Essence of the Great Expanse, the *Sublime Path to Omniscience*, was written by the great tantric yogi Jigme Trinle Ozer, who was nurtured by the kindness of the Vidyadhara Jigme Lingpa and many other holy masters, and gained determination in the samaya. By this merit, may followers see the lama as a Buddha, by which result, self-aware rigpa, Samantabhadra's own face, becomes apparent, and may they become of ceaseless benefit to oceanic beings and worlds! Sarva mangalam! Virtue!

www.ingramcontent.com/pod-product-compliance
Lightning Source LLC
Chambersburg PA
CBHW030602230426
43661CB00053B/1805